Changing Perceptions, Altered Reality

Pakistan's Economy under Musharraf, 1999–2006

Changing Perceptions, Altered Reality

Pakistan's Economy under Musharraf, 1999–2006

SHAHID JAVED BURKI

OXFORD
UNIVERSITY PRESS

Great Clarendon Street, Oxford OX2 6DP

Oxford University Press is a department of the University of Oxford.
It furthers the University's objective of excellence in research, scholarship,
and education by publishing worldwide in

Oxford New York

Auckland Cape Town Dar es Salaam Hong Kong Karachi
Kuala Lumpur Madrid Melbourne Mexico City Nairobi
New Delhi Shanghai Taipei Toronto

with offices in

Argentina Austria Brazil Chile Czech Republic France Greece
Guatemala Hungary Italy Japan Poland Portugal Singapore
South Korea Switzerland Turkey Ukraine Vietnam

Oxford is a registered trade mark of Oxford University Press
in the UK and in certain other countries

ISBN 978-0-19-547507-4

Typeset in Adobe Garamond Pro
Printed in Pakistan by
Kagzi Printers, Karachi.
Published by
Ameena Saiyid, Oxford University Press
No. 38, Sector 15, Korangi Industrial Area, PO Box 8214
Karachi-74900, Pakistan.

Dedication

The book is dedicated to
Shaafi Javed Burki, my 9-year-old grandson,
who wants to inherit my entire library of books and reads
everything I write.

Contents

Acknowledgements

I have been contributing a weekly column to the op-ed pages of *Dawn* for almost seven years. Although I have not kept a count, I must have, by now, published 350 articles and written 750,000 words. The topics I touched upon have ranged over a wide front. I am an economist and my main interest was to write about economics. Since I have lived outside Pakistan for more than forty years, of which I spent more than twenty-five years at the World Bank, I was able to bring to my writings some perspectives that were different from those who write on economic issues pertaining to Pakistan from within Pakistan. My readers tell me that they find it interesting when I look at Pakistan from the outside, bringing to their attention certain developments in economic thinking and how those would apply to Pakistan.

Sometimes I also wrote on international politics, in the belief that some of these developments had a direct bearing on the way the Pakistani economy was developing. Globalization was touched upon in several contributions for the reason that the processes this term implies affects Pakistan in many different ways. Pakistan is now less dependent on official development assistance than on the amounts remitted by the people who left the country and live abroad but send money back home. It has also begun to receive foreign direct investment (FDI), but not of the type that would ensure high levels of sustainable economic growth.

I believe I have, in my columns, been able to introduce some new ways of looking at the economic and social progress of the economy. I have, for instance, maintained that Pakistan should not treat its large population as a burden but as an asset. I have argued that the policymakers in Islamabad should get to know the many diasporas formed by Pakistanis in many continents. I have suggested that a number of significant structural changes are required if the country is to move forward steadily and that the opportunity cost of the conflict in Kashmir should be calculated to devise a strategy for the future. These and several other issues are discussed at some length in the book.

The idea for writing this book came from two brothers in Lahore, journalist Fakhar Malik of the daily *Jang*, and Mohammad Saeed, an official in the excise and customs department. In the spring of last year they presented me with bound volumes of my articles and asked my permission to translate them into Urdu. I did not agree since I don't believe newspaper columns make good reading between the covers of a book. Instead, I agreed to develop some of the themes in the articles as chapters in a book. The result of that effort is this volume. I am grateful to them for getting me to do this work.

I am also thankful to the editors of *Dawn* for allowing me to use the material they have published in their pages. I am grateful to Virginia Baker, my assistant in Washington who worked diligently through the various drafts of the chapters.

I hope the readers will find that there is useful material in these pages to have them reflect on the difficult problems Pakistan faces in the sixtieth year of its existence as an independent state.

Shahid Javed Burki
Potomac, Maryland,
USA
May 2007

Introduction

The main purpose of this book is to help both policymakers and policy-thinkers debate the various issues of importance for Pakistan as it lurches forward from one period of uncertainty to another. For a number of reasons—and these too can be debated at length—the country was not given the luxury of time to settle down and construct durable economic and political systems. Over a period of time a number of political and economic developments and some interactions with the world outside produced many tensions in the society. These could be released only with the development of durable institutions that allowed people to interact with one another within rule-bound frameworks. These institutions were not developed.

The result of all this is that in the winter of 2006–2007, when this book was finalized for publication, there were several areas of social, political, and economic turbulence that were already visible or lay just under the surface. How to deal with this uneasy situation? In a series of articles written for the daily *Dawn* some years ago, I had identified a number of faultlines on which the Pakistani state and society were attempting to construct what they hoped would become durable economic, political, and social structures. That struggle continues unabated even sixty years after independence. In this book, I have shifted my emphasis to the identification of the areas of promise. My hope is that by working in them and on them, the people of Pakistan as well as those who govern from Islamabad and various provincial capitals will succeed in setting the country on a course that will provide certainty and some measure of tranquillity. But a great deal of additional work needs to be done and there has to be informed dialogue among different segments of the society on a number of issues before productive public policy emanates from Islamabad. I hope this book will make a contribution to that discourse.

Although the book draws upon more than 70 articles of the 250 I have contributed to the op-ed pages of *Dawn* over the last five years, this is not a compilation of newspaper columns. While some of the material presented in the book is taken from these articles— the original sources are identified in the footnotes—there is considerable amount of new writing and considerable rearrangement of the material published in the newspaper articles. I have done this as I feel that there is good reason to revisit and update some of the arguments I presented in the form of newspaper columns over a period of several years.

Since there was not much point in including all that I have written for *Dawn*, I have selected those articles for use in this volume that are pertinent for understanding Pakistan's current economic situation, the problems it faces today, the opportunities available for improving the well-being of the people and the orientation of public policy aimed at economic reform. Pakistan's future as a nation-state and its place in an increasingly 'globalized' world economy depends to some considerable extent on the choice of public policies. Will the current set of policymakers working in Islamabad succeed in developing the country's immense resource base and handling the various problems that need to be overcome in order to secure the country's economic and political future? I have a strong belief—not because my discipline is economics—that economics has a strong influence on politics and on social development. In spite of the political uncertainty the country faces sixty years after gaining independence, not withstanding a great deal of experimentation in the area of political development, Pakistan may be on the way to creating the structure that would define politics in the country. If such a transition takes place and a durable political system finally gets established, that process would be facilitated if the country continues to make economic progress, succeeds in providing for the poorer segments of the population, addresses the growing problem posed by inter-provincial inequality, and finds a place for itself in the global economic system. Failure to achieve these objectives will hinder progress in the political field by giving voice to those segments of the population who are seeking an entirely different political structure than the one supported by the majority. Those who wish to disturb the process of adjustment to a durable political and social order would like to create a structure in which they will have a larger space for themselves. However, one of the themes developed in this book is that economic progress will help the majority to prevail upon the disruptive minority.

The essays in this book are arranged to bring into focus half a dozen subjects of paramount interest for the people of Pakistan at this time in their history. The subjects covered include economic growth, poverty and inequality; the advantages bestowed by the country's unique geographical situation; the advantage of having a large and young population at a time when rates of fertility and population growth had begun to decline in the industrial world; the enormous but still to be tapped potential of the sector of agriculture; and, finally, how the presence of large Pakistani diasporas in three parts of the globe provide another set of opportunities for economic development. I call these the 'positives' in the structure of the Pakistani economy. The underlying theme that runs through this work is that Pakistan has the potential to join the more rapidly growing parts of Asia if it is able to put to productive use the country's many assets. Once again, there has to be focus on the design of the right kind of public policies.

What is exactly the role of public policy, how should it be played, how should policymakers equip themselves to put into place the right kinds of policies and programmes? These are some of the many questions asked—and sometimes answered—in the book. Some of the discussion uses the year 2006 as the vantage point for reviewing the situation in different parts of the economy and in analyzing how the government was approaching them.

Looking back, it appears that 2005 may well turn out to be one more defining moment in Pakistan's history. The economy had begun to grow rapidly. There was considerable economic activity in the country, fuelled in part by increase in consumption. Would the economy continue to grow or was the growth the consequence of a number of happy circumstances that may not come together again? The process economists described as 'globalization' continued to change the international economic system. International trade was the glue that was increasingly binding the various parts of the global system. Will Pakistan be able to play an important part in this system?

In 2006, the administration headed by General Pervez Musharraf began to prepare the country for another set of elections. Would it succeed in establishing a new political order or would its attempts lead to another period of political turmoil? There was growing hostility towards the Muslim world in many parts of the globe as the conflict between the West and Islamic militants continued unabated. Some of the western citizens of Pakistani origin had become actively engaged in this struggle. How would this affect Pakistan, the world's second largest Muslim country? The visit in March 2006 to South Asia—to Afghanistan, India and Pakistan—by George W. Bush, the American president, brought about a significant change in the way Washington viewed India, Pakistan's large neighbour and the country with which it had fought three wars and numerous near-wars. The Americans began to look upon India as a strategic partner; a country that had become increasingly integrated into the American economic system and one on which the United States could rely as a partner in the growing competition with China. How would America's new relations with India affect Pakistan? In 2006, President Musharraf, while pressing ahead with a number of confidence building measures in developing a new relationship with India, began to show impatience with the slow progress being made. In spite of several proposals made by him to resolve the long-enduring dispute over Kashmir, India seemed interested in moving at its own slow and deliberate pace. Could the Kashmir issue be resolved in order to reduce its economic cost for Pakistan?

The book opens with a brief discussion of the country's economic history; the roller coaster ride the economy has taken over the last several years. It then discusses the current situation—the situation in 2006—when high rates of growth in the preceding two years persuaded Islamabad that it had managed to place the economy on a trajectory of sustainable growth. The country has had two periods of rapid growth in the past—in 1958–69 and again in 1977–88—when rapid increase in GDP (gross domestic product) produced complacency in Islamabad, but a high level of expectation on the part of the population that benefits of growth should accrue to them. This did not happen. It is therefore important for policymakers to understand the true nature of what economists call the 'determinants of growth' and how they will affect the incidence of poverty and equality of opportunity.

Chapter 2 deals with Pakistan's geographical situation which has bestowed advantages to the country not enjoyed by many states in the developing world. Economists have begun to emphasize the role of geography and location in understanding the structure of economies and their development over time. This approach was popularized by David Landes in his widely read book, *The Wealth and Poverty of Nations*.[1] In Pakistan's case, geography could indeed be destiny, but to turn it into that would require two things: understanding the neighbourhood in which Pakistan is situated and devising state policies to take advantage of the country's geographical location. In this context three sections in this part examine in depth the region and the countries in Pakistan's proximity—West and Central Asia, China and India. The chapter also has a section on the United States and how the sole superpower approaches the world as it tackles the problem of international terrorism.

Chapter 3 deals with international commerce, an area in which the country has done poorly. This is unfortunate since trade can be—in fact has been in the case of the 'miracle economies' of East Asia—a very important determinant of growth and poverty alleviation.[2] There are several options available to the policymakers as they participate in the multilateral trade negotiations called the Doha Round, take part in defining and evolving the South Asia Free Trade Area (SAFTA), attempt to conclude other free trade areas (FTAs) with some countries based on the one signed with Sri Lanka in 2005 and another with China in November 2006. Once again, I do not believe that the discussion offered in the book will be dated even if the current round of multilateral trade negotiations—the Doha Round—are brought to a successful conclusion before this book is published. The debate between policymakers and economists on the pros and cons of multilateral versus regional trading arrangements will continue for many years beyond the Doha Round and the inauguration of SAFTA.

Chapter 4 treats the country's large and young population as a resource rather than as a burden. However, for the population to become a determinant of development, it must be educated and trained and must also be equipped to take part in the new system of industrial and services production that is evolving globally.

Chapter 5 deals with the importance of agriculture, a sector much neglected by a succession of regimes that have governed Pakistan. Had Pakistan not fought a trade war with India in 1949—a conflict provoked by Delhi—agriculture would have remained the economy's dominant sector. Could it achieve that status and would that be beneficial for Pakistan? I will suggest a substantial reorientation of the government's approach towards agriculture in the next several years and decades.

Chapter 6 deals with a subject mostly ignored by policymakers and policy-thinkers, the subject of migration of workers to other parts of the world. For many years, economists were concerned with the leakage of human capital—they called it the 'brain drain'. The argument advanced against what was perceived as a serious loss was a simple one. A society spends large amounts of resources to educate the young, some of this resource is contributed directly by the state; some is provided by the families; and some, on occasion, is provided by the students themselves. There is a simple cost-benefit analysis behind the decision to educate the young: once educated they will return benefits to the society at large and also to the families from which they come. By leaving the country and settling abroad, this investment is lost. A serious drain has occurred. Over the years, I have questioned this line of argument by suggesting that those who migrate contribute to the society but in a different way, and the sum total of their contributions may be even greater than would have been the case had these individuals stayed behind. This line of analysis is what I have called in my writings 'diaspora economics'.

Chapter 7 deals with one issue—or more appropriately one problem—that Pakistan has faced ever since it came into existence. This is the problem of Kashmir. Why include a discussion of the Kashmir issue in a book that deals essentially with economic policymaking? The material included in this part seeks to provide an answer to this question. It points to the enormous cost the country has borne by keeping the Kashmir problem on the front burner. It is important to provide a rough estimate of the economic damage done by the policymaker's proclivity to keep alive the Kashmir issue and to use it as a device for constituency building. I do not suggest that Pakistan should give up the effort to find a solution to the enduring problem of Kashmir. My suggestion is that Islamabad should try some other approaches—perhaps using trade as a lever for drawing Kashmir closer to Pakistan and thus essentially nullifying the impact of the decision taken by the maharaja of the state in late 1947 to join India. That move essentially cut Kashmir off from Pakistan. The solution I propose could restore those links.

Chapter 8, pulls together some of the themes developed in the earlier chapters. It suggests that Pakistan in 2005 may have reached what economist Walt Whitman Rostow in 1960 called the stage of take-off.[3] It had been there before in 1965 but it pulled back then for a variety of reasons, among them the war with India over Kashmir. It seems to be pulling back again in 2006, this time because of the inability or perhaps unwillingness on the part of the policymakers in Islamabad to allow the political and social development in the country to proceed at the same pace as the modernization of the economy.

As this introduction indicates, the main purpose behind this book is to help to formulate debate on at least six important issues dealing with economic development. In selecting the articles originally published in *Dawn* for use in this book and extensively reworking them, I have focused on those that are as pertinent today as they were when they were originally written and published. But they have been largely rewritten and integrated into the book to bring out more clearly the issues discussed above. It is my hope that the book will lead to an informed discourse on a number of economic issues vital for Pakistan's economic and political development and social stability as the country continues with the unfinished task of nation building.

NOTES

1. David S. Landes, *The Wealth and Poverty of Nations: Why Some Are So Rich and Some So Poor*, New York: W.W. Norton, 1998.
2. See for instance the important work of William Cline linking trade with poverty alleviation done under the auspices of the Washington based think tank, the Institute of International Economics.
3. W.W. Rostow, *The Stages of Economic Growth: A Non-Communist Manifesto*, Cambridge: Cambridge University Press, 1960.

1

Growth, Inequality, and Poverty

In the literature on Pakistan's economy the subjects of growth, poverty and income distribution have received considerable attention. However, various authors who have studied the subject did so from the perspective of the period or periods they were analyzing. Relatively little was said by them on the three issues that receive emphasis in this chapter: sustainability of growth at a level sufficiently high to alleviate poverty and reduce income inequality, the importance of understanding the factors that produce inequality of opportunity for various segments of society and, finally, the political and social consequences of the inability to sustain growth, alleviate poverty and reduce inequality.

The chapter is divided into seven sections. The first, following this brief introduction, provides a historical background to the economic situation the country currently (the winter of 2006) faces. The main point made in this section is that the country has been on a roller coaster economic ride since it gained independence in 1947. Section 2 discusses the current situation and offers a brief analysis of the factors that contributed to the sharp rise in the rate of GDP growth in 2004–5. Section 3 analyzes how politics and economics interacted in Pakistan's history. Section 4 discusses why the policymakers have a great deal more to do before the economy can be said to have been set on a course of a high level of sustainable growth. Section 5 analyses some of the obstacles that stand in the way of Pakistan achieving sustainable growth at a level that would bring it on par with other rapidly developing countries of Asia. Section 6 examines the situation of poverty and inequality in the country and discusses the millennium development goals (MDGs), that define the donor's agenda in the developing world and which

Pakistan has not been able to follow. Section 7 offers some thoughts on the changes in public policy that need to be made for Pakistan to achieve high growth, alleviate poverty and improve equality.

1. Economic History: A Roller Coaster Ride (1947–2006)

On several occasions Pakistan's economy has been on the verge of take-off. The term take-off was first used by the economist W.W. Rostow to describe a situation reached by a developing economy when it could sustain a reasonably high level of growth rate without the need for extraordinary measures—state policy explicitly directed at achieving growth and modernization supported by external assistance to augment poor domestic savings. 'The take-off is the interval when the old blocks and resistance for steady growth are finally overcome,' wrote Rostow in 1953 when the discipline of development economics was young. In the take-off stage,

> the forces making for economic progress, which yielded limited bursts and enclaves of modern activity, expand and come to dominate the society. Growth becomes its normal condition. Compound interest becomes, as it were, into its habits and institutional structure.[1]

That Pakistan was at that point in the mid-1960s was generally accepted by most development economists. Several books were written on why Pakistan had succeeded while a number of other countries, including those in East Asia but certainly India, right next door to Pakistan, seemed to be still struggling. The most articulate exponent of this point of view was Pakistan's own Mahbub ul Haq who was then working as the chief economist of the powerful Planning Commission, and Gustav F. Papanek who was advising the Commission as the chief of a group of experts provided by Harvard University.

Haq's book, *Strategy of Economic Growth*,[2] famously argued that a country in Pakistan's situation should concentrate on achieving rapid economic growth, and allow the trickle-down effect to carry the benefits of a rapid increase in the size of the economy to the less-advantaged segments of the population. It did not seem to concern the chief economist that the trickle down could take a long time to work, and the imbalances that growth without explicit attention given to the problems of growing inequality and persistent poverty could prove to be politically and socially destabilizing. That, in fact, was the conventional wisdom at that time articulated by two economists who went on to win Nobel prizes for their work on growth and income distribution. In a 1954 article, Arthur Lewis argued that growth begins in the industrial sector as surplus labour moves from the countryside to towns and cities.[3] He assumed the supply of labour to be unlimited for a while; it would be hired at a given wage for as long as the surplus lasted. Once it was exhausted, wages would begin to rise and the poor would begin to draw benefits from growth. This model seemed to work well for Pakistan, which was just beginning the process of industrialization while the size of population and labour supply continued to increase beyond agriculture's capacity to absorb it. The Lewis model did not see real wages increasing for as long as there was abundance of labour available in the countryside to man the mills and the factories. Approaching the issue of growth and equality from an econometric angle, Simon Kuznets invented his famous 'inverted U-curve' which, using data from a number of countries, showed that inequality increased during initial phases of growth. Haq, therefore, had solid economic theory of the time to back his strategy for growth. It was later that economists began to focus on other determinants growth not just accumulation of capital and movement of labour from less productive to more productive jobs. In the 1980s and 1990s, a great deal of empirical work done at the World Bank demonstrated quite unequivocally that persistent inequality could be an obstacle to growth and not necessarily one of its unavoidable consequences. Manifestations of inequality are 'likely to lead to wasted human potential and thus to missed development opportunities. That is why *World Development Report 2006* analyzes the relationship between equity and development,' wrote the World Bank in 2006.[4]

At the same time, development thinking began to look at technological improvements, and human development as direct— *endogenous*, in the language of economics—determinants of development.[5] Using that as the perspective, it is easier to understand why spurts in growth such as those experienced during the period of Ayub Khan could not be sustained over time.

While Mahbub ul Haq provided the analytical underpinnings of the model of growth that brought about President Ayub Khan's 'decade of development', Papanek provided details of the way the model actually worked. He extolled the work done by various instruments of government in wisely allocating the resources available to the government (the Planning Commission and the Planning and Development Department of West Pakistan). These resources were put to good use by a number of public sector agencies (in particular the Water and Power Development Authority [WAPDA] and the Pakistan Industrial Development Corporation [PIDC]). Papanek was also enthusiastic about the commitment and hard work put in by a number of senior civil servants. He singled out one of them, Ghulam Faruque, who was at that time the chairman of PIDC, comparing him to the legendary Robert Moses of New York who had built much of New York city's transport infrastructure.

> Like Enrico Mattei in Italy, Robert Moses in New York, or Abol Hassan Ebtehaj in Iran, Ghulam Faruque, the first head of the PIDC, was a strong-willed, powerful individual who made rapid decisions, saw them carried out, and worried about government rules, procedures, or approval only afterwards, if at all.[6]

It took a political scientist, Samuel P. Huntington of Harvard University who later gained fame by predicting a clash of civilizations between the West and the world of Islam[7] to point out that rapid economic growth without spreading widely the benefits of development, could create serious and destructive tensions within societies. Most societies were poorly equipped to handle the changes that inevitably occurred with development. The most serious source of these tensions is 'relative deprivation'. This situation results when some segments of the society move much faster than others. This causes resentment. Therefore, it is not only absolute deprivation—or extreme poverty those who hold power must worry about, but also widening disparities in the distribution of income and wealth. His book, *Political Order in Changing Societies* appeared in 1968 and emphasized the important role of institutions in economic development decades before economists began to incorporate it in their thinking.[8]

While giving comfort to the policymakers whose efforts at promoting growth may have been rewarded, Huntington suggested that large segments of the citizenry are less impressed with the outcome. He argued that political order is threatened when the level of mobilization for economic activities exceeds the level of institutionalization within a society. He was concerned that, as result of economic development political mobilization would increase faster than the rise of appropriate institutions, thus leading to instability. How could societies guard against disruption? Huntington advocated emphasis on institution building, most importantly the establishment of stable party systems. While Ayub Khan, his political associates and the economic advisers who had built his model of development or provided it with intellectual backing, were clearly surprised by the vehemence of the political movement that gained momentum in the early months of 1969, one community of political scientists saw their predictions come true. The movement eventually led to the overthrow of Ayub Khan and the military president's replacement in a palace coup by another man in uniform. Unlike Ayub Khan, Agha Mohammad Yahya Khan was less interested in economic development.

Before describing Pakistan's ride on the economic roller coaster, it would be useful to say a word about the country's colonial heritage. Indian nationalists while they were campaigning for independence from British rule, used to argue that all colonial powers were essentially predators. Britain, they claimed, was no exception. It adopted policies and established programmes that transferred enormous amounts of resources from India to Britain. The demise of the small scale Indian textile industry was usually held out as an example of how Britain had exploited the subcontinent. It turned India from a significant producer and exporter of textiles to one that became a net importer. Most of India's textile imports came from the mills established in Lancashire. India exported raw cotton to these mills; the mills spun cotton into yarn, wove the yarn into fabrics, and exported the fabrics back to India. Tens of thousands of jobs were lost in India while the mill towns in Britain prospered.

Some revisionist modern-day historians have begun to argue that Britain's colonial rule of the Indian subcontinent did more good than harm. If the costs and benefits to India of rule by Britain are measured in a dispassionate way, the scale tilts in favour of the benefits they claim. The most vigorous exponent of this point of view is the British historian Niall Ferguson, the author of a highly influential book titled *Empire*.[9] According to him if we draw up a balance sheet for the rule by the British over the areas that make up today's Pakistan, benefits will far outweigh the costs. This may be one reason why the leaders of Punjab, the North West Frontier Province and Sindh were not active participants in the Indian independence movement. They were also, at best, lukewarm supporters of the 'idea of Pakistan'. They supported Britain's rule over India long after it was being challenged elsewhere, primarily for the reason that British gave a great deal of attention to these provinces. London was interested in this part of its Indian empire for three reasons, all of them important to understand in order to develop a better comprehension of Pakistan's economic history.

Britain's paramount interest was that it wanted to recruit soldiers from this area for their army. They had convinced the people of these provinces that they belonged to what the British had begun to call the 'martial races'. Volunteers from these martial races were needed to protect Britain's Indian empire from encroachment by other imperial powers. London was already engaged in the 'Great Game' to keep Imperial Russia from controlling the several Muslim kingdoms of Central Asia. Many influential British policymakers were convinced that this was a necessary game to play in order to keep the Russians from advancing towards India, the 'jewel' in the British Crown.

Second, the British administration in India became very concerned as the country's capacity to produce food was overtaken by the increase in its population. In the late nineteenth and early twentieth century, a number of provinces of British India were rocked by famines that took a heavy human toll. The increase in population was itself a consequence of the rule over India by Britain. 'Pax Britannia' had replaced wars and insecurity that had been the norm in India for more than a thousand years. Freed from these concerns, people could turn their attention towards increasing the size of their families.

Looking for a strategy to deal with the growing food problem, the British began to focus their attention on bringing under cultivation the vast empty tracts of land in the Punjab and Sindh. There was plenty of water available in the Indus River system to irrigate this empty space. The British administrations in the Punjab and Sindh went to work to lay the foundations of what was to become one of the largest irrigation systems in the world. A series of barrages were constructed to impound enough water in the six rivers of the region—the Indus and its five large tributaries—to feed the feeder canals that began to spread out over the area. Generous offers of land grants were made to induce people who knew agriculture to settle in the 'colonies' that sprang up all over the region. Within a few decades Punjab and Sindh had become the granaries of British India.

Third, in order to provide troops for the Great Game and to supply surplus food grains from the Punjab and Sindh to the rest of India, the British built a network of roads and railways. There were few areas in Sindh, the Punjab and the Frontier Province that this communication network did not reach. In sum, if we look only at what the British government gave to this part of their Indian empire, it is not too difficult to agree with the argument advanced by Ferguson. Having inherited this impressive irrigation and communication network, Pakistan began to 'decapitalize' it.

The various administrations that were in office in the half century between 1947 and 1999 did little to save the system inherited from British rule from deterioration, let alone augment it. In fact, this was one reason why with a relatively low level of investment Pakistan was able to produce relatively high rates of GDP growth in the 1960s. It did not have to invest large amounts of resources in building the physical infrastructure that was required. The British had left one behind. Had Pakistan built upon the colonial legacy, its economic performance would have been more even. It might also have reached a higher stage of development than it actually did.

A quick look at Pakistan's economy since the country gained independence in 1947 reveals an interesting pattern with respect to growth and incidence of poverty. In terms of the growth in GDP and increase in per capita income, the economy did very well in the 1960s, and again, in the 1980s. Once again, there was a noticeable pick up in the financial years 2002–6. In the first full year of Ayub Khan's stewardship, the GDP increased by 4.9 per cent compared to only 0.9 per cent the year before. In Ziaul Haq's first year in office, growth in the GDP climbed to 7.7 per cent compared to only 2.8 per cent the year before. In 2000–1, the first year of General Musharraf's rule, the GDP increased by only 2.2 per cent as against 3.9 per cent in the year before. The rate of economic growth picked up in 2003–4 and averaged about 6.5 per cent a year in the three year period since 2003.

Yearly growth data can be very misleading and should not be used to draw firm conclusions. In other words, the economy did well under the rule of the military. But rates of growth are not the only determinants of development. How did Pakistan fare in terms of alleviating poverty, improving income distribution and providing people access to basic goods and services? After digging a bit deeper into the performance of the economy, and looking at it from the perspective of the poorer segments of the population, what emerges is the same pattern as in GDP growth rates. Once again, the incidence of poverty declined when the military was in charge.

At the time of independence some 60 per cent of the population lived in absolute poverty, a condition of life in which the basic needs of those who are affected by it are not fulfilled.[10] Those who are absolute poor go hungry most of the time; they cannot provide basic health care to themselves and their families; children cannot be sent to schools; and jobs, even if available, are mostly in the low-wage informal sectors of the economy. With 60 per cent of the population living in poverty, Pakistan in 1947 had as many as 21 million people who suffered from this kind of deprivation.[11] In the period 1947–58—the period during which politicians ruled with the help of the civil bureaucracy—the country added eight million people to its population. There was no decline in the incidence of poverty, in part because of the arrival of millions of people as refugees from India. A very large number of these people came as destitutes, leaving behind their properties and most of their possessions.

It took about a decade and a half to settle these people on the lands and businesses left behind by the six million Hindus and Sikhs who had gone to India. When Ayub Khan put Pakistan under martial law in October 1958, the pool of poverty had increased by another five million, to about 26 million people in a population of some 44 million. Economists have disputed the impact of Ayub Khan's model of economic growth on the incidence of poverty as well as on income inequality.[12] The government, while celebrating the 'decade of development', maintained that its policies had resulted in improving the economic well being of a vast majority of the country's citizens. This was disputed by Mahbub ul Haq, the chief economist of the Planning Commission in a speech given in Karachi in 1969. He suggested that growth during this period had mostly enriched the well-to-do. No firm data is available to determine what really happened to the various measures of welfare during this period. My own estimate is that while inequality increased, the incidence of poverty declined significantly. It couldn't have been otherwise. There is much empirical evidence gathered by the World Bank and other development institutions to suggest that rapid economic growth, even with some worsening in income distribution, reduces the number of people living below the poverty line.

Even more important, agriculture contributed significantly to Pakistan's economic growth during this period. The green revolution was led by the small and medium-sized landholders, and they were much more inclined to use labour-intensive techniques than large farms. Also, the Ayub government launched an ambitious programme of rural works which was focused on building infrastructure in the countryside by using surplus labour.[13] When Ayub Khan was forced out of office in March 1969, Pakistan's population had increased to 56 million. Of this some 40 per cent or 22 million people lived in poverty. This was a generally accepted estimate. In fact, it was this estimate, made popular by Mahbub ul Haq in his writings and speeches, which introduced the concept of the 'bottom 40 per cent' in development thinking.

The collapse in December 1971 of the second military government headed by General Yahya Khan brought the civilians back to power. It also saw some increase in the incidence of poverty, which can be attributed in part to the sharp slowdown in economic growth, the result of a series of failed monsoons, and the outcome of the deep restructuring of the economy undertaken by the government of Zulfikar Ali Bhutto. A committed Fabian socialist, Bhutto brought dirigistic management to the economy.[14] There were far-reaching consequences of this structural change, including the impact on the poorer segments of the population. A reduction in GDP growth and a decline in the rate of growth of agricultural output contributed to keeping the incidence of poverty at the level reached at the conclusion of the Ayub Khan period. In July 1977, when General Ziaul Haq removed Bhutto from power, Pakistan's population had increased to 72 million, of which 28 million were absolute poor. This was six million more than in 1969.

With the advent of the Ziaul Haq rule, a firmer statistical picture is available in so far as the incidence of poverty is concerned. More systematic surveys were conducted in this period that provided a better indication not only about the number of people living in poverty but also the characteristics of the poor. This period not only saw a sharp pick-up in economic growth, it also witnessed Pakistan's second green revolution, this time centred around increasing the production and productivity of cotton, the country's main cash crop. Since cotton is grown in the areas that are poorer compared to those producing rice and wheat, and since women are employed as 'pickers', there was a tremendously positive impact on the incidence of poverty because of this development.

The Zia period ended in August 1988, with his death in an air crash. At that time Pakistan had a population of 97 million, of which about 18 per cent or 17 million were poor. This was a remarkable development. While the size of the population in this 11-year period increased by 25 million, the number of poor declined by 11 million. Or putting it differently, the economy was able to help some 36 million people obtain a living standard above the line of poverty. Was the state under General Ziaul Haq responsible for these happy results? Zia himself suggested that his Islamization programme, much of which was focused on the introduction of *zakat*, a tax collected from the rich for distribution to the poor, contributed significantly to this development. This Islamic tax may have contributed a little to the decline in poverty. However, the two more important reasons were the growth rates based on agriculture and the large amounts of remittances sent by Pakistani workers in the Middle East.

The majority of the Pakistani workers in the Middle East, the most important source of remittances, came from very poor households; they mainly remitted the bulk of their large earnings to their families; and, contrary to some impressions at that time, most of this money was used to meet the basic needs of the recipients. More than anything else, remittances played a significant role in reducing the level of poverty.

This trend towards reduction in the incidence of poverty was reversed during the decade of the 1990s. Once again a slowdown in the rate of economic growth played an important role. This period also saw a significant decline in remittances, particularly after the first Gulf War in 1991, when a large number of Pakistani workers in the Middle East were sent back home. By 1999, the incidence of poverty had climbed back to 36 per cent of the population. Since the population increased to 131 million, the number of people living in poverty reached 47 million.

The size of the poverty pool began to increase at the rate of 10 per cent a year, or at a rate four times the growth of the population. This is when the military returned to power under General Pervez Musharraf in October 1999. On the eve of Pakistan's fourth military rule, the country was faced with an extremely serious crisis of poverty. However, unlike the performance of the economy under General Ayub Khan and Ziaul Haq, growth did not immediately pick up with the transfer of power back to the military in 1999.

How did the poor fare under President Pervez Musharraf? Slow recovery from the economic slump in the 1990s which was the result of the economic stabilization policies adopted by Islamabad under the pressure of the International Monetary Fund had one serious negative consequence. It exacerbated the situation of poverty; although firm estimates are not available, the number of people living in absolute poverty continued to increase at the rate of 10 million a year from 1999 to 2002. The deteriorating poverty situation was the subject of two reports, one produced by the Karachi-based Social Policy and Development Centre[15] and the other prepared under the auspices of the UNDP.[16] Both reports were critical that the government had not given much attention to the fact that the incidence of poverty was increasing significantly. Both reports were ignored by Islamabad.

Nonetheless, the economic strategy followed by the Musharraf government put emphasis initially on stabilization rather than growth and poverty alleviation. In the first two years of Musharraf's rule, the incidence of poverty probably increased. In the middle of 2003 when growth returned to the country, there were some 50 million people living in the pool of poverty, the largest number in the country's history.

It would be tempting to conclude from these broad trends about GDP growth and changes in the incidence of poverty that the military was much more adept at economic management than the civilians; that democracy failed to deliver growth and bring about palpable improvement in the lives of ordinary citizens. Economic performance was particularly poor in the first post-independence decade and again in the 1970s and 1990s—the three periods when politicians were in charge. In the 1950s and 1990s, the economy suffered because of the quick changes in governments which meant that a consistent set of policies could not be followed. In the 1970s, while there was political stability, the economy was profoundly restructured by an expansion in the role of the state. Also, the political administration at that time was deeply suspicious of private enterprise, and private entrepreneurs were fearful that their investment could be subject to expropriation by the government. What this points to is not that the military was necessarily a better manager of the economy. It indicates that military rule brought political stability and a continuity of economic policies and these always help economic growth.

The periods of Ayub Khan and Ziaul Haq saw the same group of civilian managers stay in charge of the economy. The military did not interfere in the day-to-day management of the economy. It only provided broad oversight. President Ayub Khan was more involved himself in economic decision-making than was General Ziaul Haq. However, even Ayub left the formulation of broad strategies in the hands of economic experts. Economists never tire of repeating that what the market dislikes the most is uncertainty. This was what troubled the Pakistani economy the most during the 1960s, 1970s and 1990s. Investors were not confident that the assumptions they were making about the future would prevail. Of these three periods, the 1990s were the most uncertain since each government that came to office was happy to change policies adopted by the one it succeeded.

2. Pakistan's Current Economic Situation[17]

President Pervez Musharraf's tenure started differently from those of his military predecessors. Whereas the rate of economic growth picked up immediately after Generals Ayub Khan and Ziaul Haq took control, the economy languished for three years under General

Musharraf. The rate of growth increased smartly in 2002–5 but began to slow down again in 2005–6. As I will indicate below, my assessment of the economic future is considerably less sanguine than that of Islamabad. What will be the political and social consequences if the economy falters once again?

Pakistan had many moments in its history when economics influenced politics in unexpected and negative ways. It happened, as discussed in the previous section in 1969, when growing discontent with the economic policies pursued by the government of President Ayub Khan created considerable discontent that ultimately led to regime change. It happened again in 1977 when Zulfikar Ali Bhutto's economic programme failed to deliver the poor from the state of burdensome poverty, failed to provide the unemployed youth productive jobs, and failed to pacify the various regions of the country that were unhappy with the way Islamabad was treating them. On at least five occasions in the 1990s economic mismanagement and rampant corruption were so disillusioning for the citizenry that they were happy to have the people they had elected and placed in high office replaced by quasi-constitutional means. Was the country headed once again in that direction seven years after President Pervez Musharraf had taken control?

This question no doubt sounded strange to the ears of Islamabad when I asked it in a series of articles published by *Dawn* in March and April of 2006.[18] The Musharraf regime was persuaded that there was much to celebrate about the economy. Why should one entertain the thought in those seemingly good times that economics could once again force political change? I thought there were good reasons to underscore why sometimes seeds of discontent get sown during what policymakers regard as happy moments. The seeds may sprout before the realization develops that all was not well with the state of the economy.

A number of positive developments and positive policies helped to revive the economy in the 2002–3 period. These included an increase in investor confidence and increase also in the level of consumption. By far the most important determinant of growth recorded in this period was the continuity in policymaking. The same set of actors dominated decision-making in politics as well as in economics. Continuity in policymaking brought foreign capital into the country—foreign flows have always been important in Pakistan's history in igniting growth. A series of successful privatizations have brought new foreign capital and the promise of new management practices into some vital industrial sub-sectors. To take just one example: the privatization of the Pakistan Telecommunications in 2005 will result in improvement in the way the sector will be managed. There was considerable visual and anecdotal evidence to suggest that some structural changes had begun to take place in the economy's real sectors as well. However the privatization of Pakistan Steel Mills was overturned by the Supreme Court in the summer of 2006 and may affect the confidence of foreign investors in the country.[19]

Changes in agriculture were also palpable as agro-processing was becoming a significant business with the entry of new capital, introduction of new technologies, and development of elaborate distribution networks. The dairy industry was at the centre of this development. Pakistanis were frequently reminded by the country's senior leaders that their country was the fifth largest producer of milk in the world. Given the fact that this business reached a large number of people, many of them poor, the modernization of the dairy industry was bound to have very positive social consequences. A growing middle class which was already fairly large—perhaps as large as 50 million—was providing the market for absorbing a number of new agro-processed products. With the base of this business expanding, its products should enter the export market.

There were some other positive changes. Two of these will be of considerable significance for the growth of the economy and prosperity of the population. Signs of change in this context were visible and they told a story still not picked up by official statistics. The construction of the Lahore–Islamabad Motorway and the way it was being operated seemed to have spawned a new business—bus services, that by providing comfort, safety and regularity, had begun to wean away passengers from the airlines. The motorway was an expensive project which could not be justified in terms of cost-benefit analysis when it was built. It siphoned away a large amount of public money that could have been used much more productively in some other activities. But economists have a way of dealing with even the most egregious mistakes. Treating the investment in the motorway as 'sunk cost' it would be useful, to note, analyze, and build upon the changes being introduced in the economy by this development and to expand it in order to increase the contribution it could make to the development of some of the modern services.

The other palpable positive development was the push towards the modernization of higher education. The initial forays into this long-neglected area were made by the private sector working either for profit or motivated by the desire to develop the country's large but neglected human resource. Under General Musharraf the government had joined in this effort after the establishment of the Higher Education Commission. The Commission's strategy, its performance to-date and how it could help to bring the higher education sector out of darkness is a subject discussed in a later chapter.

Considering these positive developments why was there the need to worry about the future? There were, in fact, four worries about the state of the economy in 2006 when the government seemed to believe that it had set it on a high growth trajectory. One, for reasons discussed later, the high rates of growth of the 2003–6 period were not sustainable in the future. Without a serious correction in the course the economy was taking, the rate of increase in the GDP was likely to fall back to somewhere in the range of 4 to 5 per cent. Given the structure of the economy this was the most it could produce. Two, at a rate of growth falling in this relatively low range, the economy will not be able to bring about a significant change in the incidence of poverty. The number of new jobs that will get created will be considerably less than needed by a rapidly growing workforce. Rural–urban migration will continue to proceed at a rate twice the rate of increase in population which in turn will place an even greater burden on large cities.

These cities were already bursting at the seams, unable to fully cater to the basic needs of the population.

Three, a combination of a large pool of poverty, increasing population of large cities, and a boom fed by speculation in the capital markets and in real estate will worsen income distribution which was already considerably skewed in favour of the rich. As noted in the previous section, a high incidence of poverty inhibits growth. This could also create the basis for social turbulence. Four, if social turbulence occurred once again, it will happen as the country moves towards the time when another set of elections must be held. These elections will be more critical than the six that were held over the last twenty years, in 1985, 1988, 1990, 1993, 1997 and 2002. These will be important since the establishment that holds the reins of power will be testing people's acceptance of the hybrid system of governance it has been using to run the country.[20] For Pakistan's political history, 2007 will be as much a turning point as were the elections of 1970 and 1977.

In 1970, the military gambled that by allowing the people to give voice to their aspirations and frustrations they will be able to produce a viable and durable political structure. That did not happen. The 1970 elections were fair but released tensions the institutions available to the society were too fragile to absorb. The rest, as they say is history. In 1977, Islamabad, was now under the control of a new political establishment that, after brushing aside the military, had gone on to introduce a number of deep social, political and economic changes. Having done that, it lost its nerve and was not prepared to test its popularity with the people based on what it had given to them in the realms of economics and politics. It was apprehensive that the old vested interests would be able to marshal enough response from the citizenry to unseat the incumbents. The party in power resorted to massive rigging. The result it produced was not acceptable to the people and the agitation that followed its declaration brought the military back to power. The rest, once again, is history.

In the early years of the twenty-first century Pakistan once again seemed to have entered the same phase of good macroeconomic performance, poor distribution of the rewards of growth to a wider section of the citizenry, and lack of absorptive capacity on the part of the political system it experienced in the mid-1960s. As was the case during the period of Ayub Khan, outside observers once again began to take note of what they perceived as positive economic developments in the country. To take one example: In its issue of 27 March 2006 *Newsweek International* wrote a very favourable story on the country's economic situation. As Ron Moreau who wrote the story put it, 'the proof is in the numbers. Last year the country's GDP growth hit 8.4 per cent, the world's second highest behind China, following two years of solid 6 per cent growth'.[21] Actually it was one year's 6 per cent growth—one of the three factual mistakes made by the magazine in its coverage—but using them as an issue would be a quibble since the correspondent was making the right point: he underscored the very important fact that growth in recent years had been accelerating, a good sign for any economy.

> This year the economy is predicted to expand by 7 per cent. After years of instability, with the government and military trying to distract people from their economic woes by waging *jihad* in Kashmir and railing against neighbouring India, a true middle class is now developing. Economic reforms have given the government money to invest in health and education, and foreign investors are eyeing Pakistan for the first time. In many ways the country has become the world's most surprising economic success story.

This, with one important difference, was an accurate reflection of the state of the economy at the time and I could add a great deal more to suggest that there was indeed an economic boom in the country. A large middle class had begun to exert its growing economic weight; it was buying cars and motorcycles in record numbers; it was purchasing 'files' to lay claim to residential plots in numerous housing estates that had sprung up in most major cities; it was sending its children to expensive private schools; it was taking vacations in Europe and the Middle East; it was going to Dubai to shop in that city's well-appointed shopping malls; it was spending enormous sums of money on weddings and other celebrations. The middle class was in a festive mood.

It was not only the middle class that had gone on a spending spree; *The Newsweek* correctly reported on the interest of foreigners in bringing money to the county. A number of Middle Eastern financial and industrial houses and real estate developers were buying and developing assets in Pakistan. Successful privatization of a number of public sector financial and public utility companies brought the Arab investors to Pakistan. More were expected to come as the country proceeded to put more publicly owned assets on the market. There was Arab interest in green-field plants. A good evidence of this was the ground-breaking ceremony performed on 29 March 2006 by President Pervez Musharraf on a steel mill project that would add a million tons of capacity to domestic production.

There was an increase in domestic investment not just in real estate but also in the economy's productive sectors. Industrialists were putting new money into textiles and cement, and investment was being made in the sector of agricultural processing. While hard numbers were difficult to come by, there was evidence of change in the major cities of the country. Large billboards announced the offerings being made aggressively by commercial banks for the purchase of homes, cars, consumer appliances and for personal consumption. Mobile phone operators offered various services at affordable prices. A number of other billboards gave information about new housing estates being developed. And, some more told of the arrival of new lines of dairy and packaged food products to the market. Specialized trucks were transporting processed chicken, milk and other agricultural products. The latter was a particularly important indicator of development. It showed that agriculture was finally being commercialized and Pakistan may finally be on the road to achieving the remarkable potential of its countryside.

The question whether Pakistan had managed to bring about the needed structural change in its economy to ensure a rate of GDP increase in the range of 7 to 8 per cent was vigorously debated after the government provided estimates of growth for the year 2004–5.

Two points of view were articulated in this debate. It is useful to recall this debate since every significant increase in GDP growth should be carefully analyzed lest it induces complacency among policymakers and results in postponing reforms without which the high rate of growth cannot be sustained.

According to one point of view in this debate, the brisk performance in 2004–5 was the consequence of the happy confluence of a number of positive events. Those who held that view—and I belong to that group—thought there was a low probability of that happening again. The government, on the other hand, maintained that the economic performance in 2004–5 signalled a significant break with the past and had set the economy on a new trajectory of growth. Islamabad maintained that growth was now built into the structure of the economy and will be sustained at a high level for years to come.

It is useful to examine both arguments in some detail not to settle the debate one way or the other but to determine whether all the changes that are needed in the structure of the economy had indeed been made. A better understanding of the factors that contributed to the remarkable economic progress in 2004–5 would help to devise public policy for sustaining growth in the next several years. This task was not undertaken by the government with the seriousness it deserved. The only piece of analysis I saw in the area of determinants of growth was done by the Higher Education Commission. The Commission was one of those relatively rare government entities that was working hard to put together a strategy for bringing about change in a vital sector of the economy. I will have more to say about this subject in another section of the book.

The 'confluence of happy circumstances' argument rested its case on factors such as the extraordinary good weather the country experienced in 2004–5 after several years of damaging drought. Drought had laid waste much of the countryside. Once it ended and rains came, agricultural production rebounded. Agricultural output increased by more than 7 per cent in 2004–5 over the previous year. Perhaps as much as 1.5 percentage points in the rate of increase of 8.4 per cent recorded in 2004–5 could be attributed to the bounce back in agricultural output. However, this was not the only fortuitous event.

Some other sectors of the economy also began the process of recovery from a decade and a half of stagnation. We know from the experience of many countries around the globe that continuity in policies and palpable efforts at economic reform can bring the economy back to its long-term growth path. This happened in country after country in Latin America in the 1990s. This is also the reason why the Indian GDP growth increased sharply once reforms were introduced in the early 1990s.[22]

If Pakistan had not been beset by political instability and poor governance in 1993–9, the economy could have grown at the rate of about 5 to 5.5 per cent a year. That was the structural rate of growth of those times. Instead the rate of increase was less than 4 per cent during this turbulent period.[23] This gap between real and possible growth resulted in 'suppressed growth' equivalent to about 20 to 25 per cent of the GDP. This began to be released once political stability returned and there was continuity in public policy. Stability was bought at the price of suspended growth. Islamabad need not have accepted the strategy forced on it by the International Monetary Fund (IMF) at that time. The IMF favoured stabilization first and resumption of growth later. Once the IMF programme was done, the authorities, concerned with low growth, decided to stimulate the economy by priming the monetary pump. I would guess that another 1.5 percentage points of the 8.4 per cent increase could be attributed to this policy stance.

Finally, we should take into account the large amount of foreign capital inflow that augmented domestic savings and increased the rate of investment in the period after September 2001. Over the 2001–5 period foreign flows amounted to some 8 per cent of the GDP a year. These added 2 percentage points to the rate of growth. Adding the contributions made by these three determinants of growth—by good weather, by monetary expansion, and by a sizeable increase in external savings—it is possible to conclude that some 5 percentage points in the increase in national output in

2004–5 can be accounted for by these essentially exogenous factors. Or, putting it differently, the economy's internal structures produced a rate of growth of only 3.5 per cent. Absent these happy circumstances, the economy would revert closer to the rates of increase experienced in what the administration headed by President General Pervez Musharraf called the 'lost decade of development', the 1990s. The rate will be a little higher but not a great deal more because of the few structural changes such as the modernization of the financial sector that were made since the military took power in October 1999. This then was the line of analysis behind the 'confluence of happy circumstances' school of thought.

The official view, of course, was very different. It attributed the performance of the economy since 2003 to good public policy. According to it the revival of the economy was owed to a number of structural changes made by Islamabad, particularly in the financial sector. The Musharraf government was confident that it had put policies in place that would continue to produce high rates of growth well into the future. My conversations with some senior policymakers during a month-long visit to the country in the spring of 2006 highlighted two beliefs strongly held by official Islamabad.

One, government's own statistics were not accurate; they under-reported the rate of investment. At the current rate, the economy's incremental capital output ratio—the amount of GDP that must be invested to produce one per cent increase in national income—was not as low as 2.5 as official statistics suggested. It was around 3.5, while even a figure of 3.5 suggested economic efficiencies that were not apparent in the country. If there was truth in that assertion then a sustainable growth rate of some 6 to 6.5 per cent was more plausible.

Two, the government believed that the unusually high amounts of foreign capital flows could be sustained well into the future. There was comfort in the belief that foreign investors had developed confidence in the economy and will bring capital into the country to benefit from the relatively high rates of return that had become available. This was particularly true for the affluent members of the Pakistani diasporas, particularly those in the United States, that had begun to invest in some sectors of the economy. There was indeed a significant structural change in the stream of remittances sent by Pakistanis living abroad and these people were investing in the country; history showed that their confidence will not survive the re-emergence of economic and political uncertainty.

Why should one be sceptical of the government's point of view? There were a number of soft spots on the economy's surface and several weaknesses in foundations on which the economy's structure was built. Among the soft spots were high inflation, an appreciated rate of exchange, rising trade deficit, possible bubbles in the real estate and capital markets. Among the structural problems were the neglect of the sectors in which the country had comparative advantage, dependence on external savings, supply constraints on exports, dependence on one set of products and a few markets for international commerce, poorly developed human resources, an outdated physical infrastructure and a poorly developed corporate sector. As discussed in the first section of this chapter, economic theory has advanced enough to suggest that Pakistan in 2006 did not have the endogenous factors present in its economy to suggest that a high level of growth rate would be sustained well into the future.

3. Interface between Politics and Economics

Given the analysis offered in the previous section, what lies in the country's economic future? It didn't seem possible, given the soft spots and structural weaknesses that public policies had indeed been adopted to ensure a high rate of economic growth in the next several years. Islamabad had begun to suggest that the country had finally left the groups of laggards and joined the club of high-performing Asian nations. That didn't seem to be the case. The government suggested that it had identified the sectors and economic activities that will ensure high rates of sustainable growth. That was not done, with a few exceptions.

Is it unrealistically optimistic to project a growth rate of up to eight per cent during good years? Not necessarily so. We need only to look at India's growth record over the last two and a half decades to suggest that an increase in GDP of this magnitude is possible in countries with significant amounts of suppressed growth. Pakistan is in the same situation today as India was in the early 1990s. Like India it could also experience a growth spurt and make it last for a while with supportive policies and a favourable domestic environment.

But it would be wrong to assume that the state of nirvana has been achieved. There are many pitfalls the economy could confront as it begins to move forward. The most serious of the difficulties it can run into is another political crisis. Such a crisis, were it to develop, will not only deflect the attention of the policymakers in Islamabad; it will also discourage new investments in the economy. We know from our experience how difficult it is to make good economic policy and invite investors to take risks when the political system is dysfunctional. To make the system work requires what the Americans began to call the process of nation-building, following their invasions of Afghanistan and Iraq. Pakistan is still at the beginning stage of that process. Poor state of law and order and an inefficient legal and judicial system is another obstacle that may slow down the rate of economic recovery. A great deal of attention is required in this area to create an investor friendly environment. I will deal with each of these two constraints in turn.

First, the possibility of the return of political instability. Let me start with a bit of history. The term nation-building had gained considerable currency in the 1950s and 1960s as scores of new states that had gained independence from colonial rule began to define themselves. In the 1970s and 1980s, interest in this process on the part of development practitioners flagged as the global economy wrestled with a number of economic problems, including inflation, a sharp increase in the price of oil, and the problem of debt that ruined a number of developing economies. In the 1990s, attention shifted to the socialist countries in Eastern Europe and

Central Asia as a score of nations, liberated from the control of Moscow, began the difficult process of making the transition to market-based economic systems.

The area of development has been subject to fads. Nation-building came back into fashion in the early years of the twenty-first century—largely due to America's preoccupation with the dangers to the global system which many Washington-based policymakers attribute to the Islamic world's underdeveloped political systems. A number of them concluded that America and the West will have to get the world of Islam to develop politically and socially in order to save themselves from the '9/11' types of horrors. Once regime changes had been brought about in Kabul and Baghdad, the administration of President George W. Bush began the process of nation-building in Afghanistan and Iraq. That process did not go too well for the reason that the goals that were to be achieved were never clearly defined.

What did nation-building actually involve? Did it mean democratization of the political system by introducing representative forms of government in countries that have only seen authoritarian rule? Or did it mean the laborious and time-consuming effort aimed at building institutions without which democracy cannot take root? Or, again, did it mean concentrating mostly on providing people with basic needs and services before inviting them to proceed to the polling booth?

It is important to answer these questions, particularly in the context of Pakistan. One major problem Pakistan's economy could run into is the possibility of another structural failure in the political system. President Pervez Musharraf and his colleagues sought to prevent that by introducing a new political order without formally changing the constitution. In a conversation with him in Islamabad in March 2005, I asked him why he was not prepared to go to the people with the suggestion that the parliamentary system had not worked in the country given the way political and economic power was distributed.[24] What was needed was a presidential system in which the people directly voted for the chief executive and then gave him the freedom to implement his mandate over a specified period of time. I suggested that the system over which he was presiding resembled a presidential form rather than a parliamentary structure that was embedded in the constitution of 1973. He accepted the argument but said that working on a new constitutional dispensation would be a risky enterprise. 'Any attempt to do that would open a Pandora's box', he said. His approach, instead, was to create a new system by stealth. A Legal Framework Order promulgated by his administration before the polls of October 2002 was a step in that direction. But the opposition led by the Islamists in the Muttahida Majlis-e-Amal refused to oblige.

They forced changes in the system President Musharraf wished to introduce. What resulted was a hybrid system of government, part presidential and part parliamentary. But a quasi-presidential system was not the only innovation introduced by the new military government. It was General Musharraf's wish to prevent another constitutional crisis in the country that prompted him to create a role for the military in the system. This was also not acceptable to the political groups that opposed him in the National Assembly elected in October 2002. There were, therefore, enough ambiguities and uncertainties in the structure of politics to warrant concerns about its stability. Given Pakistan's past history, there was a real danger that politics could cause the economy to stumble once again. And, given the fact that after three years of hard work by Islamabad, the economy began to recover, it would be unfortunate if this opportunity was sacrificed at the altar of politics.

It is interesting that after 9/11 even the liberal community in the West that had actively espoused the cause of democracy in the developing world began to develop serious doubts about the wisdom of forcing change at a pace faster than permitted by local circumstances. In a widely read book, Fareed Zakaria, a member of the liberal establishment, presented a convincing case for adopting a more measured approach in introducing democracy in developing countries. 'For people in the West, democracy means "liberal democracy", a political system marked not only by free and fair elections but also by the rule of law, a separation of powers, and the protection of basic liberties of speech, assembly, religion, and property. But this bundle of freedoms—what might be called "constitutional liberalism"—has nothing intrinsically to do with democracy, and the two have not always gone together, even in the West,' wrote Zakaria in his 2003 book.[25] In 2006, as Pakistan began to prepare for another election, it was clear that its political system was nowhere close to constitutional liberalism.

America's experiences in Afghanistan and Iraq led even those who had always voted for democracy as the best form of government in all societies to begin to talk about a phased approach. In an article published in *The New Yorker* in January 2006, Hendrik Herzberg drew an interesting lesson for nation-building in the developing world from the history of Chicago.

> The quintessential city that works is, of course, Chicago. The ward heelers and alderman of that city understand that political power flows not from the barrel of a gun and not even necessarily from the ballot box, but from the ability to fix potholes. Garbage that gets collected, buses and trains that take people to places, cops that whack bad guys upside the head, taps that yield water when you turn them on, lights that go on when you flip the switch, all lubricated by taxes and a bit of honest graft—these are what keep streets calm, voters pacified, and righteous reformers out of City Hall.

Much the same point was made to me in a conversation by a senior member of the new political administration in Islamabad.

> When I go campaigning in the streets I notice people don't worry about Pakistan's foreign policy or about the way America is treating the Muslim world. They don't even talk about Kashmir. They are not even bothered by a little bit of corruption on the part of poorly paid government officials. Their main concern is with the availability of services—health, education, clean water, reliable electric power, city lights—they expect from the government and their representatives. If you don't meet their expectations they will ... switch their votes [away from you] and go for a new face. If you deny them these services for a long time, they will get sufficiently agitated and throw out the entire system.[26]

It is precisely the services that *The New Yorker* wrote about and the Islamabad-based politician talked about that suffered in Pakistan during the chaotic nineties. They will suffer again if the opposition to General Musharraf manages to have its way. Another politically induced economic downturn will, ultimately, cause grievous damage to politics and set back by years the prospects of democracy's eventual return. At this moment in time what Pakistan needs the most is economic growth and all its attendant benefits.

The second pitfall the economy faced in 2006 was the prospect that investment, both domestic and foreign, may not come back in the amounts needed for sustained growth. Uncertainty is the enemy of investment and nothing produces greater uncertainty than the prospect of danger to life and property. That danger may not be real; it has only to be apprehended for the investor to become reluctant to risk his capital. There was a widely held perception, particularly outside the country, that Pakistan was not a safe place in which to do business; that the state was unable to provide adequate protection to the lives and assets of business people, particularly foreigners; that the legal and judicial systems were difficult to work to enforce contracts; that the country, in spite of all the efforts made by the government of President Musharraf, had turned xenophobic. The fact that the US State Department's 'travel advisory' continued to apply to Pakistan five years after 9/11 and the invasion of Afghanistan did not help remove that perception. Pakistan was no more violent than a number of other developing countries which continued to attract foreign investors. In the case of Pakistan, however, reports of violence in the western press were invariably put in the context of the activities of such anti-western groups as Al Qaeda.

A sense of insecurity about life and property also inhibited investment by domestic entrepreneurs. In their case, however, poorly functioning legal and regulatory systems were more problematic. Foreign investors could always rely on courts and arbitration mechanisms outside the country. These options were not available to local businesses. These problems needed the government's attention for domestic and foreign investment to increase by significant amounts, a condition that must be met for the economy to grow at the rate for which it clearly had the potential.

4. Sustaining a High Level of GDP Growth[27]

Economic situation in the fall of 2006 looked reasonably good but it raised three queries about the future. One, was the present a good predictor of the future? Two, could the economy achieve sustainable growth based on consumption, the main determinant of growth during 2003–6? Three, should the nation sit back and enjoy as the future unfolded, or was there a good deal of additional work that needed to be done before it could be said that the country had finally secured its economic future? To more discerning observers it was clear that the boom of 2003–6 rested on weak foundations; it could not be sustained unless a number of structural reforms were undertaken. The structures that need to be rebuilt or demolished altogether were created over a long time and a number of vested interests had developed around them to protect them from being changed. There were a number of weaknesses in the economy that needed the urgent attention of the policymakers in Islamabad. The most glaring of these was that the boom rested mostly on consumption and not on investment. The time available for setting the economy on the right course was not all that long, perhaps no longer than a couple of years.

What complicated the situation for the policymakers in Islamabad was the fact that the period during which adjustments had to be made was the period when the country had to prepare for another set of elections. These were scheduled for the fall of 2007. Correcting the economic course when elections were just around the corner was a difficult enterprise even for a mature political system. It would be extremely difficult for a country that was still trying to find political legs on which to stand. There was, therefore, not much time left to smoothen all the economic wrinkles in the economic fabric.

The economic story would have been a success if the rate of growth in per capita income in 2003–6 could be sustained over a reasonable period of time; if significant reductions were occurring in the incidence of poverty; if policymaking in Islamabad had been thoroughly institutionalized; if economic decision-making had been decentralized to lower tiers of government that were closer to the people and if capacity had been created at these levels to deliver services and development to the people. There were very few signs of any of these things happening. Unless the course on which the economy was set was changed quite significantly, the country could run into rough political and social weather as it did in the closing years of the Ayub Khan regime.

'Staying the course' was a phrase popularized by George W. Bush in relation to his country's policies towards Iraq. But sometimes policymakers must take a deep breadth, reflect carefully on the situation they were dealing with, and change the direction being pursued. The moment for doing precisely that had arrived in Pakistan in 2006 with respect to the management of the economy. There were many examples of good economic situations turning sour quite quickly; that happened not only in Pakistan in the 1960s but in a number of countries in other parts of the developing world.

When I looked at Pakistan's economic situation in 2006, I was reminded of what I saw in Latin America in 1994. It was early in that year that I was appointed vice president at the World Bank in charge of that continent and began to study the economies of the major Latin American countries. Latin America then was buoyant; that was particularly the case with Mexico which was entering into a free trade arrangement with Canada and the United States, where large amounts of investment had begun to arrive from the United States, where the financial markets in New York were opening themselves for access to the Mexican government and to indigenous Mexican enterprises.

During a visit to Mexico City in the spring of 1994 and discussions with a number of senior officials, I compared the Mexican situation with those that I had seen in East Asia, the region where I had worked before moving to Latin America. I saw many weaknesses in the Mexican economy, in particular the un-sustainability of its external accounts, the increasing reliance on external borrowings to finance trade deficit, the exposure of the banking system to high risk borrowers, and poor productivity of the industrial sector which made it difficult to compete in the international market. In a meeting with Carlos Salinas, then president of Mexico in January 1994 and later with Pedro Aspe, an accomplished economist who was then serving as finance minister, I expressed some apprehensions about the future of the country's economy. They dismissed my concerns and told me that Mexico should not be compared with the countries of East Asia. The economic, social and political fundamentals of the two regions were so different that lessons could not be drawn from the one for the other. Within less than a year of these conversations, however, Mexico was in a deep crisis; its banking system collapsed, the value of the currency plummeted, inflation increased significantly, and the government's financing spun out of control. Not only did the Mexican economy go into a tailspin; the country pulled down with it other countries of the region as well.

I compared the Pakistani situation with the one I found in Mexico in 1994 in a brief comment on the presentations made by Pakistan's State Bank Governor Shamshad Akhtar in Washington in April 2006. The Governor was speaking at a seminar organized by the Woodrow Wilson Center. I said that there were a number of developments in the Pakistani economy that threatened not only growth but could result in instability: Inflation had increased; trade deficit had grown to the point where balance of payments were becoming a burden for the health of the economy; a number of commercial banks, exposed to a wide variety of consumer loans, had a weak and weakening asset base; investments were being made in the more speculative parts of the economy; and the gap between national savings and investment was increasing. In many ways Pakistan, I said, was operating a casino economy. That comment was picked up by the Pakistani press and caused considerable discomfort in Islamabad.

All that having been said, Pakistan in 2006 did not appear to be headed towards an economic crisis. There was still time to correct the course. Pakistan's economy had been on a roller coaster ride all through its nearly sixty years of development; it once again showed signs of having reached a height from which it could fall. There were many weaknesses from which the economy suffered and which could stall growth and begin the process of a serious reduction in the rate of expansion. These included fiscal policy and government expenditures in non-productive activities, insufficient public investment in several critical sectors, severe trade imbalances, an energy crisis that was just around the corner, slow moving exports with heavy reliance on textiles and dependence on access to the United States' market, choking of traffic on the main roads in many large cities with heavy associated costs to the businesses. The list did not end with these; it went on and on. These weaknesses could be overcome reasonably quickly but that would need the government's attention within a well thought-out medium term framework. A framework did exist; it was developed under the aegis of the World Bank but that was a hurried job for which several ministries and development agencies provided inputs that were assembled within the covers of one document that lacked coherence, imagination and foresight.

These were good days but good days could turn into difficult times if public policy neglected to deal with the problems that lay just under the surface. The country faced numerous problems which required serious thought and action. There was considerable political uncertainty as the country headed towards another set of elections in 2007. The war against terrorism was heating up along the border with Afghanistan. Afghanistan itself was becoming more unsettled with every passing day. Relations with Washington appeared to have been strained, particularly after the visit to South Asia in March 2006 by George W. Bush, the American president.

The links between groups of radicals that operated in several Muslim communities in Britain and Pakistani Islamic extremists were exposed by two incidents that shook the world: the bombing of the London mass transport system on 7 July 2005 by four suicide bombers that claimed the lives of fifty-two innocent commuters, and the revelation on 10 August 2006 of a plot to bomb American airliners bound for various destinations in the United States. The airliners plot involved two dozen young people, most of them from the Pakistani diaspora in Britain. The wide media coverage received by these two events did not increase the confidence of the investors in Pakistan. And yet Pakistan in 2006 was even more dependent on foreign capital flows than was the case in several other periods when the confluence of events plunged the economy into severe crises. There was no doubt that as 2006 drew to a close, a number of dark clouds were appearing on the economic horizon. The country seemed headed towards another period of economic difficulties if not a crisis. There could be a repeat of what happened in 1969 and 1977 when popular discontent led to prolonged political difficulties. That could happen again, and the reason for it would be the economy's inability to deliver the poor from poverty and to close the widening gap between the bottom 20 and top 20 per cent of the population.

Since Pakistan's population was increasing at the rate of over 2 per cent a year, the GDP growth rate of 5 per cent could stop any further increase in the number of people living in poverty. But arresting the incidence of poverty at a high level would not buy time for the administration in power. It needed a GDP increase three times the rate of growth of population to have the poverty pool shrink by 10 per cent a year. If Pakistan managed a growth rate of 6.5 to 7.5 per cent in its GDP in the period 2005–10, the number of people living in poverty could decline to 34 million, or under 20 per cent of the expected size of the population of 172 million people in 2010. It was, therefore, gratifying for the policymakers in Islamabad that the Pakistani economy, having gone through a fairly long period of stagnation, began to grow, starting in 2003–4. If what we have learnt from the experience of other countries holds true for Pakistan, the pick up in the rate of growth should begin to see a decline in the incidence of poverty. How rapidly the pool of poverty shrinks will depend on how fast the economy grows in the future and for how long a high growth rate could be sustained. As discussed in Section 1 above, Pakistan has experienced growth spurts in the past. In two periods—in both of them the military was in charge—Pakistan's GDP grew by more than 6 per cent a year. During the eleven years of the period of Ayub Khan, the GDP increased at the rate of 6.7 per cent a year. In the Ziaul Haq period, which lasted also for eleven years, the GDP grew at 6.4 per cent a year. This should not imply that the Pakistani economy does well when men in uniform are in control. What it does show though is that during the periods of military rule Pakistan was able to draw significant amounts of foreign capital which augmented its low rate of domestic savings, and produced reasonable amounts of investment. But during military rule the economy also became extremely dependent on external capital flows. This created enormous vulnerability.

During the period of Ayub Khan Pakistan invested 21.1 per cent of its GDP. In the Zia period, the rate of investment was 18 per cent. These rates fell significantly when the flow of foreign capital declined as it did beginning in 1965 and again in 1989. Should we attribute the more recent increase to GDP growth to a larger flow of external savings? How precarious is this flow and could a significant reduction in it bring the economy down to its knees once again?

There is no doubt that the inflow of foreign capital increased after 9/11. This happened for three reasons. Considerably larger amounts of American aid became available after General Pervez Musharraf took the decision to side with Washington in its war against international terrorism. The US also cracked down on the remittances sent by Pakistani expatriates through the *hundi* system. And, the government was able to negotiate a significant amount of reduction in the stock of debt which helped it to save large amounts of money that was used for servicing it. If the Americans pull out of Afghanistan and if aid flows from Washington cease once again as they did in 1965 and 1989, would the rate of economic growth plummet to the levels of the 1990s? Could the rate of growth be sustained without large official capital flows?

The management of the economy under President Musharraf has resulted in a number of structural changes that could provide the basis for sustainable growth. These include the transfer of most commercial banking from public to private hands. In 2006, less than one-fifth of banking assets were with the government-owned banks and even in that rapidly shrinking sector the government had a programme to increase the share of private ownership. The State Bank of Pakistan had gone through a period of significant reforms. It had improved not only monetary management but also kept a watchful eye on the performance of the banking sector with the help of strengthened supervisory and regulatory mechanisms. The regulation of the banking and the non-banking sectors was now in the hands of separate agencies—the State Bank and the Security Exchange Commission of Pakistan (SECP). The SECP had introduced a number of reforms to strengthen the internal management of the corporations listed on the various stock exchanges.

There were a number of reforms in the area of fiscal management. The government had reduced fiscal deficit to below 4 per cent of the GDP thus creating, for a while, a non-inflationary economic environment. With the government's financing needs reduced significantly, there was little need for it to go to the banks or the capital markets to borrow money. That reduced pressure in the money markets and made it possible to lower interest rates. One of the most important reforms introduced by the Musharraf regime was to rationalize the National Savings Scheme (NSS). The rates offered on various NSS instruments were brought close to those on offer to savers by the market. At the same time, banks and other financial institutions were barred from investing in the NSS. That forced these institutions to make their resources available to the private sector.

The creation of fiscal space as a result of a lessened debt burden resulted in some increase—albeit a modest one—in the Public Sector Development Programme (PSDP). The programme gave much needed financial support to both human resource development and to improving the country's physical infrastructure.

These were steps in the right direction. Nonetheless, the Musharraf government did not recognize that it needed to develop a consistent strategy for ensuring sustainable increase in the size of the economy if it wished to avoid the sputtering out of growth. This happened in the past when, for some reason or the other, external capital flows declined precipitously.

In addition to continued dependence on external flows because of a low level of domestic savings, Pakistan's economy continued to suffer from three other structural weaknesses. It had a weak human resource, it had a poorly developed physical infrastructure particularly in the sectors of electric power, railways and ports; and the quality of governance remained poor in spite of the efforts made at bringing some sense of accountability to the upper levels of decision-making.

In order to address the long-standing problem of low domestic savings, the country needed to develop institutions that encouraged people to save more. We know from the experience of some Latin American countries that the creation of private pension plans resulted in significant improvements in domestic saving rates. Pakistan had pension schemes that covered the employees of the public sector and those working for large private companies. Nothing was available for other workers. The establishment of private equity funds could also help small and medium enterprises scale up. These enterprises are funded by the owners; another source of capital such as private equity would draw more resources into these companies.

Attention also needs to be given to improving the quality of human resource.[28] This should cover not only primary education and basic health care. It should also deal with secondary, tertiary, and technical education and the capacity to do research and development. The government's effort is needed to touch upon all institutional improvements, including the development of the private sector.

5. Obstacles to Sustainable Growth

Two areas—improvements in physical infrastructure and the quality of governance—need to receive an equal amount of government attention. Let me begin with the infrastructure area, as discussed in Section 1 above, in which the colonial administration had made considerable amounts of investment. These provided a rich inheritance for Pakistan which it did little to develop. The only significant investment made in the irrigation system was done in the context of the Indus Basin Replacement Works. As the programme's name suggests, these works did not add much to the system. Their primary purpose was to replace the water that was allocated to India. The network of communications was similarly neglected. In the fifty-year period between 1947 and 1997, Pakistan added only a couple of hundred kilometres of new railway track to the vast network left behind by the British. The road building record was better but the major investment in this period was the construction of the Lahore–Islamabad motorway that remained underused half a dozen years after it was opened to traffic. Pakistan did not invest much in power and telecommunications, either. The country was briefly surplus in electric power after a score of generation units were built in the 1990s under the independent power producers' programme. The programme was expensive in the sense that it obliged WAPDA to purchase power from private producers at a price higher than its average cost of production. This meant that WAPDA ended up subsidizing the independent generators, and weakening its own financial situation. Although Pakistan had invested a significant amount of public money in developing the telecommunication network, it was done in a haphazard way. The country was also slow to reform the Pakistan Telecommunication Corporation which performed inefficiently, not unlike most public sector enterprises.

Pakistan will have to build fast the infrastructure it needs to support a growing economy. It also needs to repair equally quickly the infrastructure that already exists. The latter—the work of repair—needs to be undertaken in particular to restore the efficiency of the large irrigation network. To do all that requires a well thought out action plan that carefully examines the demands of a growing economy and then find sources for funding it. It was fortunate for Pakistan that the World Bank had decided to concentrate once again on infrastructure development as a high priority at the time the country's resource needs for investment in this area were very large.

Some of what I discussed in Section 1 above about the rich inheritance from the British in terms of physical infrastructure also applied to matters concerning governance. At the time of independence, Pakistan had a functioning bureaucratic system, a legal system that worked reasonably well, an administrative system that maintained law and order with a fair amount of efficiency in most parts of the country, and a system of local government that looked after the needs of most of the population. Most of these institutions were allowed to wither away or were deliberately abolished by a series of administrations that governed the country over the last half century. Little new was created in their place. The poor quality of governance was one painful consequence of this neglect of institutions. It is not surprising that in the 1990s Pakistan came to be identified as one of the most corrupt places on earth. The rebuilding of the instruments of governance was needed, since good governance is an important determinant of economic growth.

To understand why this is the case, it will be helpful to compare the situation in Pakistan with that in India. India will succeed economically in spite of the fact that some of the economic and social problems it faces were more serious than those Pakistan confronted. India was much more crowded than Pakistan. With some 15 to 20 per cent of the world's poor, the burden of poverty it carried was also much heavier. There was great inequality not just among its more than one billion people. Some of the Indian states in the country's north and east had a per capita income one-fourth of the average in some of those in the west and south. There were serious social and political problems in the country that the various systems in play were barely able to handle.

In many parts of the country, women faced great discrimination; wife-burning to punish young women for not bringing sufficient dowry for the groom's household was sufficiently common to worry sociologists and social workers. The system of roads, railways, bridges and ports was straining under the impact of a rapidly growing economy. India had done even less than Pakistan to improve the physical infrastructure it inherited from the British. The Indian bureaucrat, in spite of all the investment the country had made in its fabled Institutions of Management, continued to believe that his job was to obstruct rather than to facilitate. And yet India had developed the reputation of a country that worked; Pakistan that of a country that was poised at the edge of an abyss.

There were many reasons for these differences in perception. The Indians did a much better job of representing themselves outside the country than was the case with the Pakistanis. This helped to bring in foreign capital, technology and management expertise. They have also invested much more—and much more intelligently than was the case with Pakistan—in creating a highly skilled and well informed work force. But most important of all, India had a much stronger institutional base than did Pakistan. Over the last half century—certainly after the assumption of power in 1971 by Zulfikar Ali Bhutto—Pakistan systematically destroyed the institutions it inherited from the British raj. India did the opposite; it significantly improved upon its institutional inheritance. In the institutional graveyard that Pakistan had become, tombstones carried such names as the civil administration and the system of governance; the judicial and legal systems; political parties, and the political system; the systems for formulating and implementing economic and social strategies; colleges, universities and the system of education. Two institutional structures that survived were the military and the press, the latter because of the relative tolerance displayed by a number of administrations that took office in the 1990s, especially the one headed by President Pervez Musharraf.

Why had Pakistan become a graveyard of institutions? Unlike the leaders and leadership groups in India, those who ruled Pakistan came to believe that the institutions that were in place stood in the way of their ability to reach their goals. Some of the time the goals were personal enrichment or concentration of power in one pair of hands. Even when the rulers' aim was to improve the welfare of common citizens, most institutions were regarded as bumps in the road to be ridden over.

The process of institutional decay began the moment Pakistan gained independence. The country's first generation of rulers did not have a firm political base. Not prepared to trust the masses, it bypassed them. Thus began the tradition of rule without consultation, discourse and representation. At the same time the urgent need to rehabilitate and resettle millions of refugees who had arrived from India, led to the use of unconstrained state power. Evacuee property—the assets left by the departing Hindus and Sikhs—was disposed of at the will of the administrators whose actions could not be easily questioned in the courts. The seeds of corruption that were to mar the Pakistani landscape in the decade of the nineties were in fact planted in the soil immediately after the country was founded.

The first seven years of President Ayub Khan's administration were committed to the economic development of the country, a goal that was achieved with considerable fanfare at home and celebration abroad. For some time Pakistan was feted as the model of development. Nonetheless, Pakistan's first military ruler did not appreciate the important point that the process he had begun could not be sustained without a functioning judicial system, representative politics, and freedom of expression. In this approach he was encouraged by a number of development theorists who believed at that time that strong military governments led ably by visionary leaders could deliver their countries from economic and social backwardness. Among them was the political scientist Samuel P. Huntington who in the work already cited suggested that the military was in a better situation to guide politically backward societies in the period of transition towards modernity.[29] There was not much point in consulting the people with the help of a representative system of government or giving them voice with the help of a free press. Even an independent judicial system was seen as obstructing the path to rapid economic development.

Ayub Khan came down hard on the judicial system, on the development of political parties, on developing a representative system of government, and on the press. On the other hand he developed a sound system of economic planning and management, a local government structure that brought the state closer to the people and an educational system that began to improve the level of human development. Had he not suppressed the first set of institutions, he and his government would not have fallen so easily to the predatory designs of an ambitious general who was much less well-equipped to govern. Ayub Khan would not have succumbed had he allowed the press to freely report on some of the economic tensions that were caused by his model of development, had he put in place a political system that could find relief for those who felt that they had been left behind by the fast pace towards reaching economic goals that were once believed to be unachievable, had he permitted the judges and the judicial system to keep the fast moving economic and social systems within legal bounds. These are some of the great 'what ifs?' in Pakistan's history.[30] Ultimately, the institutions he did not build or those that he did not develop destroyed those he had created with tender loving care.

The destruction of institutions continued under Ayub Khan's successors, General Yahya Khan and Zulfikar Ali Bhutto. The two together discarded the system of bureaucratic management. That system may have had many faults but it also attracted high quality human resource to its ranks and provided reasonably good governance. It worked well in the area of economic management. And Bhutto's heavy hand fell on the system of education, bringing politics into college and university campuses. Bhutto also continued the Ayubian practice of suppressing the freedom of expression and manipulating political processes to achieve personal goals. Once again, as had happened to Ayub Khan and Yahya Khan before him, the institutions that could have saved him from being dislodged by the military were simply absent when they could have served a useful purpose for him. In fact, tragically, Bhutto was sent to the gallows by an institution—the judiciary—that he had himself subverted.

President Zia continued to show not only the same disdain for institution building that was shown by his predecessors but went one step further and began to use the state to bring religion into politics, the economy and society. In doing so Zia was not responding to public demand; he, like some of his predecessors, was putting in place what he thought the people needed or should require. Zia's Islamization programme left a legacy with which the country is still trying to come to terms sixty years after its creation. While bringing religion into many spheres of public life, the Zia administration did practically nothing to resurrect the institutions without which societies simply cannot develop. The political system remained largely unrepresentative, political parties continued to be manipulated to serve the ruling master, the judiciary was forced into submission and the legal system was allowed to atrophy.

Eleven years of civilian rule interspersed with five general elections underscored one important point about institutional development: that periodic reference to the people, without the support of institutions, is not a recipe for the development of a representative form of government. The two mainstream political parties that were given the opportunity to govern made no effort to prepare the ground for erecting a permanent structure of governance in which people would openly participate. That had been accomplished in India; given the chance once again, the Pakistani leaders let the country down once more. Theirs was total failure which once again encouraged the military to step in. A break was needed in the trajectory the country was pursuing at that time. But the question is whether progress has been made since 12 October 1999?

The answer has to be in the negative. Once again there was a belief that institutions are not important; what was needed was the leader's goodwill, determination and vision. Under President Pervez Musharraf there has been no progress in terms of developing civilian institutions, improving the state of the judiciary, strengthening the legal system, developing the capacity to do strategic thinking in economic affairs, encouraging the development of political parties, and laying down rules for succession. And by requiring the military to enter not only politics but also many civilian activities, he may have hurt the one institution that had survived the general decay in the country's institutional foundation.

The overall disdain towards institution building notwithstanding, the Musharraf government took two important steps in the area of institutional development. It established—or, more accurately, reconfigured—a system of accountability that applied to all segments of society. It also introduced a far-reaching change in the system of local government that has transferred a significant amount of authority to elected people at the local level. The *Nazims* (mayors), elected by the people, were much closer to the citizenry than any other official chosen by the people with a wide array of authority ever was in the country's history.

While these were moves in the right direction, there were some problems with both initiatives. These need to be corrected. The law that governed the accountability system did not provide the types of safeguards all citizens need when they are deemed to have done some wrong. The basic tenet of all well functioning legal systems is that the accused are treated as innocent unless proven to be guilty. The Musharraf government's accountability law made the opposite assumption. It assumed that the burden of proof rested on those charged with bad behaviour.

In so far as the *Nazim*-based system of local government was concerned, it also ran into some teething problems. Elected members of the provincial and national legislatures resented the power wielded by the local elected officials. During the period of transition from a system of administration in which the office of the deputy commissioner also controlled the magistracy and the police force, it was clear where the responsibility for maintaining law and order actually resided. Under the new system, there was some confusion as to who is responsible in this area.

It would be fair to assert that the Musharraf government has some distance to go before it can be sure that it has placed the economy on the trajectory of high growth. It introduced a number of important structural reforms that would ensure that the revival of the economy was not based on the largess of a few foreign friends. But it had to work on a number of structural reforms not seriously addressed by any of the past administrations. As 2006 drew towards a close, it appeared that Pakistan was once again entering a period of political and economic uncertainty.

6. Poverty, Inequality and the Millennium Development Goals

In an important article by Dr Parvez Hasan published by *Dawn* in its business pages in March 2006, the author presented a sobering picture of the state of poverty in the country. He drew attention to the fact that the government's claim that there had been a sizeable reduction in the incidence of poverty needed to be checked carefully with respect to the base year used for drawing the trend line, and the methodology employed for analyzing the data that had still to be released.[31]

What did the numbers released by the government show? According to a household income survey carried out by the government in 2005, the incidence of poverty declined by 20 per cent in the four year period between 2001 and 2005, from 32.1 to 25.4 per cent. Rural poverty declined from 39 to 31.8 per cent in the same period. Do these numbers really indicate a reduction in poverty? There was considerable scepticism among the analysts outside the government about the government's assertion, that its policies had made a significant contribution to addressing the problem of poverty. One reason for doubt was the choice of the base year for the survey. The year 2001 was exceptionally bad for agriculture; a major drought had taken a heavy toll on agricultural output. Rains came in 2005 and agricultural output rebounded; value added in agriculture increased by 7.6 per cent compared to the previous year. As pointed out by Hasan, choosing a bad year as the base and a good year as the end point for drawing conclusions about trends is not an exercise that can lend credibility to it.

That notwithstanding, it was not surprising that the government's survey showed a significant decline in the incidence of poverty. A sharp pick-up in growth during this period was one important reason; growth, as was recognized by development economists, was a necessary, albeit not a sufficient, condition for reducing the incidence of poverty. In the 1997–2001 period, four years prior to the base year used for the survey, the GDP increased at the annual rate of 3.3 per cent. In the period covered by the survey the increase was of the order of 6 per cent a year, almost twice as high as in the previous period. In Pakistan's case one other development also helped. In 2001–5, non-defence public expenditure increased by 50 per cent in real terms compared to its total stagnation in the 1990s. The fiscal space that become available to Islamabad because of the large flows of external capital and a significant reduction in the burden of debt was put to use in some of the sectors important for poverty alleviation. By 2006, Islamabad along with the four provinces was spending much more on education and health, sectors that, over time, would help to reduce the incidence of poverty.

The reduction in the incidence of poverty noted in the previous section, would have been much more significant but wasn't on account of inherent inequalities in existing power and asset structures. The concentration of power in the hands of a few elites meant that public policy was skewed in their favour. As the World Bank wrote in the *World Development Report 2006*, which dealt with the subject of inequality, 'the adverse effects of unequal opportunity and political power on development are all the more damaging because economic, political and social inequalities tend to reproduce themselves over time and across generations. We call such phenomena "inequality traps".'[32] How inequality traps have impacted on Pakistan's development is a subject I will address in a later section.

What was worrying was the growing income inequality, if political scientist Samuel Huntington's line of argument was to be taken seriously. As already discussed in Section 1 of this chapter, Huntington argued in his seminal work that increase in inequality, even if it is perceived and not real, can be politically and socially destabilizing. Whether income inequalities worsened in the 2001–6 period when economic growth began to pick up was something only detailed data on household income and expenditure could show. However, given that speculative investments in real estate and in the stock market were behind some of the boom noticeable in the economy there was, in all probability, a significant increase in inequality.

Some simple calculations help to explain why some of these speculative activities did not produce incomes for the poorer segments of the population. If an investor put down one crore rupees to buy a canal of land in one of the large cities of the country and invested another half a crore to build a house on it, he (or she) must obtain a minimum return of 1.25 lakh a month to justify this outlay. This would be the case whether the property was rented or not. Even if it was self-occupied, the foregone income was of the order of 1.25 lakh a month. There were very few households in the country that could afford to pay this amount of rent or to forego this amount of income. And yet plots continued to sell. They were being bought in the expectation of appreciation. However, these kinds of speculative activities did not produce employment and income for the poor; they only added to the incomes and wealth of the rich.

Pakistan has done a poor job of analyzing the situation of poverty. The subject was ignored by all administrations that were in office since the country achieved independence. The reason for this neglect is obvious: a strong political and social constituency in favour of focusing public policy on addressing the problem of poverty did not develop. The elites who dominated the corridors of power—whether these corridors were walked by men in uniform or those who wore civilian clothes—were neither interested nor committed to taking care of the poor. Even when some senior officials got involved in studying the reasons for persistent poverty, they invited either ridicule (as was the case with Masud Khadarposh) or suspicion (as was the case with Akhtar Hameed Khan) about their motives.[33]

While the subject of poverty invited little interest, that of inequality was totally ignored by various governments. This has contributed to a serious absence of information and knowledge about a subject that has contributed considerably to political and social instability in the country. As the World Bank writes in the already cited *World Development Report 2006* that dealt with the issue of inequality, 'only in Pakistan is the evolution of inequality not clear, because of difficulties with data comparability.'[34]

With the international community giving greater attention to poverty alleviation, it should be possible for Pakistan to attract a larger amount of assistance if it structured its policies to meet donor expectations. The most important set of expectations were embedded in a programme titled the 'Millennium Development Goals' (MDGs). The MDGs were adopted in September 2000 by the heads of government and state who attended a session of the UN held in New York. General Pervez Musharraf was among those who were present at the meeting and he put Pakistan's signature on what came to be called the Millennium Declaration. What did the declaration say, what are the targets it endorsed and what is the relevance of the declaration and the targets for Pakistan's economic future? These questions have acquired special significance after the transfer of executive authority to an elected government. 'We will spare no effort to promote democracy as well as respect for all internationally recognized human rights and fundamental freedoms,' promised the signatories of the declaration. But these were not the only commitments the world's statesmen made. Eight specific goals were incorporated in the document endorsed by the millennium special session. The first, and by far the most important of these, was the promise to eradicate extreme poverty and hunger.

The most commonly used measure of extreme poverty was to count the number of people with incomes of less than one dollar a day or $365 a year, with the value of the dollar calculated in 'purchasing power' terms rather than in terms of the official rate of exchange. By that count there were some 1.2 billion people living in absolute poverty across the globe when the twentieth century closed. The millennium target was to reduce their number by one-half, to no more than 600 million, by the year 2015. This meant increasing the incomes of 600 million people to beyond $365 a year over the 15-year period between 2000 and 2015. One important consequence of increasing incomes would be a reduction in hunger since the poor spend more than four-fifths of their earnings on food. Halving the incidence of poverty would result in reducing the level of hunger in the world also by one-half.

The second millennium goal related to education. As explained in the Millennium Declaration, education was important in its own right and had strong spillover benefits to mortality rates, income and even social cohesion. Worldwide, of the 680 million children of primary school age, 113 million were not attending school. Of these, not surprisingly, 97 per cent were in developing countries. However, getting children to go to school was only half the battle because they benefited only if they stayed in the educational system and completed the cycle of primary education. And, it was important that the effort to educate children included both sexes. Accordingly, the Millennium Declaration promised that children everywhere—boys and girls alike—would complete a full course of primary education.

The third millennium development goal specifically addressed the problem of gender inequality, the consequence of utter disregard of the rights of girls and women in many parts of the world. This discrimination was blatant in all aspects of human development—education, health, access to employment, disparities in wages and salaries, etc. The millennium signatories focused their attention on education and promised that gender disparities in primary and secondary education would be eliminated, preferably by 2005, and at all levels of education, but certainly by 2015.

That this would not be an easy target to achieve could be appreciated by looking at some statistics on the prevalence and extent of gender inequality. For instance, of the world's 854 million illiterate adults, 544 million (64 per cent) were women and of the

113 million children not in primary school, 68 million (60 per cent) were girls. Education was just one aspect of human development in which women, often deliberately and sometimes by the action of the state, had been left behind. Around the world, including developed countries, women earned about 75 per cent as much as men when performing the same jobs. Domestic violence was common—and tolerated—against women in many societies. 'Honour killings' of women in Pakistan and 'bride burning' in India were especially gruesome examples of the rough justice meted out to women in many parts of the world. And around the world there were an estimated 100 million 'missing' women who would be alive today but for infanticide, neglect or sex-selective abortions.

The Millennium Declaration, after committing itself to a series of goals directed at improving the well-being of the world's women, turned its attention to children. The fourth millennium goal committed the nations of the world to reduce infant and child (children under the age of five) mortality rates by two-thirds by the year 2015. That there existed, even after a number of impressive advances in health science, a wide gap in life expectancy at birth in developed and developing countries was largely the consequence of high rates of infant and child mortality in the world's poor areas. A girl born at the start of the twenty-first century in Japan had a 50 per cent chance of seeing the dawn of the twenty-second century. A child born in Afghanistan today had only a one in four chance of reaching the age of five—or putting it differently—a 75 per cent chance of dying before reaching that age. The most unfortunate aspect of a large incidence of infant and child death was that a significant number of them were preventable. Every year about 11 million children perished from preventable causes, often for want of simple and easily furnished improvements in nutrition, sanitation and maternal health and education. Immunizations against leading diseases were an important element in improving child survival. After making significant gains in the 1980s, largely the consequence of a series of efforts mounted by such international organizations as WHO and UNICEF, immunizations in developing countries levelled off at about 75 per cent in the 1990s. In other words, 25 per cent of all children in the developing world do not receive protection against communicable diseases. The rapid spread of AIDS in Africa and Asia is further affecting the health and the rate of survival of children.

The fifth millennium goal encompassed improving maternal health. The UN declaration committed the world's nations to reducing maternal mortality rates by three-quarters by 2015. Most of these deaths occurred for two reasons: repeated pregnancies that took a heavy toll on women's health, and millions of women having to give birth without being attended by skilled health professionals.

The sixth millennium target dealt with an area still not well understood—HIV/AIDS, malaria and tuberculosis and other diseases that continued to disable and kill millions of people in the developing world. According to one UN report,

> by the end of 2000 almost 22 million people had died of AIDS, 13 million children had lost their mother or both parents to the disease and more than 40 million people were living with the HIV virus—90 per cent of them in developing countries, 75 per cent in Sub-Saharan Africa.

But, increasingly, AIDS was no longer an African disease. It was fast spreading to Asia with China and India destined to become its next big victims. One UN estimate put the number of HIV infected people in India alone at four million and in China at one million.

AIDS was not the only big killer in the developing world. Every year there were more than 300 million cases of malaria, and 60 million people were infected with tuberculosis. While there was still no cure for AIDS, medical technologies available at the time the Millennium Declaration was adopted could prevent malaria and tuberculosis from being fatal. However, the lack of access to these treatments results in tuberculosis that killed two million people a year and malaria another one million people. This crisis had both humanitarian and economic dimensions. Some years ago the World

Bank developed a methodology to estimate the economic loss caused by such debilitating diseases as malaria and tuberculosis.[35] When these potential killers were present in an endemic form, the loss they caused could shave off a couple of percentage points from the rate of economic growth. Recognizing all this, the world leaders who put their signatures on the Millennium Declaration pledged to halt and reverse the spread of HIV/AIDS by 2015 and—also by the same year—to halt and begin to reverse the incidences of tuberculosis, malaria and other major diseases.

Having promised a great deal of action to directly address the problem posed by persistent poverty and to provide better educational and health coverage to the more underprivileged segments of the world's population, the leaders from across the globe turned their attention to the steady deterioration of the physical environment. They promised to integrate the principles of sustainable development into country policies and programmes and reverse the loss of environmental resources. The leaders recognized that global warming was a universal concern and that carbon dioxide emissions were one of its principal causes. The emission of this gas had increased quite dramatically in recent decades, from 5.3 billion tons in 1980 to an estimated 6.6 billion tons in 1998. Much of this emission came from sources in high-income countries. Nonetheless, there was a fear that as rates of economic growth continue to be sustained at a high level in China and continue to increase in India—the two most populous countries of the world—the share of developing countries in carbon dioxide emissions would increase quite significantly. One way of stopping, if not reversing, global warming was to create carbon dioxide sinks—trees and forests that absorb this gas and discharge oxygen into the atmosphere. Unfortunately, the forest cover in most parts of the developing world was decreasing at an alarming rate.

But global environmental deterioration was not the only concern addressed by the world's leaders at the millennium conference. They also looked at the local environment in which the world's poor spent their lives. Accordingly, they pledged to halve the proportion of people without sustainable safe drinking water by 2015. They also promised to achieve, by 2020, a significant improvement in the lives of at least 100 million slum dwellers living in the developing world.

These seven sets of goals were ambitious. If realized they could bring about a profound improvement in the lives of hundreds of millions of the world's poor people. Would these targets be attained simply because the leaders of the world had gathered in New York to celebrate the dawn of the new millennium? The world leaders themselves provided the answer to this question. They recognized the need for developing a global partnership for development—a key component of which would be finding additional financial resources for the countries and people faced with economic and social distress. Some consensus was reached that it would take a total of $40-60 billion a year in addition to the current $56 billion already being provided. With this additional amount factored in, the world's rich countries will be providing 0.5 per cent of their combined GNP (gross national product) as development assistance.

The signing of the Millennium Declaration signalled a major change in the way the world's rich nations looked at economic backwardness in the developing world. The fight against poverty, hunger, disease and discrimination was seen as an effort in which all countries and all the world's people needed to get involved. The moral compulsion to help the countries emerging from decades— if not centuries—of colonial domination that motivated much of the aid effort by the rich countries was now gone. Also gone were the imperatives dictated by the cold war in which the world's two superpowers—the United States and the Soviet Union—used aid and other ways to find friends and allies across the globe.

By the time the 'millennium conferees' met in New York in September 2000, colonialism was a distant memory and the political compulsions that motivated a number of rich nations to aid poor countries were no longer there. Nonetheless, the rich were not prepared to forsake the poor. They were looking for a new set of imperatives to assist the world's poor. The leaders of the world's rich nations were now motivated by moral compulsions. They understood that it was morally repugnant to have so much poverty coexist with so much abundance enjoyed by their own citizens.

The awareness among the rich of extreme poverty and deprivation was heightened by a remarkable development in the post-Cold War era—the growth in importance of civil society. Civil society, made up of thousands of institutions that had learnt to use the Internet to mobilize support for the multitudes of causes they pursued, had come to influence public policy. Democracies must deal with pressures and those brought to bear by civil society could not be ignored by policymakers. Western governments responded whenever civil society coalesced around a deeply felt objective.

The path to the MDG programme took the international development community through two decades of intense debate. It is useful to describe the way the approach to alleviating global poverty developed over time in order to understand what the donors expect of a country such as Pakistan. Much of the conceptual work preceding the MDG programme was done at the World Bank and the various organizations of the UN system.

In the *World Development Report* published in 1980,[36] the World Bank emphasized the importance of what it called the 'seamless approach to development' in which progress in one area (such as a concerted programme for improving the access of the poor to such basic needs as food, water, shelter, education and health) contributed to other economic objectives (such as improving productivity and accelerating economic growth).[37] In its dialogue with the policymakers and in developing some of the projects and programmes it financed, the World Bank emphasized the importance of simultaneously addressing the circumstances that, working together, kept millions of people in the world desperately poor. There were important synergies in the efforts the countries were asked to mount—in education, health, employment generation, shelter, etc.

In the *World Development Report* of 1990,[38] the World Bank went back to a discussion of global poverty. This time around its approach to the subject was influenced by the way a number of countries had handled the problem of extreme economic disequilibria—rampant inflation, growing burden of external debt, large and unsustainable increases in budgetary deficits. The Bank now emphasized that in the situations marked by such disequilibria it was the poor who suffered the most. The rich had ways to protect themselves against the ravages of hyperinflation but the poor bore the bulk of the brunt. For poverty to be addressed, the governments had first to set their fiscal and monetary houses in order. The World Bank—and with it the development community—moved from the seamless web approach of the 1980 *World Development Report* to the sequential approach of the 1990 document.

It was with great fanfare that the World Bank began the analytical work that was to result in the third report on global poverty scheduled for publication in 2000, the beginning of the new millennium. A large team was assembled and was given two years—instead of the customary one year—to write the new document. The team headed by Ravi Kanbur, a highly respected development economist who had once worked at the World Bank as the chief economist of Africa, began an ambitious work programme to understand what had happened to poverty and income distribution in various parts of the world in the two decades since the World Bank wrote its first report.

As new data and information poured in, Kanbur and his team began to appreciate that the set of policies advocated by the Washington-based financial and economic institutions had delivered neither economic growth nor poverty alleviation. A new approach—or, at any rate, a new emphasis—was needed to bring about a profound change in the conditions in which the vast majority of the world's population was maintaining its existence. The popular dogma—sometimes called *The Washington Consensus*—had not been of much help to the poor. Kanbur and his team wished to emphasize not just economic openness and a greater role for the private sector. They wished also to promote the role of the state in providing social services to the poor. In other words, the new team was going back to the emphasis placed in the 1980 report.

But the Kanbur approach proved difficult for the development establishment at the World Bank to swallow. It had been fed on the diet of *The Washington Consensus*. Kanbur, under pressure, resigned and the document the World Bank finally published was a compromise between those who advocated growth as the only way to address poverty and those who believed that along with growth governments had to put programmes in place aimed at directly aiding the poor.

While the World Bank was engaged in this debate, the UNDP pressed ahead with an approach that took a broader view of development. Like the Bank, the UNDP was also presenting its ideas on development in a series of annual documents that appeared under the title of *Human Development Reports* (HDRs). Mahbub ul Haq who by then had left the World Bank and had served the government of President Ziaul Haq as planning and finance minister, had joined the UNDP to help it to produce these reports.

The main contribution made by the HDRs was to include a number of measures in addition to gross domestic product to determine the stage of development of countries around the globe. A new index—the human development index (HDI)—was devised for this purpose. In the report published in 2005, Pakistan's HDI was estimated at 0.527, ranking it at 135 among 177 countries for which data was provided. In terms of income per head of the population, Pakistan's ranking was 130. The implication was clear. Even at its level of development as measured by per capita income, Pakistan was doing less well for its population. Sri Lanka—to take a counter example—was in the opposite situation. Its ranking on the HDI scale was 17 positions better than its ranking on the scale of GDP per capita. In other words, Sri Lanka had done much better for its population than was expected of a country at its income level. It is interesting and disturbing to note that most large Muslim countries were in Pakistan's situation. The only comforting development for Pakistan was that it had graduated from the ranks of low human development to those of medium human development countries.[39]

The analyses carried out by institutions such as the World Bank and UNDP set the stage for the Millennium Declaration and the goals identified in it. For Pakistan and countries in a similar situation it had become critically important to strive to meet these goals in order to receive foreign assistance they so desperately need. Public policy needed to be directed not only at increasing the rate of economic growth but also at reducing the incidence of poverty and increasing equality of opportunity. Unfortunately even taking into account the decline in the incidence of poverty suggested by the recent surveys carried out by the government, it seems extremely unlikely that Pakistan will achieve most of the millennium development targets. Even if the country remains on the rapid growth trajectory it has followed since 2003, the problem of poverty and income inequality will remain. The government's ability to provide services to the poorer segments of the population will remain weak. It is likely that some of the more disadvantaged groups (for instance women residing in the countryside) and some of the more backward areas (for instance Balochistan and the tribal areas of the North West Frontier Province) will continue to perform poorly, particularly in the areas that are the focus of attention in the millennium growth strategy.

7. Public Policy and Structural Change[40]

There was reluctance on the part of policymakers in Islamabad to address the problems the country faced. They seemed willing only to talk about and discuss the good things that have happened to the economy. But the fault lines that existed just below the surface could not be wished away; they had to be located and the structures that were built on top of them had to be secured against the tremors that the weaknesses were bound to, produce from time to time.

Islamabad could take action provided it did two other things first. It had first to shed the notion that all was well with the economy and society and, two, it had to be willing to move in a totally different direction from the one it had taken. Senior policymakers had spent too much time applauding some of the achievements of the 2003–6 period; they had to realize that the indicators they used in their public pronouncement did not point to the possibility of sustainable growth. The high rate of increase in GDP of 2003–6 could not be treated as the start of a new trend.

The sharp increase in foreign exchange reserves—another development, other than the high rate of GDP increase, to which Islamabad attached great significance and which was mentioned repeatedly by the senior leaders in their speeches—was a good development but it would prove to be ephemeral if the rate of increase in exports did not keep pace with the increase in imports, if the quantum of foreign capital flows was not enough to cover the trade deficit, if the foreigners' confidence was jolted and the flows were reduced, as had happened in the country's history so many times before.

What had been gained could be easily lost if the people under the weight of inflation, or resentful at not being able to find productive jobs, or deeply disturbed by the growing inequalities in income and wealth, or apprehensive that political uncertainty was once again appearing on the horizon became restless and began to turn to the streets to vent their anger. These and other fears and apprehensions could lead important segments in society to become restive; so restive that they could begin to crave for a new political order. This had happened before and there was no reason why history would not repeat itself especially when policymakers showed little interest in studying it or drawing lessons from it.

By the end of 2006 the only manifestation of extreme discontent was to be found in the country's remote areas. The heartland remained untouched. There were active insurgencies in Balochistan and Waziristan. In late August, the discontent in Balochistan took a nasty turn when Sardar Akbar Khan Bugti, the 79-year-old leader of an important tribe in the province, was killed in a confrontation with the military. The news of his death reminded many people of the events that led to the civil war between East and West Pakistan and the emergence in December 1971 of the country's eastern wing as Bangladesh. The government of General Pervez Musharraf justified the action in Balochistan that led to Sardar Bugti's death by citing his group's unwillingness to accept the writ of the state. But as the economist Akmal Hussain pointed out in a newspaper article,

> the writ of the state is based not on armed force but on justice. Underlying the 'writ' is an unwritten social contract between the citizens and the state, in terms of which the state is granted monopoly over the use of armed force in return for guaranteeing certain basic rights to citizens. Therefore if the state is seen to deprive the citizens of a particular province of their rights or is seen to exercise force without justice, then the underlying social contract that is vital to sustaining the writ of the state is violated. In such a circumstance the state is pitted against its own citizens as a militant provincial nationalism emerges and the state loses its monopoly over military force. The response to this confrontation must be to establish the writ of the state by establishing the underlying social contract. Military action cannot be a sustainable basis for determining the relationship between a state and its citizens.[41]

Compared to the country's size and the size of its population these problems could be brushed aside as minor irritations that could be taken care of by a resolute authority willing not only to display the enormous might at its disposal but, if need be, to use it. States do this all the time and there was no reason why Pakistan should act any differently. On several occasions President Pervez Musharraf had said that the writ of the state would be made to run no matter how remote the area and how powerful those that resisted it, that he would not countenance those who were advancing their own petty interests by threatening the state, that he was not reluctant to use force to restore law and order. There may be some justice in this argument, but as Akmal Hussain points out in the lengthy quote I have used from his article, the state also had a responsibility in terms of granting people their rights.

There was another problem: both situations had seeds in them that could sprout elsewhere in the country. As already noted, Pakistan was already faced with the problem posed by Islamic extremism that gained strength largely because of the policies pursued in the Muslim world by the US administration headed by President George W. Bush. These two problems had different origins: the rise of Islamic extremism, particularly in the areas on Pakistan's border with Afghanistan but not entirely confined to them, and the resentment at the growing inequality in wealth and income among different regions and groups in the country. The first problem affected Waziristan, the second Balochistan. But there was no reason why these problems would—or should—remain confined to these areas. Their seeds could be carried by the strong winds of resentment that had begun to blow in the country produced by events, some of which were under Islamabad's control and some which were coming from the areas near as well as distant from the country's borders. The biggest threat the country faced was that these two sources of discontent—radical Islam's unhappiness with the policies adopted by the Bush regime, and growing inter-regional and inter-personal inequalities—could begin to feed on one another, thus gaining strength and threatening those who would rather not follow their social and political programmes.

Economics is at the bottom of almost all the unhappiness that prevailed, in spite of Islamabad's belief that it had set the country on the trajectory of growth on which it will stay over a long period of time. The healthy growth rate of 2003–6 would only become sustainable if it rested on domestic investment and not on consumption, if it was the product of domestic fundamentals and not external capital flows whose quantum and timing will remain uncertain. Also the widening trade deficit needed to be closed not by gaining access into the saturated western markets for products that added not a great deal of value to the economy but by developing new products and services for which there was good external demand, if the large and young population could be educated and trained and if the country could offer attractive opportunities for investment to people with capital not just in the Arab world but also in the West and Japan.

There were at least eight areas of public policy that needed urgent attention but this attention had to come out of deep and thoughtful analysis of the problems that were to be addressed. The areas that required policymakers' attention included land policy, water policy, low agricultural productivity, industrial policy, further development of the financial sector, trade policy, human resource development and the role of the state for providing basic services to all segments of the population. Some of these areas will be covered in some detail in the chapters that follow. The main purpose of this opening part of the book is to identify the areas that should become the focus of public policy over the next few years. Islamabad must realize that Pakistan's economy would be put on a high and sustainable growth strategy if serious structural adjustments are made. This will be a recurrent theme to be developed in the book.

NOTES

1. W.W. Rostow, *The Stages of Economic Growth: A Non-Communist Manifesto*, New York: Oxford University Press, 1953.
2. Mahbub ul Haq, *The Strategy of Economic Planning: A Case Study of Pakistan*, Karachi: Oxford University Press, 1963.
3. Arthur Lewis, 'Economic Development with Unlimited Supply of Labour', *Manchester School of Economic and Social Studies*, 1954, Volume 22(2), pp. 139–91.
4. The World Bank, *World Development Report 2006: Equity and Development*, Washington, DC, 2006, p. 2.
5. Technology as an endogenous determinant of growth was first conceived by Paul Roemer. This story is well told in David Warsch, *Knowledge and the Wealth of Nations: A Story of Economic Discovery*, New York: W.W. Norton, 2006.
6. Gustav F. Papanek, *Pakistan's Development: Social Goals and Private Incentives*, Cambridge, Mass.: Harvard University Press, 1967.
7. Samuel P. Huntington, *The Clash of Civilization and the Remaking of World Order*, New York: Simon and Schuster, 1996.
8. Samuel P. Huntington, *Political Order in Changing Societies*, New Haven: Yale University Press, 1968.
9. Niall Ferguson, *Empire: How Britain Made the Modern World*, London: Allen Lane, 2003.

10. This is my estimate; no official estimates are available of the incidence of poverty at that time.

11. When I refer to Pakistan even in the period between 1947–71, it means today's Pakistan. I have factored out of this analysis what became Bangladesh in December 1971 following a bitterly fought civil war between what were then East and West Pakistan.

12. The most detailed chronicle of the achievements of the regime headed by President Ayub Khan was offered in a three-volume study of the period by Herbert Feldman, a British journalist who spent a long time in Pakistan. See his books, *Revolution in Pakistan: A Study of the Martial Law Administration*, Karachi: Oxford University Press, 1967; *From Crisis to Crisis: Pakistan 1962–1969*, Karachi: Oxford University Press, 1972; *The End and the Beginning, 1969–1972*, Karachi, Oxford University Press, 1972.

13. The suggestion that the green revolution was led by middle-sized farmers was offered by me in a number of studies published in the 1970s. This was contested by Hamza Alavi who maintained that the revolution was led by large landlords who used capital intensive techniques to produce increases in output and productivity. The two points of view were presented in one volume of essays. See Shahid Javed Burki, 'The development of Pakistan's agriculture: An interdisciplinary explanation' and Hamza Alavi, 'The rural elite and agricultural development in Pakistan' both in Robert D. Stevens, Hamza Alavi, and Peter Bertocci (eds), *Rural Development in Bangladesh and Pakistan*, Honolulu: University of Hawaii, 1976.

14. In some of my earlier works, I have suggested that Zulfikar Ali Bhutto's programme of socialization had motivations other than the pursuit of ideology. By nationalizing industries, Bhutto also hit at the power base of the industrial and financial elites who may have challenged him. See Shahid Javed Burki, *Pakistan under Bhutto, 1971–77*, London: Macmillan, 1980.

15. Social Policy and Development Centre, *Combating Poverty: Is Growth Sufficient? Annual Review*, Karachi, 2004.

16. UNDP, *Pakistan: National Human Development Report, 2003: Poverty, Growth and Governance*, Karachi: Oxford University Press, 2004.

17. This section draws upon three articles by me published by *Dawn* in March and April 2006: 'The Growth Story', 28 March 2006, 'The future of the economy', 4 April 2006, and 'Interplay between economics and politics', 11 April 2006.

18. See footnote 12 above.

19. The opposition built a strong case against the administration headed by Prime Minister Shaukat Aziz. In a 500-page document filed in August 2006 in the National Assembly as part of its no-confidence resolution against the Prime Minister, the opposition argued that the market price of the physical assets owned by Pakistan Steel Mills was several times more than the price of the sale accepted by the government from a consortium headed by a Saudi Arabian company.

20. I call the system hybrid since the 17th amendment to the constitution passed in early 2003 as President Musharraf surrendered some of his power to the National Assembly resulted in the creation of a presidential system with a hint—but only a hint—of parliamentary oversight of the executive branch.

21. Ron Moreau, 'Pakistan's turnaround economy', *Newsweek International*, 27 March 2006.

22. The Indian experience with reforms in 1991 is well recorded in a collection of articles written by a number of experts directly associated with the effort launched. The effort was launched under the direction of then Finance Minister Manmohan Singh, who went on to become the country's prime minister in 2004. See Bimal Jalan (ed.), *The Indian Economy: Problems and Prospects*, Delhi: Penguin Books, 2004.

23. Notice that I have excluded the first Nawaz Sharif period from the period of economic turbulence, since some serious reforms were then successfully carried out.

24. I pick up this argument in the section on land reforms in the chapter dealing with education and agriculture.

25. Fareed Zakaria, *The Future of Freedom: Illiberal Democracy at Home and Abroad*. New York: W.W. Norton, 2003.

26. Conversation with a senator who was also a senior officer holder of the ruling party, Pakistan Muslim League (Q).

27. This section draws upon a number of articles published by me in *Dawn* over the last three years including 'Reviving economic growth', *Dawn*, 26 November 2002; 'Outlook better, brighter', *Dawn*, 20 May 2003 and 'Institutional graveyard', *Dawn*, 29 November 2005.

28. This subject is discussed in considerably greater detail in a later chapter.

29. Samuel P. Huntington, *Political Order in Changing Societies*, op. cit.

30. The use of 'what ifs' to understand the influence of leaders and unforeseen events on history was popularized by a number of modern historians including Niall Ferguson and Robert Cowley. See Niall Ferguson (ed.), *Virtual History*, New York: Basic Books, 1997 and Robert Cowley (ed.), *The Collected What If?: Eminent Historians Imagine What Might Have Been*, New York: G.P. Putnam, 1999.

31. Parvez Hasan, 'Mixed Messages in Poverty Numbers', *Dawn: Business,* 3 April 2006.

32. The World Bank, *World Development Report, 2006: Equity and Development*, Washington DC, p. 2.

33. See the entries on these individuals in Shahid Javed Burki, *A Historical Dictionary of Pakistan*, London: The Scarecrow Press, 1999.

34. The World Bank, *World Development Report, 2006*, op. cit., p. 45.

35. The World Bank, *World Development Report, 1993: Investing in Health*, Washington DC: Oxford University Press, 1993.

36. The World Bank, *World Development Report 1980: Poverty and Human Development*, Washington DC, 1980.

37. Much of the conceptual work behind this report was done by a group that I headed at the World Bank. The group included Paul Streeten who had done some pioneering work in the areas of poverty and inequality. The analytical work done by our group was put together by the World Bank in a book. See Paul Streeten, Shahid Javed Burki and Mahbub ul Haq, *First Things First: Meeting Basic Needs*, New York: Oxford University Press, 1982.
38. The World Bank, *World Development Report, 1990: Poverty*, Washington DC, 1990.
39. UNDP, *Human Development Report 2005: International Cooperation at a Cross Roads*, New York: Oxford University Press, 2005.
40. This section draws upon my article published in *Dawn*, 18 April 2006, under the title of 'Setting the Course Right'.
41. Akmal Hussain, 'Bugti killings and the Echoes of History,' *The Daily Times*, 30 August 2006.

2

The Question of 'Location'

Location has two meanings: the geographic location—the space a country really occupies, and the location a country can assign itself by the way it conducts its relations with the world outside. Britain, for instance, is in Europe but it remains strongly attached to America, once its colony. My purpose is to explore how '11 September' may have altered Pakistan's location in this wider sense. The terrorist attack of 11 September 2001 has changed the world, including Pakistan. In the early years of the twenty-first century, Pakistan is a very different country. It is different because President Pervez Musharraf was prepared to reorient the country's foreign policy and several aspects of its domestic policies. With the suddenness that surprised even the West, which had long sought Pakistan's dissociation from the Taliban regime in Afghanistan, the country gave up on what was once its protégé. 'Musharraf to [General Colin] Powell's surprise said that Pakistan would support the United States with each of the seven actions the United States wished him to take.'[1] Not only did Pakistan abandon the Taliban, but it also took an active role initially in their destruction and elimination from Afghanistan. Only two days after the terrorist attacks, the Pakistani president changed in a fundamental way his country's approach towards Afghanistan. The change in policy, he declared, was being introduced in Pakistan's national interest.

Equally suddenly, President Musharraf turned on Islamic extremists in his own country. In a historic speech to the nation on 12 January 2002 he declared war on the organizations that had not only brought terrorism to some of Pakistan's neighbours but had also terrorized the people of Pakistan. In clear and unambiguous terms, he launched a new policy toward Islamic extremism in the country. All citizens of Pakistan, no matter how actively and diligently they pursued Islam, were required to function within the prescribed legal framework, he declared.

After abandoning the Taliban in Afghanistan and after laying down a new and restrictive law within which extremist organizations could legitimately function in Pakistan, General Musharraf seemed prepared to move in one other different direction. He wished to factor Pakistan's geographic situation into an economic strategy.

In this chapter, I will deal with the important subject of economic geography—how a country's location can affect its economic prospects. In Section 1, the opening part of the chapter, I will explore how Pakistan's geographic situation has placed it right next to two economic giants—India and China—and how the restructuring of the global order following the demise of the Soviet Union and the emergence of the United States as the sole super-power increased America's influence on the country. In Section 2, I will provide an overview of Pakistan's relations with India, focusing on the changing Indian situation in the global economy and the emerging world political order. In Section 3, I will look at China as Pakistan's other large neighbour. In Section 4, I will explore Pakistan's emerging relations with the countries in West Asia and in that context analyze how it could build a new partnership with the Muslim countries of Central Asia. In Section 5, I will deal with the new American approach towards the Muslim world and towards Pakistan, that has the world's second largest Muslim population. Section 6 will provide a brief conclusion to the main themes explored in the chapter.

1. Among the Giants[2]

Even a cursory look at the world map highlights the uniqueness of Pakistan's geopolitical situation. It is one of three countries that sits on the borders of two giants—China and India. What makes these two countries giants is a combination of their large populations—both have more than a billion people each and both have seen rapid growth in their economies. The other two countries that also border on China and India are small and as such both—Bhutan and Nepal—are of little consequence for the future of the global economic and political systems.

But Pakistan is different. It is a relatively large country with a population of close to 160 million in 2006. The current size of the population ranks it among the seven largest countries in the world. Given that the population continues to increase at a relatively rapid pace, in twenty years time—in the year 2030—Pakistan will be the world's fifth largest country after China, India, the United States and Indonesia. It will once again occupy the position it had when Bangladesh was the country's eastern part.

The size of the population is not the only thing that enhances Pakistan's geopolitical importance. China, India and Pakistan are all recognized nuclear powers. Each country has two nuclear-armed nations sitting on its borders. China borders with India and Pakistan; India with Pakistan and China; and Pakistan with China and India. This is not the case with other nations armed with nuclear weapons. The United States, Russia and Israel don't have nuclear-armed neighbours looking down at them from just across the border. It is only Britain and France that exist in close proximity but even in their case a deep-water channel separates them. At the hottest point in the Cold War—the Cuban Missile Crisis in 1961—both Washington and Moscow operated with some comfort knowing that the two countries, no matter which side of the border was looked at, were separated by the vast expanse of two oceans. Such a luxury of time between the firing of a missile armed with nuclear weapons and its arrival at the designated target is not available to Pakistan and its neighbours. Given the speeds at which missiles travel, these two events—the firing and the landing—occur almost simultaneously.

Not only does Pakistan have a couple of billion-plus people countries as its neighbours, both China and India also aspire to superpower status. Both realize that this status won't be achieved suddenly or that the United States, currently the only surviving superpower, will be eager to allow rivals to emerge. In the National Security Strategy issued by Washington in September 2002, it was stated clearly that America would not like to accommodate other countries on the pinnacle of the global power it occupied. But even if it did not suit the American purpose to have company, it may not be easy for it to stop some countries from trying to get there. China, India, the European Union, Russia—perhaps even Brazil and Japan—would want to scale those heights. In fact, following the visit by President George W. Bush to South Asia in March 2006, the United States began to actively promote the development of India into a near superpower.

China had already achieved that status given the size of its economy and the breakneck speed at which it was growing. Chinese authorities had plans to double the size of the country's GDP between 2005 and 2015. But India was also going through a period of economic expansion and a profound restructuring of its economy. In the financial year 2006 that ended on 31 March, Indian GDP grew by more than 8 per cent, one of the highest rates ever. The future rates of growth would probably be a bit lower than that of China's, but were expected to be high enough to provide space within which to restructure and modernize the economy. This was required in order to place the country on the path of high levels of growth rates that could be sustained well into the future. Sometime in the not too distant future India could become a serious player in the global economy. This position was articulated most persuasively by two newspaper columnists who published well-received books on India's place in the global economy. While *The New York Times* Thomas Friedman built the case of India on the basis of that country's capacity to marshal a very large army of well-trained engineers and computer scientists to advance its position in information technology,[3] Edward Luce placed emphasis on the overall dynamism of the Indian entrepreneur.[4] Both saw India becoming a major player in the global economy within a matter of a decade or two.

In its quest for quasi superpower status, China had seriously revised its worldview. It no longer saw itself as the champion of the developing world as it did during the period of Chairman Mao Zedong and Prime Minster Zhou Enlai, the founding fathers of modern China. Instead, it was now focused much more on pursuing its own strategic interests and on creating relations with other large powers—the United States in particular but also Russia, Japan, the European Union, India, and Brazil. As a Chinese scholar of foreign affairs wrote before the visit to Washington by President Hu Jintao in April 2006, his country had begun to distinguish between 'hegemonic power' and 'hegemonic behaviour'. It was prepared to accept the former but will resist the latter. The hegemon in question was obviously the United States and China was prepared to check Washington's hegemonic behaviour.

Three examples of foreign policy conduct and foreign economic relations from this perspective were the Chinese stance on the North Korean nuclear issue, the World Trade Organization (WTO) trade negotiations under the Doha Round, and its approach towards Taiwan. Although China was uncomfortable at the US insistence on not having bilateral discussions with the North Koreans, it played host to the six-party discussions in 2005. Nonetheless, it distanced itself from the US position when it saw that the line being followed was not in its own long-term strategic interests. In the trade talks, China withstood the American pressure and joined with three other regional powers—Brazil, India and South Africa—to go against the positions taken on agricultural trade by the US and the European Union. This position contributed to the collapse of the Doha Round of negotiations in July 2006. On Taiwan, Beijing showed a remarkable amount of pragmatism. It responded to Taiwan's provocation by not becoming bellicose as it did in the 1990s. In 1995 and 1996 China conducted aggressive missile tests in the hope of cowing Taiwanese and American leaders. Instead, it evoked the opposite results from those intended by Beijing. Rather than let Beijing handle relations with Taiwan on its own terms, the US sent two aircraft carriers to the Taiwan Strait. The Chinese got the message. After that experience China became much more accommodating with respect to Taiwan, looked at the long-term aspects of the relationship, and was prepared not to ruffle too many feathers in Washington, not even in Taipei. China believed that time was on its side. It was convinced that ultimately the island of Taiwan would become a part of China, much as Hong Kong and Macao did over the last decade.

Watching carefully and obviously with some envy at China's rise to a near great power status, India also made some significant adjustments in its foreign policy stance. The beginning of the process of rapprochement with Pakistan—a process launched by Delhi in April 2003 when then Prime Minister Atal Bihari Vajpayee extended his hand of friendship to Pakistan in a speech given in Srinagar, the capital of the disputed state of Kashmir—should be seen in this context. In agreeing to talk about Kashmir after recognizing that that dispute was central to its uneasy relations with Pakistan, India was beginning to move along the path of pragmatism pursued with such success by China.

For Pakistan, it was important to fashion its foreign policy not only by taking full cognizance of the two emerging near-superpowers in its immediate neighbourhood. It had also to factor in the interests of the only real superpower, the United States.

Islamabad, for the third time in its 60-year history, had close relations with Washington. Each time Pakistan responded to America's strategic interests and not to its own national concerns. The first occasion Pakistan was drawn close to America was in the 1950s and early 1960s when it did the American bidding in the cold war. A slight display of independence on Pakistan's part irked Washington. That happened when President Ayub Khan and his foreign minister, Zulfikar Ali Bhutto, sought to get close to China. Washington's unhappiness with this move was expressed openly to such an extent that President Ayub Khan worried about its consequences for the security of his own country. He made his position clear by choosing the title of *Friends Not Masters* for his political autobiography published in 1967.[5] The Pakistani president was signalling, at least to his own people, that for him America was a friend and a useful ally, not a master that could dictate policy. The riposte to this position came from Zulfikar Ali Bhutto, once the foreign minister in Ayub Khan's administration. He published, a year later, his own interpretation of Pakistan's relations with the United States and provocatively titled his book, *The Myth of*

Independence.[6] The fact that the warm relations between Beijing and Islamabad helped President Richard Nixon to open a window to China in 1971 went more or less unrecognized by Washington.

The second time Islamabad was pulled into America's orbit was in the 1980s when it fought alongside Washington to force the Soviet Union out of Afghanistan. The benefits to the US of the help given by Pakistan were enormous.[7] The Soviet defeat in Afghanistan would not have been possible without Pakistan's assistance. Moscow's defeat in Afghanistan contributed to the collapse of communism in Eastern Europe and the break up of the Soviet Union. 'The operation certainly contributed to the collapse of the Soviet Union; how critical a role it played is still being debated. But without doubt the Soviet invasion of Afghanistan and the Red Army's defeat at the hands of the CIA-backed Afghan rebels was a world-changing event,' wrote George Crile in his dramatic account of the role played by Charlie Wilson, a US Congressman from Texas in mobilizing America's support in the war against the Soviet Union's occupation of Afghanistan.[8] However, Pakistan gained little—if anything at all—from partnering with America in its first foray into Afghanistan. Instead it paid a heavy price when that war and the way it was fought led to the rise of Islamic extremism in the country.

With America's war against international terrorism, launched after the Al Qaeda sponsored attacks of 11 September 2001, Pakistan was once again back in the US orbit as a valued ally. This time, however, it was in Pakistan's strategic interest to pursue some of the goals the US was following. It was vital for Islamabad to curb the rise of Islamic extremism—a goal to which President Pervez Musharraf committed himself with renewed vigour following the two attempts on his life in December of 2003. But the American preoccupation with curbing terrorism unleashed a number of forces that will have profound implications for Pakistan. I will look at some of them.

Washington's single-minded preoccupation with the war on terrorism created tremendous opportunities for other near great powers such as China, India, Japan, Brazil and Russia. With

America so distracted, these countries began to carve out their own spheres of influence. China was now a predominant player in East Asia but its national interests were bound to come into conflict with those of Japan. Russia was aggressively pursuing its interests in Eastern Europe and Central Asia. That began to happen as Tokyo, under the leadership of Prime Minister Junichiro Koizumi became worried about China's rise and increasing economic strength and was willing to openly confront Beijing. Brazil would want to be a dominant player in South America. Its pursuit of that strategy has already brought it into conflict with the United States on matters relating to trade and Washington's relations with Cuba and Venezuela. And, finally, India had interests in South Asia. Its peace overtures towards Islamabad that began in April 2003 should be viewed in that context. As India and Pakistan drew closer, China will have to satisfy itself that this burgeoning relationship will not hurt Beijing's strategic interests.

There was one common force present explicitly or implicitly in all these spheres of influence—the United States. As Henry Kissinger pointed out in his book, *Does America Need a Foreign Policy*,

> at the dawn of the new millennium, the United States is enjoying a pre-eminence unrivalled by even the greatest of empires of the past. From weaponry to entrepreneurship, from science to technology, from higher education to popular culture, America exercises an unparalleled ascendancy around the globe. During the last decade of the twentieth century, America's preponderant position rendered it in the indispensable component of international stability.[9]

What this meant was that the US will not want any of the near-superpowers to carve out their sphere of influence that did not incorporate the US's strategic interests.

In the period following 11 September 2001 the United States was totally concentrated on achieving three objectives: defeating international terrorism, curbing the spread of weapons of mass destruction and bringing democracy to the world of Islam. The last of these three objectives lost some of its salience as America got bogged down in Iraq, as forces of radical Islam gained strength in Egypt, Lebanon and Palestine through democratic means, and as Islamic extremists continued to mount attacks, particularly in Britain, regarded as the closest American ally. The bombings of London's underground trains and a bus on 7 July 2005 that claimed fifty-two lives along with the death of four suicide bombers, and the thwarting, on 10 August 2006, of the alleged plans to bomb commercial airliners bound from London to various destinations in the United States had the involvement of people of Pakistani origin. Pakistan had become a central player in helping Washington's war on global terrorism. If it faltered in this endeavour, it was clear that it would invite the wrath of Washington which during the presidency of George W. Bush showed that it could be totally unforgiving if it determined that nations, people or leaders were getting in its way. Living among the giants had many advantages. But it also could be perilous—Pakistan had to be aware of the pitfalls.

2. India as a Giant Neighbour

For almost six decades after achieving independence, Pakistan conducted its foreign policy to achieve two declared objectives. One, to secure Kashmir's accession to Pakistan. Most Pakistanis felt that Kashmir was the unfinished business which resulted in the division of British India into two countries—a predominantly Hindu India and a predominantly Muslim Pakistan. By bringing Kashmir into Pakistan, the two-nation theory so powerfully enunciated and so brilliantly advocated by Mohammad Ali Jinnah would have arrived at its logical conclusion.

Pakistan had attempted to achieve this aim of its foreign policy by pursuing another objective: to counter India's growing influence in the world. For India to formally gain the status of a great power—by being included, for instance, in the UN Security Council as a permanent member—it had to be economically strong. It had also to be at peace with its neighbours. Pakistan's leaders believed that by bleeding India in Kashmir, they could continue to deny this ambition to New Delhi. If Pakistan could somehow contain India, it could perhaps also force it to give up control of the state of Kashmir and allow it to be assimilated into Pakistan. The Pakistani strategists calculated that India may ultimately be prepared to use Kashmir as a price to gain entry into the club of superpowers.

But in the Indian mind Kashmir represented something even more important than its quest for a superpower. Kashmir was an important part of what Sunil Khilnani, an Indian historian, called the 'idea of India'.[10] India's opposition to the two-nation theory was as passionate as Pakistan's subscription to it. Indian scholars and statesmen claimed that the break-up of Pakistan in 1971 and the independence gained by its 'eastern wing' as the state of Bangladesh, showed that there was, in fact, not much substance in Jinnah's two-nation theory. The continuing Indian antipathy towards Pakistan—or at least that of some of its senior statesmen— was vividly reflected in one of several conversations Jaswant Singh, the powerful minister of external affairs in the government of Prime Minister Atal Bihari Vajpayee had with Strobe Talbott. Talbott then was deputy secretary in the Department of State, the second ranking US diplomat in the administration of President Bill Clinton. Singh and Talbott negotiated for several years on how the United States could come to terms with India as a nuclear power. In one of these conversations Jaswant Singh talked about the place of Pakistan in the community of world nations. He saw Pakistan's 'predicament as a lost soul among nations, an ersatz country whose founders' only real legacy was a permanent reminder of what a tragic mistake partition had been'.[11]

But the advocates of the two-nation theory—a group of which I regard myself to be a member—could equally convincingly argue that the departure of Muslim Bengalis had not proven Jinnah wrong. He had argued that the Muslims of British India were socially, culturally and religiously so different from the country's Hindu majority that the two nations could not live in harmony within the boundaries of one state. Muslims in what were once the Muslim majority areas of British India now lived not in one country but two. If Kashmir was not allowed to join Pakistan but became independent instead, the British Indian Muslims would be living in three different countries, separate from Hindu-dominated India. I will discuss the conflict with India over Kashmir in more detail in a later chapter of the book in which I will focus on the enormous economic cost Pakistan incurred because of this long-enduring conflict.

The idea of India was based on the belief that the citizenship of the state of India was not defined by religion, caste or social class. All Indians were Indians since they inhabited the same geographical space. In pursuit of that idea, India crafted a secular state which was maintained in its original form in spite of the emergence in the 1990s of a virulent form of Hindu fundamentalism that targeted not only Muslims living in India but other religious communities as well. The destruction of the Babri mosque in Uttar Pradesh was the work of a group closely associated with the Bharatiya Janata Party, the party which dominated the coalition headed then by Prime Minister Atal Bihari Vajpayee. But the Babri mosque was not the only incident against the non-Hindu communities of India. In 2001, fundamentalist Hindus directed their campaign against the Christian community and the churches in which they worshipped.

Nonetheless, the world images that India and Pakistan created were very different. Pakistani society got increasingly identified with an extreme form of Islam, intolerant towards its own people who did not subscribe to whatever version of the religion was advocated by the most vocal group. And abroad, by championing the cause of the Taliban in Afghanistan in the 1990s, it created the strong impression that it stood for an extreme form of Islam which sought to return to the world that existed 1,400 years ago. This impression was created precisely at the time when globalization was reducing the real and the virtual distances among different countries and communities. In that increasingly integrated world a world that *The New York Times* columnist called 'flat' in his best selling book—Pakistan was being left hopelessly behind.

The first war in Afghanistan—the one fought by the Afghan Mujahideen but assisted by Pakistan, Saudi Arabia and the United States—contributed to the demise of the Soviet Union and the collapse of European communism. While most of the world was prepared to take advantage of this breathtaking change, Pakistan remained mired in solving two seemingly unsolvable problems: one, the role of Islam in the way it governed itself; and two, its relations with India. It was the latter, in particular, that consumed so much of Islamabad's attention and—as it turned out—exhausted the country's energy, its economy and many of its options. It was in the pursuit of this approach that Pakistan followed a foreign policy that became increasingly India-centric.[12] It was because of this policy that Pakistan fought three hot wars with India and participated in several 'near-wars' with its neighbour. The last of these 'near wars' was in the winter of 2001–2002. For Pakistan—presumably also for India—this near-war was a costly business. A fully mobilized army costs money and a weakened Pakistani economy could not afford to have this confrontation extend over too long a period of time. And India could not also afford to have an army of one million soldiers in a state of deployment.

While Pakistan was so engaged in defining its role in the world of Islam, in devising a political structure that would adequately serve its diverse population, in pulling its economy out of a deep trough, India was more positively occupied. It had gradually begun to lift its sights beyond Pakistan to the dramatically reshaped world following the collapse of European communism and the disintegration of the Soviet Union. It was now looking to play a serious role in global affairs. It was convinced that its size, the mastery by it of several new technologies and its impressive rate of economic growth entitled it to play such a role. This was also recognized and endorsed by President George W. Bush during his visit to South Asia in March 2006.

Just about the time the world was beginning to acquire a new shape and a new character, the Indian economy began to grow at an unprecedented rate. After a deep economic crisis that nearly bankrupted the economy in the early 1990s, New Delhi, under the capable leadership of two farsighted men—Prime Minister Narasimha Rao and Finance Minister Manmohan Singh—decided to break with the past and opt for economic modernization. In order to get out of this crisis, India, in 1991, very deliberately and very quickly abandoned Jawaharlal Nehru's socialism in favour of gradually opening its economy to the world outside. While it did not adopt all the aspects of the policy framework that had been assembled under the title of *The Washington Consensus* in the mid-1980s, it accepted its basic approach. India recognized that it could grow and economically prosper only if it became a part of the rapidly changing global economic system. To gain full membership into the system required the acceptance of globalization as a process dictating the change in economic relations among the nations of the world.

Indians however are cautious people. They did not move at the pace adopted by several countries of Latin America for whom *The Washington Consensus* had been crafted in the first place. Most Latin countries threw open their doors quickly as a part of the policy they called the *apertura*—openness. This brought them a great deal of foreign investment. It also brought to their shores a large number of transnational corporations which picked up the assets the over-burdened public sector was offering at cheap prices. The American, Spanish, French and Dutch financial, manufacturing, and public utility companies came into Latin America and 'globalized the region.' But their entry also brought volatility and with volatility came a series of economic crises that nearly wrecked Mexico in 1994–95, Argentina in 1995, Brazil in 1999. In 2001–2002, the Argentinean economy was not nearly but completely destroyed. But by not completely opening its economy, India escaped the volatility that had buffeted other major emerging economies. In this it seems to have taken the cue from China, its neighbour to the northeast.

With a rapprochement of sorts in place begun, as noted above, by overtures made in April 2003 by Vajpayee, Pakistan and India seem to be moving along three parallel tracks. They are consciously attempting to develop a relationship that would stand the shocks of unpleasant developments. It was such an occurrence—the terrorist attack on the Indian parliament in December 2001—that brought the two nuclear-armed nations to the verge of yet another open conflict. The near-war of 2001–2002 lasted more than a year and took a heavy economic toll on both countries. The governments in Delhi and Islamabad seemed to have concluded that they could not afford another confrontation of this type. That notwithstanding, there was a high level of probability that some hardliner groups on both sides of the border would make a serious attempt to disrupt the process that was started following the SAARC summit in Islamabad in January 2004 when President Pervez Musharraf, responding to the initiative taken by Vajpayee, signed the Islamabad Declaration with the Indian prime minister. The two countries promised to begin a 'composite dialogue'—a term favoured by the Indians, on solving all outstanding issues between the two countries, including the long-enduring problem of Kashmir.

A terrorist attack by a Pakistan based group on some place in India could not be ruled out. The coordinated attacks on commuter trains in Mumbai in August 2006, India's financial sector, by Islamic terrorists once again soured relations between the two countries and slowed down the process of reconciliation. Similarly an Ayodhya mosque type incident could occur on the other side of the border, engineered by some elements in the Indian political system for whom friendly relations with Pakistan remained distasteful. It would take resolve from both Islamabad and Delhi to withstand these pressures.

It was heartening that the senior leaders of the BJP had indicated that they would fight the April 2004 national elections on the basis of their party's economic record rather than continuing animosity with Pakistan. Similarly, President Pervez Musharraf's speech to the Pakistani parliament on 17 January 2004 was a clear indication that he had set his administration's course towards creating a working relationship with India.

What was the first track on which the Pakistani and Indian diplomats could begin to move? A knee-jerk reaction to some unpleasant development could be prevented by the adoption of what were rightly called 'confidence-building measures.' The Indian government appeared to have recognized that it was dangerous to completely isolate Pakistan—to build an impenetrable wall between itself and its Muslim neighbour to the north. Isolation bred suspicion; it also strengthened those forces that had an interest in widening the gulf between the two sides. Regular contacts between the citizens of the two nations would be extremely helpful in moving along the process of reconciliation. Given the troubled history of the subcontinent, it will take a long time to normalize relations between India and Pakistan. But the process could be hastened by confidence-building measures. They could encompass sporting events between the teams from the two countries; exchange of writers, academics, teachers, and journalists; exchange of books, magazines, newspapers, and journals; visits by musicians, movie stars and special screenings of movies made by the two countries. Such contacts could also help to prevent another 'near war.'

The second parallel track on which the two countries launched themselves was to find a solution to the long-surviving Kashmir problem. Pakistan had moved further on this track than India. Shortly before the SAARC summit held in Islamabad in early January 2004 President Musharraf hinted that Pakistan would no longer insist on a UN supervised plebiscite in Kashmir as mandated by the Security Council resolutions of the late 1940s. This was the basis of Pakistan's position for a long time. Various Pakistani governments had maintained that implementing the UN resolutions was the only way of solving the Kashmir dispute. In the Islamabad agreement in order to begin negotiations between the two countries, Pakistan gave, for the first time, a pledge in writing that it will not allow its territory to be used to launch attacks on Indian-occupied Kashmir. This was a long standing demand on India's part, one that had kept it from discussing bilateral issues with the Musharraf government.

Finally, Islamabad reiterated that it would honour the commitment made at Simla by Prime Minister Zulfikar Ali Bhutto that all India–Pakistan disputes would be tackled and solved through bilateral negotiations. This was a major concession by Islamabad. On several occasions after Simla, Pakistan had attempted to internationalize the Kashmir dispute by involving a third party as a mediator. There was some hope among Pakistan's policymakers that after 9/11 Washington may be willing to become such a party. It could play the role of a broker to do a deal between the two long-time antagonists. Islamabad believed that it was in Washington's interests to play this roles since it would get Pakistan's undivided attention as a partner in the war against international terrorism once the Kashmir problem was resolved. Or, if the US was not willing to go alone into this area, it could perhaps do it in the context of the United Nations involvement. The hard-hitting speech given in September 2003 by President Musharraf at the opening session of the UN General Assembly was to get that agency's attention focused once again on Kashmir. Musharraf's address provoked an equally strong response from Atal Bihari Vajpayee, the Indian prime minister.

What did India offer in return for these Pakistani concessions? For the first time it recognized that Kashmir was a central element in the uneasy relationship with Pakistan. This recognition suggested some shift away from the long-held Indian position that Kashmir was an integral part of the country and its status was not open to negotiations.

In fact, the Indians have often claimed that any compromise on Kashmir would undermine what historian Sunil Khilnani had called the 'idea of India.' That idea encompasses nation building, not on the basis of any form of identity—religious, linguistic, caste, etc.—but on geography, plurality and accommodation. According to this line of thinking, letting Kashmir leave the Indian union would weaken the 'idea' and encourage other fissiparous tendencies to flourish. There were many of those in India, and the argument was that by providing Kashmir some special treatment, Delhi would encourage other groups to demand something similar for themselves. There was a similar 'idea of Pakistan' argument on the Pakistani side. Pakistan, after all, was created as a homeland for the Muslims of British India. By accepting the partition of the provinces of Punjab and Bengal, Mohammad Ali Jinnah and his associates agreed to create Pakistan only in the areas in which the

Muslims had a majority. Kashmir was one such area and the logic that had resulted in the partition of India on religious lines should have brought the state into the Pakistani fold. That, of course, did not happen.

The third track was that of regional trade. At the time of the Islamabad summit in January 2004, the seven SAARC nations agreed to work towards the creation of a free trade zone in South Asia. They set themselves the target of 1 January 2006 by which time the South Asian Free Trade Area (SAFTA), would come into force, allowing goods and commodities to move freely among the countries in the region. This was a good move since the trade track held the greatest promise for bringing about peace in the South Asian subcontinent. There were plenty of examples around the world to suggest that deep animosities among nations can be dissolved once trade begins to move freely.

This happened, of course, in Europe which, after two catastrophic wars in the twentieth century, was now a zone of peace. This also happened in the Mercosur, a trading arrangement among the nations in the southern cone of South America. The countries in this area had fought several wars and they continued to view one another with deep suspicion for a very long time. The birth of Mercosur helped to change this mindset. In fact, warming of relations between Argentina and Brazil, the two largest regional economies, ultimately led to both sides giving up their nuclear ambitions. The same could be said to be true for the North American Free Trade area that brought Mexico closer to the United States and was likely to stay that way in spite of the uneven progress made by the trading arrangement during its first ten years.

In what way should SAFTA evolve? In working out a plan for its development and evolution how carefully should the founding countries look at the experience of other successful regional trading arrangements? What are the lessons that could be drawn from what has happened in other parts of the world? How much focus should be placed on moving beyond trade to other issues that have stood in the way of regional integration in South Asia? These are important questions and are discussed in the chapter on trade and development. For the moment, I will return to the subject of rapprochement between India and Pakistan and discuss the very different sets of motives that persuaded the leadership on both sides of the border to begin to think in terms of launching an era of peace in the subcontinent.

Historians of deep conflicts between nations tell us that accommodation can be reached once the motives for doing so begin to coincide. The resolution of the sharp animosity between Germany and France occurred when the two countries recognized that they would gain enormously if they lifted their sights beyond narrow national interests and started to focus, instead, on the economic future of continental Europe. Once that happened, the rest was easy. However, the further expansion of Europe became somewhat problematic since there was a clear divergence of motives on the part of the continent's core (France and Germany) and its periphery (countries such as Portugal and Poland). The core would like to see the new institutions of the European Union develop in a way that it gave it greater weight in the arrangement than the periphery, including the ten countries that were added to the expanded union in 2004. The peripheral countries wanted equality in the contemplated set-up.

Unfortunately, India's and Pakistan's motives were different in seeking some kind of accommodation. Of the many different motives that propelled the two countries to seek rapprochement, two were compelling. On the Indian side, the ongoing conflict with Pakistan was a major distraction in its quest for global play. The BJP leaders who governed until their party's defeat in 2004, began to recognize that they could not place India on the global map as a near-superpower as long as it remained entangled with Pakistan. On the Pakistani side of the border, President Pervez Musharraf began to appreciate how big a menace the rise of Islamic fundamentalism and *jihadi* groups had become. The two assassination attempts on him seemed to have convinced him to focus on eliminating one of the reasons that provided these groups their *raison d'être*. Peace with India would accomplish that.

Could these two motives be aligned in some way that they began to be seen as a part of a plus-sum game in which neither side loses and both sides gain. That could happen if the building of trade between the countries—rather than solving the Kashmir problem—is placed at the centre of the evolving detente. I have devoted Chapter 7 to a discussion of this problem.

3. China, the Other Giant Neighbour

Pakistan has had cordial relations with China, one of the two economic giants in its immediate neighbourhood, for almost half a century. Starting in the early 1960s, during the period of President Ayub Khan and under the prodding of Zulfikar Ali Bhutto, his foreign minister, Pakistan assiduously cultivated China as a friend. It did that for essentially two reasons. First, was the perceived need to find a balance for India. As discussed in the previous section, until about 2004, Pakistan's approach to the world was determined by what I described there as an 'India centric' strategy. That was the test all policies towards the world outside had to meet. Second, with Zulfikar Ali Bhutto in charge of foreign affairs in the early 1960s—a position to which he was elevated after the death of Mohammad Ali Bogra, Ayub Khan's first foreign minister—Pakistan's foreign policy acquired an ideological tinge. This was the first time in the country's history that diplomacy began to be looked at through the prism of ideology. As Bhutto was to argue in his little book, *The Myth of Independence,* published after he left office, there was great need for Pakistan to move out of the sphere of influence of the United States. Relations with China would be a part of that strategy. 'China's dominant place in Asia is assured; Pakistan is an Asian state, whose destinies are forever linked with those of Asia, and it is vital for Pakistan to maintain friendly relations with China for strengthening Asian unity. As members of the community of Asia and Africa, our countries have a common interest in the promotion of Afro–Asian solidarity—a further reason why they must maintain friendly relations with each other. As underdeveloped countries, China and

Pakistan seek to cooperate with other such countries for obtaining better international trading terms and for a more equitable participation with the developed states in the economic and social advancement of the underdeveloped nations,' wrote Bhutto in 1968, two years after his departure from the administration of President Ayub Khan and three years before he returned to power as Pakistan's chief executive.[13] He was advocating a foreign policy for his country in which China rather than the United States would become a central player.

In the early 2000s, Islamabad had to develop a different rationale for its China policy. With President Pervez Musharraf prepared to recognize that Pakistan's relations with the world had to be structured on grounds other than its concerns about India, China began to figure in a different way in foreign policy. A part of this recognition was the adjustment Islamabad was making to the way the United States was conceiving its role in the world. In the strategy document published in September 2002, a year after the attacks of 11 September 2001, Washington made it clear that it would not accept any challenge to its status as the only surviving superpower. China was the only country that could offer such a challenge in some distant future. Also, as I will discuss in a later section, the American approach towards the Muslim world changed from year to year. By the time President George W. Bush visited South Asia in March 2006, Washington seemed to have decided that the Muslim world had to be isolated since it could neither be politically or socially reformed at the pace desired by America nor cowed into submission through the display and use of force. Thus buffeted, China offered an opportunity for the Muslim world.

International terrorism and the pressure on the sources of energy became the two principal motives for international affairs for most countries in the early 2000s. China figured prominently in this new set of calculations. In defining its own relations with Beijing, Islamabad had to factor this changed calculus. For the first time in human history, a country that will remain 'developing' for many decades to come had become the world's premier economy. What will be the impact of this development on the rest of the world? In particular, how will the developing world be affected by the rise of China's economic power? These important questions did not have easy answers since what was happening in China and what China was doing to the world outside its borders did not have many historical parallels.

This was not the first time in history that a country, in terms of the size of its economy, had caught up in some respects with those that were in the lead. The United States overtook Britain to become the world's largest economy in the closing years of the nineteenth century. Although it has remained in that position since then, in the 1960s Japan began to close the gap with America and within a decade became the world's second largest economy. In spite of very sluggish growth for more than a decade, Japan remained in that position. A couple of decades after Japan did its catching-up, a number of small countries of East Asia acquired all the attributes of developed economies. This was another 'catching-up' period in the global economic system and it too had considerable consequences for the world economy. In the case of China, however, the economy that was engaged in catching-up was not 'developed' according to the usual meaning of that word—its income was still at the bottom of the range of incomes of middle income countries—or was fully industrialized. It will remain developing for many years into the twenty-first century in the sense that the structure of its economy, the location of its population, the rate of increase of its GDP will continue to be similar to those of developing countries than match those of the mature industrial nations.

China's rise as a global economic power will be as consequential for the global economy as was the rise of the United States after the Second World War. But it is unlikely China will ever dominate the world as completely as the United States did after the collapse of the Soviet Union. For one, the US will remain the world's dominant economy for a number of decades to come even if it lost to China the status of being the largest. Even if China's GDP overtook that of the US in the next few decades—something that is likely to happen sometime in the next half century—its income per capita will still be only a fraction of the American, no more than about one-twentieth of the US.

Global economy also required military prowess. It was unlikely that China will be able, any time soon, to deploy the amount of resources the Americans were committing to defence and developing new military technologies. Also, China, even as a global economic power, will not be able to equal the American social and cultural influence. For that, the English language was a pre-requisite. If there were ever a lingua franca, it would not be an exaggeration to say that English is such a language. It is the language of global culture and the language in which the world communicates over the Internet. Even where English is not the mother tongue—as is the case in continental Europe and Latin America—it is being learnt at an increasing rate. However, the Chinese have a long way to go before they acquire the kind of facility the Indians and other South Asians have in English. China will have to compete with the South Asians in the modern service sector, much of which relies on communicating in English.

All these caveats notwithstanding, the Chinese presence has been profoundly felt in the global economy. There are several reasons for this; all of them the consequence of China's amazing rate of economic growth. The country's economy continued to expand at an impressive rate. It grew at a blistering pace in 2003–2006. The GDP—the total output of goods and services—soared at an annual rate of 9.5 per cent during this period. China's official statistics indicated that its economy was growing much faster than those of the industrial world. The US economy did better in this period than that of many other developed countries—better than that of Continental Europe and Japan—but the rate of growth was not anywhere near that of China's. In 2003, China crossed a milestone; its GDP was estimated at $1.43 trillion, or $1000 per head of the population. It was, in other words, no longer a poor country. It had entered the ranks of middle-income nations.

Not only did China cross the $1,000 threshold in income per head of its very large population, but growth also brought about a number of structural improvements. By 2005 China had built an additional 4,600 kilometres of motorway, bringing the network's total to 30,000 kilometres, second only to that of the United States. During the year, 112 million people obtained mobile phones, bringing subscribers to 532 million, and about 30 million kilowatts of power capacity was installed. China also had the second largest Internet system in terms of the number of domestic subscribers. It was likely to soon over take America in this area. This was, of course, of great relevance for Pakistan, one of the dozen countries in China's immediate neighbourhood.

Of great significance was the subtle change taking place in the Chinese countryside. The breakneck speed at which the urban economy was growing, created an income and wage differential between cities and towns on the one side and thousands of villages in the middle part of the country on the other. This was drawing workers away from the country and into the urban areas. The number of workers who left their fields and went to better paid jobs in cities climbed to 120 million in 2003, up from around 94 million in 2002. In 2004 and 2005, another 50 million migrated from villages to towns and cities. This meant within four years some 100 million people migrated within China every year. This must count as one of the largest movements of people within such a short period of time anywhere in the world at any time in history. The arrival of such a large number of workers from the countryside to towns and cities in which much of China's industrial sector was located helped to keep industrial wages low and consequently, the prices of a large variety of goods produced for export. This made China very competitive for countries such as Pakistan that also relied on labour-intensive products for much of their exports. But this situation may not last for long, and will provide some relief to Pakistan and other large developing nations.

The Chinese researchers estimated that these workers typically sent about half of their annual salaries to their families back home. This amounted to an infusion of $70 to $80 billion of capital to the countryside, translating into a significant improvement in the standard of living in what was still a fairly impoverished part of the world. In spite of this rural–urban migration, China still had 800 million people living in its villages. The Chinese authorities indicated that they planned to move as many as 500 million of them to the urban areas. If these plans materialized, a large majority of them will go to China's eastern coast. This movement of people will continue to affect wages of semi-skilled people around the world including in countries such as Pakistan which had begun to feel the challenge posed by China in industries such as textiles, leather and sports goods, and consumer electronics. There have been reports that some of the industries in the Gujranwala–Gujrat industrial corridor have succumbed to the pressure from China.

It is not inconceivable that in the next half century, some 750 million people will live on the Chinese coast, from the city of Dalian in the north to Hong Kong and Macao in the south. Their incomes will be several times the average income of that area today. In today's dollars, the east coast Chinese by 2050 may be earning $20,000 a year, which will translate into an aggregate income of $15 trillion, about one and a half times the GDP of America in 2005 but produced in a space less than one-two-hundredth of that of America.

That transformation in and of itself will have enormous consequences for the global economy. For the moment, it was industrial growth that had begun to reshape not only the country's own economy but that of the rest of the world as well. The Chinese growth was the consequence, in large measure, of the very sharp increase in industrial output, not an unusual event for a developing economy with the exception of India where services constituted the leading sector. Industrial output accounted for nearly two-thirds of economic growth in 2005 with heavy manufacturing—chiefly steel, petrochemicals and machinery building—making up more than one-half of the increase in industrial production. The rapid increase in industrial production put considerable pressure on the use of natural resources. Given the size of the economy and given also the fact that China was importing most industrial inputs, the rapid expansion in industrial output created pressures on global commodity markets. The country became a large consumer of raw materials.

It was the rapid increase in China's consumption of energy that created economic, political and diplomatic ripples across the world. In 1995, the country was a net exporter of oil. It also had large quantities of untapped coal reserves. Chinese customs figures showed that the country imported a record 91 million tons of crude oil in 2003. This was 31 per cent more than in 2002. However, by 2005 China's net imports of oil reached 10 million barrels a day, which met as much as 80 per cent of its demand compared with only 35 per cent in 2000. China was the reason for the relentless increase in oil prices in the spring of 2006, as the scramble for oil on the part of the major consumers became a frenzy. Latest estimates from the International Energy Agency showed that the Chinese consumed 5.46 million barrels of crude oil a day compared with Japan's 5.43 million. Oil demand increased fast because of rapid growth in electricity generation and the dramatic increase in the number of vehicles on China's rapidly expanding road and motorways networks. Sales of new cars and light trucks in the country increased by 86 per cent in 2003, and by another 36 per cent in 2004. This rate of increase was maintained in 2005. China's auto production surpassed that of South Korea but, given the growth in demand, its import of cars as well as auto parts was rapidly increasing—by as much as 84 per cent in 2005. China spent $14.45 billion on these imports, with $5.25 billion on new cars.

What China did to the world energy market was not short of what the Middle East did in 1973 and 1979. The main difference was that the twin oil price shocks of 1973 and 1979 were delivered by the exporters, curtailing output. In 2005–2006, the shock was the consequence of an enormous increase in demand occasioned by the rapid expansion of the Chinese economy. But oil was not the only source of energy that came under pressure because of the increase in Chinese consumption. Surprisingly for the Chinese, the country may also become a net importer of coal. China accounted for 30 per cent of global production of coal in 2006. Most of it came from its own mines. With the prospect that the country would run out of the domestic supply of coal, China began to look outside its own borders for new sources of supply. Pakistan was one of the countries to which it turned. It began to show interest in developing the large coal deposits in Pakistan's Thar Desert in Sindh province.

Coal was the only major industrial input in which China had abundant supplies of its own, but that may not last for very long. For most other products, China was dependent upon outside suppliers. In 2005, China consumed 36 per cent of the world's steel and 55 per cent of the world's cement. It also became the largest consumer of copper, the price of which hit a record high in the spring of 2006. Once again Pakistan was one of the countries to which it turned for a possible source of copper. It acquired the Sandak mines in Balochistan in 2003 when they were privatized by Islamabad. China's enormous appetite for industrial raw materials produced a boom in commodity prices across the world in the early 2000s. No major commodity was left untouched and no major exporter of commodities reaped large benefits. However, the pace with which the Chinese economy continues to expand will have an enormous bearing on global energy supplies, on the prices of major energy products, and on the distribution of income and wealth across the world.

The increasing dependence on raw material imports affected China's external relations and its view of the world. The politics of oil—and, ultimately, also of coal—will shape how China related with the rest of the world. For instance in January 2004, China's President Hu Jintao travelled to three African countries—Algeria, Egypt and Gabon—all oil exporters. These countries did not figure predominantly in China's foreign relations in the previous half-century. And, in March 2006, President Hu Jintao combined his visit to Washington with calls on the leaders of Saudi Arabia and Nigeria. The message from China was clear. Its relations with the outside world would not be dictated by the concerns of the United States; they will be determined by China's strategic interests, in particular access to sources of energy and industrial raw materials.

There were a number of questions pertaining to the economic and political role of the state that would have a bearing on its economic relations with the outside world. The future role of the state in the economy is a work in progress; the Chinese themselves have not yet determined how the state's role will—or should—evolve over time. The ultimate role of the Chinese state will be of consequence not only for the country's large citizenry. It will also affect how China related to the rest of the world. In that context, the state's role in four areas was of considerable interest for the world outside China: how it would manage external finance including the exchange rate, how it would improve its economic statistical base, how it would overcome the physical constraints the economy was facing and how it would reform the state-owned enterprises. Policies in all these areas would be of consequence for Pakistan.

The issue of the exchange rate acquired considerable importance in 2005–6, as China built up its trade deficit with the United States and as more industries and jobs migrated from the American manufacturing sector to the growing industrial belt of China. That the exchange rate had remained almost unchanged at 8.62 yuan to a dollar for more than a decade became a contentious issue between Washington and Beijing. The de-linking of the yuan from the dollar and the use of a basket of currencies to peg the value of the domestic currency brought about a very minor revaluation of the Chinese currency. Its rate with respect to the American dollar increased by a bare 2 per cent in 2005 and a similar amount in 2006. The Americans maintained that China, by keeping the value of its currency depressed with respect to the dollar, had managed to penetrate their markets with relatively cheap manufactures. They wanted Beijing to float the currency. If that was not possible since it would result in a serious shock to some parts of the Chinese system, the Americans wanted the authorities to at least revalue the yuan well beyond the minor adjustment made in 2005. If the Chinese allowed the value of their currency to appreciate, there was little doubt that the yuan would become considerably more expensive. Some financial experts believed that the country's currency was undervalued by anywhere between 20 to 35 per cent. Letting it find its own value in the market would bring it to between 6.5 to 7.0 yuan to a dollar. At that rate of exchange, China's GDP of 12.3 trillion yuan would not measure at $1.43 trillion but would be anywhere between $1.75 trillion and $2 trillion. With these reworked numbers, per capita income would not be just $1,000 but between $1,300 and $1,500. Knowing with greater accuracy Chinese per capita income and hence the purchasing power of the country's citizens, would be helpful to those who are interested in selling goods to China.

These are the tricks estimating the size of the economies in terms of fixed exchange rates can play. But accurately estimating China's per capita income was not the reason for the world's interest in the rate of exchange. The main reason was that an upward valuation of the Chinese currency would make the country's products more expensive in the markets overseas and, possibly, save manufacturing jobs in America and several European countries, perhaps also in Pakistan where China's competition was being felt in many industries, particularly textiles.

The exchange rate issue reflected on another problem with the Chinese economy: its statistical base. What was known was that the Chinese economy was big and had been growing rapidly at rates much faster than the rates of GDP increase of all other major economies in the world. However, given the way various estimates were made, it was not easy to be precise about a number of important measures: exactly how large was the economy; what was the average income of a Chinese citizen; what was the distribution of the GDP among different sectors of the economy; how fast was the rate of growth from quarter to quarter of the economy and its various components?

All these questions were difficult to answer. There was a widespread belief among China scholars that the officials in the country responsible for assembling economic and financial data tended to smoothen out economic fluctuations. The official figures about GDP growth at any given point in time gave the impression of economic stability whereas, experts suggested, the economy went through wide fluctuations from quarter to quarter, not just year to year. That the Chinese economy was fairly volatile mattered not only to the students of the Chinese economy and to economic historians. It was also of great concern and interest to the policymakers in places such as Islamabad who had to make adjustments in public policy to what was happening in China.

Some of these statistical problems were not unique to China; the country shared many of them with other developing countries. What was important was that in considering the impact of the Chinese economy on other parts of the world, policymakers had to recognize that all analysis must be based on caution. As the future was always hard to predict, it was even more difficult to be accurate when the statistics on which the projection must be based were subject to considerable errors of estimation.

Another puzzle about the future of the Chinese economy was how the state will perform its role. There were several areas in which the state's role was acquiring great importance. Among them was managing the severe transport bottlenecks that had emerged as a result of the rapid expansion in the economy. Why should the world be interested in how the Chinese state dealt with the logjam for transportation? It was not easily obvious why this should be a major concern outside China unless we looked at the peculiarities of the Chinese system of transport. A rise in freight costs as a result of congestion should increase the price of the goods from China in external markets and, therefore, reduce the need for revaluing the currency. But that did not happen for the reason that China effectively had two transport systems, one for exports and the other for imports. It was the only major economy in the world that had organized itself in that way. Given China's focus on exports, it had invested heavily in the system that moved goods out of the country and not into the system used for bringing commodities into the country. Exports moved mostly in steel containers on trucks travelling on highways in which the Chinese authorities invested large amounts of resources. Trucks offloaded containers at special ports that received considerable investment, including from foreign firms. But for imported commodities, the story was different. They passed through old ports and were loaded on railway wagons that travelled on a slow and antiquated system that had not received the same sort of investment lavished on highways. An important consequence of this asymmetrical development was that it had begun to affect world commodity prices in a way that provided protection to China's agriculture. For instance, shipping rates for grain moving from the Gulf Coast of the United States to China climbed to $70 a ton from only $18 two years ago. This way nobody outside China really benefited from the significant increases in the country's demand for farm products.

Although China abandoned socialism as an economic ideology, it had still to make full transition to a market economy. A significant part of the economy was still managed by the state. This was in part the consequence of state-owned enterprises (SOEs), providing all kinds of social cover to their employees that the government was unable to do. The Chinese were wary that by rapidly privatizing the SOEs, they might have a social problem on their hands.

One area where the Chinese will have to take some quick decisions was in finance where the large banks were still under state control. As was the case with most state-owned banks, the Chinese institutions also built large portfolios of non-performing loans. After joining WTO, the government was under pressure to reform this part of the economy, since this sector had become available for foreign entry. The government began to move. In 2004, it injected $45 billion into the Bank of China and the China Construction Bank to help prepare the ground for their listing in Hong Kong and possibly New York. The authorities also laid down targets for the banks that must be reached—11 per cent return on equity by 2005, 13 per cent by 2007 and a return on assets close to the average of the top 100 banks in the world.

The precise effect of the Chinese economy on the rest of the world can only be gauged if we have a good measure of its size, its sector distribution, its per capita income and how the state was going to solve some of the structural problems it must address. That said, Pakistan must keep a careful watch over developments in

China. This is not only because a country of China's size sits on Pakistan's eastern border. It is also because the peculiarities of the Chinese economy, its future prospects, the value of its currency, the demand it places on the world's sources of commodities, the pressure China's growing demand for energy is placing on the international price of oil are all areas of considerable concern for policymakers in Islamabad.

From the time of Zulfikar Ali Bhutto when Pakistan began to leave the American orbit and entered the Chinese sphere of influence, the role China has played in foreign policy was mostly to counter the weight of India. That China can perform such a balancing role is an important consideration for policymakers in Islamabad. However, as the preceding discussion of the performance, character and prospects of the Chinese economy suggests, Pakistan must also take advantage of, as well as, protect itself from the growing weight of the Chinese economy.

4. West Asia: The New Great Game

Some fifteen years ago—in the fall of 1986—Barber Conable, who was then the president of the World Bank, invited me to join a group of twenty-one senior managers assembled to draw up a new organizational make-up for the institution. We worked for three months and came up with an entirely new structure. According to our scheme, the Bank was to be divided into three parts: one responsible for all lending operations, the second for the Bank's finances and the third for formulating development policy. One of my contributions to the new structure was to persuade the Bank's new management to move Pakistan from Asia and to place it in the Europe, the Middle East and North Africa (EMENA) region. I was convinced then—and I am convinced now—that that was the right geographic place for Pakistan. That is where Pakistan remained for almost five years. In the middle of 1991, the Bank got a new president who carried out another re-organization. Pakistan went back to South Asia and this is where it remains today. But this is not where it completely belongs.

In fact, in the IMF's geography, Pakistan is in the Middle East department. Lately, economists have begun to put emphasis on geography, in part because of the importance regional trading arrangements are acquiring in the global economy. The European Union evolved from a trading association founded soon after the end of the Second World War. East Asia has a couple of trading arrangements in place. One of them, the Asia Pacific Economic Cooperation (APEC), was considered important enough for President George W. Bush to leave Washington while his country was at war to attend the organization's summit meeting held in Shanghai in September 2003. Africa also had a number of arrangements in place. It was only South and West Asia in which regional cooperation had not flourished. That was mostly because of inter-country rivalries. That may change as a result of the current war in Afghanistan.

The terrorist attacks on New York and Washington on 11 September 2001, the ensuing war in Afghanistan, the collapse of the Taliban regime, and the resumption of inter-tribal and inter-ethnic conflict in Afghanistan brought the spotlight to shine on the Muslim world of West Asia. My purpose in this section is to highlight some of the economic, social and political characteristics of this region.

There were many reasons why West Asia could make an economic, social and political success of itself provided it took note of the evolving global situation and provided it carefully assessed its own potential. For that to happen, a great deal had to change in the region, including the structure of the economy and the shape of politics. At the same time, the business community in the region had to equip itself to play an active role. If the business community were to get mobilized and if it was supported by the various states of the region, there could be a quick economic response helped in part by international investors.

To reach these three conclusions, I will present my argument in three parts. I will identify the main economic, political and social characteristics of the region. I will then focus on what I consider to be the region's main problems. Finally, I will indicate what I regard as the region's main economic assets, suggest how these assets could be developed to benefit the area, and speculate on how the community of international investors may respond once the region began to work on the realization of its considerable but yet to be fully tapped potential.

West Asia could be defined to include twenty-five countries; this was the region that President George W. Bush began to call the Greater Middle East, when he presented his programme for the political and social development of the Muslim world. The region began in the west with Morocco and included all countries of the Maghreb, Turkey, the nations of Central Asia, Afghanistan, Iran, the Saudi Arabian Peninsula and ended with Pakistan in the east. It was a sizable region in terms of both area and population. Nearly 650 million people lived in the region in 2006. Other than its size, what were its main characteristics?

Islam was the predominant religion of the region. Nearly 90 per cent of the population—585 million people—were Muslims. In other words, nearly one-half of the world's total Muslim population lived in this area. But with the exception of Saudi Arabia, Iran and a few small countries in the Gulf, Islam had not influenced the region's political structure. The region also had a very young population—in fact, the youngest in the world. Some 52 per cent of the people in the region were below the age of 18. America, with 282 million people, had 72 million young people—those under the age of 18. West Asia had more than four times as many young people as America—more than 300 million.

In terms of population, Pakistan, with 160 million people in 2006, was the region's largest country. Although several countries in the region saw fairly significant declines in fertility—for instance, Saudi Arabia's population growth declined from 5.2 to 3.4 per cent a year within one decade—the region continued to have the most rapidly growing population in the world. In 2005, there were only two countries in the world with population growth rates of more than 4 per cent. Both Jordan and Yemen were in this region. That was the reason why the region had such a young population. By 2050, the region will more than double its population to 1.25 billion, with Pakistan at 350 million people, still the largest country.

West Asia was a relatively well-to-do region with a combined gross domestic product of close to a trillion dollars in 2005. The regional per capita income was close to $1,450, which placed it in the World Bank's category of middle-income countries. But there were considerable differences in the levels of income. The UAE, with income per head of $20,000, was the region's richest country. Afghanistan, with per capita income of $150, was the poorest. In addition to the UAE, there were four relatively prosperous countries: Saudi Arabia ($7200), Oman ($6070), Lebanon ($3,750), and Turkey ($3,300).

West Asia was a male-dominated region with one of the lowest participation rates for women in the workforce. In middle-income countries, it was normal for over 40 per cent of all women to be working. In West Asia, the average was only 28 per cent with Saudi Arabia registering the lowest level—only 5 per cent—of any country in the world. By keeping such a large number of women out of the workforce, the region was constraining its economic development.

The region had some of the most unevenly distributed incomes in the world. When income distribution was measured as the ratio between the shares of the top 10 per cent of the population to the bottom 10 per cent, anything more than six to seven connoted a less than satisfactory situation. In other words, there were reasons to worry if the rich—the top 10 per cent of the population—earned more than six to seven times the incomes of the poor—the bottom 10 per cent. However, the regional average was more than 10. In Turkey, which had the worst income distribution of all countries for which data were available, the rich received more than fourteen times the share of the poor.

Turkey was the only country in the region which had a functioning democracy. All other countries had political systems that were considerably less than fully representative. An analysis in *The New York Times* placed the political systems in the region's countries into nine categories ranging from the democratic (Turkey) to the totally dysfunctional (Afghanistan). Most of the countries in the region were either monarchies or 'limited' democracies.

What were the region's main problems? Much of the region was politically unsettled. When the following five features—a very young population, a population that was rapidly urbanizing, a population which discriminated against women, a population in which the distribution of income was highly skewed, and a population that had to endure highly repressive political systems—were combined, it was not surprising that there was so much turmoil in the region.

That this was indeed the case came to be appreciated following the terrorist attacks of 11 September. 'Why do they hate us so much?' was a question that was repeatedly asked. The 'they' in this question were the young people of West Asia, some of whom were responsible for the terrorist attacks. The 'us' in the question referred to the country, America, and the people, the Americans. The common perception in many of these countries was that somehow the Americans were responsible for the glaring income inequality and poorly representative political systems.

The region's economy had a very narrow base and was excessively dependent on one natural resource, oil. The oil exporting countries of the Middle East were sitting on the largest remaining global oil reserves in the world. Saudi Arabia did not only have the largest reserve, it was also the largest producer and exporter of oil. Iran, Iraq, Kuwait were all major oil-dependent economies. Qatar had a lot of gas. And, the states around the Caspian Sea were becoming major oil producers. Depending on how the world—the world of politics as well as the global economy—reshaped itself, the Central Asian states could also become major exporters of oil and gas.

Geographically, the West Asian region is well placed to become an important part of the global economy. It borders on the European Union, China and India—three of the world's largest economies. It is well positioned to meet the resource requirements of China and India which, by 2025, will be very large economies but with serious shortages of energy and a number of agricultural products. The large textile industries of China and India could be fed by the cotton surpluses of Pakistan and Central Asia, and the emerging food deficit of China could be catered to by the vast irrigated lands in various parts of West Asia. The West Asian region has good ports, is strategically located on a number of airline routes, and could develop a good land-based communication system by integrating its road and railway networks.

However, a great deal of work will have to be done before West Asia could be turned into a well-integrated economic and trading zone. Pakistan could perhaps take the lead in turning this prospect into a reality. China could be brought in as an economic partner.

Whether Pakistan will gain entry into such an organization will depend upon the success it achieves in handling the forces of Islamic militancy within its own borders. It is probably because Pakistan was coming increasingly under the influence of militant Islam that China did not invite it to become a member of the Shanghai group. That may change as a result of the initiatives taken by the administration of General Pervez Musharraf. Another approach Pakistan could follow is to reactivate the Regional Cooperation for Development (RCD), an association formed decades ago by Iran, Pakistan and Turkey. The RCD never developed beyond an organization for exchanging visits among the officials of the three member countries. After the departure of President Ayub Khan from the Pakistani political scene, the organization became moribund. Ayub Khan was the main architect of the RCD. No other leader was prepared to put life into it once he was gone.

There is another option—Pakistan's membership in an association much larger than SAARC, the Shanghai group or the RCD. The Pakistani leadership could take the initiative of assembling the Muslim countries of West Asia into an economic and trading bloc.

5. The United States, the Muslim World and Pakistan[14]

Rather than trace the entire history of America's relations with the Muslim world and Pakistan—a subject of several important books in the early 2000s[15]—I will focus this section on the visit by President George W. Bush to South Asia in early March 2006. In several ways this visit redefined the way Washington looked at the Muslim world in general and Pakistan in particular.

President Bush came stealthily to South Asia and, after spending four days, went back to Washington equally stealthily. He arrived in Afghanistan unannounced and spent a few hours in Kabul and the American airbase in Bagram. His plane landed in Islamabad–Rawalpindi Chaklala air force base at an unannounced time with the cabin blacked out so that the plane's contour would not be visible to anybody wishing to do harm. He left Pakistan in the same way a day later.

This manner of comings and goings served as a symbol of the way America had come to be perceived in the Muslim world. The only way now for the American head of state to be physically present in the Muslim world was to slip in and out unnoticed by the population. Could America continue to conduct business this way? Did the visit to the world's second largest Muslim state start the process of reconciliation between the United States and the Muslim *Ummah*? The answers to both questions had to be 'no', one reason why it was necessary to examine in somewhat greater detail the full impact of President Bush's visit to this part of the world.

During this brief visit, President Bush went to four cities, one each in Afghanistan and Pakistan and two in India. He went to Kabul and Rawalpindi–Islamabad as a war president meeting with his soldiers in Afghanistan and the soldier-president in Pakistan. He went to Delhi and Hyderabad in India as the leader of the world's largest economy which was at the frontline of creating a new global economic order. He talked war and military action in Afghanistan and Pakistan but economic and human development in India. While talking about war, he seemed more comfortable in

Kabul, a willing and enthusiastic ally, than in Islamabad, a somewhat sullen and increasingly disenchanted partner.

In this process, President Bush left behind a greatly uncomfortable Pakistan. This was the first time he was visiting this part of the world. While his impressions about India were formed by the contacts he had with the members of that country's diaspora in Texas, his impression about Pakistan was limited to his dealings with President Pervez Musharraf. Both impressions were highly positive in the sense that he was impressed with the people of Indian origin living and working in the state of Texas and he was comfortable in his dealings with the Pakistani president. These impressions became the basis of his approach towards the two countries of the South Asian subcontinent. He talked to the Indian people in India but only to the Pakistani president in Pakistan.

He was impressed with the levels of skills, dexterity and enterprise the Indians possessed. He believed that such a population would not only help the country to which they belonged and make it possible for it to climb great heights. He was also convinced that the Indians could contribute massively to global prosperity and peace. He saw this kind of Indian in the various audiences he addressed in Delhi and Hyderabad. The only 'common people' he came face to face with in Pakistan were a bunch of cricketers; he was kept safely away from the rest of the population.

With President Musharraf, George Bush had developed a relationship of trust. Here was a man who had risked his life to join America's war on terrorism. If his resolve was weakening, as was sometimes suggested by some of President Bush's advisors and some parts of the American press, it was not because the Pakistani president was being devious and was playing tricks. It was because he had to take into account his own internal compulsions. President Bush understood his mission to Islamabad as a part of the American effort to get Pakistan and its leader even more committed to the fight against terrorism.

These impressions were reinforced by the senior members of corporate America with whom President Bush and his administration were in close touch. They saw enormous opportunities in India but only visible as well as hidden dangers in Pakistan. Political analysts based in Pakistan did not fully comprehend the enormous influence of corporate America on public policymaking in the United States. India Inc., the term which was used to identify the corporate leaders of Indian origin in the United States, had cultivated very close relations with their American-born counterparts. They were at the forefront of the Washington effort to assign India a role in the American administration's vision of a new world order during the Bush presidency. No such corporate constituency existed for Pakistan.

During President Bush's visit to South Asia, America's task in India, therefore, was to help that country become an even more effective player in the global economy, the global political system and the global society. Having already invested heavily in the country, the American corporations wanted India to become a part of the global production system. This involved not only the IT sector and the sector of health sciences. It also included industries such as automobiles, steel, chemicals, and oil and gas. To take only one example: Indian exports of automobile parts in 2006 were likely to exceed $1 billion.

Corporate America did not have significant investments in Pakistan—and consequently no such interest—in the country, other than putting a lid on Islamic terrorism which threatened economic activity in the vital Middle East and in South Asia. With this as the background it should be easy to understand why President Bush took such different positions in India and Pakistan. In Pakistan he understood his task to help Islamabad contain the menace posed by the rise of Islamic extremism, in India he wished to help the country move to the front of the global economic system.

What did President George Bush leave behind after his four-day visit to South Asia? This was the second presidential visit in five years. On the previous occasion not much was expected in Pakistan from President Bill Clinton.[16] At that time, the West was not happy with General Musharraf; he was generally regarded as a military usurper who had set back by years—if not by decades—Pakistan's political development. India, of course, was different. The Americans saw it as the world's largest democracy managed with the same kind of chaos and panache with which they ran their own government. The American corporations, after having gone to China, had begun to discover India. In discovering it they found the two giants to be very different. China offered a workplace where a disciplined labour force could efficiently produce the goods needed by American consumers, and parts and components required by American manufacturers. India was different. Whereas China had the industrial muscle, India had the brains; China produced the machines that worked in its factories to produce all kinds of products for export, India first developed and then deployed brains to produce softwares that made the machines and the factories work. Pakistan was nowhere to be found in this new order of industrial and service production.

Accordingly, in his visit to India, President Clinton assiduously courted the Indian academia and its industry. He went to Pakistan simply for the sake of history; after all, that country was once an important ally of the United States. More recently it was from across the Pakistani border with Afghanistan that Osama bin Laden had planned attacks on such American assets as two embassies in East Africa and a ship of the US navy in the Arabian Sea. It would do no harm to warn Pakistan about its support for the regime in Kabul that harboured Osama bin Laden, perhaps even to get the country's help to bring him to justice. A more spectacular terrorist attack, this time on American soil, put Pakistan on America's radar screen. After 11 September 2001, literally overnight, Pakistan became a valued ally of the United States and President Musharraf a sought after world leader. There was also a different president in office in Washington at that time.

But a great deal has happened since that fateful day. For several years President Musharraf was feted by America and most Western powers for the contribution he and his country made to the war against global terrorism. However, after some initial successes, the war did not go well. The Taliban resurged in Afghanistan; Iraq got close to widespread civil strife; Al Qaeda or its associates were able to strike at the heart of two large European cities, Madrid and London; and Al Qaeda still had its senior leaders in place, sending messages from their hideouts to their followers across the globe. In a long message carried by world televisions, on 2 September 2006, Ayman Al-Zawahiri, Osama bin Laden's deputy invited Americans to convert to Islam to save themselves from acts of terrorism. This was seen as a serious affront on the eve of the fifth anniversary of the 11 September 2001 attack. These were not the only setbacks. The Islamic extremists were seen to be succeeding in their effort to widen the rift between the West and the Muslim *Ummah*. The way the Muslim world reacted in early 2006 to the publication of cartoons depicting the Prophet Muhammad (PBUH) took the western world by surprise.

In this changed context it was legitimate for the leaders in Pakistan to believe that Washington would pay special heed to their claim that their country could become the model of political, social and economic development for the rest of the Muslim world. The country seemed to be set on achieving a high rate of economic growth, it had begun to reduce the size of the large pool of poverty, it was working on several initiatives to improve the quality of education and increase the number of people with world class skills, and it was moving towards the creation of a political system that combined the need for a strong executive and broad participation. All these were some of the elements in the strategy President Musharraf had described as 'enlightened moderation'.

But Washington had begun to sing from a different sheet of music. After having recognized that the global war on terror would be a long-drawn-out affair, it began to focus on a number of other concerns. It was prepared to put on hold its attempts to remould the Muslim world. There was a growing feeling in the American capital that the war on terrorism had distracted it for so long that it was not properly focused on other urgent issues of the day. Four of these were of particular importance. One, the growing strength of China, the second the increasing competition among the world's major economic powers for access to reliable sources of energy; the third, to protect access to these resources; and the fourth a strong and growing corporate interest in India which had begun to match that in China.

It is these interests that informed President Bush's new India policy and the one that he brought with him and the one that he clearly articulated during his short visit to South Asia. What are the implications of this policy for Pakistan in particular and South Asia in general, and also for the Muslim world? Bush had in mind two new pillars of his administration's evolving world view and an associated foreign policy. There cannot be any doubt that India was ready to fill many roles Washington wished to assign to its partners. There is also a hint of a new way the Americans were looking at the Muslim world in light of the various setbacks they had suffered since 11 September 2001. The first pillar of the new American world view was viewed at length by numerous Pakistani commentators who wrote thoughtfully about the significance of what President Bush said and did in South Asia.[17] It was the second, even more worrying, aspect of the new American foreign policy that escaped the attention of almost all commentators.

Pakistan and India were indeed two different countries, as President Bush pointed out in his statement at Islamabad. One had a majority of Muslims in its population, many of whom were not just contemptuous of the West and its values; they were openly hostile to it. The philosophies they followed and sought to inspire were being called several names, including Islamo-nazism and Islamo-fascism. After 9/11, 3/11 (in Madrid), 7/7 (in London), and the plan to bomb US-bound commercial airliners revealed in August 2006, they could not be dismissed as nonsensical. This assault on the West needed to be beaten back. The other country—India—was a multi-racial, multi-ethnic and multi-religious democratic society that did not openly discriminate against minorities. It gave them the opportunity to advance and assimilate without giving up on the differences in culture, religion and language. In 2006, India had a president who was a Muslim scientist of some repute who had helped with the country's effort to become a nuclear power of some significance. The prime minister was a Sikh economist with a PhD from Oxford who observed his religion. The chairman of the main political party in the coalition that governed in New Delhi was a former housewife of Italian origin and the widow of an assassinated prime minister. What could be more diverse than this coterie of leaders?

Indians are argumentative by nature, as we were reminded recently by Amartya Sen, the Nobel Prize winning economist.[18] They are also assimilative. Pakistanis, on the other hand, give the impression of extreme intolerance towards intelligent discourse. This attitude no longer emanates from the corridors of power as President Musharraf rightly pointed out in his talk with the editors after the departure of the American president. It comes from the religious right that had increasingly come to influence society. In sum, the Indian culture was interested in 'inclusion', the developing Pakistani culture was increasingly focused on exclusion. The two countries were, indeed are very different and Washington was prepared to look at them from very different angles.

Indians have also developed a political and legal and system that can, at least most of the time, address the social ills the society faced. India's problems are no less severe than those Pakistan faces; in many respects the country has to deal with situations more difficult than those found in Pakistan. That side of India has been hidden from the view of the West for the reason that the problem do not become crises. They get handled through discourse and accommodation. Pakistan's way of dealing with difficult social issues were essentially ad hoc and authoritarian.

Pakistan's politicians and opinion-makers were surprised by what President Bush said and did in Delhi and Islamabad. They need not have been had they been paying attention to what was being done and said by the West with respect to South Asia's two largest countries and the region's two largest economies. India was seen correctly as the world's largest democracy and, once again, correctly as the world's second most populous country. It was viewed, correctly one more time, as a country on the way to becoming a major global economic power. That was likely to happen largely on account of its rapid rate of economic growth since the mid-1980s, which averaged about 6 per cent a year. This meant that the size of its economy has quadrupled since 1986. It is the world's largest producer of engineering graduates, many of whom come equipped with world-class skills, particularly in computer sciences. Most large western corporations were knocking on the Indian door to get in, apprehensive that the Indian train would soon leave the station without them having climbed on it. It was that India that President Bush wished to embrace and cultivate.

By the fall of 2006 when the work on this book was concluded, official Washington had decided that it was engaged in an ideological struggle with some parts of the Muslim world that was similar to the one it faced with the Nazis in the 1930s and 1940s and with the communists for almost half a century after the Second World War. 'The war we fight today is more than a military conflict, it is the decisive ideological struggle of the twenty-first century,' President Bush told a meeting of American veterans of wars on 31 July 2006.

On one side are those who believe in the values of freedom and moderation—the right of the people to speak and worship, and live in liberty. And on the other side are those driven by the values of tyranny and extremism—the right of a self-appointed few to impose their fanatical views on all the rest. As veterans you have seen this kind of enemy before. They are successors to Fascists, to Nazis, to Communists, and other totalitarians of the twentieth century. And history shows what the outcome will be. This war will be difficult, this was will be long, and the war will end in the defeat of the terrorists and totalitarians, and a victory for the cause of freedom and liberty.

By casting the struggle against Islamic extremists in such ideological terms, President Bush was attempting to deflect attention away from the policies pursued by Washington in the Middle East for decades, and also by its failure in Iraq and possibly in Afghanistan. If this approach is sustained beyond the term of President Bush, it will have difficult consequences for Pakistan, the Muslim world's second most populous country and one with a growing appeal for Islamic extremists.

6. Conclusion

In the early 2000s, in particular after the 11 September 2001 attacks on the United States by a group of radicals who operated out of Afghanistan and had a large number of sympathizers in Pakistan, foreign policy making by Islamabad acquired a number of objectives that were not previously pursued. For half a century after the country gained independence, foreign affairs were dominated by concerns about India: that country's perceived and, at times, real threat to Pakistan. This changed once the United States became actively engaged in the war against terrorism, once China became a near-super economic power, once India got aligned with the United States as a strategic power, and once the countries of Central Asia entered a new version of the old 'great game'. All this demanded a delicate balancing act on the part of Islamabad. To a great extent, Pakistan's economic success and its ability to develop a viable political system that provided representation to a diverse population, and its own war against Islamic extremism will depend on how well these new considerations are factored into the making of a foreign policy.

NOTES

1. The type of pressure put on President Pervez Musharraf by the administration of President George W. Bush is related in Bob Woodward, *Bush at War*, New York: Simon and Schuster, 2002, pp. 58–59.
2. This section is based on my article published in *Dawn* under the title 'The Question of Location' on 29 January 2002.
3. Thomas L. Friedman, *The World is Flat: A Brief History of the Twenty-First Century*, New York: Farrar, Straus and Giroux, 2005.
4. Edward Luce, *In Spite of the Gods: The Rise of Modern India*, New York: Doubleday, 2006.
5. Mohammad Ayub Khan, *Friends Not Masters: A Political Autobiography*, Karachi: Oxford University Press.
6. Zulfikar Ali Bhutto, *The Myth of Independence*, Karachi: Oxford University Press, 1968.
7. The partnership among Pakistan, Saudi Arabia and the United States in the war against the Soviet Union's occupation of Afghanistan received considerable analytical attention. See in particular, Steve Coll, *Ghost Wars:*

The Secret History of the CIA, Afghanistan, and Bin laden, from the Soviet Invasion to September 11, 2001, New York: The Penguin Press, 2004.

8. George Crile, *Charlie Wilson's War: The Extraordinary Story of the Largest Covert Operation in History*, New York: Atlantic Monthly Press, 2003, p. 5.

9. Henry Kissinger, *Does America Need a Foreign Policy: Toward a Diplomacy for the 21st Century*, New York: Simon and Schuster, 2001, p. 17.

10. Sunil Khilnani, *The Idea of India*, New York: Farrar Straus Giroux, 1997.

11. Strobe Talbott, *Engaging India: Diplomacy, Democracy and the Bomb*, New Delhi, Penguin, 2004.

12. I find it interesting that President Musharraf adopted this phrase—'India eccentric'—I had used in my *Dawn* article to portray his approach towards his neighbour following the visit in March 2006 by President George W. Bush to South Asia.

13. Zulfikar Ali Bhutto, *The Myth of Independence*, Karachi: Oxford University Press, 1968, p. 131.

14. This section draws upon the material covered by me in three articles. See Shahid Javed Burki, 'West Asia: New Great Game', *Dawn*, 16 December 2001; 'The Question of Location', *Dawn*, 29 January 2002; 'Pakistan and West Asia', *Dawn*, 5 February 2002.

15. See in particular, John L. Esposito, *Islam: The Straight Path*, New York: Oxford University Press, 1998; Rashid Khalidi, *Resurrecting Empire: Western Footprints and America's Perilous Path in the Middle East*, Boston: Beacon Press, 2004; and Dennis Kux, *The United States and Pakistan: Disenchanted Allies*, Baltimore, Md.: The Johns Hopkins University Press, 2001.

16. The visit by President Bill Clinton to South Asia was well covered in two books written by two persons closely involved in the visit, including the president himself. See William Jefferson Clinton, *My Story*, New York: Alfred A. Knopf, 2004, and Strobe Talbott, *Engaging India: Diplomacy, Democracy, and the Bomb*, Delhi: Penguin, 2004.

17. See for instance articles by Tanvir Ahmad Khan, 'For a better South Asia', *Dawn*, 6 March 2006; Mohammad Waseem, 'Implications of the Bush Visit', *Dawn*, 7 March 2006; and F.S. Aijazuddin, 'Bush's Crucial Visit', *Dawn*, 9 March 2006.

18. Amartya Sen, *The Argumentative Indian: Writings on Indian History, Culture and Identity*, London: Allen Pane, 2005.

3

Trade and Development

In the 1990s and the early 2000s, a number of significant structural changes occurred in the global economy, particularly in the way various countries and regions of the world interacted with one another. According to Thomas Friedman, *The New York Times* columnist and the author of a book that attracted a great deal of attention when it appeared in 2005, the world was becoming flat in the sense that the peaks and troughs that marked the structure of the global economy since the advent of the industrial revolution were evened out largely as a result of the development of technologies that could be easily transported.[1] More trade took place among the regions and countries of the world than ever before. For 2003, the last year for which complete data was available, the World Bank estimated the global output at $34.76 trillion. Of this, $9.31 trillion was traded, amounting to nearly 27 per cent of the total.[2] How did Pakistan fare in this respect? The answer to this question is the subject of this chapter.

The evolution in the structure of Pakistan's trade can only be understood in the context of political and economic developments in South Asia. The long-enduring hostility between India and Pakistan reduced intra-regional trade to insignificance. It is clear to all but the most nationalistic that Pakistan will not make much economic progress without easing tensions with India. For that to happen, as discussed in Chapter 7, a workable solution will have to be found for the Kashmir problem. This will need India's full cooperation rather than continued confrontation with it. This conclusion—one of the several presented in this book—will not be well received by those who believe that Pakistan and India have irreconcilable differences; any effort to resolve them will diminish

Pakistan and increase India's stature. I believe that this approach will in fact weaken Pakistan; no small country located next to a large one has prospered economically by confronting rather than working with its neighbour. This is as true for Mexico and Canada in relation to the United States, for Argentina, Bolivia and Uruguay in relation to Brazil, for the Netherlands and Poland in relation to Germany, for Zimbabwe and Namibia in relation to South Africa, as it is for Bangladesh, Nepal, Pakistan and Sri Lanka in relation to India.

This does not mean that any of these countries should sacrifice their interests and subject them to those of the larger neighbour. What it means is that differences must be resolved through dialogue rather than confrontation. One more conclusion I will reach in this chapter is that a multilateral framework such as the one provided by the fledgling SAFTA offers a very good opportunity for all Indian neighbours to work with India. It is for the reasons cited above that the discussion of trade and development in this chapter will be in the context of regional trends. How South Asia has performed with respect to international trade, why it has lagged so far behind other world regions in terms of its share in international trade, how can the countries in the region work with one another to promote greater regional trade and increase the region's presence in the global market, are some of the questions that will be addressed in this chapter.

Apart from the damage done by the long-enduring hostility between India and Pakistan, the import substitution policies followed by the countries in the region were also responsible in reducing the role of trade in economic development. Could the region catch up with the rest of the world in terms of using trade as a factor in economic growth? How important is the multilateral system as administered by the WTO in promoting trade in the countries of the region? Should South Asia follow the example of other regions in the developing world and increase intra-regional trade by creating a free trade area? This is another set of questions to be asked and answered in this chapter.

In the chapter's first section I will provide a quick overview of South Asia's approach towards international commerce. As we will see, history—both political and economic—played a large part in determining the pattern of trade, the destination of exports and the origin of imports for the countries of the region. In Section 2, I will provide a brief overview of the economy of and patterns of trade in the region. In Section 3, I discuss the reasons why South Asia was so poorly integrated into the world economy. In Section 4, I will look at the attempts made to-date by the region to overcome the legacy of history and promote intra-regional trade. In Section 5, I will examine the role the developing global trading system could play in increasing regional trade. In Section 6, I will discuss the importance of the WTO for the conduct of trade by Pakistan and other countries of South Asia. The last section provides a brief conclusion.

1. The South Asian Economy and the Structure of Trade

South Asia has a relatively smaller share of global trade compared to other parts of the developing world. In 2003, the last year for which data is available, the area's combined GDP was only 2.1 per cent of the world total (3.7 per cent in terms of purchasing power parity[3]), its share in merchandise trade was only 1.1 per cent. The region's share in trade in services was slightly higher; about 1.7 per cent, primarily because of the large information technology (IT) exports by India. South Asia is a large region in terms of population but is still relatively poor compared to other parts of Asia. In 2003, the region's estimated population was 1.4 billion and its combined gross domestic product was $728 billion, measured at market exchange rates, or $3.74 trillion in terms of purchasing power parity (PPP). Average per capita income was only $530 in conventional terms and $2493 in PPP terms. India was the region's predominant country and its largest economy. For the last decade and a half, it was also the region's most rapidly growing economy. With 1,064 million people, it had 77.5 per cent of the population.

In purchasing power terms India accounted for 82 per cent of the region's total income, but 68 per cent of the total regional trade. Given the size of the Indian economy it was clear that for Pakistan it had to be the largest trading partner. That, as I will discuss below, was not to be the case.

While trade-to-GDP ratios were relatively low in South Asia, growth of trade in all countries in the region, barring Pakistan, was much higher than the increase in domestic output. This meant that the trade-to-GDP ratios for Pakistan were even lower a decade and a half ago than was the case in the early 2000s. Pakistan began to play catch-up beginning with the 2003–2004 financial year. In 2004–2006, both exports and imports increased by double-digit rates.

2. The Weight of History

Under colonial rule, most of the South Asian region was one country with much of the physical infrastructure built specifically to allow easy flow of goods and commodities among the provinces of British India. In fact, the British administration in India invested heavily in developing the irrigation systems in the provinces of Punjab and Sindh to feed the food-deficient parts of the empire. I will discuss this feature of colonial rule in some detail in Chapter 5. For the purpose of the discussion here, it would suffice to recall that in order to save their Indian empire from the repeated ravages of famines that took a heavy toll in the eighteenth and nineteenth centuries, the British adopted a strategy for increasing the domestic supply of food grain by developing the vast tracts of virgin land in Punjab and Sindh. The strategy worked and within a few decades, Punjab and Sindh were able to produce vast quantities of food grains that were surplus to their needs. But this surplus had to be transported to the northeast, especially the heavily populated provinces of Bengal and Bihar. To do this, the British invested heavily in transport infrastructure, in particular farm-to-market roads, a system of roads linked with the fabled Grand Trunk Road that linked Kabul with Calcutta, railways, and the port of Karachi.

These investments formed the basis for close economic integration of the various parts of what was then the British Indian Empire and later became parts of the independent states of Bangladesh, India, and Pakistan. One of the themes to be explored in this chapter is that if regional economic integration succeeds, it should be able to restore quickly the economic and trading system that existed before British India was divided into independent countries. It was *politics* that severed these links; it will take *politics* to restore them.

Politics intervened most dramatically in the way the waters of the Indus River system were divided between the successor states of India and Pakistan. The water dispute surfaced in the early 1950s and almost resulted in war between India and Pakistan. In fact, when India threatened to cut off water supplies to Pakistan in 1951 by blocking the flow of water in the Ravi and the Sutlej, Liaquat Ali Khan, Pakistan's first prime minister, went to the balcony of his house in Karachi, then the capital of the country, and raised his fist and threatened war. Intense international diplomacy and the involvement of a consortium led by the World Bank salvaged the situation. The Indus Water Treaty of 1960 led to the assignment of three western rivers of the system to Pakistan and three eastern rivers to India.[4]

This was not the only dispute between India and Pakistan that had profound economic consequences for the region and inhibited trade between the two countries. For example, the 1947 partition of British India into India and Pakistan need not have resulted in the sharp decline in trade between these new political entities. Trade declined mostly because of political reasons. In 1949, Pakistan refused to follow other countries of the 'Sterling Area'[5] in devaluing its currency with respect to the US dollar; India, in return, refused to recognize the new exchange rate of 144 of its rupees to 100 Pakistani rupees and halted all trade with its neighbour. 'India', declared Sardar Vallabhbhai Patel, the powerful home minister in Prime Minister Jawaharlal Nehru's cabinet, 'will not pay 144 Indian rupees for 100 rupees from Pakistan'.[6] Trade between the two countries was reduced to a trickle; nothing flowed through official channels. Pakistan, starved of most manufactured goods of daily consumption launched a programme of industrialization to achieve a measure of self-sufficiency. Had this trade war not occurred, Pakistan would not have industrialized as rapidly as it did, and would not have forsaken its comparative advantage in agriculture.[7]

With this inauspicious beginning, trade between India and Pakistan declined rapidly and remained insignificant until the beginning of this century when the two countries began to work to resolve their outstanding issues, including the problem of Kashmir, while attempting to use a series of regional arrangements to promote intra-regional trade. However, given the weight of history on the relations between the two countries, the easing of tensions occurred slowly and ran into several obstacles, disappointing those who had hoped for a rapid development of various exchanges between the two countries.

The growing political problems between India and Pakistan were not the only reason for the poor performance of intra-regional trade in the South Asia region. All countries in the region had pursued import-substitution approaches toward economic development for nearly forty years, from independence in the late 1940s to the adoption of greater openness in trade beginning in the mid-1980s. Consequently, following independence from British rule, trade among the countries declined from about 19 per cent of the total in 1948, to about 4 per cent by the end of the 1950s, and to 2 per cent by 1967.[8] Trade between India and Pakistan was reduced to practically nothing. As discussed below, the share of intra-regional trade in total trade began to increase only after the countries abandoned import substitution in favour of general trade liberalization. In the early 2000s, the share of intra-regional trade in total trade increased to 5 per cent.

Another pertinent legacy was the dirigistic economic policies adopted by all countries in the region. Jawaharlal Nehru, India's first prime minister, taking the advice of senior Indian economists and following his own instincts, brought socialist economic management to his country. As a result of the support it had provided to Britain in fighting the Second World War, India had a highly developed bureaucratic system that could quickly establish controls over the economy. During the war, India's bureaucrats were responsible for setting up public sector enterprises for producing goods for the war effort that could not be obtained readily from the market. They were also responsible for procuring supplies for the fighting men while ensuring that domestic shortages did not occur. To prevent price gouging, they ran an elaborate system of rationing and price controls. This bureaucracy and its elaborate systems were at hand when Nehru launched the 'license raj'. Developed over three decades, the tentacles of this system left no corner of the Indian economy—old and established or new and modern—untouched.[9]

For a decade and half, Pakistan followed a different route, encouraging the private sector to help meet the enormous shortages of consumer goods created by the 1949 trade war with India. While encouraging private entrepreneurship, the state also insulated it from foreign competition by building a high wall of protection around it. It also established state-owned financial institutions to provide the private sector cheap and long-term capital. Institutions such as the Pakistan Industrial Corporation for Investment and Credit (PICIC) and the Industrial Development Bank of Pakistan (IDBP) on-lent money obtained from the World Bank and other development banks to aspiring entrepreneurs. And, for a time, Pakistan operated a dual exchange rate system that gave rich incentives to those who set up import-substituting industries while punishing those who wanted to sell their products in the international market.

In the two-year period between 1972 and 1974 Zulfikar Ali Bhutto, an avowed socialist, took Pakistan in a sharply different direction. He undertook a programme of extensive nationalization of private assets soon after assuming office. His administration took control of thirty-one large-scale industries, virtually all financial institutions, all large-scale trading companies and eventually even small agro-production enterprises. By the middle of the 1970s, the grip of the Pakistani state on the economy was as tight as the hold of the state in India. When Bhutto was done with his programme of nationalization, the entire financial sector and most of the large-scale industry was in the hands of the government. The state had intruded as deeply into the economy as it did in neighbouring India.

Sheikh Mujibur Rahman, the first President of Bangladesh, finding no reason to experiment with a system of economic governance different from those followed by his neighbours, also brought bureaucratic-socialism to his country. Thus, by about the mid-1970s, South Asia had closed itself off to the outside world. The region had followed an entirely different trajectory of development than the one pursued by East Asia and the tiger economies of that region. Consequently, East Asia took off, industrialized and got integrated into the global economy. South Asia, on the other hand, stagnated and became progressively poor under the watch of the state.

The relatively poor performance of South Asia in carving out a greater role for itself in international trade was due in part to protectionist trade policies pursued until recently by all countries in the region. It was also the consequence of the failure of the region to develop an industrial structure that was well integrated into the international production system. The region's stilted growth patterns was largely reinforced by protectionist trade policies pursued for more than four decades by regional governments. Fortunately, this stance began to change in the 1990s and change was accelerated in the early 2000s.

As a result of some of the recent changes in trade policy, larger countries in the region became reasonably open to international trade. In 2003, Sri Lanka was the most open, with trade-to-GDP ratio of 66 per cent. The corresponding ratios for Nepal was 42 per cent; for Pakistan, 32 per cent; for Bangladesh, 30 per cent; and for India, 22 per cent. The relatively lower figure for India was typical for most large countries with the exception of China. However, as already indicated, there was relatively little trade among the countries of the region. Will the reforms undertaken in the mid-1980s, but not always pursued with the single-minded commitment shown by the leadership groups in East Asia, and the promise of greater intra-regional trade enable South Asians to close the yawning gap between their economic situation and that of East Asia? This will depend upon continued policy reforms leading towards even greater openness, better integration into the global economic system and greater regional integration.

First Sri Lanka in the 1970s and then India, Bangladesh, and Pakistan in the early 1990s abandoned trade protectionism in favour of openness as the strategy for development and poverty alleviation. India's greater openness was prompted by the foreign exchange crisis in 1991 and the prodding of the IMF, which had developed a new approach subsumed by most commentators under the title of *The Washington Consensus*. Fiscal austerity, privatization, and market liberalization were the three pillars of this programme of economic adjustment. While the countries of Latin America plunged into these reforms, the South Asians adopted a measured—perhaps too measured an approach. The more deliberate pace of opening the economies received some support from the academic community. According to Joseph Stiglitz, the Nobel Prize winning economist,

> the Washington Consensus policies were designed to respond to the very real problems in Latin America, and made considerable sense... When trade liberalization—the lowering of tariffs and elimination of other protectionist measures—is done the right way and at the right pace, so that new jobs are created as inefficient jobs are destroyed, there can be significant efficiency gains.[10]

For a decade—from the mid-1980s to about the mid-1990s—most major economies of the South Asian region undertook reforms to achieve greater openness. But the effort stalled, particularly in India, after 2000. Unfortunately, old habits die-hard and strong vested interests that had survived the demise of the 'license raj' brought to bear political pressure to slow the reform process. Reformists, however, persisted. Liberalizing momentum resumed with large cuts in industrial tariffs by India between 2002 and February 2006. According to a World Bank study, 'other developments—Pakistan's comprehensive liberalization of its trade policies since 1996/97 (including its agricultural trade policies), and Sri Lanka's potential to resume long-deferred reforms as prospects improve of ending its civil war—contribute to a regional picture of very mixed achievement but widely shared responsibility.'[11] As a result of these measures, Pakistan and Sri Lanka became the least protected markets in the region with a top custom's duty rate of 25 per cent and average custom's duty, including other protective rates, of 18.8 per cent for Pakistan. Bangladesh was the region's most protected economy with an average tariff rate of 26.5 per cent. India, the region's largest economy also had a relatively higher rate of protection.

3. South Asia's Failure to get Integrated in the Global Economic System

Over the period of some three and a half decades, starting with the early 1970s, developing countries carved out a prominent place for themselves in the evolving global production system and in world trade. The two developments were closely linked. The global production system was based on the activities of some 60,000 transnational corporations (TNCs). That system encompassed a number of East Asian countries other than those in the developed world, but did not include South Asia.[12] India was the only South Asian country that attracted some TNC attention; Pakistan was largely ignored. TNCs' choice of location was sometimes dictated by fiscal environment but usually by factor endowments. Even the simplest operations, such as the production of garments, were split into several steps. According to a story in *The Economist*, published on the eve of the lapse of the Multi-fibre Arrangement (MFA) that governed trade in textiles for several decades, 'the shirt on your back probably had an exotic life. Say you bought it in America and the label said it was "Made in Sri Lanka".'[13] However, before leaving Sri Lanka for the United States, it may already have travelled to many places across the developing world. It may well have been made from Chinese fabric, woven in China from fibre imported from Pakistan, cut in China, sewn in Sri Lanka with buttons imported from China. Final packing may have been done in Hong Kong. What was true for shirts was also true for a number of other products, particularly consumer electronics. Even the automobile industry in all parts of the world depended on hundreds of suppliers located in many distant places.

By splitting the final product into several intermediate products and components, TNCs maximized returns on investments. That way they were able to play on various kinds of arbitrages—wage, skill, and knowledge being the most important ones—locating the manufacture of parts and components in countries that had a comparative advantage in producing them. Parts were then sent for assembly into final products and shipment to customers all over the globe. East Asian countries became major suppliers of parts and components that made up final products produced in this dispersed system. This was one reason why China ran a sizeable trade deficit with the countries of East Asia but had a large trade surplus with the United States. In 2005 while China ran a trade surplus of $202 billion with the United States, the most important destination of final products it produced, it had significant deficits with the countries from which it imported intermediate products. It had a combined deficit of $105.8 billion with four East Asian countries— $52.1 billion with Taiwan, $38.0 billion with South Korea, $8.4 billion with Malaysia, and $5.5 billion with Thailand. The countries that had large trade surpluses and deficits with China—in particular the United States, Taiwan and South Korea—invested heavily in the country. Most of these investments were made by the TNCs that had their headquarters located in the territories of China's main trading partners. The East Asians specialized in the production of parts and components while the United States was the largest consumer of final products. China emerged as the major 'assembler' of parts and components and the 'shipper' of the final product to various parts of the world, especially the United States. It was a 'go-between' economy.

Under this system of production, much international trade took place within firms. The direction of trade was also profoundly influenced by this system—which partly explained why the developing world's share of world trade increased from about one-fifth of the total in 1960 to about one-third in 2005. During this time, international trade as a whole was increasing at unprecedented rates. Growth in exports outpaced growth in output in every region. Among developing countries, the East Asian region outperformed the rest. Latin American exports also grew as a share of the world market in the 1990s but not as sharply as in East Asia. South Asia, on the other hand, did relatively less well. Although the region's GDP growth in 1980–2000 and the share of exports in output increased—particularly in the latter part of this period of two decades—South Asia had the lowest share of trade in the aggregate GDP of any region, barring the Middle East and North Africa. Non-oil export shares of the East Asia and Pacific region increased from 18 per cent in 1980, to 25 per cent in 1990, to 34 per cent in 2000. The corresponding shares for the South Asia region were 8, 8.5, and 14 per cent, respectively.

As indicated above, India was the only South Asian country that succeeded in carving out a place for itself in the rapidly changing global economy. However, even in its case it succeeded only in one part of the global economy—the information technology or the IT sector. In the early 2000s, it became a major source of outsourcing for most large corporations based in America and Europe. For example, in the space of a few days in December 2005, three of the biggest companies in the US, viz. JP Morgan Chase, Intel, and Microsoft announced plans to create a total of more than 7,500 jobs in India in high-value areas such as research and development, and processing complex derivative trades. This move signalled that outsourcing to India was moving beyond relocating simple, labour intensive but relatively low skill activities such as call centres and medical and legal transactions, to high skill areas. For some big US companies, what began as an interesting experience became a core strategy. Under JP Morgan's plans, 20 per cent of the global workforce of its investment bank was expected to be in India by the end of 2007.

Why were American and European corporations, in particular those operating in the fast developing and changing service sector, being attracted to India? For JP Morgan, the attractions of India were not just costs—which industry analysts estimated at about 40 per cent below the levels in the industrial world[14]—but also the calibre of staff being produced. According to the head of operations at JP Morgan's investment bank, 'the quality of people we hire is extraordinary and their level of loyalty to the company unbeatable.'[15]

Could the rest of South Asia benefit from the increasing integration of India in the high technology end of the service sector? Benefits could flow to other populous countries in the region provided the economies in the area got better integrated. That could happen, as discussed below, with the successful launch of the SAFTA.

4. Hesitant Steps Towards Regional Integration

While regional governments in South Asia were reducing protection, some also took steps to encourage intra-regional trade. The major economies of the region directed their exports at several countries distant from their borders which led to the development of an uncommon pattern of trade. The United States was the major importer of South Asian goods and commodities; it accounted for 36 per cent of Bangladesh's total exports, 29 per cent of Pakistan's, and 21 per cent of India's. There was a different pattern for the points of origin for South Asian imports. For both Bangladesh and Pakistan, China became the single most important source of imports. For India, the United States was the largest single supplier. It would appear from the structure of South Asian trade that the 'gravity model' was not working for the region.[16] According to this model, widely accepted by trade economists, commerce between two countries is determined by two factors; the mass (or size) of the economies and the distance between them. While the United States had a large mass, its distance from South Asia was long enough to reduce its presence as a destination of exports and origin for imports for the countries in the region. India with a relatively larger mass than other countries in the South Asian region, should have been the most important trading partner for all countries in South Asia. That this was not the case was largely on account of regional politics.

In 1985, largely at the urging of President Ziaur Rahman of Bangladesh, the South Asian countries decided to establish a regional arrangement intended to produce greater economic cooperation among them. The South Asian Association for Regional Cooperation (SAARC) gave membership to seven countries— Bangladesh, Bhutan, India, Maldives, Nepal, Pakistan, and Sri Lanka. The seven members of SAARC agreed to a charter with the following objectives: (a) to promote the welfare of the peoples of South Asia and to improve their quality of life; (b) to accelerate economic growth, social progress and cultural development in the region and to provide all individuals the opportunity to live in dignity and to realize their full potentials; (c) to promote and strengthen collective self reliance among the countries of South Asia; (d) to contribute to mutual trust, understanding and appreciation of one another's problems; (e) to promote active and mutual assistance in the economic, social, cultural, technical and scientific fields; (f) to strengthen cooperation with other developing countries; (g) to strengthen cooperation among themselves in international forums on matters of common interest; and (h) to cooperate with international and regional organizations with similar aims and purposes.[17]

A secretariat was set up in 1986 at Kathmandu, the capital of Nepal, headed by a secretary general and one director from each member country to facilitate the work of the organization. Until the mid-1990s, the secretariat was not required to work on issues related to economic cooperation and integration. However, in April 1993, the Council of Ministers signed an agreement to form the South Asian Preferential Trading Arrangement (SAPTA), and mandated the secretariat to watch over its progress. The agreement became operational in December 1995. Following SAPTA's establishment, three rounds of preferential tariff reductions were implemented. Concluded in 1995, SAPTA-1 covered only 6 per cent of traded goods (about 226 products at the 6-digit level of the Harmonized System of Tariffs [HS]). The important issue of non-tariff barriers was left to be dealt with at a later date. SAPTA-2, concluded in 1997, was slightly more ambitious; it covered 1,800 six-digit HS items and incorporated provisions about easing some non-tariff barriers. SAPTA-3, signed in 1998, was the most ambitious of the three agreements. It covered 2,700 items. Work on SAPTA-4 was initiated in 1999 but was put on hold after the military takeover in Pakistan on 12 October 1999. Politics had once again halted the advance of regional integration in South Asia.

Since the SAARC was stalled because of continuing hostility between India and Pakistan, India concluded bilateral agreements with its smaller neighbours to increase trade. As a consequence, the total value of regional trade increased rapidly during the late 1980s and most of the 1990s, but not the share of regional trade in total trade. This was principally because of unilateral trade liberalization by countries on India's borders and large appreciations of the exchange rates of the peripheral countries relative to the Indian rupee. Most of the increased trade was one way, with large increases in exports from India, especially to Bangladesh and Sri Lanka. This growth in regional trade had little to do with the granting of regional trade preferences under the SAPTA which did little to increase intra-regional trade. The implementation of SAPTA agreements at best were hesitant steps towards increasing the flow of commerce among the countries of the South Asia region.

5. Move Towards the Creation of South Asia Free Trade Area

Among the three approaches to increasing trade between countries, purists preferred unilateral action not contingent on the granting of reciprocity by trading partners.[18] The second-best approach was to conduct negotiations on removing barriers to cross-border trade in the context of such 'international rounds' as the Tokyo and the

Uruguay Round multilateral discussions and the Doha parleys that started in 2001. According to this line of thinking, the least satisfactory approach was to start with regional integration as the first step in easing constraints on global trade.

Notwithstanding the disdain with which purists regard regional integration, such agreements proliferated as has the literature analyzing their contribution to promoting international trade. The number of regional trading arrangements (RTAs) had more than quadrupled since 1990, rising to about 230 by 2004.[19] By 2005, trade between RTA partners made up nearly 40 per cent of the world total. As countries reduced tariffs across the board, however, the value of preferences declined and trade facilitation acquired more importance. A World Bank study emphasized that 'trade policies are one element—and often a relatively minor one—of the overall costs of trade.'[20] Three key issues related to trade facilitation were worthy of attention: customs clearance, transport, and standards and their conformity assessment. Costs of trade, which included custom procedures, bottlenecks and adoptions of standards, could amount to 30 to 105 per cent of the tax on trade. Lowering these costs can have beneficial impacts much more significant than those accruing from reducing tariffs.

With tariff reductions, non-trade issues became important and RTAs became more ambitious in scope.[21] New agreements, including those between developed and developing countries—or North–South agreements—were addressing issues that went beyond trade—investment, labour and environmental laws, and, in some cases, political openness. Most South–South agreements, however, focused on merchandise trade, and tended to treat services, investment, and intellectual property rights unevenly, or ignored such subjects altogether. Agreements such as the Association of South East Asian Nations (ASEAN) and Mercosur did not provide specifically for liberalization of services beyond what was already available as a result of unilateral actions by the member states or were included in multilateral accords such as the General Agreement on Trade in Services (GATS) in the context of the World Trade Organization (WTO).

There was consensus among experts that modern services needed to be included in RTAs because services played a large role in the economies of developing countries and attracted foreign investment. According to one study on economic integration in Latin America, controlling for other factors, countries with fully liberalized financial and telecommunications sectors grew annually on average about 1.5 percentage points faster than other countries.[22] This was because preferential treatment of services allowed more suppliers to compete in the regional market, lowering prices and increasing efficiency. Including services in trading agreements did not erode government revenues because, in contrast to goods, the movement of services across international borders was normally not taxed.

Do RTAs attract more investment? That they should encourage domestic investment was obvious but their impact on foreign direct investment (FDI) inflows was less so. In a study completed in 2005, the World Bank investigated the effects of 238 RTAs and other variables on FDI flows for 152 countries over a period of twenty-two years, from 1980 to 2002. In general the Bank found that the countries that were open (measured as the ratio of trade to GDP), grew more rapidly, were more stable (measured by rates of inflation), and attracted greater amounts of FDI. On average, a 10-per cent increase in market size associated with an RTA produces a 5-per cent increase in FDI. However, the study underscored that an RTA could not substitute for an adequate investment climate.[23]

Analysts who supported RTAs as stepping-stones toward free international trade maintained that geographic proximity was a good reason to encourage them. In supporting the 'natural bloc' concept, some trade experts used 'gravity models' to argue that geography was a good determinant of the quantum of trade.[24] It was natural for neighbouring countries to extensively trade among themselves. As discussed above in Sections 2 and 3, proximity did not work in South Asia where intra-regional trade remained an insignificant component of total trade. This 'inverse regionalism'— a term coined by some trade economists working on South Asia— was not necessarily the result of political problems between India and Pakistan.[25] Proximity, it was argued, was not a good enough reason to deploy a great deal of political and bureaucratic energy in moving toward regional integration in South Asia. This position is hard to justify. Given the long history of intra-regional trade when the now independent states of South Asia were part of the British Indian Empire, some of the old patterns of exchanges of goods and commodities could be established once the right environment for them was created.

In light of the above, how successful will be South Asia's effort to create a regional trading arrangement? The Islamabad Declaration of 2004—issued after the twelfth summit of the SAARC nations— set into motion a process that may culminate in the creation of a vibrant SAFTA. Would this improve South Asia's economic performance and assist the region's integration into the rapidly evolving global economic system? Should the success of the proposed SAFTA be measured only in economic terms?

Even at this early stage of analysis of the possible outcome of SAFTA and its impact on the economies of the region, it was important to underscore that the success of the contemplated regional arrangement will depend on non-economic outcomes. As the late Robin Cook, former foreign minister of Britain, said of the signing of the European Constitution,

> pause for a while to contemplate the remarkable transformation of European politics which made this event possible. Most of the countries sitting together in the same council chamber have been at war with each other in living memory and in the century that preceded it.

But the progress towards increasing economic and political association among the countries of Europe was not always easy: '[T]heir appeal to past millennium betrays what derives their resistance to European integration—a misplaced nostalgia for the outdated world of free standing nations. It is an era that has vanished. We are all interdependent now.'[26] At their twelfth summit held in Islamabad, Pakistan in January 2004, the seven heads of state of the SAARC nations took a major step toward regional economic integration. They agreed to launch the SAFTA by 1 January 2006. This step should have been taken earlier. At their summit in 1997, SAARC leaders had agreed to launch the SAFTA by 2001. The five-year delay was caused by the rapid deterioration of relations between India and Pakistan following nuclear tests by the two countries in May 1998, the military takeover in Pakistan in October 1999, and the near-war between the two nations in 2001–2002 when more than a million soldiers were massed along the India–Pakistan border. Tensions eased starting in April 2003 when Atal Bihari Vajpayee, then prime minister of India, pledged to work toward creating a peaceful South Asian region.

The SAFTA, as defined at the Islamabad summit, was a traditional trade agreement in that it did not include some of the non-trade issues incorporated in many RTAs in other parts of the world. In that sense, South Asia was playing catch-up with other developing regions. The framers of SAFTA—mostly government officials representing the Ministries of Foreign Affairs and Commerce in the SAARC countries— could learn from the experience of other RTAs.

The SAFTA covered tariff reductions, rules of origin, safeguards, institutional structures, and dispute settlement. It also called for the adoption of various trade facilitation measures such as harmonization of standards and mutual recognition of test results, harmonization of customs procedures, and cooperation in improving transport infrastructure. These measures could help significantly reduce the cost of international trade, especially regional trade.

The SAFTA tariff reduction programme stipulated average weighted tariffs of no more than 20 per cent by the region's more developed economies—India, Pakistan, and Sri Lanka—within two years of the entry into force of the agreement. Within five years after the completion of the first phase, India and Pakistan were required to adjust their tariffs to the 0 to 5 per cent range. The region's least developed countries—Bangladesh, Bhutan, Maldives, and Nepal—were required to have average weighted tariffs of no more than 30 per cent within two years, but would be allowed longer periods for the second downward adjustment: Sri Lanka in six years and Bangladesh, Bhutan, Maldives and Nepal in eight years. India, Pakistan, and Sri Lanka committed themselves to reduce their tariffs to the agreed low levels on imports from other countries no later than 1 January 2009. The agreement also called for the elimination of all quantitative restrictions for products on the tariff liberalization list. While member states were allowed to develop lists of sensitive items that would not be subjected fully to the stipulated tariff cuts, the number of products to be included in the country lists were subject to review every four years.

The Islamabad Declaration established a number of institutional devices to oversee the implementation of SAFTA. A ministerial council was to be the highest decision-making authority while a Committee of Experts (COE) was to monitor in detail the implementation of the agreement and resolve disputes. The COE was to report to the ministers every six months on the progress of the agreement. The agreement, to become effective on 1 January 2006, was to be fully implemented by 2015.[27]

Could a regional trading arrangement in South Asia such as the one envisaged under the framework of the SAFTA set in motion the same kind of dynamism that brought Europe to its present situation? The answer to this question will have to wait the passage of time. However, the brief overview of economic development in the South Asian region, in sections 2 and 3 of this chapter, underscored the point made by Robin Cook: a great deal of historical baggage has to be cast off before countries in the region that has suffered a great deal of conflict can begin to work together. Progress in intra-regional trade should help in creating a sense of dynamism that, in turn, could improve relations in other areas.

Pakistan would benefit greatly from the successful implementation of SAFTA. Some of the changes in the projected value of Pakistan's exports and their destinations were estimated by me and an economist working from Islamabad as a part of a study financed by the US AID. According to our calculations, the value of total exports by Pakistan would increase at the rate of 10 to 12 per cent a year in real terms over the 2005–2015 period, reaching $90

billion; India–Pakistan trade would increase ten-fold; and the share
of the United States in Pakistan's exports would decline from one-
fifth of the total to less than one-eighth while that of India increases
more than four-fold.[28]

The SAFTA was not formally launched on 1 January 2006, the
target set in the Islamabad Declaration of January 2004. It was
inaugurated instead on 1 July 2006. The delay occurred because of
some misgivings on the part of Islamabad. There were some
troubling indications in February 2006 that Pakistan may be
contemplating pulling out of the regional trading arrangement
altogether. That would have been very unfortunate from Pakistan's
perspective. It would have done little damage to India, but it would
have been a highly imprudent use of economic policy in an area in
which Pakistan had little leverage. While most countries that were
members of the SAARC had ratified the SAFTA treaty, Pakistan
was reluctant to follow, arguing that ratification would involve
granting the 'most favoured nation' (MFN) status to India. This
was the wrong approach to adopt. Neither pulling out of SAFTA
nor continuing to deny India the MFN status would have helped
Islamabad achieve the objectives it was seeking. Let me first deal
with the MFN issue.

According to the rules of the WTO and obligation of
membership in that organization, all member states must give the
MFN status to each other. The failure to comply can lead to a
complaint by a state that has not been given the status by another
member. In response to a reference by the aggrieved party, the
WTO can impose sanctions on the offending member. The
principle of MFN—that the same treatment has to be granted to
all members of the organization and that no member can be
discriminated against—was one of the pillars on which the WTO
was built and on which it stands. I will trace the history of WTO
in Section 6 below in greater detail. It came into being in 1995
following the conclusion of the Uruguay round of negotiations and
the signing of the Marrakech treaty. Both India and Pakistan were
the original signatories. Pakistan, in other words, was obliged to

give the MFN status to India as it had given it to all other countries that are WTO's members.

India, observing the rules of membership, gave the MFN status to all the countries it traded with; Pakistan refused to reciprocate and kept India out of its list. Several arguments were put forward since that decision was taken as to why Pakistan was not ready to comply. Some of them were political and some economic. It was said that the term 'most favoured nation' did not translate well into Urdu and that the grant of the status to India by Pakistan would lead to headlines in the Urdu press that would not be comfortable for Islamabad. The headlines would proclaim that Pakistan had declared India to be its most *pasandeeda mulk*, a description that would not sit well with some anti-India elements in the society.

Some years ago Washington had the same problem with reference to China. Since China at that time was not a member of WTO, the grant of the MFN status to it from the United States could only be done by legislative action. The US Congress had to pass a bill every year to authorize the grant of the MFN status to China. Every time it was done, the anti-China lobby in Washington raised hackles its accusing the administration of insensitivity to China's alleged abysmal record in areas such as human rights, environmental protection, treatment of minorities, subjugation of Tibet and a host of other actions by Beijing that were considered deplorable by some group or other in the United States. The MFN question, in other words, became an important lever in the hands of Washington in conducting its relations with Beijing.

Washington handled this recurrent problem by dropping the 'most favoured nation' term from its legislative lexicon altogether. The term was replaced with the less emotive 'normal trading relations' and the strategy worked. Pakistan could perhaps take a leaf out of Washington's diplomatic playbook and designate its relations as being 'normal' with India rather than being subject to conditions and barriers that do not have the sanction of the WTO. Besides trade with Pakistan was of little consequence for India. Pakistan did not have any leverage over India in terms of the markets that India coveted or the markets in India that would be starved if Pakistan blocked the supply of its goods to them. Trade was a poor and ineffective leverage to use for Pakistan in its relations with India. That was also not the case with India, which was the reason why the two countries did so little trade.

Politics, however, was not the only reason why Pakistan continued to stall the normalization of trade relations with India so that they meet the obligation of membership in the WTO. Islamabad claimed—and in this respect it had a fair amount of evidence on its side—that even after granting Pakistan the MFN status, India had continued to discriminate against its neighbour by putting in place all kinds of non-tariff barriers. These covered a wide front. Merchandise entering India from Pakistan had to meet certain standards which were prescribed by Indian laboratories, and these were located at some considerable distance from the Pakistani border. Pakistani exporters had to incur fairly large costs to meet these requirements. This condition served as a quasi tax on imports from Pakistan.

Another popular form of non-tariff barrier was the category of sanitary and phyto-sanitary (SPS) regulations that pertained to agricultural products. The SPS was a common non-tariff barrier used by most countries that wished to protect their agriculture sector. India was no different in that respect and it had applied this type of trade restricting measure in its trade with all its neighbours. Both Bangladesh and Nepal were very resentful of the way Delhi was using SPS to constraint imports from these two countries, particularly of perishable commodities.

India had also become an enthusiastic user of anti-dumping measures to limit imports. These measures were allowed under the WTO; the problem with them was that they imposed a great administrative burden and expense on the countries that were subjected to them. The main problem with the way anti-dumping provisions worked was that the burden of providing proof that the sanction applied was wrongly used, rested on the shoulders of the country against which it was deployed. It was not surprising that large countries that had the bureaucratic and legal infrastructure to sustain anti-dumping remedies were its most frequent users. The countries that were adversely affected were those that did not have the administrative, legal and financial means to challenge these activities.[29]

And India had also used the grant of transit rights as a way of reflecting its influence in trade matters in the region in which it was an economic and military colossus. It played with transit rights if it wished to discourage the export of some goods that would gain a market share in third countries on the part of some of its small neighbours. India was known to direct the Nepalese traders to use the ports most distant from the places where goods were manufactured. It was also not willing to grant Nepal access by road for some of its products that had a market in Pakistan. It was much cheaper for the Nepalese and Pakistani traders to use land rather than sea transport for trade, rather than go through a combination of road and ocean transport. In other words, India had successfully used its control over transit routes in intra-regional trade to achieve its narrow economic objectives.

However, by holding back on MFN status Pakistan was not able to strengthen its position with respect to India. It did not acquire a weapon whose use would prompt the right economic behaviour on the part of India. The same applied to membership in SAARC and ultimately in SAFTA. By threatening to quit SAFTA, Pakistan, instead of weakening the Indian hand, would only strengthen it. This was particularly the case if Pakistan wished to produce a forward movement on India's part in resolving the long-festering problem of Kashmir. SAFTA should not and must not be used as a lever by Islamabad over Kashmir.

One of the long-term Indian goals was to isolate Pakistan in the region that encompassed both countries, as well as in the region in which Pakistan had a more significant presence than India. Ever since the idea of a regional cooperation mechanism was floated by Bangladesh, which eventually led to the creation of SAARC, India was reluctant to give much authority to the organization. Delhi had deliberately kept the SAARC secretariat located in Kathmandu, Nepal weak. The secretariat could not undertake any independent work unless it had the sanction of the capitals of the entire membership. This was one way of giving India a veto over all actions by the secretariat. Delhi was the most difficult capital to please for the SAARC bureaucracy; it had even blocked the flow of grants from institutions such as the World Bank, the Asian Development Bank, and the British Department for International Development to allow the secretariat to do independent analytical work. One reason why the SAARC had remained weak was that India wished it to be that way.[30]

While participating in SAFTA, Delhi was simultaneously—but more aggressively—promoting another regional grouping, the BIMSTEC (The Bay of Bengal Initiative for Multi-Sectoral Technical and Economic Cooperation). This organization had all countries of the SAARC minus Maldives and Pakistan as its members. In addition it included Myanmar and Thailand. The BIMSTEC was following a more aggressive timeline than SAFTA. If it was established before SAFTA the latter would become largely meaningless. Indian trade diplomacy was engaged in other ways to isolate Pakistan. It was successful in keeping Pakistan from associating with the ASEAN. India also managed to exclude Pakistan from the forum of large Asian and African countries that had the ambition to create a large trans-continental free trade area. With this as the background, it was difficult to comprehend why Pakistan would seriously contemplate walking out of SAFTA in early 2006. As it turned out, such a threat did not get India to move on Kashmir—the ostensible reason for such a move. It only further isolated Pakistan in the South Asian region at the time when India was gaining more strength every day. Instead of leaving SAFTA, Pakistan should have been working hard to strengthen the organization. I took up this matter during a visit to Pakistan in February 2006 and gave three seminars, two in Karachi and one in Islamabad. The Karachi seminars were attended by a large number of business executives, while the seminar in Islamabad drew government officials as well as analysts from a number of think tanks based in the city. I also gave a number of TV interviews. The theme of all these presentations was the same: it was not in Pakistan's interest to use trade as a lever to obtain political concessions from India. I followed up these public events with a long meeting with Commerce Minister Humayun Akhtar Khan, who told me that there was an intense and earnest debate in the cabinet about the right course Pakistan should pursue. He himself was of the view that while he was interested in turning SAFTA into a meaningful regional trading arrangement, it was also in Pakistan's interest to conclude bilateral agreements with a number of countries who were important trading partners of Pakistan. A free trade agreement (FTA) was concluded under his watch with Sri Lanka, while work was proceeding on FTAs with China and the United States.

It would have been useful if the Pakistani authorities had spent some time studying the experiences of other successful regional trading organizations, in particular those which had one relatively large economy in the centre surrounded by smaller ones. The European Union was a classic case of an economic and trade organization that was able to constrain the region's largest economy, Germany, and to force it to play by the rules that were acceptable to all member states. The same was true for Mercosur in which Brazil, the organization's largest economy and the region's most powerful country, was bound to good political and economic behaviour by a system of rules. The small countries in Southern Africa were working hard to create a similar organization in which South Africa will be embedded.

If India worked at times to the disadvantage of its neighbours by using non-tariff barriers to constrain trade, or harassed them by anti-dumping measures, or used transition restrictions to achieve narrow national interests, an organization such as SAFTA would be an ideal forum within which to correct such errant behaviour. Pakistan was South Asia's second largest economy and it was incumbent upon it to play a role that would encourage all member countries to work for the common good rather than promote narrow national interests. Quitting SAFTA and not playing that role would be a mindless policy to follow.

6. WTO, South Asia and Pakistan

Should Islamabad concentrate its energies on creating a workable regional trading arrangement such as SAFTA and thus remove the distortions created in the pattern of its international trade as a result of the long-enduring hostility with India, or should it take the multilateral route and participate actively in creating a trading environment which would meet its needs? Before answering this question, it would be useful to provide a brief overview of the evolution of the international system of trade.

The multilateral financial, economic and trading system took half a century to form. The work on it began even after the Second World War was over and continued until 1995. In the first phase, agreement was reached to form two institutions each with a well specified objective. The IMF was set up to ensure that the world would not suffer from the type of financial crises that did so much damage before the world went to war. The International Bank for Reconstruction and Development (IBRD) was set up to aid the rebuilding of war-torn Europe and Japan and assist the development of the countries that were on the verge of gaining independence from centuries of colonial rule and domination. The institutional framework for aiding the development of nations emerging from decades, if not centuries of colonial rule, was developed further by adding the International Development Association (IDA) and the International Finance Corporation (IFC) as affiliates to IBRD. Collectively, this set of institutions came to be called the World Bank. A number of regional development banks such as the Interamerican Development Bank (IDB), the Asian Development Bank (ADB), the African Development Bank (AFDB) and, much later, the Islamic Development Bank were added to the multi-lateral system. However, agreement could not be reached on the creation of the third institution, a world trade organization. That had to wait for another fifty years; it was only after the Uruguay Round of trade negotiations that the international community agreed to set up the World Trade Organization (WTO) to regulate international commerce.

That it took fifty years to create the third leg of the system to regulate commercial relations among nations was not surprising. It was largely due to the reluctance of governments to accept some encroachment on their authority on matters relating to trade. International commerce was too political a subject to be let into the control of an international bureaucracy. However, by the mid-1990s, the process of globalization had advanced sufficiently to lead to some worry that some aspects of it had to be subject to regulation. Accordingly, at Marrakech, Morocco, the world's major trading nations—the European Union, Japan and the United States—agreed to create a framework that would not only regulate trade but also create a mechanism for the resolution of disputes.

Regulating trade meant essentially prescribing the tariffs that could be levied by the members of the WTO and governing the use of non-tariff barriers to trade. The most important organizing principle for the WTO was the MFN approach according to which access given to one country—the MFN—had to be shared with all others. Members could not discriminate among themselves; however, some margin was left for giving 'favoured treatment' to groups of countries. This is the way the countries regarded as 'developing' were allowed to maintain higher tariffs and other constraints on trade than allowed to developed nations.

All countries that were the contracting parties of the General Agreement on Trade and Tariffs (GATT) were invited to become members of the WTO as long as they signed the treaty concluded at Marrakech in the final round of the Uruguay negotiations. Those that had not joined GATT but wished to become members of WTO had to agree to the conditions set by the existing membership. These could be extremely rigorous and took a long time to negotiate as happened in the case of China. A country such as Pakistan, having joined the GATT, was not subject to this additional conditionality.

Once the WTO was up and running, it was clear that another set of negotiations was needed to smoothen out the various wrinkles that remained in the international trading system. Three of these were important. One, some of the sectors of vital interest to the developing world had been left out of the Marrakech treaty. Most important of these was agriculture. To bring this sector in line with other sectors, some of the protectionist policies pursued by the developed world had to be abandoned. This was politically not easy since the voting blocks in America, Europe and Japan that benefited from these policies had considerable political clout. Second, some of the rapidly growing developing countries now had a place in international commerce that did not justify the continuation of preferential treatment that was initially given to this group. Brazil, China, India and South Africa belonged to this group of countries. Third, some of the more rapidly growing parts of the global economy were not under the purview of WTO. The ICT (information and communication technology) was foremost among these. To fill these gaps there was agreement among developed countries that a new round of trade negotiations had to be inaugurated. This was resisted by the developing world for as long as it was not promised what it termed as fairer treatment in international commerce. The next phase of the evolution of the multilateral system began in 2001, with the inauguration of the Doha Round.

The Doha Round of negotiations had an inauspicious beginning. The first attempt to begin the dialogue in 1999 ran into stiff resistance from a variety of non-governmental groups. They arrived at Seattle, the site of the meeting, determined to stop the start of a new set of discussions among the worlds' trading nations. Those who were against the launch of yet another round of negotiations had several grievances. They ranged from the belief that the previous round—the Uruguay Round—concluded in 1995 created a world trading regime that did very little for the world's poor. In fact, according to this line of thinking, the world trading order that resulted from the Marrakech Treaty created an un-level playing field, tilted away from the developing world. The tilt was particularly sharp in two sectors of enormous interest for the developing world, agriculture and textiles. Both sectors were of great significance for Pakistan.

There were also other reasons for the opposition by the non-government organizations (NGOs) to another global trade round. Many of them believed that by creating an elaborate system of international trade rules, the Marrakech Treaty provided considerable space to the large transnational corporations (TNCs) that dominated the world production system. This space was used to exploit the poor. Some NGOs that appeared at Seattle were concerned that the outsourcing of production that was resulting from the process of globalization and had the support of the WTO resulted in poor working conditions and low wages for the workers employed by the TNCs.

Several others were troubled by the fact that the Uruguay process had provided considerable authority to the world's rich nations to protect patents—or intellectual rights—even at the cost of not providing cheap medicines to the sick in the developing world. For instance, the drugs needed for slowing down the progress of AIDs could be produced in the developing world at a fraction of the cost charged by the large pharmaceutical companies. That this could be done was demonstrated by some pharmaceutical companies in India who defied the rules and supplied cheap AIDs drugs to the poor countries of Africa. This could not be done more openly since any infringement of patents could be severely punished by the WTO.

And then there were NGOs who went to Seattle to make the point that the rules governing the international production system allowed considerable latitude to the TNCs to exploit physical resources in a way that caused grievous harm to the global environment. These corporations had to be constrained and made accountable to the civil society since the world governments had failed to draw up a programme for protecting the environment. For these and other reasons the demonstrations in Seattle turned violent and blood flowed in the streets of this attractive city on America's west coast. The ministers who had assembled at Seattle slipped out of the city without coming to any agreement.

They met again at Doha, the capital of Qatar, in November 2001. They succeeded this time in launching a new round for two reasons. The Qataris were able to use the limited access to their capital to keep out potential trouble makers from the city. And, the terrorist attacks of 11 September 2001 on the United States had convinced Washington that something quite significant had to be done to reduce the level of resentment that existed in the Muslim world against the West—particularly against America. There was a widespread feeling not only in the Muslim countries but in all parts of the developing world that the global trading system discriminated against them.

This discrimination had taken at least three different forms. The tariffs against the exports from the developing world were considerably higher than on the trade between developed countries. In some cases, the use of tariffs was coupled with the use of quotas against the developing world's exports. This was the second cause of the developing countries' resentment. The quotas were directed mostly at clothing and textiles. Even before the launch of the Uruguay Round, industrial countries had operated a system called the Multi-fibre Arrangement (MFA) that allowed limited exports of various items of textiles and clothing from poor to rich countries to come under quotas. The developing countries agreed to the conclusion of the Uruguay Round and the establishment of the WTO only after it was promised that the MFA would be phased out over a ten year period and by 1 January 2005 the MFA would be completely eliminated. This was done and the textile industry in the developing world began to quickly restructure and grow. Pakistan's textile industry is still coming to terms with the post-quota environment in which it must now operate.[31]

The third area of unhappiness among the developing countries was the subsidies given by rich counties to their farmers, and the constraints placed on developing countries' exports to the markets in rich countries. Under the European Union's Common Agricultural Policy (CAP) a large amounts of subsidies were given for the production of agricultural products such as rice, sugar and dairy products in which the developing world had a distinct comparative advantage. The United States also operated a farm support programme in which the items entering world trade fetched relatively low prices because of the subsidies given by Washington. The subsidies to the cotton producers were by far the most important policy that had a negative impact on the incomes of farmers in the developing world.

These unfriendly policies toward the developing world had one important consequence: they hurt the poorest people in the developing world. They hurt the semi-skilled workers employed in the developing countries' textile sector, a high proportion of whom were women. They hurt the poor cotton farmers of West Africa whose incomes fell because of the low price in the international market that resulted from cotton subsidies in the United States. They hurt those parts of the developing world in which farmers could produce such high value crops as fruits and vegetables for export to the high income markets, but market access was denied to them for various reasons. Phyto-sanitary regulations—regulations against plant products—were the most often used non-tariff barrier to keep out exports from the developing world.

It was the decision by the developed world—by the United States in particular—that the new round of negotiations would pay special attention to the demands of developing countries that led to the agreement to launch the Doha Round. The United States, traumatized by the terrorist attacks on its territory on 11 September 2001 identified continuing slow growth, persistent poverty and deteriorating income distribution in the developing world as the reasons for the alienation of the youth and the direction of their anger at Washington. Trade therefore became one of the many weapons the United States was prepared to use in order to win over the hearts and minds of the people of the developing world.

However, trade is one area where good intentions seldom translate into intended actions. The decision to focus the Doha Round on the issues of interest to the developing world had the backing of economic theory. By addressing these issues rich nations, wedded to the principles of free markets, would be removing a number of serious distortions in international trade that hurt the developing world. It was calculated by a number of individuals and institutions that by removing these distortions, the developed world would be transferring incomes to the developing world that would be many times more than the official aid they provided. Not only that; by removing these distortions, rich countries would be putting additional incomes directly into the pockets of the people. Administration of aid required governments as intermediaries, and governments were often inefficient and corrupt. By allowing the poor to trade openly in world markets, incomes would flow to them without much intermediation.

The World Bank estimated in a study published in 2002 that freeing international trade of all barriers and subsidies would lift 320 million people above the $2 a day poverty line.[32] This could be achieved by 2015, the year set by the United Nations for achieving what were designated as the Millennium Development Goals (MDGs) by the world leaders in their 2000 summit held in New York.[33] The Bank's estimate was vindicated by William Cline, a highly respected economist who had worked in several think tanks. In a widely read book among policy circles in the United States, Cline reached a higher figure—440 million—of the number of people who would be helped by free trade, in particular free trade between poor and rich nations.[34]

While the principles on which the Doha Round was to proceed were supported by theory, politics had its own goals. Most developed countries found it difficult to overcome the opposition of the small number of people in their countries who would have been temporarily hurt by the removal of farm subsidies. Also opposed to the easing of some of the constraints were the influential pharmaceutical companies who were not prepared to lose their patents and reduce the price of their drugs even if that meant not delivering relief to the poor people facing certain death from such communicable diseases as AIDs. For these reasons, as the ministers planned their trips to Hong Kong, the site of the December 2005 ministerial meeting connected with the Doha Round, there was not a great deal of hope of success.[35] Pascal Lamy, the new Director General of WTO, feared that the Hong Kong meeting could result in a total impasse unless the ministers from the developed countries were prepared to make some commitments that would meet the goals of the Doha Round when it was initially launched.

Pakistan did not go to Hong Kong with a great deal of hope. Humayun Akhtar Khan, its energetic and knowledgeable commerce minister, had carved out good space for himself as a designated negotiator for G-20, a group of large and influential developing countries who, by virtue of their size, carried considerable weight in international trade matters. The group had worked hard to develop a common position which would have positive consequences for its members. Non-agricultural market access (NAMA) was the area of greatest interest to this group of countries. But in pursuing this line, the G-20 faced two conflicting interests. There was the interest of the countries such as Brazil, the world's most efficient producer of agricultural products, to gain an even playing field in trade in agriculture, undistorted by subsidies and other forms of state assistance. If this were to happen, large agriculture exporting countries such as Brazil would most certainly benefit, while countries such as Pakistan that had begun to rely on importing commodities such as cotton for providing inputs to a rapidly growing industry, would pay a higher price for the needed raw materials.

There was one other contentious issue the G-20 had to deal with. This concerned the willingness on the part of the developed world to permit duty free imports of textile and clothing from the least developed countries, while levying heavy tariffs from the producers in the relatively more developed developing countries that included Pakistan. How to reconcile these opposing interests? How to ensure that the evolving global trading system moved forward even after the shaky push received at Hong Kong, and that it would bring benefits to Pakistan which was only now, nearly sixty years after becoming a state, beginning to draw developmental benefit from international trade?

The discussions at Hong Kong were aimed at further improvements in the multilateral trading system. At issue were a series of actions the developed world had promised it would take to create a system that did not discriminate against the world's poorer nations. For most developing countries what mattered most was the elimination of protective measures that kept the farmers in rich countries in agriculture producing the products in which the developing world had a clear comparative advantage.

What was the outcome of Hong Kong? The question has some importance since the answer to it provided some insights into the way international trade negotiations were conducted. This question produced two answers. According to Professor Jagdish Bhagwati of Columbia University, who is a leading exponent of multilateralism in trade, the summit was a great success. It was a success for the simple reason that it did not produce a deadlock among so many different trading interests represented at Hong Kong. Bhagwati was also pleased that one of the decisions taken at Hong Kong was the agreement to create a new global financing facility that would provide 'aid for trade'. He had argued for the establishment of such a facility for a long time, suggesting that one way of appeasing the potential losers from the furtherance of multilateralism was to help them adjust to free and open trade.

The other view to which I subscribe was that only small steps were taken at Hong Kong; the objective was to save the talks from collapse and hope that time will narrow the considerable differences that remained among important trading nations. This was unlikely to happen in the time available. The Doha Round has to be concluded by the end of 2006 since the authority given to President George W. Bush to negotiate a deal was set to expire in the middle of 2007 and was not likely to be renewed. It did not seem much could be achieved in the short time that was available unless Europe, America and large developing countries were prepared to accept some fundamental changes in their trading systems.

What was the position taken by Pakistan at the meetings and why did it differ from the one assumed by much of the developing world? Pakistan went to the trade summit with the belief that its economic future depended on its ability to create a larger market share in textiles, and that in textiles the United States and the European Union will remain the dominant markets for many years to come. Both assumptions were questionable. It was not a sound economic strategy to put all economic eggs in the textile basket, and it was equally imprudent to ignore the fact that the fastest developing markets in the world were in Pakistan's immediate neighbourhood and not in distant Europe and America. Reading global economic trends from a static angle and not from a dynamic perspective was a big mistake. Looking at the world from the more dynamic perspective should have resulted in Pakistan pursuing a different approach at Hong Kong than the one it actually followed.

The previous rounds of negotiations had made significant progress in reducing the level of tariffs on industrial products particularly among developed countries. Developing countries were permitted to maintain higher tariffs in order to give them the time to prepare their industries for competition from rich countries. Before Hong Kong, there was pressure on more developed developing countries to lower their tariffs if not for the goods produced in developed countries then at least for the products of less developed countries. There was a demand that countries like Brazil, China, India and South Africa that had, by now, well developed industrial sectors, should grant preferential access to less developed countries. However, rich countries did not make much progress in further splitting the developing world. There was agreement that developed countries will not demand from the developing world more than they were prepared to give themselves. Rich countries, given the way they had handled trade in textiles and clothing for more than four decades, were playing on a weak wicket. Developing countries forced them to concentrate their attention on the opening up of the sector of agriculture.

After a series of all night sessions that engaged most of the ministers who were present at the meeting, Pascal Lamy was able to come out of Hong Kong with a declaration that provided nothing more than a hint of progress. The only achievement was to keep the talks alive. Another failure after the debacle at Seattle in 1999 and Cancun in 2003 would have killed the Doha Round of negotiations and probably also killed the WTO. The ministers made little tangible progress. Those representing developing countries were able to secure a promise from the developed countries that agricultural export subsidies would be abolished by the end of 2013. There was an additional promise that a substantial part of the subsidies would be scrapped before 2011 and that there will be a parallel elimination of indirect subsidies. The choice of the timetable was forced on Hong Kong by the budgetary cycle followed by the European Union (EU). The EU was following a seven-year budgetary cycle. Instead of going through the pain of agreeing on a budget every year, it was adopting fiscal parameters every seven years. This was done at a summit of the EU leaders held shortly before the meeting in Hong Kong, which in itself was an indication that for Europe promoting integration in Europe had a much higher priority than promoting multilateralism in trade. The EU could have waited for the outcome of the Hong Kong meeting before setting its own budgetary policy. Instead it chose to dictate to the WTO its own timetable. Since the next round of budgetary talks will take place in Brussels only in 2012, the EU was not prepared to accept any WTO deadline that came before that time. Hence the choice of 2013 as the deadline for the removal of agricultural subsidies.

Agricultural subsidies take several forms including export credits, food aid and trading through state enterprises. It was agreed that in the coming months, WTO member nations will agree on the value of indirect subsidies, since at Hong Kong they were unable even to define state policies that could be described as subsidies. Governments pledged that they would also draw up a time table for phasing out subsidies.

The Europeans, led by France, had declared that any attempt to force them to drastically reduce subsidies could mean the end of the Doha Round. At Hong Kong, the Europeans agreed to a three-tier classification which placed them at the top, the United States in the middle and all other nations at the bottom. The members with the highest subsidies—meaning the Europeans—agreed to cut the trade-distorting subsidies the most. Having agreed to this qualification, governments will need to determine the size of the cuts and to devise rules to stop them from reclassifying subsidies into categories that could shelter them from future cuts.

A multi-tier formula agreed at Hong Kong set bigger cuts in higher tariff, smaller cuts for 'sensitive' products produced in developed countries and exemption for 'special' products grown in developing countries. A mechanism was also agreed upon, that would allow poor nations to raise duties in case there was a surge in imports following the implementation of the tariff structure at the conclusion of the Doha Round. These agreements notwithstanding, a great deal of work remained to be done in 2006. WTO members had to decide on the size of tariff cuts and on the number and treatment of 'sensitive' and 'special' products. For a country such as Pakistan the Doha Round had to produce a sizeable market access for the various fruits, vegetables and flowers it could grow for export to developed country markets.

The Hong Kong negotiators dealt with the sensitive subject of cotton subsidies by giving concession only to African countries and to least developed nations, but not to countries such as Pakistan. They agreed to eliminate subsidies in 2006 and grant unrestricted access to the countries in these two categories. The United States indicated that it would further cut its $4 billion subsidy to cotton growers and also promised to reduce its farm support programme for cotton producers.

The process begun at Hong Kong aimed at bringing trade in agricultural products into the multilateral framework was perhaps the most notable achievement of the trade talks. Pakistan adopted a different posture; it decided to pursue market access in textiles as its main objective. As such it showed little interest in the development of trade in agriculture. To neglect the opportunities agriculture offered and to concentrate entirely on developing long-distance foreign markets in textiles meant neglecting Pakistan's real comparative advantage in favour of a sector that was over-crowded with competitors, and the development of which in Pakistan was the result of faulty policies adopted in the past rather than the exploitation of the country's real potential.

The other area where action was promised at Hong Kong was of direct interest to Pakistan. This concerned the grant of privileged access in rich markets to the goods from the countries designated by the international community as 'least developed'. The group included Bangladesh which had, over the years, become an important exporter of garments, both to the European Union and the United States. As such it was a significant competitor for Pakistan in these markets. It stood in the way of Pakistan's efforts to gain better access for its textiles and garments to these countries.

The emergence of Bangladesh as an important garment exporter offered an interesting case study of how concessions granted with the purpose of helping poor countries had introduced or could introduce distortions in the multilateral trading system. These distortions benefited one group of poor people at the expense of another—a case of a poor Peter being taxed to pay a poor Paul.

The development of the garment industry in Bangladesh was the consequence of the decision taken by the United States and the European Union to grant to the new country a significant proportion of the export quota available to Pakistan within the framework of the MFA. This decision was taken in spite of the fact that the newly independent state of Bangladesh did not have much of a textile industry at the time of its birth. This was done for two reasons. One was to punish Pakistan, which had not won many friends as a result of the way it had conducted itself in the civil war that resulted in the creation of Bangladesh. The other reason was that by dividing Pakistan's textile export quota into two parts, the United States and Europe were effectively reducing the access of a country—Pakistan—that had a clear comparative advantage in the business of textiles, and which had the demonstrated ability to gain access to markets in rich countries.

The net result of this policy was to encourage a significant amount of foreign investment in Bangladesh by mostly East Asian textile entrepreneurs who, because of the quotas assigned to them, could not increase their own exports. Bangladesh's quota offered a tempting opportunity which was successfully exploited by them.

Over time Pakistan came to face stiff competition from the new garment producers of Bangladesh. After the end of the quotas following the termination of the MFA regime, competition from countries such as Bangladesh continued. This time around, Pakistan and other non-LDCs (least developed countries) faced much higher tariffs in the importing countries. Tariff concessions were granted by all rich counties to the least developed countries in the name of poverty alleviation. This was a convenient posture to take. It satisfied the demands made by many vocal non-government organizations to help poor nations while, at the same time, protecting the domestic textile and garment industry.

At the meeting in Hong Kong, trade ministers agreed to continue the practice of duty-free access for least developed countries. There was pressure on the United States to allow all exports by LDCs into the country free of duties and quotas. This was being done by the European Union. The US resisted the pressure and, with Pakistan endorsing its position, it agreed to permit 97 per cent of LDC imports free of duty. The LDCs had campaigned hard for a 99 per cent quota. Following the collapse of the talks in Geneva, Europe proposed that this measure should be adopted by all rich countries. But the US refused. It took the position that extracting individual strands from the Doha talks violated the long-standing practice that trade agreements are a 'single undertaking in which nothing is agreed until everything is agreed.'

Before the Hong Kong meeting there was agreement that talks would be intensified bilaterally between various groups of countries to liberalize trade in services. At Hong Kong the Europeans pressed for liberalization targets, and that position was opposed by most developing countries that feared that their underdeveloped service industry would be swamped by such developed country institutions as banks and insurance companies. Instead, developing countries wanted greater access for their workers to the service sector even on a temporary basis. It is hard to understand the strong protectionist sentiment in the developing world in the service sector. Instead of seeking protection and long periods of time for opening the sector, the developing world—in particular the countries that have large and young populations, a category of countries that included Pakistan—should have asked for opening markets in the developed world for services such as airlines and shipping.

The next stop after Hong Kong for the Doha Round was Geneva. When the world's trade ministers assembled in November 2001 to launch a new round of trade negotiations, they agreed to focus on the demands of the developing world. Meeting in Doha, the gleaming capital of the tiny Gulf state of Qatar, they had underscored their intention to aid developing countries by calling the new set of negotiations the 'development round'. They chose that description in spite of the fact that the WTO, under whose auspices the new round was to be negotiated, is not a development institution. In the multilateral economic system that task is assigned to the World Bank and a number of regional banks such as the Asian Development Bank.

Nonetheless, the developing world pinned a great deal of hope on the Doha Round. There was an expectation that they would really gain from this dialogue, making up for the previous rounds that focused almost entirely on the trade interests of industrial countries. As discussed above, economists recognize that trade not only helped in increasing the rate of growth of gross domestic product of all countries, including those that are still developing. It also helped to alleviate poverty and reduce income inequality if the markets of rich countries were opened to receive goods manufactured and commodities produced by the poor workers of the developing world.

Why is the Doha Round close to a collapse? The latest setback was caused by the inability on the part of a small group of countries that sent their trade ministers to Geneva in late July 2006, to move the round forward by resolving the differences that separated them. But the talks failed. Although most of the criticism for the failure at Geneva was directed towards the Americans, other participants could not be absolved of blame. Agriculture proved to be the stumbling bloc. Washington refused to accommodate the demand for reducing subsides to its farmers valued by some at $20 billion a year. However, America was not the only country at fault. Rich countries poured nearly $1 billion a day into propping up their farmers. That fuelled overproduction, drove down prices, and made it impossible for poor farmers to sell their products abroad or even at home. For instance, an increase in the price of internationally traded cotton would certainly help the poor farmers of Africa. It would also help the poor producers in cotton producing countries such as Pakistan and India.

While Washington balked at the issue of agricultural subsidies, the European Union refused to lower tariffs on farm imports as demanded by the United States. The Americans wanted a reduction of 60 per cent. Tariff reductions by Europe would have helped the farmers in America increase their exports, thus compensating for the losses that would have resulted from a reduction in subsidies. The European Union offered a reduction of 50 per cent in tariffs but wanted to protect 5 per cent of its products as a part of a 'sensitive list'. Some large developing countries, Brazil and India included, were happy to support the European position. However, the wall of protection that would have remained would not have helped the really poor farmers of the developing world.

India was the third country that dug in its heels in Geneva. There were demands on the large and rapidly developing countries such as India to also open their economies, particularly to trade in agriculture. While Brazil was prepared to be more accommodating, India was not ready to oblige. According to one observer at Geneva, 'the Indian government, acutely aware that its predecessor lost an election by ignoring the villages, pandered shamelessly to its protectionist farmers and seemed almost gleeful when the talks broke up.'

International trade negotiations are always conducted on the basis of a simple promise; there will be gainers and losers in any final outcome but the gainers' benefits would outweigh the losses of the losers and the governments would find a way of compensating those who lost. In the Doha discussions, however, those who represented potential losers were able to dominate the agenda while those who would have gained stayed on the sidelines. For instance, big transnational corporations who had actively supported the previous round of discussions—the Uruguay Round—and had gained the most from the easing of restrictions on global trade were not involved this time around. They were of the view that world trade in products of interest to them would continue to increase even if the Doha Round failed. On the other hand, agricultural producers in all major economies, developed and developing, took an active part in setting the agenda for the talks and standing in the way of progress towards open and freer trade in the sector.

Washington, distracted by the events in the Middle East, did not spend much time on preparing the political ground for reaching a compromise. Some Republican and Democratic senators urged President George W. Bush not to make further concessions on agriculture to the Europeans until they showed flexibility in return. With the mid-term elections due in November 2006 in which the president's party was expected to lose some ground to the Democrats, there was pressure on President Bush not to be too accommodating on trade.

There was a considerable exchange of accusations following the collapse of the Geneva talks. Europe blamed the United States, the United States held the Europeans and the Indians responsible, and the Brazilians blamed every body. 'Blamesmanship is not going to sell one ton of beef or remove one trade subsidy' said Susan Schwab, the US Trade Representative, after the collapse of the Geneva parleys. 'We need to focus now on what is doable'. Peter Mandelson, the European counterpart of Schwab had an answer. He suggested that the WTO members should take the steps agreed at the ministerial meeting in Hong Kong in December 2005.

One area on which there was agreement concerned 'trade facilitation', the business of setting rules for getting goods through customs cheaply and quickly. There was a consensus among trade economists that the cost of doing business at the borders was now a more important obstacle to trade than tariffs. But, as in most things concerning trade, even this seemingly obvious area for governmental action was not devoid of controversy. Many governments were using customs regulations as quasi-protective barriers. India, for instance had mastered the area. Even though it had reduced tariffs on the trade with the countries of South Asia, it continued to use a number of non-trade barriers to inhibit imports from its neighbours. The ministers' meeting in Hong Kong had resolved to smoothen the flow of goods across international borders by developing a series of trade facilitation measures. However, the United States was not prepared to back the Hong Kong agenda without a comprehensive agreement.

The moment of truth had arrived after the failure of the Geneva talks. There was a need to answer a number of important questions and base public policy on these answers. What would be the impact of the failure at Geneva? Within a period of four years, from 2000 to 2004, the value of international commerce increased from $6.45 trillion to $9.12 trillion. Would this kind of expansion continue? Would the poor countries be hurt more by the likely demise of the Doha Round? Would the multilateral trade system, without the benefits promised by the Doha Round materializing, hinder the development of poor countries and delay their efforts to reduce the proportion of poor in their populations? What should Pakistan do in terms of increasing its exports?

7. Conclusion

What would happen if the Doha Round totally collapses? As already indicated, it faces the deadline of July 2007 when the administration of President George W. Bush will no longer have the fast-track trade promotion authority granted by Congress. There was some talk of getting Congress to extend that authority by one year. In an increasingly politicized environment it was unlikely that President Bush would succeed in getting this approval. The other option—at least for the United States—was to go ahead with bilateral trade deals it was negotiating with a number of its trading partners. Some dozen agreements were under negotiation in 2006. Work had also begun on free trade agreement between the United States and Pakistan.

Washington had long pursued a strategy of negotiating trade agreements at three different levels. It had worked on an all-encompassing multilateral deal in the context of the Doha Round. It had also made some efforts at the regional level. In December 1994, then President Bill Clinton initiated work on the Free Trade Agreement for the Americas (FTAA) that would have created a free trade area in the western hemisphere, stretching between the North and South Poles. In 2005 it concluded a free trade accord with five Central American countries plus the Dominican Republic. And, as mentioned above, it was working on bilateral arrangements with a number of countries.

This approach, labelled 'competitive liberalization' by trade officials, was based on the theory that smaller pacts would lead to bigger ones. Washington has dismissed concerns that the proliferation of two-way accords would undercut the authority of the WTO. But that authority may have already been compromised by the failure of the talks at Geneva in late July 2006.

With the near failure of the Doha Round of trade negotiations, what are the public policy choices available to Pakistan? Should it follow the United States and seek to expand the markets for its exports by entering into bilateral and regional trading arrangements? In choosing the partners with which to work, should it concentrate on the countries nearer home and the regions to which it belongs, or should it cultivate a special relationship with the world's largest markets, the United States, the European Union, Japan, and China? How much emphasis should it place on restoring India as its largest trading partner?

Before attempting answers to these questions, it would be useful to highlight an important aberration in the pattern of Pakistan's international trade. As discussed earlier in this chapter, it was history rather than economics that degraded India's position as a trading partner for Pakistan. The situation was very different in the late 1940s. Then, for what is Pakistan today, more than 40 per cent of exports went to India and more than 20 per cent of imports came from that country. For a few years after the two countries gained independence, India continued to use Pakistan's road and railway network for its exports and imports. Karachi remained an important port of entry and exit for international trade for northern India. Indian trade with Afghanistan also flowed through Pakistan. But in 1949 India and Pakistan became hostile neighbours and have remained that way for almost six decades.

The two countries drifted apart and sought markets outside the region for their exports and imports. That began to change, but slowly. In 2004–5, India–Pakistan trade through formal channels was estimated at $600 million, almost two and a half times more than the level reached in 2000–1. The amount of trade that flowed through informal channels was perhaps three to four times more than formal trade. Much of it was in the form of smuggling across the poorly patrolled Sindh–Rajasthan border. A significant amount moved through Dubai but got included in trade statistics as Dubai–Pakistan trade. It was for that reason that in 2004–5, Dubai was Pakistan's third largest trading partner, accounting for 6 per cent of total trade. The United States was the largest with 19 per cent share and Saudi Arabia was in the second place with 10 per cent of the total. India and Afghanistan were in the fourth place, each accounting for 5 per cent.

The direction of trade, therefore, did not reflect Pakistan's geographical position nor its comparative advantage. The question for the policymakers is whether they should focus their energies on reviving trade with India. The recent cooling of relations between the two neighbours, following the terrorist attacks on the commuter trains in Bombay in the summer of 2006, underscored an important fact about India–Pakistan trade. It will not be governed by economics alone; it will always be subject to politics. However, building trade relations between the two countries will help enormously in easing political tensions. An editorial in the *Financial Times* published soon after the Mumbai attacks, reminded policymakers in both Islamabad and New Delhi of what Cordell Hull, the US Secretary of State under President Franklin Roosevelt, said about the importance of trade in relations among nations. 'If goods do not pass frontiers, armies will,' he said. 'It is not an absolute truth but India and Pakistan should recall Hull's wisdom as they contemplate the dangers of sliding into a deeper crisis,' concluded the newspaper's editorial.[36]

The launch of the SAFTA offered an opportunity to the South Asian neighbours to reorient their economic relations. However, for different reasons, both Islamabad and New Delhi did not give much attention to the potential of SAFTA. New Delhi was more interested in creating space for itself in other regional trading arrangements, in particular those being developed in Southeast Asia. It believed that the economic opportunities available in that region were more meaningful than those on offer in South Asia. It was also promoting BIMSTEC, a regional arrangement that incorporated all of SAARC but not Pakistan and also included Myanmar and Thailand. BIMSTEC would serve two objectives of New Delhi's approach towards the region in which it was attempting to carve for itself the position of an economic and political superpower. It would exclude Pakistan and build an economic bridge between South and Southeast Asia.

Pakistan's lukewarm approach towards SAFTA was the result of an extraordinary belief that it could use the arrangement as a lever to obtain concessions from India. This was a misguided approach since, as discussed above, India continued to work on Pakistan's political and economic isolation rather than its incorporation in regional bodies. Instead of allowing itself to fall into this trap, Pakistan should put a great deal of political and bureaucratic effort into promoting SAFTA. It could use the fledgling regional pact to constrain India's growing influence in the area.

In a study on the prospects of SAFTA and its economic potential, a group of economists led by me worked out the structural changes that could occur in the pattern of Pakistan's international trade if this regional arrangement was to be correctly developed.[37] We determined that the most significant impact of SAFTA on Pakistan would be a sharp increase in international trade as a proportion of gross domestic product.

In 2004–5, the trade-to-GDP ratio was on the order of 30 per cent, with trade defined as including trade through informal channels and GDP measured according to updated 2001 national income accounts. With SAFTA successfully implemented and with trade with Afghanistan conducted mostly through formal channels, total trade could increase at a rate of 10 to 12 per cent per year in the next ten years. Total trade in real dollars (2004–05 dollars) could increase from the present $33.5 billion to $90 billion. With the economy more open and with trade with India allowed, India–Pakistan trade could increase tenfold, from the current $2 billion (including informal trade) to $20 billion. In other words, of the $58 billion increase in total trade projected for this period, $18 billion—or almost 31 per cent of the increase—could come from increased exports to and imports from India.

With the successful implementation of SAFTA, the structure, destination, and origin of Pakistan's international trade will change profoundly. Agricultural and light engineering products will become important export items, while industrial raw material and capital equipment will become important import items. With Pakistan able to meet a significant proportion of its energy needs by tapping the gas pipelines from Iran, Central Asia and the Middle East connecting to India, the share of fuel imports in total trade should decline. And, with Pakistan able to earn large transit fees from the use of its territory for gas pipelines to India, the share of the service sector in export earnings should increase significantly.

New trading opportunities with the countries in the region will change the structure of the Pakistani economy. Agriculture should regain some of the importance it had at the time of independence from Britain. But Pakistan will not become the granary for the rest of South Asia as it was then. Its agricultural system, with its year-round supply of water, should be able to provide high value-added output to the growing Indian and Middle Eastern markets. With transit trade earning more foreign exchange, the transport sector should feel the impact, through the modernization of trucking, processing, repackaging, and warehousing industries. The banking sector will also have to develop new product lines to provide financing for new lines of export to India as well as for servicing transit trade. And Pakistan could see a major expansion in tourism as Indians begin to visit holy sites in Pakistan that have been inaccessible to them as well as other sites in the country's picturesque northern areas. Lahore is already preparing for the arrival of Indian tourists. According to one British newspaper account 'the city is sprucing itself up for a growing flow of visitors from Delhi—many of whom have memories or relatives there— with a fancy new airport, refurbished colonial buildings, and ambitious hotel projects.' An increase in tourism will result in a rapid expansion of the hotel, restaurant and entertainment industries.

The main point made in this chapter is that increasing the quantum and value of international trade is vital for the acceleration of the rate of growth of the Pakistani economy and for sustaining it over a period of time. The most important instrument of policy available to Islamabad for achieving this objective is to take an active part in developing SAFTA as a regional trading arrangement. SAFTA offers a framework within which India's trade policies could be made more friendly towards its neighbours. While Pakistan is engaged in promoting SAFTA into an arrangement that is more ambitious in its reach and scope than the one conceived in January 2004 by the SAARC leaders, it should continue to take an active interest in creating an international environment in the context of the WTO. In this effort, it should not only seek a better access for textiles, its major industry, but seek to diversify the content of its international commerce as well as the destination of its exports.

NOTES

1. Thomas L. Friedman, *The World is Flat: A Brief History of the Twenty-First Century*, New York: Farrar, Straus and Giroux, 2005.
2. The World Bank, *World Development Indicators 2005*, Washington DC, 2005, various tables.
3. The purchasing power parity measure converts the value of the gross domestic product at the rate which is comparable to the purchasing power in the country in question when related to the United States. This gives a rate of exchange which is considerably different from the official rate of exchange. In the case of Pakistan, the PPP exchange rate is about Rs 16 to a dollar rather than Rs 60, the rate at the time of this writing (September 2006).

4. For a detailed account of the development of the dispute and its ultimate resolution see Aloys Mitchell, *The Indus River,* New Haven, Conn.: Yale University Press, 1969.

5. The Sterling Area was made up of the countries of the British colonies that had linked their currencies to the 'sterling' or the British pound. The Sterling Area is roughly equivalent to today's Commonwealth.

6. That was not the only area of India's policy towards Pakistan in which Patel took a more belligerent view towards the Muslim state. 'Nehru and Patel came dangerously close to a public clash only once,' writes Shashi Tharoor in his biography of Nehru. 'In 1950, under pressure from the right to intervene militarily in East Pakistan where a massacre of Hindus had begun, Jawaharlal first tried to work with his Pakistani counterpart, Liaquat Ali Khan, on a joint approach to communal disturbance, and when this had been ignored by Liaquat offered President Prasad his resignation. But when Patel called a meeting of Congressmen at his home, Nehru fought back, withdrawing his offer of resignation, challenging Patel to a public debate on Pakistan policy, and even writing to Patel to express doubt whether the two of them could work together anymore.' Shashi Tharoor, *Nehru: The Invention of India,* New York: Arcade Publishing, 2003, p. 169.

7. For an elaboration of this view see Shahid Javed Burki, *Pakistan: A Nation in the Making,* Boulder, Colorado: Westview Press, 1980.

8. The World Bank, *Trade Policy in South Asia: An Overview,* (Report No. 29949), Washington DC, 7 September 2004, p. 20.

9. An excellent description of the license raj and the damage it did to the Indian economy is in Gurucharan Das, *India Unbound,* Delhi: Penguin, 2003.

10. Joseph Stiglitz, *Globalization and its Discontents,* New York: W.W. Norton Columbia, 2002, p. 85.

11. The World Bank, 2004, op. cit., p. 1.

12. The term 'global production system' is used by UNCTAD in its annual *World Investment Reports* to describe the way a large number of US, Western European and Japanese firms have evolved into TNCs.

13. *The Economist,* 'The Looming Revolution,' 13 November 2004, p. 91.

14. David Wighton, 'Movement of tasks overseas jump up skill claim relentlessly', *Financial Times Survey: The World 2006,* 25 January 2006, p. 4.

15. Veronique Weil, as quoted in David Weighton, op. cit.

16. These models draw their name from Newtonian physics in that trade flows between two countries increase in proportion to their economic mass (as measured by their respective GDPs) and are constrained by the friction between them (proxied by the distance between them) due to the transaction and other costs.

17. http://www.saarc-sec.org

18. The American-Indian economist Jagdish Bhagwati is one of the most articulate exponents of this point of view. For his approach to international trade see his recent book, *In Defense of Globalization,* New York: Oxford

University Press, 2004. He also contributes regularly to the *Financial Times* on trade issues.

19. The World Bank, *Global Economic Prospects: Trade, Regionalism and Development*, Washington DC, October 2004, pp. 2–1.

20. See the citation in footnote 16 above.

21. Although some North-North agreements, such as the recent expansion of the European Union, have incorporated labour movements, most North-South and South-South agreements are confined to intra-firm movements of professionals, and do not focus on increasing access for temporary workers, skilled or unskilled.

22. Aaditya Mattoo and Pierre Sauve, 'Regionalism and Trade in Services in Western Hemisphere: A Policy Agenda', in A. Estvadeodal, Dani Rodrik, Alan Taylor and Andres Velasco (eds), *Integrating the Americas*, Cambridge, Mass.: Harvard University Press, 2004.

23. The results of the study are reported in The World Bank, Global Economic Prospects, 2005. Washington DC, 2004, pp. 5–12.

24. See, for instance, J.A. Frankel, E. Stein and S.J. Wei, *Regional Trading Blocs in the World Economic System*, 1997, Washington DC, Institute for International Economics.

25. See S. Lahiri, 'Controversy: Regionalism Versus Multilateralism' *The Economic Journal*, 1998, Vol. 108, pp. 1126–1127.

26. Robin Cook, 'A Strong Europe—or Bush's Feral US Capitalism' *The Guardian*, 29 October 2004, p. 26.

27. Details are from the SAARC Ministerial Declaration, January 2004.

28. United States Agency for International Development, *South Asian Free Trade Area: Opportunities and Challenges*, Washington, DC, 2006.

29. The subject of non-tariff barriers to trade was covered by my team in the final report prepared for the US AID project on SAFTA. See Shahid Javed Burki, 'SAFTA: A concluding word' mimeo, Nathan Associates, Washington DC, June 2006.

30. These impressions are based on the interviews conducted by me at the SAARC Secretariat during a visit to Kathmandu, Nepal in December 2004. I then met with the Secretary-General of SAARC and a number of directors representing the member countries.

31. The textile industry must also deal with the challenge posed by China, a subject covered in Chapter 2.

32. The World Bank, *International Trade and Global Poverty*, Washington DC, 2002

33. UNDP, *Human Development Report 2002*, New York, Oxford University Press, 2002. The subject of MDGs was discussed in Chapter 1.

34. William Cline, *Trade Policy and Global Poverty*, Washington DC, International Institute of Economics, 2004.

35. The world's commerce ministers had met every two years since the 2001 launch of the Doha Round. The 2003 meeting was held at Cancun, Mexico

which resulted in failure largely because of the insistence of a small group of West African nations that the United States remove or at least significantly reduce subsidies it gave its farmers.

36. *Financial Times,* 9 August 2006.
37. US Aid, *South Asian Free Trade Area: Opportunities and Challenges,* 2006, op. cit.

4

Developing Human Capital

For the last couple of decades, policymakers in Pakistan have recognized that they had failed to develop their country's large human resource. In terms of human development, when measured using the human development index developed by Pakistan's own Mahbub ul Haq,[1] the country had fallen behind much of the developing world. Pakistan had become a laggard even in South Asia. With this recognition came the realization that public policy must be reshaped and designed to close the gap between Pakistan and other rapidly developing countries by investing in education and training. This led to the launching of several programmes aimed at bringing education to the masses. But no consistent approach was followed. There was a great deal of experimentation, considerable waste of public resources and loss of precious time. For more than a decade, Islamabad accepted the approach advocated by the World Bank that the state's principal preoccupation should be with promoting primary education. According to this line of thinking, expanding school enrolment to the point that universal primary education was achieved was the most important contribution the state could make to the development of its human resource. The government was to concentrate in particular on the more neglected segments of the population, in particular women and people living in the more backward areas.

As I will discuss in this chapter,[2] this approach deflected attention from other equally important components of the sector, in particular higher education. Implicit in this emphasis on primary education was the belief that much of higher education could be left to the private sector. The state's failure in the sector of education brought the private sector into Pakistan's education in a number of significant ways. Some had entered to fill the gaps left by the state, some others came for profit. I will call the later group 'educational entrepreneurs'. However, even with the entry of the private sector, the country continued to fall behind. It was only after the induction of the second administration headed by President Pervez Musharraf that state policy towards education began to acquire a degree of coherence. Two initiatives in particular began to make a considerable difference. One was to develop the capacity to deliver basic education at the local level. This began to be done under the auspices of the Human Development Foundation. The other was to develop higher education under the direction as well as involvement of the Higher Education Commission.

This chapter is divided into eight sections. In Section 1, I will discuss the state of education in the country, relying not only on the data provided by the government but also assembled by a number of non-government organizations that became active in education in the 1990s. In Section 2, I will describe the evolution of the sector of education over the last several decades and assess the contribution being made by its many components. In this section I will underscore the important role politics played in shaping the sector. In Section 3, I will discuss the state of education in the Muslim world, since I believe that some of the problems the sector faces in Pakistan are because of the way Islam is being interpreted by some of its more radical followers who have gained in influence in many Muslim countries. In Section 4, I will indicate how some of the donors who have been active in Pakistan have influenced the development of education in the country. This discussion will focus in particular on the respective roles of the World Bank and the United States Agency for International Development. In Section 5, I will deal with the important subject of knowledge accumulation and the contribution it makes not only to sustaining growth at high levels but also to integrating the domestic economy with the rest of the world. In Section 6, I will investigate the role of higher education in knowledge accumulation and how the state can help in this process. The role assigned to the Higher Education Commission by the government of President

Pervez Musharraf will be discussed in this context. In Section 7, I will use 'outsourcing' as an example of how population can be turned into an economic asset, not only for increasing the productivity of the domestic economy but also for export. This section will use India as an example of a country that was able to develop its human resource as an 'exportable commodity'. In Section 8, I will offer some suggestions for the design of public policy for promoting higher education.

1. The State of Education

It would be appropriate to begin this discussion by looking at Pakistan's demographic situation in 2006. In that year, Pakistan was already the world's sixth largest country, after China, India, the United States, Indonesia, and Brazil. Its population was estimated at 160 million. With a male/female ratio of 103.7, the country also had a larger number of males in its population. Pakistan had one of the world's youngest populations. One half, or 77 million, of the population was below the age of 18 years. The number of people below the age of 18 in the United States was less than those in Pakistan, and yet, the American population was almost twice as large as that of Pakistan. What is more, with each passing year, Pakistan's population was getting younger. Out of a population of some 255 million projected for 2030, about 180 million will be below the age of 18.

In spite of a significant decline in the level of fertility in recent years, Pakistan's population will continue to grow at a rate well above 2 per cent a year for several years. Even with some further reduction in the birth rate, by 2030 Pakistan could—less than a quarter century from now—overtake Brazil and become the world's fifth most populous country, with a population of 255 million. Or, put in another way, Pakistan was set to add another 100 million people to its already large population over the next twenty-five years. In two to three decades, Pakistan will have the largest concentration of Muslims in the world, more than in Indonesia and in India. Although Indonesia in 2030 will still have a larger population than Pakistan, it has a higher proportion of non-Muslims than is the case for Pakistan. In 2006, an estimated 95 per cent of the Pakistani population was Muslim.

A significant number of this additional population will end up in the already crowded cities of the country, in particular Karachi, Lahore, and the urban centres on the periphery of Lahore. Karachi already has more than 13 million people; by 2030 it could have a population of 25 million. By the same time, Greater Lahore may have a population of 15 million. Will such large urban populations live in peace and become active contributors to Pakistan's economic growth and development? Or will they become increasingly restive and disturb peace not only within the country but also outside the country's borders? The answers to these two questions will depend on the way the authorities and people of Pakistan approach the subject of education and what kind of assistance they can receive from the world outside. Unless an ambitious programme is launched soon and implemented with the government's full attention and energy, a significant proportion of the young will be poorly educated and will have skills that will not be of much use in a modern economy. The numbers involved are large.

An indifferently educated workforce made up of millions of young people living in a few crowded mega cities, will become attractive recruits for groups and organizations that are alienated from the global economic, political and social systems. In a Muslim country such as Pakistan, the groups that will be able to attract the young espouse various radical Islamic causes. In 2006, the situation in Pakistan was delicate. There was the possibility that the continuation of the high rate of growth registered in 2003–6 could be sustained and create opportunities for the young in an expanding market place. There was an equally strong possibility that the economy would stall and the incidents of poverty would increase.[3] Which way the country would go would depend on state policy. Policy towards education will be important.

In 2006, some 75 million people were at the school and university-going age, defined as between 5 to 24 years old. Of these only 27 million, or 36 per cent, were attending various educational institutions: 20 million in primary schools; 6.5 million in middle, high, vocational and technical schools; but only 0.5 million in university and professional schools. The enrolment rates, therefore, were 83 per cent in primary schools, but only 18.6 per cent in the middle, high and technical schools. However, it was at the university level that enrolment had seriously lagged behind, with only 2.3 per cent of the young in that age group attending educational institutions.[4]

While the general enrolment rate increased by an impressive 23 per cent in 1990–97— equivalent to a growth rate of 5 per cent a year—the dropout rate remained very high. By the end of the 1990s, the primary gross enrolment rate had reached 83 per cent, but only 48 per cent of the age group reached grade five. The enrolment and retention rates taken together gave some indication of the amount of resources wasted in the educational sector. Illiteracy among women in Pakistan was twice as high as among men. Pakistan's poor were so poorly educated that they could not lift themselves out of poverty. Until 2003 when the rate of economic growth picked up, the incidence of poverty was increasing at a rate of four times the increase in population, 10 per cent a year compared to 2.5 per cent. In 2006 there were an estimated 50 million people living in poverty.

Finally, the development of tertiary education needed to be addressed. In 1995, only 2.3 per cent of the relevant cohort was in tertiary institutions in Pakistan compared to 6.6 per cent in India. In the same year, India spent 13.7 per cent of the public sector expenditure committed to education on the institutions devoted to tertiary education. The comparable figure for Pakistan was only 4 per cent. Pakistan, therefore, had a long way to go before it could begin to catch up with its neighbour.

2. The Structure of a Fractured Sector

In the late 1940s and up to the early 1970s, Pakistan had a reasonably efficient system of education, not much different from other countries of the South Asian subcontinent. It was dominated by the public sector; educational departments in the provinces administered schools and colleges while a small number of public sector universities provided postgraduate instruction. A few schools were run by local governments. The public sector also had teacher training schools and colleges. The main purpose of the system was to prepare students for government service. The government, including the military, was the single largest employer in the country.

There were not many private schools within the system of education for several decades following the birth of Pakistan. Those that existed were run mostly by Christian missionaries and Islamic organizations, each producing graduates for two completely different segments of society. The first set of schools catered mostly to the elite. They followed their own curricula, taught from the text books written mostly by foreign authors. They imported experienced teachers from outside. The students who graduated from these schools usually took examinations administered by Cambridge University in England. A significant number of graduates from these schools went abroad for higher education. Upon return, or after graduating from institutions such as Lahore's Government College and Forman Christian College, they joined one of the superior civil services or entered the army.

At the opposite end of the educational spectrum were religious schools, called *deeni madrassas* that imparted religious instruction. Some of the better institutions belonging to this genre were either imports from India or were patterned after the old *madrassas* in what was now the Indian state of Uttar Pradesh. The best known of these was the Darul Uloom at Deoband that had developed its own curriculum and taught a highly orthodox or fundamentalist interpretation of Islam. Following the partition of India and the birth of Pakistan, a number of *ulema* (Islamic scholars) from Deoband migrated to Pakistan and established seminaries in the new country. Two of these, a *madrassa* at Akora Khattak near Islamabad called Darul Uloom Haqqania and the other in Banori township of Karachi played a prominent role in bringing an austere form of Islam to Pakistan. This was not the type of Islam that had previously been practiced in the country. Islam was brought to the areas that now constituted the state of Pakistan by a number of Sufi saints from Afghanistan and Central Asia. The religion they spread was not by force of arms but by setting a personal example of piety, simplicity, and respect for the members of other faiths. Consequently, even to this day non-Muslims visit shrines such as that of Khwaja Mueenuddin Chishti at Ajmer Sharif in Rajasthan. This was not the version of Islam that appealed to the seminaries patterned after Deoband. I will return to the subject of these *madrassas* a little later.

The private schooling system of that era imparting western style education, therefore, produced members of what later came to be known as the Pakistani establishment—the military and the civil services. The religious schools, on the other hand, produced *imams* (preachers) for the mosques, teachers for the *madrassa* system of education and political workers in the Islamic parties. These two very different systems with very different ideologies and pedagogic techniques produced two very different social classes with very different world views and views about the way Pakistan should be governed. The two groups clashed on many occasions in the political and social arena. One example of this was the controversy in 2005 over the deletion of a box in the newly designed and machine-readable passport that initially did not have a column indicating the religious affiliation of the passport holder. This move was taken by the government headed by President General Pervez Musharraf as one small step towards what he had called 'enlightened moderation'. He was, however, beaten back by the religious parties and the 'religion column' was reinserted in the passport. Another example was the amount of street violence religious groups were prepared to resort to in order to stop women from participating in sporting events in Gujranwala. Once again the government stepped back rather than pressing forward with the modernization of society. A third example was the violence in January 2006 in many major cities of the country to protest against the publication of cartoons in a Danish newspaper that ridiculed the Prophet Muhammad [PBUH]. The students in the *madrassas* played an important role in these conflicts. Education, therefore, had begun to play a divisive role in the Pakistani society.

In between these two active social classes was a large inert group, the product of a large public school system that included all aspects of education. It started with kindergarten and primary schools at the bottom, included secondary and higher schools, and, at its apex, had semi-autonomous but publicly-funded universities. For several decades the standard of instruction provided by this system was adequate; the system's graduates were able to provide the needed workforce for the large public sector and also for the rapidly growing private sector of the economy. Those graduates of the system who went abroad for further education either at their own expense or relying on the funds provided by various donor-supported scholarship schemes did not experience much difficulty in getting adjusted to the foreign systems. Some of Pakistan's better known scholars and professionals such as the Nobel Prize winning physicist, Professor Abdul Salaam, and the well known economist Mahbub ul Haq were the products of this system.

However, the system deteriorated over time to the extent that it became common to describe Pakistan as the country that had done the least for the social development of its large population. It was also common to fear that without major investment in education, Pakistan could become a large exporter of manpower to the stateless Islamic organizations—Al Qaeda being the most prominent among them—that would continue their battle against the West, western values, and anything else they saw from their narrow prism as anti-Islamic.

How did Pakistan travel the distance from a moderate Muslim country with a reasonably efficient educational system to a country in which the public system of education has virtually broken down and in which a large number of educational institutions are providing instruction that teach hate for those who hold different points of view and encourage *jihad* against them? Pakistan's gradual transformation from one state to the other occurred slowly under many different impulses. As such the country offers a good case study of how a society can get derailed.

The Pakistani educational system collapsed slowly; at times its progressive deterioration was not even noticed by the people who later were to be most seriously affected by it. The collapse basically occurred for four reasons. The first jolt was given in the early 1970s by the government headed by Prime Minister Zulfikar Ali Bhutto. Bhutto decided to nationalize private schools, in particular those run by various Christian missionary orders. His motive was simple. He was of the view that private schools encouraged elitism in society whereas he wanted equality and equal opportunity for all. This action increased the size of the public sector without increasing the size of public funds made available to education.

Bhutto was also responsible for delivering the system the second shock and this time around the motive was political expediency. His rise to political power was viewed with great apprehension by the religious forces in the country. They considered the socialism Bhutto espoused as 'godless' and were determined to prevent him and the Pakistan People's Party founded by him from gaining ground. The two sides—Bhutto and the Islamists—chose to use the college and university campuses to fight the battle for the control of the political mind in the country. Both sought to mobilize the student body by establishing student organizations representative of their different points of view. For a number of years campuses of the publicly run institutions became the battleground for gaining political influence at the expense of providing education. It was in this battle, waged in educational institutions, that Pakistan witnessed the birth of another organization—the Muhajir Qaumi Movement[5]—that was to use violence in order to spread its word and make its presence felt. The MQM was not a religious organization. It did not espouse a religious cause. But it used educational institutions in the public sector to energize its base.

The third development to make the system of education dysfunctional occurred in the 1980s when a coalition led by the United States and including Pakistan and Saudi Arabia decided to use the seminaries as training grounds for the *mujahideen* who were being instructed to battle the Soviet Union's troops occupying Afghanistan. There was an unspoken understanding about their respective roles among these three partners. The United States was to provide equipment and training for the foot soldiers of the *jihad*. Pakistan was to set up *madrassas* in the Afghan refugee camps and along the country's long border with Afghanistan. According to *The Washington Post*, the United States government even supplied texts to the *madrassas*, 'glorifying and sanctioning war in the name of Islam'.[6] Pakistan's military, with good knowledge of the Afghan terrain, was to be actively involved in training the *mujahideen*. The government of Islamabad also reserved the right to choose among the various groups that were prepared to do battle in Afghanistan. The Saudis were happy to aid the effort with money, as long as they were allowed to teach *Wahabism,* the brand of Islam they favoured and espoused, in the seminaries that were to be used for training the *jihadis*. This proved to be a potent mix of motives: the United States was able to recruit highly motivated fighters to battle the occupying forces of the Soviet Union in Afghanistan, Pakistan was able to further its influence in Afghanistan and Saudi Arabia was able to introduce its extremely conservative interpretation of Islam into a large Muslim country that had hitherto subscribed to a relatively liberal, accommodating and assimilative form of the religion. The strategy worked in so far as the objective of expunging the Soviet Union was concerned. But it left a legacy: an educational system that continued to produce *jihadis* for various Islamic causes.

Even without the intervention by the United States, President Ziaul Haq would have brought religion into education. But the war in Afghanistan provided him with more resources to invest in his programme. *Madrassas* have a long tradition in the Muslim world, including Pakistan. The way the system is structured and the way it works is not always understood, not even by the policymakers entrusted to reform it. The *madrassa* is the foundation of the system, providing ten years of schooling. Those who attend it are provided food and sometimes also lodging. For study beyond the *madrassa* level, students go on to a Darul Uloom, for two years of instruction. For further specialization, students can get enrolled in a *jamia* for four years of instruction. According to one estimate there were in 2002 some 10,000 institutions of Islamic education registered with five boards that supervised their activities. Roughly 70 per cent were Deobandi, 16 per cent Barelvi, 5 per cent Jamaat-e-Islami, 4 per cent Ahl-e-Hadith and 3 per cent Shia.[7]

The fourth unhappy development to affect the sector of education was the political confusion that prevailed in the country for more than a decade, from the time of the death of President Ziaul Haq in August 1988 to the return of the military under General Pervez Musharraf in October 1999. In this period four elected governments and three interim administrations governed the country. Preoccupied with prolonging their stay, the elected governments paid little attention to economic development in general and social development in particular. Under the watch of these administrations, public sector education deteriorated significantly. The donor community took cognizance of this situation and sought to help Pakistan reform its educational system. The aim of the World Bank's Social Action Programme (SAP) was to improve the provision of primary education through the public sector. Women and people in the disadvantaged areas were particularly targeted for help. But, as discussed later, the programme failed since the public sector institutions were poorly equipped to handle it.

By the time General Musharraf assumed power in October 1999, it was clear that more than money to put back public sector education on the right track was needed. It required a change in the way society viewed education and in the way it was prepared to impart knowledge that would be useful in the market place. The education system had to aim to change the mindset so that all citizens began to recognize that it was not right to declare your religion on the front page of the passport, or to stop women from participating in public supporting events, or to turn to extreme violence whenever Islam was disparaged or mocked in the West.

As a result of these four developments—or phases as I have characterized them—Pakistan in 2006 had a highly fractured system of education. The country, in fact, had three educational systems operating in parallel. The largest of these was the system of public education managed by the departments of education in the country's four provinces and a number of autonomous universities funded, in part, by the public sector. About three-fourths of the population was served by this system. The quality of education provided was generally poor. There were some exceptions but these were at the tertiary level. At the primary and secondary level, the system was not doing a good job.

Largely as a response to the failure of the public educational system, space was created for 'educational entrepreneurs' to enter the sector. The institutions they established were for profit. Hundreds—if not thousands—of schools were founded, mostly in the country's large cities and mostly providing education based on curricula developed in Britain and the United States. These entrepreneurs also established some institutions in the tertiary sector. For some time there was a flurry of activity in the area of information technology but, following the collapse of the technology boom in America in 2001, there was considerable slackening of interest in this part of the educational sector. Private sectors reverted back to the provision of general education, mostly in English medium schools. The private sector accounts for about one-fifth of the school-going population.

While, as indicated above, religious schools have existed for a long time in the subcontinent, many institutions founded during the struggle of the Afghan *mujahideen* against the occupation forces of the Soviet Union were not interested in teaching modern subjects; their main aim was to produce an army of young men deeply influenced by a highly conservative form of Islam. The graduates of these schools not only fought in Afghanistan but also participated in what they called *jihads* in Bosnia, Kosovo, Chechnya and Kashmir. Over time these schools began to prepare young men not only for helping with armed resistance but also for carrying out acts of terrorism in the Western world. *Madrassa*-trained young men, for instance, were behind some of the suicide bombings in London in 2005. London was not the only city that was targeted. According to one account, 'of the four suspects named in the bombings that traumatized Istanbul, three hailed from Bingol, a gritty mountain town about 1,000 miles away in Turkey's eastern mountains. Notably religious, each of these suspects bore the markers of Islamic militancy familiar in biographies of suicide bombers, including travel to Pakistan for religious training.'

There was considerable debate amongst analysts of the educational system about the share of *madrassas* in total enrolment at the primary level. Estimates varied widely from 1 per cent of the total to 33 per cent of enrolment. The higher figure was provided by the International Crisis Group in its report on the *madrassas* and was widely quoted by the western press.[8] According to a study sponsored by the World Bank, the suggestion that one-third of school enrolment was accounted for by the *madrassas* was the result of a serious arithmetical error.[9] The fact that there was such a range of estimates means that public policy concerning education was being made in the dark. There were perhaps two million students in *madrassas* out of a school enrolment—not just primary but up to the tenth grade—of some 27 million, or 7.4 per cent of those in all schools. At the primary level, *madrassa* enrolment accounted for about a half of this proportion, about 3.5 per cent of the total enrolment.

The fourth and final part of the system was made up of the institutions providing technical education in disciplines such as health sciences, business management, accounting, banking and finance and information and technology. These institutions also provided workers for the modern sector in Pakistan. The total number of students graduating from these institutions, however, remained very small.

The most authoritative estimate of the distribution of primary enrolment in government, private and *madrassa* schools was provided by Ishrat Husain, then governor of the State Bank of Pakistan, the country's central bank. He provided these estimates in a presentation at the Woodrow Wilson International Center for Scholars that organized several workshops in 2004–2006 focusing on various aspects of development in Pakistan. According to Husain, 73 per cent of the primary school enrolment was accounted for by government institutions, 26.1 per cent by private schools, and only 0.9 per cent by *madrassas*. Both government schools and *madrassas* had a larger presence in the countryside, accounting for 81.8 per cent of total enrolment. *Madrassas'* share was 1.1 per cent while private institutions catered for the remaining 17.1 per cent. In cities and towns the corresponding shares were as follows: government, 62.4 per cent; private, 36.9 per cent; and *madrassas*, 0.7 per cent.[10]

The four-part system described above was not working for Pakistan. How should it be restructured? This became an important question not only in Pakistan but in the West as well, as it began to address the problem posed by militant Islam. One manifestation of this interest was to provide a fairly significant amount of aid for reforming the educational system in the Muslim world. However, the donors were doing what they did in the past—pour large amounts of money into governments' coffers. What they were not likely to do was something they don't have much experience in doing—help the Muslim world to reform the entire system of education—to adopt a holistic approach towards educating the Muslim masses. Before turning to the role the donor community could play in Pakistan, I will discuss the state of education in the Muslim world.

3. Education in the Muslim World[11]

In an earlier section, I identified the increasing influence of Islamic radicalism as an impediment for the development of Pakistan's educational sector. I will develop that point further in the context of education in the Muslim world. Why should the subject 'education in the Muslim world' be different from simply education in developing countries? What is it that warrants the problem of education in the world of Islam a separate treatment? Why has fresh money from western donors begun to support reform of the educational systems in the Muslim world as a part of the former's war against radical Islam?

The United States in particular got seriously committed and involved in reforming educational systems in many Muslim countries. It indicated its willingness to provide $100 million in grants to Pakistan for this purpose. But Pakistan was not the only country receiving assistance from America for education. During a three-hour visit by George W. Bush to the island of Bali on 21 October 2004, the United States president promised to provide $250 million to improve the quality of education in the schools run by the public sector as well as those managed by Islamic charities in Indonesia, the Muslim world's largest country in terms of population. Bali was the scene of a terrorist attack in October 2002 in which more than two hundred people were killed.

It is significant that the US announcement for assistance to Indonesia was made in the meeting President Bush held with a group of moderate Muslim leaders of that country. Washington, in other words, was making an explicit connection between its declared war on international terrorism and the quality of education being provided by the schooling systems in the Muslim world. Was it correct to make this connection especially when it was recognized soon after the attacks occurred, that the nineteen hijackers who flew planes into the World Trade Centre and the Pentagon on 11 September 2001 were not the products of the *madrassa* system of education? Several were educated in the West and most belonged to the upper strata of society in Saudi Arabia, UAE and Egypt, the countries from which they came. Nonetheless, it is legitimate to address the subject of educating the Muslim populations, not just as a part of the problem confronted by the rest of the developing world.

There are significant differences in the way education has been handled by Muslim countries and there are also significant differences in the results that have been achieved. I will take up these two issues in turn; first, the approach to education in the Muslim world and, second, the outcome of that approach. There are three things that stand out which are different from the way in which the Muslim state and society has educated its citizenry. One, there is a much closer association between religion and teaching in general in most Muslim countries. Even in a system such as that in Pakistan which was built upon the approach the British had adopted in developing education through the public sector, Islamiyat—the study of Islam—was introduced as a compulsory part of the curriculum in the 1970s and the 1980s. This was done by the state in order to placate a small but influential segment of society, people who believed that the curricula in public schools must teach the basic tenets of Islam. This concession may have won the leaders of the day some political returns but it resulted in seriously distorting the curriculum. There is, of course, nothing wrong with teaching religion in schools. It is done in thousands of parochial institutions in the West, in particular in the United States. What is important is to ensure that instruction in religion does not give a message that conflicts with the teaching of science and other modern subjects. This separation has to be made explicitly and deliberately. Unfortunately this did not happen in Pakistan.

Two, in most of the Muslim world non-government organizations—in particular the charities funded by Islamic societies—have traditionally played a significant role in providing education. This is the origin of the *madrassas* as an educational institution and its advent goes back many decades. The curricula followed by the *madrassas* reflect the value systems of the sources of the funds they receive. In more recent times many *madrassas* were established with support from Saudi Arabia to teach Islam along *Wahabi* lines, an extremely conservative variant of the religion. This was done to the neglect of other subjects that were vital for training and educating people so that they could operate in the modern economy and become members of a global economic and social system.

Three, female education received much lower priority in Muslim countries, in large part because of the way the Islamic faith was interpreted by many influential scholars over the last several decades. This was particularly problematic since economists have recognized for sometime now that of the many determinants of economic growth and social change, none was more important than the education of women. Societies that neglect female education were condemning themselves to eternal backwardness.

What have been the major outcomes of these approaches to education? One way of answering this question is to look at the several measures of education—in particular adult literacy rates, youth literacy rates, the rates of participation at various levels of schooling, the expected years of schooling and the amount of public sector expenditure on education in the Muslim world. In order to draw some important conclusions it will be useful to compare the situation in Muslim and non-Muslim countries.

Before providing a whole set of numbers, it is interesting—and distressing—to note that the statistics from the Muslim world about the various aspects of education are not as good as those from the non-Muslim world. This is an indication of the relatively low priority given to education by Muslim societies, including the governments of these countries. Even when information is available, its coverage is poor and the data not very reliable. One thing the governments could do is to improve the database without which good and effective policies cannot be developed and implemented.

In the early years of the twenty-first century adult illiteracy rates were still very high in Muslim countries—50 per cent for males in Bangladesh, 42 per cent in Pakistan, 33 per cent in Egypt compared with 31 per cent in India, 13 per cent in Brazil and only 5 per cent in the Philippines. What was even more troubling was that adult female illiteracy rates were considerably greater than that of males, indicating a strong bias against educating women. The ratio was very high for Saudi Arabia. For every illiterate male adult there were two illiterate females in that country. The ratios for Pakistan and Bangladesh were 1.7 and 1.4 respectively.

While youth illiteracy rates—youth being defined as persons between the ages of 15 and 24—signifying the efforts made in recent years to bring education to the masses, were considerably lower than adult illiteracy rates, they were still higher in the Muslim world than in non-Muslim countries. A fairly significant difference between adult and youth illiteracy rates is a good indicator of the progress being made and this is noticeable in many Muslim societies. In Bangladesh, 43 per cent of male youth were illiterate, while the proportion for Pakistan was 20 per cent. The comparable figures for India, Brazil and the Philippines were 20, 6 and 1 per cent. What was worrying, however, was the ratio between female and male youth illiteracy—the ratio for Pakistan was more than 2, in Bangladesh it was 1.4. For Pakistan, for every illiterate male youth there were young females who were not literate.

Improvement in youth literacy is largely the outcome of increased participation by various age groups in education. Of the eight large Muslim countries, four—Bangladesh, Egypt, Indonesia and Turkey—had achieved universal primary education with participation rates of 100 per cent or more. A rate of more than 100 per cent implied that the country was catching up with what was neglected in the past; that the students were attending school even though they had passed the age group for that particular level of education. The fact that Indonesia had a participation rate of 110 per cent for primary schools meant that 10 per cent of the students at this level were older than the relevant age group. Saudi Arabia, Pakistan and Iran were three countries that had participation rates of well below 100 per cent which meant that they continued to add to the pool of illiterates. The primary enrolment rates for these countries were 68, 77 and 86 per cent, respectively in 2003. This relatively poor performance was the result of low enrolment rates for girls.

The available date on expected years of schooling in the Muslim world was very spotty. In the *World Development Indicators* published by the World Bank every year, there were no entries for Pakistan. But for Bangladesh there was an indication according to which the expected years of schooling for both boys and girls was 8 years in 2003, while it was 12 years for Malaysia. It was interesting and encouraging that for Bangladesh girls had caught up with boys; in their case the time they could expect to spend in school had doubled from 4 to 8 years over the last one decade. Since this was also the period when Bangladesh saw an explosion in the output of its garment industry, and since this industry employed a large number of young women, a connection could be made between the demand for education and the prospect for finding well-paying jobs. Since the labour participation rates for women in Pakistan was still very low, families didn't have the incentive to send their girls to school or to keep them there for a reasonable period of time. One policy implication of this finding was that increasing employment opportunities for women create incentives for educating them.

Although participation rates at the primary level had improved considerably, there was evidence that in the Muslim world the quality of education provided remained poor. With the increasing importance of *madrassa* education in some of the Muslim countries, particularly in Pakistan, these ratios didn't indicate that the educational system was producing students who would, over time, be able to play a meaningful role in economic development and modernization.

Noticeable improvements in participation rates at various levels of education and a considerable decline in youth illiteracy were achieved as a result of increase in inputs into the educational system, the consequence of a significant commitment of public sector expenditure in education. Malaysia and Iran were two large Muslim countries that had made education a high public sector priority. In 2000, the latest year for which statistics are available, nearly 27 per cent of the government's budget was spent on education in Malaysia. The proportion for Iran was a bit more than 20 per cent. In this respect two Muslim countries had done very poorly. In Egypt only 8 per cent of total public sector expenditure was committed to education. In Pakistan the share was even lower—only 7.8 per cent. With the donor community—in particular the United States but also institutions such as the World Bank—providing more money for education there will probably be some improvement in the flow of public funds into education. However the real change will only come when Muslim countries change their culture and go back to the original teaching of Islam in which the importance of education was emphasized and in which no gender distinction was made concerning the need for educating the people.

4. Development of Education and the Donor Community

The growing recognition that Pakistan was failing in the effort to educate its large and growing population, that the religious schools had grown in importance, and that some graduates from the religious schools were turning towards Islamic extremism placed education at the centre of the donor community's agenda. In September 2001, Pakistan returned as a frontline state in a new war—this time a war against terrorism—and the donors began to reward it with more economic assistance. Education had returned as a priority for the donor community. Some of the donors, in particular the United States and the World Bank, made available large amounts of resources to the country on the condition that they be spent by the public sector on education. However, the donors' past involvement in education had not been very productive. The result of these efforts was the waste of public resources and breeding of political and bureaucratic corruption, but little improvement in the state of education.

One example of the programme that failed to meet its ambitious objectives was the World Bank sponsored Social Action Programme (SAP). It was launched with considerable enthusiasm in 1988 in association with several other donors to Pakistan. It had three basic purposes: to increase the amount of public money spent on education; to bring about a significant increase in school attendance by persuading parents to send their girls to school; and to bring education to the more backward areas of the country. These were all laudable objectives but the donor community—including the World Bank—did not recognize that pouring money into the government's coffers when the government's institutions were extraordinarily weak would only result in waste. That was exactly what happened. The SAP did increase for a while by one full percentage point of the gross domestic product the amount of public money going into education. But that, unfortunately, was its only success. The SAP failed to bring education to the people of Pakistan. It only created a system that became increasingly corrupt, with 'ghost schools', 'ghost teachers' and 'ghost students'. After the SAP monies were exhausted, even the World Bank admitted that a good part of the aid provided by it and other donors was wasted. What went wrong with the SAP?[12]

Would that experience be repeated with new donor money pouring in into the education sector? Much of the new money was intended to be spent on primary schools, both in the public sector and in the reform of the *madrassa* system. Was that the right way to obtain the best results from this additional resource? The SAP's design had one major fault. It relied upon a dysfunctional bureaucratic system to deliver a series of well-intentioned objectives. That couldn't—and didn't—happen. The departments of education that became the principal implementing agents for the programme needed to be reformed before they could implement such an ambitious undertaking. As is now well known, in spite of the enormous amount of money provided for social development, Pakistan's social indicators showed no improvement after the programme was terminated, compared to the situation before its start.

The World Bank and the community of donors it had assembled to support the SAP recognized, midway through the implementation of the programme, that some corrections were needed to be made. To understand what was going on, it created a large implementation office as a part of its resident mission in Islamabad. That was not the right step to take since the Bank should have known, as its own documents had begun to recognize, that no programme aimed at bringing about massive social change would succeed without the full ownership and commitment of the recipient agencies. The Pakistani departments involved with implementing the SAP had shown neither.

Even after the end of the SAP the Bank continued to emphasize education in its lending and analytical work but changed its strategy in three ways. It shifted its attention from the national to the provincial level, it designed the programme keeping the need of the individual provinces, and it built a strong monitoring and system management into the programme. The SAP was a national programme although education under the constitution was the responsibility of the provinces. Accordingly the Bank decided to work with the provinces. Recognizing that there were considerable differences in the implementation capacity of the various provinces, it made education a part of the provincial development strategy. In 2005–6, the institution produced provincial strategies for the four provinces and tailored its lending programme to local needs as well as political commitment of those in power. Under this approach, Punjab became the first province for the Bank's attention. According to one foreign analyst:

> The presence of a very reform-minded chief minister at the head of the province of Punjab opened the way for new support. When the chief minister took office in 2002, he immediately recognized education as the area that needed drastic improvements.[13]

The Bank was satisfied with the initial results of its strategy in the province. Within one year of the start of the programme in 2003, enrolment in government primary schools increased by 13 per cent (compared to the previous trend of less than 2 per cent increase per year). Girls enrolment in 6–8 grades in the low-literacy districts receiving the stipends [under the programme] increased by 23 per cent. Recent household survey data shows that net primary enrolment rates in the province increased from 45 per cent in 2001 to 58 per cent in 2004–2005. The initial positive results from the Punjab Education Sector Reform Programme seem to confirm that success greatly depends on several key factors: highest level political commitment, ownership at all levels, and robust monitoring. For its current engagement in the education sector, the World Bank is now looking for these conditions to be met.[14]

That the emphasis on primary education was at the core of the SAP and the provincial programmes that succeeded it was laudable, provided this form of instruction was seen as one small part of the process of educating and training people to participate not only in their own economic betterment, but also to play an important role in the economic and social modernization of the countries to which they belonged. By just focusing on primary education, governments in the developing world were not preparing their people for taking advantage of the opportunities offered by the evolution of what is sometimes called the 'new economy'.

A World Bank report, *Constructing Knowledge Societies: New Challenges for Tertiary Education* accepted some of the criticism levied against it by some practitioners of development.

> The Bank is commonly viewed as supporting only basic education; systematically advocating the reallocation of public expenditures from tertiary to basic education; promoting cost recovery and private sector expansion, and discouraging low-income countries from considering any investment in advanced human capital.[15]

The Bank, by implication, accepted the need for reorienting its approach. The reorientation required emphasis on knowledge accumulation, the subject of the next section.

5. Development of a Knowledge-Based Economy

Broadening the scope of intervention in the sector of education acquired great importance in view of the significant changes that had occurred in the global economy in the closing years of the twentieth century. These changes opened new opportunities for developing countries. Knowledge became the most important contributor to economic development. A study by the Organization for Economic Cooperation and Development, a Paris-based organization that coordinates development work by rich countries, concluded that underlying long-term growth rates in its member states depend on maintaining and expanding the knowledge base. The same conclusion was reached by the World Bank's *World Development Report 1998/1999*, according to which 'today's most technologically advanced economies are truly knowledge-based... creating millions of knowledge related jobs in an array of disciplines that have emerged overnight.'[16]

These conclusions were supported by a number of trends. For instance, in the world's more developed countries, growth of value added for the 1986–94 period was 3 per cent for knowledge industries compared with only 2.3 per cent for the business sector as a whole. Between 1985 and 1997, the share of knowledge-based industries in total value added rose from 51 to 59 per cent in Germany, from 45 to 51 per cent in the United Kingdom, and from 34 to 42 per cent in Finland. Therefore, in order to accelerate the rate of economic growth, emphasis in public policy on knowledge accumulation acquired considerable importance.

Another indication of how knowledge was changing the fortunes of many countries across the globe was the composition of goods traded among nations. The proportion of goods in international trade with a medium-high or high level of technology content rose from 33 per cent in 1976 to as much as 54 per cent in 1996. The message conveyed by these numbers was clear: economic growth had become dependent on knowledge accumulation as much as on capital accumulation. In rich countries, investment in the intangibles that make up the knowledge base—education, software development, research and development—exceeded investment in physical equipment. Again, the message policymakers needed to receive from this finding was that they had to shift their focus from capital accumulation as such, to policies that promote the use of capital and labour in a more productive way. This could only happen with an improvement in society's base of knowledge.

The significance for the developing economies of the increasing share of knowledge in the global economy is because of two developments. The first was perhaps best described as 'demographic asymmetry', a subject on which I have written extensively elsewhere. The second reason was a link between human development and economic growth, whose existence was postulated many decades ago by economist Robert Lucas. Lucas's main contribution was to recognize that output increases are not entirely the result of greater application of labour and capital to production processes. Something additional was at work, and that was human development technological improvement.

The total productivity of an economy, or of a sector, or of an individual enterprise was the consequence of a combination of labour, capital and technology. Take two countries with exactly the same amount of labour and capital. The one that is more technically sophisticated will always outperform the one that is relatively backward. That was why India was likely to do better than Pakistan unless Pakistan succeeded in closing the technology gap. This effort was started in 2003 with the establishment of the Higher Education Commission as an entity with considerable autonomy in the allocation of large amounts of resources that were put at its disposal. The Commission's programme and its likely contribution to developing human capital is a subject to which I will return later in this chapter.

But let us look at the work of another economist, Robert Solow of MIT. He had looked at capital in the traditional way. It was defined as land and machinery. Later capital came to be treated in much broader terms than the original Solow construct. It was not just machinery in the case of non-agricultural pursuits that qualified as 'capital' but also such intangibles as human and social capital. Human capital formation was the result of investments in health, education and training. Social capital was the product of how individuals and groups of individuals related and worked with one another. Education and knowledge accumulation was a critical input in the formation of all types of capital.

How much of the productivity increase and corresponding growth in national output should be attributed to such intangibles as human and social capital? This question became increasingly important as the rapid evolution of information and communication technology made a tremendous amount of difference to the way human and social capitals develop. In fact, information and communication technology contributed significantly to the amounts of these two 'capitals'. This was not anticipated by Professor Solow.

Solow's work on the link between human capital and economic development did not stop with the identification of total factor productivity as an important element in the growth equation. In 1987, the MIT professor, who in the meantime, had gone on to win the Nobel Prize in economics, developed what came to be known as 'the productivity paradox.' He puzzled why when you could see the computer age everywhere, it was not visible in productivity statistics. The first commercial computer was installed in the early 1950s by General Electric and tens of thousands of companies had followed suit. American firms in particular—but those in other countries as well—had invested heavily in successive generations of IBM 360s, Univacs and Digital Equipment mini computers. However, all the investment in computing did not immediately yield productivity gains. In fact, productivity growth in all developed economies slowed significantly after the introduction of these machines into the workplace. In the United States, the annual rate of increase in output per hour—one common measure of productivity—during the 1960s was 2.6 per cent. From 1973 to 1995 it dropped to an abysmally low 1.5 per cent in spite of the mass arrival of personal computers and the development of the Internet. In the 1985–1995 period, computers migrated from the data centres in the firms to office desks and most homes. Why didn't the investment in computers show up in estimates of increase in productivity? This was Solow's paradox.

But then after 1995, growth in productivity suddenly picked up. Again to use America as an example, productivity growth increased from 1.5 per cent per year in the previous two decades to 2.5 per cent. Noticing this change several prominent economists, the then US federal chairman, Alan Greenspan, included, began to talk about the dawn of a new economy. But why did this increase in productivity happen after such a long time lag? Technology gurus had an answer that seemed plausible. They hypothesized that technology's impact is felt when investments in any particular innovation reaches a critical mass. They pointed out that in the decade before productivity increases began to appear, capital investment in computers and telecommunications equipment was on a rising trend, peaking in the United States at 50 per cent of all business capital spending. But economists were not impressed with this line of thinking. They failed to see a causal link between information and communications technology (ICT) on the one hand and growth and development on the other.

Solow was one of the many sceptics. Another doubter, Robert Gordon at Northwestern University in Chicago, pointed to a number of alternative explanations such as normal variations in the pace of productivity growth through the business cycle. He didn't think that the ICT revolution had much to contribute to a sharp rise in productivity in the late 1990s. But productivity increases persisted. While business investment in ICT fell sharply all over the world and the rate of economic growth slowed, productivity improvements continued, reaching 5.3 per cent in the US in 2003 and a scorching annualized rate of 9.4 per cent in the third quarter of 2003. It was clear that all these developments needed a theory.

It came from Erik Brynjolfsson, a young MIT economist working at the Sloan School, whose ideas seemed to convince the doubters. He argued that productivity gains following investments in ICT can take more than five years—sometimes even longer. This happens since ancillary changes must accompany investments in ICT hardware and software. 'IT is just the tip of the iceberg in terms of the investment that goes into these projects. Ninety per cent of the investment—literally, 90 per cent—goes into creating new organizational and human capital,' he argued.[17] Without intangible capital—human and social in particular—which takes time to form, investment in ICT does not produce productivity increases.

There were many examples available to those who like to study these developments of how human and social capital can combine with investment in ICT to produce extraordinary increases in productivity. One illustration of this was 'swarming,' a technique pioneered, like so many others in this field, by the US army. The technique was based on peer-to-peer networking in which employees in an organization—an army, a government department, an NGO, a firm—pulled together to form an ad hoc team from anywhere to work on a specific task. According to one account,

swarming was developed as a tactic by the US army to enable separate units to come together for a particular attack. By enabling small forces to co-ordinate with each other directly, rather than through a central command post, the army has cut the time needed to plan military operations from ten hours during the first Gulf War to just ten minutes in Afghanistan.

Scores of businesses adopted 'swarming' as a way of applying knowledge to various processes. Hewlett-Packard (HP) was one such business. According to Craig Samuel, the company's chief knowledge officer,

> the potential prize is worth billions of dollars to companies like HP if we can collaborate in the right manner, and the breakthrough technology is the flow of person-to-person (or P2P) information. Napster showed that by using P2P it is possible to link individuals around the world into a unit with a common focus very quickly.

According to this way of thinking, ICT alone did not contribute to productivity increases and economic growth. The use of computers and the Internet produced positive economic effects only when people working with them adopted new approaches. They can 'swarm' over finding solutions to the problems that would have taken a long time to solve even with computers especially if work habits had not changed. It took education and knowledge accumulation to make an effective use of the ubiquitous computer. But knowledge has to be constantly acquired to make an effective use of computational power and the rapid flow of information made possible by ICT.

The implications for the developing world of combining rapid-fire developments in ICT with human development were obvious. Countries in this part of the world could help themselves in two ways. Through sharp increases in productivity, they could bring about significant increases in the rates of economic growth. This had already begun to happen in the places where large investments were made in developing ICT, not only by the private sector, as in India and to a lesser extent in Brazil, but also by the government, as in China. Pakistan had fallen way behind these countries. The investments made by countries such as China and India will produce productivity increases down the road which, in turn, will contribute to increase in GDP growth. For Pakistan to take the same route it would have to invest heavily in building both human and social capital. This requires emphasis on higher education, on developing an interface between research and industry, on building and developing institutions that make it possible for individuals to work together.

There are estimates that the extraordinary developments in India's IT sector had already added at least a one percentage point to its rate of GDP growth. That the Indian policymakers in 2006 were talking confidently about achieving and sustaining rates of GDP growth of 7 to 8 per cent a year was because of the extraordinary inroads knowledge-based technologies were making in the country's economy. China will draw similar benefits once its large investments in the ICT sector begin to bear fruit.

Another important contribution the ICT sector could make in the developing world is to allow the dispersal of production processes. This would be similar to what transnational corporations have begun to do as a part of the process generally called 'globalization'. Producers in developing countries, by using ICT, could take work to the places where people live rather than have them congregate to towns and cities which are the centres of economic activity. By using ICT, developing countries can slow down the rate of rural to urban migration and constrain the further growth of such mega cities as Karachi, Calcutta, Lahore and Bombay.

By far the most important contribution of ICT is to better integrate the developing world with the global production system. Rather than worry about the digital divide that would, as some had feared, result in producing a further gap in the incomes of developed and developing countries, ICT could help to narrow the differences. Once again, India and China offer good illustrations of the positive consequences of ICT for economic growth and development. But for all that to happen, developing countries have to prepare their workforce by educating and training them and by making it possible for them to accumulate knowledge. By introducing networking arrangements among people they could introduce new forms of teaching, instruction and knowledge accumulation. The most important ingredient in this knowledge and networking-based strategy for economic growth is education, in particular at the tertiary level.

A well-educated workforce is of tremendous use to the countries that have deliberately promoted the sectors of the economy that are dependent more on human skills than on capital equipment. This was the secret of the success of the 'miracle economies' of East Asia in the last quarter of the twentieth century. The same strategy was repeated with spectacular results by China at the start of the twenty-first century. Pakistan's neighbour India was not far behind. India's IT industry has created a large presence for itself in the world's markets. In 2005, Indian IT exports were closer to $18 billion, almost equal to Pakistan's total exports. India expected to increase exports in this sector by fourfold and reach $80 billion in 2015.

India is the current favourite for outsourcing, and presents Pakistan with a model that it can replicate. India has more than half a million IT professionals. It is adding two million graduates a year, many of whom are attached to the IT sector. The starting salary of a software engineer in India is $500 a month, about one-eight to one-tenth of the US. This makes it attractive for foreign companies to outsource work to India. This then is the route Pakistan should take, but it will need a great deal of government attention and a considerable amount of public and private sector investment in institutions of technology and higher learning.

6. The Role of Higher Education[18]

As has been emphasized in this chapter, economic growth suffered in Pakistan because of the neglect by the government of human resource development. The government did poorly not only in moving towards universal primary education for both girls and boys—an objective to which it committed itself with President Pervez Musharraf's signature on the Millennium Declaration issued by world leaders in September 2000, aimed at achieving a number of targets by specified periods—it also neglected higher and technical education. As was discussed in the previous section, without making knowledge accumulation a focus of public policy, Pakistan will not be able to achieve the high rates of growth to which it aspires and which have become possible in India. What is the most appropriate strategy to follow in this context, what is the role of the state in this area, what role can the private sector play in this field, how has the Higher Education Commission fared in this respect since its establishment in 2003? These are some of the questions addressed in this section.

Economists and planners long accustomed to using the state to address problems posed by economic backwardness are tempted to rely on government action to deal with sectors such as education. The question of the role of the state in education, a question that has been the subject of much attention for decades and an issue about which there have been wide swings of the pendulum including that of informed opinion, remains central in Pakistan. 'Public goods, quasi-public goods, and externalities are fairly common in the real world,' wrote economist Paul Krugman in one of his books on development.

> They are common enough for it to be necessary to take proposals for government intervention in the economy on a case-by-case basis. Government action can never be ruled in or ruled out on principle. Only with attention to detail and prudent judgment based on the facts of the case can we hope to approach an optimal allocation of resources. That means the government will always have a full agenda for reform— and in some cases, as in deregulation, that will mean undoing the actions of government in an earlier generation. This is not evidence of failure but of an alert, active government aware of changing circumstances.[19]

This long quotation from the writings of a highly respected economist helps to focus attention on a number of issues that have bedevilled the role of the state in economic matters, not just in the sector of education. Krugman was right in emphasizing pragmatism over ideology, a dynamic approach over the one that did not change, and the recognition that governments can never—in fact, should never—totally step aside from participating in the economic lives of the citizens they govern. It was wrong for development practitioners to insist during the time the policy agenda associated with *The Washington Consensus* held sway, that good economic governance meant little, and argue for a very spare role of the state.

In this context, it was interesting to note that while much of *The Washington Consensus* advice to the developing world emanated from rich countries, public funding remained the main source of support for higher education in that part of the world. But that began to change and in a way that had lessons for the developing world. According to a 2001 OECD (Organization for Economic Cooperation and Development) study, of the eight rich countries for which data was then available, private expenditures for tertiary education grew faster than public expenditures in seven countries—France, with a strong tradition of high quality government-financed tertiary education, was the sole exception. In Canada, Italy, the Netherlands and Switzerland public expenditures actually decreased in real terms. This happened because of a sharp increase in private participation in this part of the educational sector, a subject to which I will return in a moment.

Not only was the state in the developed world contributing a smaller proportion of the total funding available for tertiary education it was also using much greater flexibility in the way government funds were provided. A number of countries switched to resource allocation formulas pegged to the value of inputs and outputs. The formula-funding approach to budgetary allocation was designed to develop greater institutional autonomy by giving more management discretion to tertiary educational institutions in the internal distribution and utilization of government funding. For instance, in Australia, Denmark, New Zealand and Sweden, tertiary education institutions were given more autonomy in allocating resources across faculties, departments and programmes. Formula funding also provided financial incentives for improved institutional performances in relation to national policy goals.

In other words, a number of rich countries treated tertiary education as a quasi-public good with important externalities that justified considerable government funding. That tertiary education had important externalities—which meant that it produced an array of social benefits that went beyond those that became available to those who were educated—had come to be well recognized. A 1998 report published by the Institute for Higher Education Policy (IHEP) based in Washington identified a number of public benefits that can be associated with tertiary education. These included nation building and development of leadership. Political development was also facilitated by higher education. Democratic participation; increased emphasis on consensus-building as a way of managing inter-personal and inter-group affairs; the perception that society was based on fairness and opportunity for all citizens were some of the developments fostered by the right kind of tertiary education.

Let me illustrate this point by taking an example from Pakistan. Sectarian violence in Pakistan was perpetrated by the groups whose members had not received higher education and whose exposure to education, at best, had been to the narrowly focused *madrassas*. Bringing modern education to these groups should make them more tolerant towards people who professed different faiths. This was an example of an externality associated with tertiary education.

Social mobility was also helped by tertiary education, a fact that was noticed by some anthropologists who had studied the composition of the labour force in India's IT sector. There was much greater mixing of the castes in this part of the economy than was the case with the old manufacturing and service sectors. The IHEP study also identified reduced crime rates, improved health and improved basic and secondary education as some of the social benefits of tertiary education.

Like so many other benefits from positive economic developments, tertiary education also had multiplier and cumulative effects. The old debate in the United States about the relatively poor performance of black Americans in racially mixed schools and colleges began to focus on the cumulative impact of tertiary education as communicated through generations. It was noted that in the affluent suburb of Shaker Heights, a community in Ohio state, middle class blacks apparently worked less hard in school and clearly lagged behind their white peers in achievement. But, race was not the determining factor. According to one expert,

> 90 per cent of the district's white students, but just 45 per cent of its black students, have two parents with college degrees. And nationally, middle income blacks are much more likely to be new to the middle class than middle income whites are, so parenting behaviours that are associated with class (such as reading nightly to children) can be mistakenly interpreted as racial in character.

Another important externality was the formation of industrial and educational clusters that are dependent on the institutions providing higher education. The existence of universities and training institutions promoted the development of high technology industries in many parts of the developed and developing world. The successful experience of technology-intensive poles such as Silicon Valley in California, Route 270 in Maryland, and Bangalore in India attested to the positive effects that the clustering of human capital alongside leading technology firms can produce. East Asia had many examples of technology intensive poles including the Daeduck Research Complex in Korea, Tsukaba Science Town in Japan and Hsinchu Science-Based Technology Industrial Park in Taiwan. The only comparable example of this in Latin America was Campinas in Sao Paulo State, Brazil. Balancing these external social benefits were economic and social advantages that became available to those who obtained higher education. Among the economic benefits for the well-educated were higher salaries, better employment opportunities and higher savings rates. Social benefits included an improved and healthier lifestyle and also higher life expectancy.

Since the benefits from tertiary education accrued to both private and public sectors, governments were prepared to allow private finance to enter this area. Nonetheless, most governments insisted on a regulatory framework within which the private sector was allowed to participate. If the development of tertiary education was to be treated as the shared responsibility of public and private sectors, how should the latter be invited to play a meaningful role? There were several options available, some more attractive than others. To start with is the entry of private players into the system as 'for-profit' operators. They can play an important role in the systems in which public institutions are particularly weak. This is the case in several South Asian countries, particularly Bangladesh and Pakistan.

How free should be the entry of private capital in tertiary education? Is there a role for the state, particularly in terms of regulating the institutions set up by 'educational entrepreneurs'? Should the state motivate the private sector to self-regulate by providing accreditation only to those institutions that meet certain prescribed standards? How should students from less well-to-do families gain access to these institutions? Answers were being found to these and many other questions by educationists across the globe. In the United States private colleges and universities conformed to certain standards laid down by various collegiate and university associations. In several Middle Eastern countries, the state granted charters for the establishment of private institutions after a thorough investigation. In some Latin American countries, student loan programmes were available to help children from poor and middle class families finance their stay in private institutions.

There is one requirement for active state participation in developing private institutions. For the state to play an effective role, government agencies assigned the task of regulation and oversight have to be technically strong and able to resist the temptation to collect rents from the entrepreneurs wanting to invest in the sector. This is not the case in countries that have weak governments and, therefore, weak ministries and departments of education. It is precisely in these countries where 'for-profit' educational institutions seem to flourish the most. This, then, poses a paradox. There are two solutions. One is to trust the private sector to regulate itself on the basis of guidelines developed in a transparent way by the public and private sectors working together. The other is to establish an autonomous institution in the public sector and entrust its management to people with good reputation in the field of education. Pakistan chose the second option by creating the Higher Education Commission in 2003.

Some lessons can be drawn from the experience of one other developing country that used education to bring about not only an acceleration in economic growth but also to become an important player in the new global economic system. The country that achieved this result was South Korea. The Korean government, while ensuring a move towards universal primary education, also focused on developing higher education. This was done in four phases, each planned with great foresight. In the first phase, in the 1950s, the Koreans expanded tertiary education in the public sector but with some cost sharing. While 70 per cent of the cost was met from the government's budget, 30 per cent came from the tuitions charged from students. In the 1960s, the Korean government encouraged the establishment of private institutions, with limited public funding for capital costs and scholarships. In the 1970s and 1980s, the government turned its attention to the expansion of engineering and technical education to meet the manpower requirements of an economy that was rapidly modernizing. Finally, in the 1990s, the government focused on improving the quality of research and development while introducing performance-based funding of all educational institutions, public and private. The government of Pakistan should take its cue from a country such as Korea that successfully modernized its economy by developing its human resources. As Seoul did, Islamabad should also turn its attention to all aspects of educational development, including higher education.

It took a long time for policymakers in Pakistan to recognize that they were losing the ground that had become available to other populous developing countries as the process of globalization began to reshape the world economy. Ground was being lost since various governments that held office over the last several decades failed to recognize the importance of education for promoting economic growth. Even the reformist regime headed by President Ayub Khan in the 1960s did not identify education as one of the areas of high priority. It set up a number of commissions to advise it on the issues in which it wished to introduce reforms but education was not one of them. It was only with the advent of the Musharraf period that the state directed its attention towards this vital area of human development.

It is interesting that even in the case of General Pervez Musharraf, his administration was slow in recognizing education as a sector deserving of government support and attention. It was not included in the seven-point plan the new military leader presented to the nation soon after taking charge of the country in October 1999. However, once he recognized that this was a sector that had long been neglected by the state, that its development could not be left to the established bureaucratic system, that some innovative programmes were needed to bring about change, and that the sector required his personal attention, President Musharraf launched a comprehensive programme under the direction of dynamic leaders.

President Musharraf recognized that the conventional approach of putting additional resources in the hands of the people and institutions that had failed to deliver in the past would not work. What was required was a revolutionary approach—and I don't use the word 'revolution' lightly—to reverse the course of history. One way of underscoring this point is to quote at some length from Stephen Cohen's 2004 book on Pakistan.

> In the case of educational reform a sceptical attitude is warranted because of past performance, the limited technocratic vision of the senior leadership, a disdain for academic freedom and scholars, the absence of strong social pressure for better education from Pakistan's citizenry and above all, a still minuscule budget for education. Foreign assistance for education makes up 76 per cent of the government's educational expenditure, and Pakistan still ranks among the fifteen worst countries as far as education is concerned. The elite will manage for itself with a few choice institutions available to the wealthy, and foreign education as an option.[20]

Some of this scepticism among foreign observers of the Pakistani scene began to dissipate after the Musharraf government took some initiatives, but they will be looking for more positive developments and credible action by the government. It was important to watch how the world outside reacted to the initiatives taken by the government inside Pakistan. A series of positive developments in the sector of education in the country would help to dispel the widespread impression that the country was plunging into darkness, that its social and political institutions had been commandeered by obscurantist forces, and that it had become a major exporter of Islamic terrorists and terrorism. As Fareed Zakaria wrote in an article for *Newsweek*, published in the spring of 2006, that while Al Qaeda was weakened considerably after 2001, the only activity that remained was by way of 'Al Qaeda Central by which I mean a dwindling band of brothers on the Afghan-Pakistan border.'[21] The western interest in Pakistan's educational sector, therefore, was prompted by some of those concerns. Not only were the donors prepared to put money into the sector, they were also organizing seminars and workshops to understand the nature of the Pakistani malaise and possible cures for it. It was at one of these workshops, held last year by the highly respected Woodrow Wilson Center at Washington, that I came across the first positive assessment by an American expert about some of the recent developments in Pakistan's educational sector. In a paper presented (and later published by Woodrow Wilson in its volume on the workshop proceedings), Grace Clark said that 'this is a very exciting time to be involved with higher education in Pakistan because there is a revolution going on in academia in Pakistan.'[22]

There were three elements in the programme launched by the Musharraf administration that were innovative and worthy of notice. The first was to identify two areas in which the state needed to move expeditiously. They were capacity building at the local level, the level at which most of the action took place in the provision of basic education, and improving the capacity to deliver higher education. The second was to establish autonomous bodies to work in these two areas. The work of capacity building at the local level was entrusted to the Human Development Foundation of Pakistan, and that of bringing about a quantum change in higher education to the Higher Education Commission. The third was to recognize that the educational sector needed a partnership between the public and private sectors. The government had neither the capacity nor the resources to handle the colossal task alone; it needed to work with the private sector that had already demonstrated the imagination, passion and resolve to improve the level of education at all levels in the country.

The Higher Education Commission began its operations in 2003 by first writing a programme for the five-year period between 2005 and 2010.[23] The *Medium Term Development Framework* identified four areas for emphasis.[24] The first was access to the institutions providing higher education. In 2005, only 2.9 per cent of 13 million people in the age group 20 to 24 years were enrolled in institutions of higher learning. This was an extraordinarily low proportion for a country at Pakistan's level of development. India had more than 7 per cent of the similar cohort receiving higher education. The countries which had succeeded in accelerating their rates of economic growth and had become active participants in the global economic system—countries such as South Korea, Malaysia and Taiwan—started the process of economic and social transformation with a much larger proportion of young people in higher education institutions. They then went on to build a robust relationship between institutions of higher learning and the modernizing sectors of the economy—industry, commerce and finance.

The Commission wrote in its programme that it would pay particular attention to increasing enrolment in institutes of higher learning. This would be done in several ways: by encouraging students to go for higher education by giving them stipends, by increasing the capacity of existing institutions to take in more students, and by establishing new universities. In March 2006, President Musharraf announced that his government would establish six new universities, each with the help of a different donor. This would be done under the Commission's auspices. It was expected that these initiatives would help to increase enrolment in higher education from 2.9 to 5 per cent by 2010 and to 10 per cent by 2015. If that happened, Pakistan should have 1.8 million students attending institutions of higher learning. If the drop out rate was not more than 10 per cent, this would mean that the country would be turning out graduates at the annual rate of 1.6 million. This, of course, would be a quantum jump in the number of graduates coming out of schools and colleges.

However, increasing the supply of higher education facilities and the number of graduates did not necessarily mean an improvement in the quality of human resources available to society and the economy. Pakistan did not have a programme in place for testing the quality of graduates at the national level, but that notwithstanding, there was an impression that the quality of education had suffered at all levels over the last several decades. The Commission's *Medium Term Development Framework* states, 'The present quality of higher education is very low. Not a single university of Pakistan is ranked among the top 500 in the world'.[25] Accordingly, the Commission began to focus on improving the quality of teachers, arguing that the first step in any programme to improve the standard of education at any level was to have more qualified teachers available to the students. This was also the part of the programme that drew the most criticism, in particular from several members of the faculties. This should have been expected, since any change—and what the Commission was intending to do was a colossal change—would be resisted by those who were likely to be hurt by it.

One of the most important changes engineered by the Commission was to de-link the pay scales of the teachers from those of the civil bureaucracy. Economists often talk about the law of unintended consequences. This pertains to the outcomes—some happy and some not so happy—that were not expected by the policymakers when they took certain initiatives. If the Commission succeeded in establishing compensation for highly qualified teachers in ranges considerably higher than those available to senior government officials and matching those the private sector was paying to qualified and experienced managers, it would have created a career stream that would attract the best and the brightest to education. If this trend continued and if, under the Commission's direction, the public sector joined it, I can see a time when the country's youth will give a career in education a very high priority. That, of course, would improve the quality of education. Some of this had already begun to happen in the private sector. On my visit to Pakistan in March 2006, I was impressed with the salaries some of the private colleges and universities were prepared to offer in order to attract highly qualified teachers to their campuses.

However, the offer of high salaries must accompany the prescription of strict criteria that should be used to identify those who would receive them. This the Commission said it would do; this was also the reason for the unhappiness of several teachers already in the profession with the contemplated reforms, since under the established criteria they would not qualify for the new pay scales. But the establishment of a new pay scale would not by itself improve the quality of the teachers in institutions of higher learning. That too was the right approach. There were a number of other initiatives the Commission started, including improving the infrastructure available for higher education, introducing scholarship programmes for higher education in foreign universities, promoting excellence in learning and research, and introducing new technologies in the provision of knowledge and information to students as well as members of faculties. Pakistan seemed to have found the political will and the resources to address a long-neglected problem.

7. Outsourcing: One Benefit from Using Population as an Economic Resource

While the people of the developed world are rapidly ageing, a number of populous countries such as Pakistan continue to have very young populations. The country's rate of fertility remains high. Although it has begun to decline in recent years, it is not likely to reach for a while the level of 2.1 births per woman. It is at that level that populations attain a steady state, when the number of births equals the number of deaths. This level was reached by the West several decades ago. Now, most developed countries have much lower fertility rates. With fewer births than deaths, populations in several European countries and in Japan will begin to decline in size. In fact Japan registered a decline in its population in 2005, the first time in world history. It is this demographic asymmetry that provides countries such as India and Pakistan windows of opportunity. India has opened this window for itself and is drawing enormous benefits already. The window remains closed for Pakistan.

To exploit the window of opportunity made available by demographic asymmetry, the developing world must take a number of positive actions.[26] By now rich countries fully recognize that they have to rely, in some way or the other, on the copious supply of young and skilled workers from poor countries. They have to do that in order to sustain the growth of their knowledge-based industries. That the developing world has many more young people than the developed world—in absolute numbers as well as their share in total population—will not automatically produce material benefits for the former.

That can only happen if people are well-educated and trained to participate in the knowledge-based economy developing around the world. A combination of demographic advantage, developments in the information and communication technology sector, the transformation of manufacturing processes by transnational corporations and their willingness to outsource a significant amount of work to the developing world have opened a number of new possibilities for the countries that are still relatively poor. To see where these opportunities lie, let us first look at the way technological development and innovation contribute to development.

While the realization that migration was bringing about a healthy change to the host economies was slow in coming to Europe, it was readily recognized in the United States that foreign workers had contributed significantly to the spectacular productivity growth in that country. The Americans were generous in admitting highly skilled workers into the country. One way of doing that was to grant H-1B visas to foreign high-tech workers in ever-increasing numbers. In 2001, the limit on the number of visas in this class was increased to 195,000 by the US Congress. And then three things happened: in March 2001, the dotcom bubble burst, reducing the demand for tech workers; in September 2001, Muslim terrorists struck America, creating a deep suspicion against migrants from the Muslim world; and in 2002, the US economy went into recession putting great pressure on wages. The most immediate impact of all this was to turn the Americans against immigration, in particular against the immigration of young males from Muslim countries. Pakistan by far was the hardest hit country because of its proximity to Taliban's Afghanistan and the perception that it was an important breeding ground for terrorists.[27]

It has now become apparent that skilled workers don't have to leave home to provide their input for the products and services being produced by the West's hi-tech industry and financial and medical institutions. The enormous amount of investment made by the large telecommunication companies in laying down fibre optic cables connecting different parts of the globe, created a capacity far beyond the demand for it. This brought down the price of connectivity. Overseas cable costs fell as much as 80 per cent since 1999. This made it possible to transmit huge amounts of data from corporate headquarters in the United States to companies doing outsourced work in the developing world. Mathew Slaughter, associate professor of business administration at Dartmouth College, said in a newspaper column that information technology work will 'move faster [than manufacturers] because it's easier to ship work across phone lines and put consultants on airplanes than it is to ship bulky raw materials across borders and build factories and deal with tariffs and transformation.'

Given the size and openness of the Pakistani economy, why are foreigners not attracted to the country? Why has India become such a flavour of the day and why does Pakistan continue to be shunned by foreign investors? Why are foreign investors attracted, but not to Pakistan? Let me briefly recount as to what is really happening with respect to foreign investors' interest in our neighbour, by offering some concrete examples. In the space of a few days in December 2005, three of the biggest companies in the United States—JP Morgan Chase, Intel, and Microsoft—announced plans to create a total of more than 7,500 jobs in high value areas such as research and development and processing of complex derivative trades. As a newspaper commentator wrote: 'But for those worried about sluggish job creation by the US economy there was an additional worry. The jobs would all be in India. Worse, they would be jobs that in the past would have been in the US.'[28]

What is even more important and impressive from the Indian perspective is the fact that some of these companies have decided to bet their future on India. Under JP Morgan's plan, 20 per cent of the global workforce of its investment bank will be in India by the end of 2007. HSBC, one of the world's largest banks operating out of London, has similar plans with regard to its requirement for financial skills. In an entirely different field—computer sciences and IT services—companies such as Microsoft, IBM, Intel, AMD, plan to locate significant parts of their research operations in India. What attracts them most to India is the quality of human resources available in that country. For foreign companies the attractions of India are not just costs—which industry analysts estimate at being about 40 per cent below US levels[29]—but also the quality of staff being produced by the Indian universities.

According to Veronique Weill, head of operations at JP Morgan's investment bank, 'the quality of people we hire [in India] is extraordinary and their level of loyalty to the company unbeatable.'[30] One of the many areas in which public policy continues to fail in Pakistan—a subject to which I will return momentarily—is the inability of the educational system to produce in significant numbers the same quality of people as those graduating from India's science and technology institutions.

What is most troubling for Pakistan is that it is losing ground not only to India, a country that also has a large and young population. It does not even figure in the 'back-up' plans drawn up by foreign corporations for addressing the growing shortage of skills in their home countries. According to one knowledgeable analyst, 'to avoid being too concentrated in one country, JP Morgan is already looking at other potential offshore locations mainly in Eastern Europe, but also China and the Philippines.'[31] How can Pakistan get on the corporate maps of American and Europe? Why has public policy failed in that respect?

The most difficult problem Pakistan faces is the perception about it being the epicentre of Islamic extremism on the verge of an explosion in both political and social spheres. Not only that; many influential voices in the United States in particular are not convinced that Islamabad is doing all it needs to put down Islamic extremists. In an editorial the day after Prime Minister Shaukat Aziz's visit to Washington, *The Washington Post* not only advocated unilateral US action against extremists if Islamabad failed to act on its own, it resorted to name-calling. Calling President Pervez Musharraf, 'a meretricious military ruler,' it advised the administration of President George W. Bush that 'if targets can be located, they should be attacked—with or without General Musharraf's cooperation.' The newspaper had a long list of complaints.

> General Musharraf has never directed his forces against the Pushtun militants who use Pakistan as a base to wage war against American and Afghan forces across the border. He has never dismantled the Islamic extremist groups that carry out terrorist attacks against India. He has never cleaned up the Islamic *madrassas* that serve as breeding ground for suicide bombers. He has pardoned and protected the greatest criminal proliferator of nuclear weapons technology in history, Abdul Qadeer Khan, who aided Libya, North Korea and Iran. And he has broken promises to give up his military office or return Pakistan to democracy.[32]

If the visit by the prime minister was meant to change some influential minds about the way they viewed his country, it cannot be counted as a great success. The *Post's* editorial could not be seen as a ringing endorsement of a country in which American corporations could do business. This segment of opinion-makers in Washington was not prepared to recognize that by following mindlessly the American dictat, President Musharraf's regime—in fact any regime in Pakistan—could not expect to stay in power by totally alienating its own people. It was also ironical that even after the occupation of Iraq and the use of lethal force against the insurgency, the US was not able to quell violence in that country. It was only after a long and hot pursuit and expenditure of a considerable amount of human and financial resources that the US succeeded in capturing the Jordanian fighter Abu Musab al-Zarqawi who had led the insurgency against the coalition troops for more than two years.

While improving Pakistan's image with respect to its participation in the struggle against Islamic extremism is not fully in Islamabad's control, what it could do is to measurably improve the quality of its human resources. Here the public policy continues to falter in spite of the large amounts of new money committed to investment in higher education and skill development. Much of the effort under President Musharraf has been directed towards the use of public funds to finance new avenues for advanced education for Pakistani students. As discussed in the previous section, the establishment of the Higher Education Commission may begin to address the problem of the low level of skill development. Only time will tell whether this initiative will bear fruit. What the government could have done but didn't do was to establish new institutions or significantly improve those that are already operating in a few areas where Pakistan could carve out a place for itself. An approach that was built on public-private partnership would have been very helpful in this area of human resource development.

Some specific initiatives could still be taken. The government could invite the private sector to establish some institutions of excellence—for instance a health sciences institute in Lahore, an advanced engineering and technology institute in Karachi, an urban planning institute at Hyderabad, a small scale engineering institute at Muzaffarabad, a transport institute at Peshawar, a banking and finance institute at Islamabad, and an agricultural sciences institute at Faisalabad. These are some examples of the kinds of initiatives the state should take to take advantage of a large and young population that could bring in immense economic benefits to the country. In not developing such a strategy Pakistan is rapidly losing ground to other populous countries. It is still not too late to plan for the future and make a real attempt to move forward.

8. Educating the Masses: Some Conclusions[33]

The conventional approach to addressing the problem posed by the underdevelopment of the educational sector was based on six assumptions. One problem—by far the most important one according to most experts—many societies faced was that the cost of sending children to school was greater than the benefit education was likely to bring. Parents incurred costs even when education was free. The perceived cost of education was likely to be more of an inhibiting factor for the attendance of girls in schools than for boys. In poor households girls helped their mothers handle a variety of chores including the care of their siblings. One way of approaching this problem was to provide monetary incentives to parents to send their children to school. School feeding programmes fell into this category of assistance; they lowered the cost of education for parents.

Two, the state may not be spending enough on education. The remedy is to increase the proportion of public resources going into education. If tax-to-GDP ratio cannot be increased, the state should be willing to divert resources into education from sectors with lower priority. The donor community was prepared to help with funds if there was the fear that the domestic resources were too constrained to allow for an increase in public sector expenditure on education. This was one reason why development institutions such as the World Bank significantly increased their lending for education.

Three, typically a state spent more on secondary, tertiary and university education than on primary education. The cure was to divert more funds into primary schooling and if need be charge students attending colleges and universities.

Four, the quality of instruction was poor. The obvious solution was to invest in teacher training, reforming the curriculum and improving the quality of textbooks. Sometimes the quality suffered because schools lacked proper physical facilities. They were poorly constructed or the buildings were poorly maintained. In some cases students did not even have chairs and desks at which they could sit and work. This problem could be handled, once again, by committing more resources for public sector education.

Five, the educational bureaucracy was too remote from the parents who wished to see an improvement in the quality of education given to their children. This gap between the provider and the receiver could be bridged by organizing parents to oversee the working of the educational system. Teachers could be made responsible to the parent's associations in addition to being responsible to the educational departments in some distant places.

Six, in highly traditional societies, parents would be prepared to send their girls to school only if they did not have to travel long distances, if they are taught by female teachers, and if the schools have appropriate toilet facilities. In some situations parents would be prepared to educate girls if there were single-sex schools. The solution for this problem was to build more schools for girls and to employ more female teachers.

All this was learned from a great deal of experience by the donor agencies from their work around the world. Most of these lessons were incorporated in a high profile programme of assistance for educational improvement launched by the World Bank in Pakistan in the late 1980s. Called the Social Action Programme, the plan developed by the Bank was supported by a number of donor agencies and billions of dollars were spent on it for over a decade. The result was disheartening. The programme was inconsequential in achieving even the most fundamental objectives: increasing the rate of enrolment in primary schools for both boys and girls and bringing education even to the more remote areas of the country.

The Bank made several attempts to correct the course during the implementation phase but the programme did not succeed. There was one simple reason for the programme's failure. It did not take full cognizance of the fact that the educational bureaucracy was so corrupt, inefficient and dysfunctional that it could not possibly deliver a programme of this size. Ultimately the donors decided to abandon the programme altogether. Given this experience and given the magnitude of the problem the country faces, what options were available to the policymakers in the country and the donor community interested in providing help to Pakistan?

A variety of donors committed large amounts of finance for helping Pakistan educate its vast population in the aftermath of the terrorists' attack of 11 September 2001. According to a count by the Ministry of Education in Islamabad, foreign commitment for education was estimated at $1.44 billion spread over a period of seven years, from 2002 to 2009. Of this $450 million was being provided as grants, with the United States at $100 million the largest donor. The remaining one billion dollars was being given in the form of soft loans by the World Bank ($650 million) and the Asian Development Bank ($339 million). These commitments amounted to some $370 million a year.

The government also announced its intention to significantly increase the amount of public funds for education. In 2000–1, funding for education amounted to only 1.96 per cent of the gross domestic product. This increased to 2.7 per cent by 2003–4 when the government spent about $2 billion on education, of which about one-quarter was provided by donors. It was the government's intention to increase the amount of public resources committed to education to about 4 per cent of the GDP by 2007–8 which would bring the expenditure at par with that of most other developing countries.

However, the experience with the World Bank funded and supervised Social Action Programme clearly indicated that a mere increase in the availability of resources would not address the problem. What was required was a multi-pronged approach in which increased resource commitment was one of the several policy initiatives. For Pakistan to succeed this time around, it would have to be imaginative and comprehensive in the strategy it adopted. There were at least ten elements of this approach which could be added to the six enumerated above.

First, the government must develop a core curriculum that must be taught in all schools up to the twelfth grade. Along with the prescription of such a core syllabus, the government should also create a body to oversee the textbooks used for instruction. There should be no restriction on the submission of books that could be used as authorized texts, and there should be a fair amount of choice available to schools. They should be able to pick from an approved list. The books selected must carry the 'good-housekeeping seal of approval' of the authority created for this purpose. The members of the authority should be selected by an autonomous body such as the Higher Education Commission whose members were nominated by the government but should be approved by the national assembly.

Second, no institution should be allowed to take in students unless it was registered with the Higher Education Commission. The Commission should issue certificates of registration to the institutions, which should indicate what kind of curriculum was being taught in addition to the core syllabus. Overtime the Commission should develop the expertise to grade schools according to their quality. A scale of the type used by credit rating agencies for assessing the performance of business and financial corporations could be used by the Commission as a way of informing the parents about the type and quality of education on offer.

Third, either the Higher Education Commission or a similar body should issue certificates to qualified teachers. No school, no matter what kind of curriculum it taught, should be allowed to hire teachers unless they were appropriately certified by the authority. The certificate should indicate which subject(s) the teacher had the competence to teach.

Fourth, in order to further encourage the participation of the private sector while lessening the burden of the public sector, the state should encourage the establishment of Private Education Foundations that should be run on a non-profit basis and should raise funds that would qualify for tax exemption. These Foundations should also be encouraged to register abroad so that they can receive contributions from the members of the Pakistani diasporas in the United States, Britain and the Middle East.[34] The government should offer for sale to the Foundations the institutions it was managing at all levels. This would be a form of privatization with the intent to encourage not only educational entrepreneurs to enter the field, but also to involve the people who were interested in improving the quality of education in the country.

Fifth, the government must reform the management of the educational system. One way of doing this is to decentralize the system's financing and supervision to the local level. The devolution of authority permitted by the reform of the local government structure creats an opportunity for the involvement of local communities in educational management. The development of the local government system as envisaged by the administration of President Pervez Musharraf was being challenged by some vested interests including the members of the National and Provincial legislatures who feared erosion of their own power as more authority flowed to the local level. The old bureaucracy that had exercised enormous power under the old structure was also reluctant to loosen its grip. This resistance needed to be overcome.

Sixth, parent-teacher-administrator associations should be created that manage funds and allocate them to the areas in which serious deficiencies exist. These associations should also have the authority to assess the performance of the teachers and administrators based on the quality of education given. Parental involvement in education, even when the parents themselves are not literate or poorly educated has yielded very positive results in several countries of Central and South America. There were lessons to be learnt from those experiences.

Seventh, the government should attempt to level the playing field by making it possible for children of less well-to-do households to gain admission into privately-managed schools. The government could initiate a programme of grants and loans that should be administered by the commercial banks. Such an approach was tried successfully in several countries, most notably Mexico. Letting the banks manage these programmes would save them from being corrupted.

Eighth, to address the serious problem of youth unemployment while the population was growing rapidly and in a society that was becoming increasingly susceptible to accepting destructive ideologies, it is important to focus a great deal of attention on skill development. This would require investment in vocational schools or adding technical skills to the school curriculum.

Ninth, in undertaking a school construction programme to improve physical facilities, special attention should be given to the needs of girls. Only then will the parents have the assurance that the schools to which they are sending their daughters could handle their special needs.

Tenth, and finally, a serious review of current expenditure on public sector education should be undertaken. It is well known that the state pays a large number of 'ghost teachers' who don't teach but turn up to collect their monthly pay cheques. It is also well known that the annual recurrent cost in well-managed private schools that were able to provide high quality education is one-half the recurrent cost of public schools. Rationalization of these expenditures would increase the productivity of resource use.

Pakistan's educational system requires an almost total overhaul. It can not be reformed simply by the deployment of additional resources. This was tried once before by the donor community under the auspices of the World Bank's Social Action Programme. That, as noted above, did not succeed. What is required now is a well thought out and comprehensive approach that deals with all facets of the system. It was right for the world to worry about the larger impact of Pakistan's dysfunctional educational system especially when it was demonstrated that poorly educated young men in a country as large as Pakistan pose a serious security threat to the rest of the world. Pakistan has a workforce of 45 million of which most are poorly educated and millions are in relatively low productivity jobs. It would be timely for the world's donor agencies to offer help to Pakistan to reform its system of education so that it could produce people who have the right kinds of skills to operate in the modern economy.

At the same time it is correct to focus on the reform of the *madrassas* but it would be imprudent to give too much attention to this part of the educational system in the country while neglecting the much larger state-run educational sector. Unfortunately, an impression has been created that religious schools in Pakistan has overwhelmed the educational system, particularly at the lower level. This is inaccurate since a report issued by the World Bank in 2005, based on a careful survey of schooling in several districts of the country showed that less than 1 per cent of the students enrolled in primary classes were attending *madrassas*, whereas 73 per cent were in public schools, and 26 per cent attended private institutions.

The part of the system that really needs attention and reform is the one managed by the public sector. This system looked after the education of a large proportion of the school-going age population. There were in all 155,000 schools in the public educational system. Most of them were poorly managed and imparted education of poor quality. Reforming the system, therefore, was of critical importance.

The problem of public education will not be solved by throwing more money into the system. It is true that the government in Pakistan spent relatively little on education compared to other developing countries—in the early 2000s, the country was committing only 2 per cent of its gross domestic product on education while the countries that had developed good educational systems spent at least twice as much. There were plans to increase the amount to 4 per cent of the GDP over the 2005–2010 period. Increasing financial support for education was one of the several solutions to the problem including money provided by donors. Western donors also made fresh commitments of money for the reform of the educational system. As already indicated, a total of $1.4 billion was to be spent over a period of seven years, the bulk of it by the World Bank and the Asian Development Bank. There were indications that more donor money would come in. By 2010, Pakistan was likely to be spending $2 billion on education, with 20 per cent provided by the donor community. All this was welcome news. What was also required was systemic reform. The government had to focus on all aspects of the system including the poor state of physical infrastructure, the poor quality of teachers, the poor quality of textbooks and a curriculum that needed to be reformed. Special attention would also need to be given to educate girls in all parts of the country.

The private sector has an important role to play in reforming the educational system. This system already had 45,000 institutions and, contrary to the general impression, thousands of them were in the rural areas providing education to the children of poor families.

A concerted effort is required at improving the standard of higher education and its reach. The Higher Education Commission, established in 2003, was working in these areas. It needs the continuing support of the government.

And those at the frontline at the effort to reform education need to focus on the areas in addition to science and technology. Attention needs to be given to the teaching of social science and developing capacity to teach and research in the relatively new discipline of public policy.

Pakistanis, both policymakers based in Islamabad and the public at large, have been slow to recognize that the country's large and increasingly young population is mostly illiterate and singularly ill-equipped to participate in the economic life of the country. It does not even have the wherewithal to participate in the process of 'outsourcing' that brought economic modernization and social improvement to many parts of India. The economic and social revolution that India was witnessing could have also occurred in Pakistan but for a number of unfortunate developments discussed above, that did not happen.

NOTES

1. In 1991, Mahbub ul Haq left Pakistan for the second time—he had earlier left in 1969 to join the World Bank—to lead an effort launched by the UNDP to analyse the link between human development on the one side and economic growth and poverty alleviation on the other. While undertaking this task, he collaborated with a number of other economists including Amartya Sen, a winner of the Nobel Prize, to develop the human development index (HDI).

2. This section is based on an article published by me in *Dawn* under the title of 'Saving education sector' on 15 January 2002 and 'A quiet revolution' published 18 November 2003.

3. See Chapter 1 for the discussion about the sustainability of the rate of growth experienced in 2003–6 over the medium term.

4. Salman Shah, 'Challenges in the Education Sector in Pakistan', in Robert M. Hathaway (ed.), *Education Reform in Pakistan: Building for the Future*, Woodrow Wilson International Center for Scholars, Washington, DC, 2006.

5. The movement became a political party in the 1990s and, in order to broaden its electoral appeal, changed its name to the Muttahida Qaumi Movement. In this way it was able to keep the same acronym, the MQM, by which it had come to be known.

6. Joe Stephens and David Ottoway, 'The ABCs of Jihad in Afghanistan: Violent Soviet Era Textbooks Complicate Afghan Education Efforts', *The Washington Post*, 23 March 2002, p. A1.

7. Tariq Rahman, *Denizens of Alien Worlds: A Study of Education, Inequality, and Polarization in Pakistan*, Karachi: Oxford University Press, 2004.

8. International Crisis Group, *Pakistan: Madrassas, Extremism and the Military*, Islamabad, 2004.

9. Tahir Andrabi, Jishnu Das, Asim Ijaz Khawaja and Tristan Zajon, *Religious School Enrollment in Pakistan: A look at the Data*, World Bank Policy Research Working Paper Series, No. 3521, Washington, DC, 2005.

10. Ishrat Husain, 'Education, employment and economic development in Pakistan,' in Robert H. Hathaway (ed.), *Education Reform in Pakistan: Building for the Future*, Woodrow Wilson International Center for Scholars, Washington, DC, 2005.

11. This section draws upon an article by me that appeared in *Dawn* under the title of 'Education in the Muslim world' on 25 November 2003.

12. The next four pages of the text are drawn upon the material in my article published in *Dawn* under the title of 'Education, key to progress' on 2 December 2003.

13. Chaudhry Pervez Ilahi, of the Pakistan Muslim League (Q) was the chief minister. See Michelle Riboud, 'Education in Pakistan and the World Bank's Programme' in Robert Hathaway (editor), *Education Reform in Pakistan:*

Building for the Future, Washington DC, Woodrow Wilson International Center for Scholars, 2006, p. 140.

14. Ibid., p. 141.
15. The World Bank, *Constructing Knowledge Societies: New Challenges for Tertiary Education*, Washington DC, 2004, p. 35.
16. The World Bank, *World Development Report 1998/1999*, New York: Oxford University Press, 1999.
17. Erik Brynjolfsson and Lorin Hitt, 'Beyond the Productivity Paradox', Communications of the ACM, Vol. 41, No. 8, pp. 49–55.
18. This section is based on two articles by me published in *Dawn* under the titles 'Role of tertiary education' on 9 December 2003 and 'Higher Education: A new beginning' on 8 May 2006.
19. Paul Krugman, *The Great Unraveling: Losing our Way in the New Century*, New York: W.W. Norton, 2004.
20. Stephen Philip Cohen, *The Idea of Pakistan*, New York: Oxford University Press, 2004, p. 247.
21. Fareed Zakaria, 'Al Qaeda Central,' *Newsweek*, 30 March 2006.
22. Grace Clark, 'Reform in Higher Education in Pakistan' in Robert M. Hathaway (ed.), *Education Reform in Pakistan: Building for the Future*, Washington DC, Woodrow Wilson International Center for Scholars, 2006, p. 56.
23. In a conversation in March 2006 Professor Ataur Rahman, Chairman of the Commission, told me of the way the idea of doing a report on higher education took shape. Professor Rahman was then minister-in-charge of information technology. While waiting for the prime minister to arrive to chair a cabinet meeting, he took the time to talk to the fellow ministers about the importance of higher education, how far Pakistan had fallen behind in this area, and what could be done to move the country forward. Impressed by what the professor said, the ministers took the decision to commission him to prepare a report on the state of higher education in Pakistan.
24. Government of Pakistan, Higher Education Commission, *Medium Term Development Framework, 2005–10*, Islamabad.
25. Ibid., p. 45.
26. The next three pages draw upon the material in my article titled 'Innovation and development' published in *Dawn* on 6 January 2004.
27. There were good reasons for this perception. On 7 July 2005 four suicide bombers bombed trains and a bus in London's transport system. Fifty-four persons, including the four bombers, were killed in this incident. Three of the four terrorists were young men of Pakistani origin and two of them had visited Pakistan while they were planning these attacks. A year later, on 10 August 2006, the British authorities foiled an alleged plot to bomb a number of American airliners while flying from London to various destinations in the United States. Two dozen persons were arrested, most of them young men of Pakistani origin.

28. David Wighton, 'Offshoring: Movement of tasks overseas jumps up skills chain relentlessly,' *Financial Times*. 'The World: 2006' survey, 25 January 2006, p. 4.

29. Quoted in David Wighton, op. cit.

30. Ibid.

31. Ibid.

32. *The Washington Post*, 'The war in Pakistan', 25 January 2006, p. A18.

33. The next four pages are based on my article published in *Dawn* under the title 'Educating the Masses' on 26 April 2005.

34. See Chapter 5 for a discussion of the role various diasporas are playing in promoting the development of education in Pakistan.

5

Agriculture and Irrigation: The Other Resource

Giving prominence to agriculture would help turn Pakistan's two important endowments—a large population and a potentially rich agricultural sector—into impressive economic assets. This would happen by recognizing that an intelligent use of a well-trained and educated workforce could increase enormously the productivity of agriculture. Policymakers and planners don't often recognize that they could use the country's rich agricultural base to build the structure of a modern economy. Pakistan's agriculture has enormous potential, not only because of the fertility of the soil but also because the land the country's diligent farmers cultivate is irrigated by one of the world's great river systems—the Indus and its tributaries. While I dealt with the subject of education and human development in the previous chapter, I will concern myself with the sector of agriculture in this chapter.

The subject is vast and full justice cannot be done in the space available in one chapter. I will, therefore, discuss some aspects of it that need to be emphasized as areas of public policymaking. That, after all, is the reason for this book. The chapter is divided into four parts. In Section 1, I will provide a brief overview of the sector of agriculture, how it developed over time and how its position in the economy got reduced over time. In Section 2, I will analyze the importance of recommitting the public sector to the maintenance and further development of the system of irrigation in which large investments were made by the British during the colonial period but which was largely ignored by most administrations in Pakistan's history. There is a long discussion in this section on the controversy regarding the building of the Kalabagh dam on the Indus river, a subject of considerable interest for the development of the irrigation system. In Section 3, I will offer some ideas on why and how Pakistan should and could move away from a land-extensive form of agriculture in which emphasis is on the production of grain crops, to the production of high value-added crops. There are several niches available which the country could exploit for increasing value-added crops from agriculture, increasing the incomes of poor farmers, and diversifying and increasing exports. In Section 4, I will deal with the important subject of the distribution of land and why greater equality in land ownership will not only improve the distribution of incomes in the countryside but will also lay the foundation for the development of a durable and representative political system. The chapter ends with a brief conclusion.

1. Agriculture: A Brief Overview

As with so many other features and characteristics of the Pakistani economy the sector of agriculture was also heavily influenced by the colonial period, the way the British administered their Indian territory. They relied on the landowners for a significant share of government revenues and the landowners, in turn, squeezed everything possible from those who actually tilled the soil. Even when the state made investments in developing the land, as it did in the provinces of Punjab and Sindh, by tapping the waters of the Indus River system for irrigation, the tax system ensured that the beneficiaries paid for the money spent. It was not a system that encouraged investment by the owners and cultivators in the land that was the major source of their income. The consequence was that both land and labour productivity remained low, and there was much poverty in the countryside.

As I will note in a moment, agriculture was by far the most important sector of the economy when Pakistan gained independence. It could have been developed more and could have become the driving force in the economy had India not moved against Pakistan in 1949. In that year Delhi launched an all-out trade war against Pakistan; the immediate reason was Pakistan's decision not to go along with other members of the Sterling Area, including India, and devalue its currency with respect to the United States dollar. Saying that 'India will not pay 144 of its rupees for Pakistan's hundred rupees',[1] Delhi stopped all trade with Pakistan. The real reason was more insidious. It was a part of the Indian plan to economically cripple Pakistan and force it back into the arms of India. There was a belief in New Delhi to which Jawaharlal Nehru, the first prime minister of India, and most certainly Sardar Vallabhbhai Patel, his powerful home minister, fully subscribed. The Indian strategy in those early years was to apply such an economic squeeze to Pakistan that it would come back into the Indian fold. The Pakistani leadership responded by putting all its energies and the modest resources at the disposal of the government for developing the new country's industrial sector. Pakistan survived the challenge but in the process reduced the importance of agriculture for the economy.

As a result of the very significant changes in Pakistan's economy since the country's birth in 1947, agriculture lost its pre-eminent position. Its share in the national output was much larger in 1947, the year Pakistan was born. Since then its contribution declined as other sectors of the economy grew in size. In 1947, agriculture accounted for 53 per cent of the Gross Domestic Product; by 2005, the last year for which data are available, its share had declined to less than 23 per cent. This notwithstanding, as a result of the two 'green revolutions'—one in the late 1960s and early 1970s, the other in the late 1980s and early 1990s—the agricultural sector progressed from a state of subsistence, to that of commercialization. This transformation had a profound impact on reducing the incidence of rural poverty.

In the late 1940s—the years immediately following partition and the birth of Pakistan—less than one-fifth of Pakistan's total land area was cultivated. Sixty years later, in the early 2000s, this proportion had increased to more than one-quarter. During this period, over six million hectares of additional land was brought under cultivation, almost entirely because of an increase in irrigation, most of it by the sinking of tens of thousands of tubewells that tapped the large reservoirs of ground water. As discussed in Section 2 below, the state invested relatively little in expanding surface irrigation. In the late 1940s, 62 per cent of the cultivated land was classified as irrigated; in the early 2000s, the proportion had increased to 76 per cent.

The output of all major crops increased by significant amounts in the period since independence. The largest percentage of increase occurred for cotton, and the least for wheat. These increases were the result of both additional land devoted to these crops, as well as increase in productivity. The sharp growth in the output of Pakistan's main crops helped to alleviate rural poverty, particularly in the 1960s, the period during which Mohammad Ayub Khan was president. In 1960–1970, for instance, food-grain output increased at the yearly rate of 5 per cent, and per capita food availability increased at the rate of 2.3 per cent a year. The most notable achievement during this period was the successful launch of what is generally referred to as the 'green revolution.' In some of my earlier works, I have identified two green revolutions, one during the period of Ayub Khan that led to quantum increases in the output of two food-grain crops, wheat and rice, and the other during the presidency of General Ziaul Haq that led to a sharp increase in cotton, the country's main cash crop and the base of its industrial sector.[2] Public policy led to the first green revolution. The second was the result of private initiative with some support from the state.

There was a combination of public policies that made the first green revolution possible. The most notable among these was the decision by the government to import new high-yielding seed varieties developed under the auspices of internationally funded research institutions in Mexico (for wheat) and the Philippines (for rice). The government imported the seeds and its extension agents distributed them to the farmers for trial and eventual use. The use of the seeds spread quickly. The system of 'basic democracies' launched by Ayub Khan helped in spreading the new technology.

There was a dramatic change in the situation in the 1970s, however, the period dominated by the socialist government of Zulfikar Ali Bhutto. In 1970–79, food-grain output increased by 3 per cent a year, but per capita food availability grew by only 0.32 per cent. During the Ayub period, therefore, Pakistan nearly achieved food self-sufficiency. During the 1970s, on the other hand, the country once again became dependent on large amounts of food imports.

In the late 1980s, Pakistan witnessed the 'second green revolution,' which saw an enormous increase in both the productivity and output of cotton, the mainstay of the country's economy. The agricultural sector came under stress in the 1990s, however. Pressure on the national budget reduced public-sector expenditure on the maintenance of the vast irrigation network, with the result that the availability of water per unit of irrigated land declined. The agricultural sector also had to deal with pest attacks, in particular on cotton. Consequently, in the 1990s, agricultural output failed to keep pace with growth in population and increase in domestic demand.

In 2004, the government of President Pervez Musharraf initiated an ambitious programme aimed at rehabilitating the vast irrigation system. The aim was not only to make the country once again self-sufficient in food, but also, to become a major exporter of agricultural products. If the programme is implemented successfully it could change the structure of this important sector of the economy.

2. Irrigation[3]

Thanks in part to the ingenuity of the engineers who developed the irrigation system from the time of the Mughals, the British and the early days of Pakistan, the country now has the largest contiguous irrigated area in the world. Water in the system is available throughout the year and in sufficient quantities to grow high value crops. Pakistan's irrigated area is much larger than that of the Colorado and California systems and the system in the Indian states of Punjab, Haryana and Rajasthan. Unfortunately, a combination of government policy and poor base of knowledge of the millions of farmers who till the soil in this system, agricultural productivity has remained low. The government could have laid down the policy framework to guide the farming community towards producing higher productivity crops. It could have set up institutes of agricultural research and technology to help the farmers move towards new patterns of production. It could have helped to create a system of finance to provide credit and management know-how to the farming community. It could have created an infrastructure to move agricultural surplus from the farmers to the market place. And it could have developed markets abroad for the country's surplus agricultural products. None of this was done systematically. But all is not lost and the extraordinary potential of the agricultural sector can still be realized.

The government of Pervez Musharraf—in fact, the president himself—has recognized that Pakistan has a great deal to do to preserve and further develop its large water resource. This will need not only the construction of new reservoirs—something that the president has repeatedly emphasized in his many public pronouncements as a high priority for his government—but also to improve the productivity of the large system that already exists. It has been known for many years that a significant amount of water is wasted because of the poorly aligned and porous primary, secondary, and tertiary canals that carry water from the four major rivers that flow through the country—the Indus, the Jhelum, the Chenab and the Ravi—to the millions of acres of land still thirsty for water.

'Water is precious, use it wisely' says a notice placed in the bathroom of a five-star hotel in Karachi.[4] There could not be a sounder piece of advice but it should be given not only to the guests at five-star hotels but to the entire citizenry of Pakistan. Pakistan is rapidly moving to a situation when it will begin to be ranked among the countries that have severe shortages of fresh water. Wise use of this precious resource is one way of dealing with this crisis.

There are three basic uses of water—agriculture, industry and human consumption. Using water wisely in these three uses is one way of saving the country from economic and social disaster. The greatest waste took place in agriculture where vast amounts of water were lost to evaporation and seepage or used in such water-intensive crops as sugar cane. Wouldn't it be more prudent to invest the government's scarce resources in improving the efficiency of water use in agriculture rather than commit them to the construction of large dams such as the one at Kalabagh? This was a fair question—one that was repeatedly asked by those who opposed the construction of the Kalabagh dam—but it should be remembered that improving the efficiency of water use and increasing its supply were not mutually exclusive solutions to the coming crisis. They should be done simultaneously.

I recall a conversation with the late S.S. Kirmani, the father of the Indus Basin Replacement Works, on how best to manage the waters of the Indus River. It was his remarkable engineering vision that gave shape to the replacement works. It was the persistence and stubbornness of Ghulam Ishaq Khan, who was then the chairman of WAPDA, and Kirmani, that finally led to the agreement of the donor community to finance the construction of the Tarbela dam on the Indus. After serving as WAPDA's chief engineer, Kirmani went to the World Bank and became director of projects in East Asia. He was of the view that by simply lining the canals and tens of thousands of distribution channels, and straightening them, and levelling the fields that received water from the irrigation system and changing the cropping pattern, Pakistan could double the availability of water for irrigation. The expenditure needed for such a programme would be considerably less than that to constantly ensure an increase in the supply of water by building additional storage capacity on the main rivers. But such a programme could only be completed over a long period of time. Its success would depend on the education and skill development of the farming community, large-scale commercializing of agriculture, and the removal of implicit and explicit government subsidies on inputs such as water and power and privatization of all commercial operations. Meanwhile water shortage will continue to become more serious. There was, therefore, the need for Islamabad to focus immediately on the supply side and to undertake the construction of large dams.

There were several reasons why the policymakers in Islamabad needed to worry about the developing shortage of water. The most significant of these related to the availability of food supply for a population that was already being fed by imports. According to the government's water sector investment planning study, unless this situation is addressed, the country will face a deficit of 12 million tons in grain output in 2013. In other words, having once become the granary for all of British India, within a matter of a few years Pakistan will become one of the largest food deficit countries in the world. In today's prices, it will have to spend $4 billion to $5 billion a year to save its population from starvation.

The immediate response to this developing crisis was to increase the supply of water by tapping what was available in the impressive system of rivers that ran through the country. That was where the construction of large dams such as the one at Kalabagh entered the picture. The proposed dam at Kalabagh was a critical component of the strategy to help Pakistan face a catastrophic shortage of water. But politics has been an obstacle in constructing the Kalabagh dam. I was reminded by a member of an audience to which I spoke in Karachi in February 2006 that I should not underestimate the sentiment in Sindh against the construction of the dam. All the more reason why we should look at some of the arguments that have been advanced against Kalabagh as well as those put forward in its favour.

The dam site is located 210 km downstream of Tarbela and 26 km upstream of Jinnah Barrage on the Indus. When completed, the rock-fill dam will rise to a height of 260 feet and will be 4,375 feet long. It will create a reservoir with a usable storage capacity of 6.1 million acre feet (MAF). This will almost fully compensate the anticipated losses at Chashma, Mangla and Tarbela on account of silting and bring back the amount of water available for use to the point reached in 2004. The dam will have spillways on either side.

On the right it will have two spillways to discharge flood waters with the capacity of two million cusecs. On the left side, a spillway will feed water to a power station that will generate 3,600 MW of electricity. The project, by adding significantly to the contribution of power from hydro sources, will bring about a significant saving in foreign exchange. Since hydro power is much cheaper than thermal power, it will also reduce the price charged to the consumers.

The entire project was estimated to cost $6.1 billion and would take six years to construct. The project was estimated to yield benefits amounting to $1 billion a year—it would pay for the cost of constructing it in six years. However, both the estimates of cost and benefits were outdated by the time the administration of President Musharraf began to seriously contemplate including the dam in its development programme. The dam would probably cost $8 billion in 2006 prices but its benefit, particularly when we factor in the changes that need to be made in the pattern of cropping, will be much higher than $1 billion, perhaps twice as high.

Kalabagh became controversial from the time it was proposed; the opposition to it was based on a number of apprehensions, some of which changed over time. Initially, the most serious objection to the dam was on the basis of the number of people who were likely to be displaced by the creation of the large reservoir. There was opposition to the project in the provinces of NWFP and Sindh. Most of the affected population was in the NWFP; there was apprehension that the lake would almost totally submerge the important city of Nowshera. However, two reports prepared by experts, one written by a Chinese expert and the other by an American, produced models to show that the lake would end about 16 km downstream of Nowshera. The city would not be inundated even by the recurrence of the record flood of August 1929. The two experts concluded that the city would not be affected even after the bed of the lake was raised by sedimentation over a period of 100 years.

Another objection to the dam was that even if Nowshera was not submerged, the sheer size of the lake—about 420 sq km—

would still displace a large number of people. My estimate is that the number of people who will have to move if the dam's construction were to start in 2007 would be about 150,000. This was not a small number but there was now enough experience from around the world to draw up a resettlement plan that would leave the displaced people economically and socially better off compared to their present situation. The Chinese, for instance, have done a commendable job of caring for the displaced population from large dams. The Three Gorges dam on the Yangtze alone displaced 1.1 million people, more than seven times the number likely to be affected by the Kalabagh dam and the Kalabagh lake. WAPDA's plans for resettlement included housing for the displaced population in new towns and villages—27 in number—to be located along the periphery of the lake. Some $800 million was allocated for resettlement works which, from the perspective of international standards, was a generous amount. It was equivalent to $550 per head of the population, an amount sufficiently large to provide adequate compensation.

Sindh's opposition to the project was based on the flow in the Indus expected after the completion of the project. Once again, expert opinion regarded these fears as largely unfounded. After the completion of Tarbela, some 35 MAF of water flowed into the sea. The Kalabagh reservoir with a total capacity of 6.1 MAF would still leave a supply of 29 MAF in the river. However, it should be recognized that dams don't consume water they only store it during periods of abundance. In fact, by regulating the flow they can actually increase the supply during dry seasons. This was amply demonstrated by the operation of the Tarbela dam. According to WAPDA, the total canal withdrawals from the Indus in 1960–67 were 35.6 MAF. These increased to 44.2 MAF after 1976, following the completion of Mangla and Tarbela. The same was likely to result from the construction of the Kalabagh dam. A computer model estimated that canal withdrawals in Sindh would increase by about 2.25 MAF after the construction of the dam, which would allow for its greater regulation.

Then there was the fear that Kalabagh, by holding back water, would affect the *sailaba* crops, watered by floods that occur practically every year along the wide banks of the Indus. There were about 660,000 acres of land under this type of cultivation but water availability remained uncertain and farmers normally augmented the supply by tube wells installed in the area. By regulating the flow in the river, Kalabagh would help this class of farmers.

There was also some apprehension that by reducing the flow in the river in the initial phase of the project when the reservoir was being filled, the construction of Kalabagh would result in a backflow of sea water into the Indus estuary. Even in this case, experts believed that the intrusion of water from the sea had already reached its maximum level and was not likely to increase further following the construction of the dam.

On the positive side, the additional storage that would become available after the construction of Kalabagh would make it possible to implement the Water Apportionment Accord of 1991 that assumed availability to be maintained rather than depleted through the anticipated silting of the Mangla and Tarbela reservoirs. Without Kalabagh, inter-provincial tensions on water distribution would be exacerbated, since the amount of water to be distributed would be significantly reduced.

Rather than allow a great deal of political emotion to seep into the debate on the construction of the dam at Kalabagh, President Musharraf needed to move forward with firmness, indicating that he had consulted, listened, reflected and decided to proceed in the larger interest of the nation. It was only with this approach and attitude that the administrations that oversaw the previous major developments of the water of the Indus river were able to succeed. There was a lesson to be learned from that experience.

President Pervez Musharraf was unable to sell the Kalabagh dam project to Pakistan's smaller provinces. While not giving up the construction of the project altogether, the dam was included in a programme of construction that would involve the building of several reservoirs on the Indus and some of its tributaries over a period of 10 to 12 years. In his address to the nation in January

2006, the president said that there was an absence of consensus among the provinces on the need for a large dam on the Indus at Kalabagh. Given that, he settled for the immediate construction of a dam on the Indus upstream of Kalabagh at Bhasha.

This must have been a painful decision to make for the general. For several years since assuming power, he had said that the building of the Kalabagh dam and other major reservoirs on the Indus and its tributaries would be one of his most important legacies. He also emphasized on several occasions that the failure to undertake these important works would bring about a crisis in Pakistan. He was right on both scores. Had he succeeded in getting work on Kalabagh started, his contribution to the economic and social development of Pakistan would have matched that of President Ayub Khan, one of his military predecessors.

In the 1960s, the then military president did not feel the need for broad political consensus to undertake the construction of the mega-projects that were included in the massive and ambitious Indus Basin Replacement works. All that was required was competent economic analysis of the projects by the powerful Planning Commission. President Ayub was convinced that by working with the technocrats he could better determine what was good for the society in the long run rather than leave those decisions to political forces. He believed that the few people that dominated the political arena were unable to think beyond their immediate and narrow interests. The Kalabagh dam issue raised the question once again whether the political structure in Pakistan was equipped to initiate major development works whose implementation could be blocked by vested interests that pursued short-term and narrow objectives.

As to the precarious situation Pakistan faced in 2006, it should be mentioned that the country in the early 2000s stood at the edge of an economic abyss. To understand why that was the case, it would be useful to go back a little to the history of irrigation development in the Indus valley and indicate how it had contributed to the development of the areas that were now part of Pakistan.

And why, by neglecting further development of the water system, Pakistan was inching towards an economic disaster.

Serious work on taming the Indus and its many tributaries began after the arrival of the British in the subcontinent. Before the advent of the British Raj in the nineteenth century, India's rulers had little knowledge of water management. The Afghan rulers of India and their successors, the Mughals, came from the highlands of Central Asia. There were few large rivers in those areas and agriculture that was practiced there depended either on rainfall or on snow melt. The economy relied much less on settled agriculture than on horticulture and animal husbandry. Irrigation was used on a very limited scale, mostly for bringing water to the gardens enjoyed by the rich.

The British came to India with much greater knowledge of water management, most of it gathered from some of the colonies they had built around the globe. The first major overseas achievements for the British were in Canada. They improved the St. Lawrence/ Great Lakes seaway system in that country. According to historian David Fieldhouse who has chronicled the achievements of the British empire, 'the British could claim to have been among the great improvers of rivers and builders of canals'.[5]

This expertise notwithstanding, it was unlikely that the British would have invested in the development of the Indus river system had they not begun to worry about the political consequences of the famines that began to take a heavy human toll in the eastern provinces of their Indian empire in the eighteenth and nineteenth centuries. Even historian Niall Ferguson, who has gone against the tide of historical thinking according to which colonization of India did more harm than good is prepared to admit that the British rule initially resulted in several human catastrophes, in particular recurrent famines. According to him, there was a huge famine in Bengal in 1780 which killed as many as a third of the population of the province. 'Another famine in 1783–84 killed more than a fifth of the population of the Indian plains; this was followed by severe scarcities in 1791, 1801, and 1805'.[6] As hundreds of thousands of people died of hunger in Bengal, Bihar, Orissa and eastern UP, the British administration began to worry about the political consequences of these tragedies. A number of Royal Famine Commissions, appointed by London, investigated the problem and reached the conclusion that the government had to invest in the relatively less populated areas of the colony to generate food grain surpluses. Once produced, these surpluses could be transported by road and rail to the food deficit provinces.

Punjab and Sindh were the obvious choice for generating exportable surpluses. The two provinces had large tracts of potentially fertile virgin land if water could be brought to them. Although there was little rainfall in these areas and most of it came in a few weeks during the summer monsoons, water was available in great abundance in the Indus and its many tributaries. The solution to the famine problem was to develop surface irrigation in these two provinces by constructing barrages and canals throughout the Indus river system. The strategy worked and by the end of the nineteenth century, fifty years after the British had consolidated their hold over Punjab and Sindh, more than 100,000 tons of wheat and rice were being transported to British India's eastern provinces. Not only had the British built a large network of canals and secondary channels that brought water to a million hectares of new land, they had also built the North Western Railways (NWR) that carried the surplus of food grains to Bengal and Bihar.

The British administration also improved the port of Karachi from where ships could carry wheat and rice to Calcutta. They improved the famed Grand Trunk Road on which trucks could ply for transporting food. They built a string of market towns which received food grain produced by the farmers who were awarded land in the recently colonized areas. All this investment and public sector attention bore fruit. There was only one major famine after these investments were made, and that was in 1943 in Bengal. As the economist Amartya Sen famously argued in the book that won him the Nobel Prize, this famine was not caused by food shortages but by the collapse of incomes in the rural areas. Food was available but people did not have the money to purchase it.[7]

Economic historians have argued that while the British contributed enormously to the economic development of the areas that now make up Pakistan, they could have done much more. They invested only the amounts that were needed to produce the required surplus. Why did the British hold back when they had the technology and there was a lot of water available in the Indus river system? There are essentially three answers to this interesting question among the many.

First, the British were not prepared to spend the money that would have been required to realize the full potential of the rivers. Their primary objective was security not economic development. Apart from a short period in the 1850s and 1860s when private companies were allowed to build canals, this kind of investment was considered to be the responsibility of the state. But the British government in India was not allowed to obtain loans for canal building in London's capital market. London was not prepared to accumulate debt which it would have had to pay to finance development works in India. The money needed had to come out of the limited budget of the public works department.

The second problem was limited knowledge about the construction and management of complex irrigation works. Although, as indicated, the British had developed some expertise in the area, particularly from their work in Canada, they did not feel comfortable with the needed technical know-how. According to one assessment by the historian D.K. Fieldhouse,

> most of those who surveyed and planned the canals, dams, and bridges were army officers with little or no specialized training, though some travelled extensively to learn how Italians and others tackled specific problems. But although many expensive mistakes were made, it has been said that the fundamentals of hydraulic science and practices of irrigation engineering came out of the great irrigation works of India itself.[8]

The third constraint was more important than the two already mentioned. Large irrigation works needed large amounts of earth to be moved, and all that had to be done by hand and draught animals. Heavy earthmoving machinery that became ubiquitous in later years and was to play such an important role in constructing dams and link canals under the Indus Basin Replacement Works carried out in the 1960s, had not yet been invented. After the conquest of the Punjab in 1849, work on the Upper Bari Doab Canal was done mostly by former soldiers from the vanquished Sikh army. Some of those who worked on the canal earned freedom once the job was done; a few were given plots of irrigated land to cultivate. To quote from Fieldhouse again,

> thus the Indian canal system could technically have been built at almost any period of known history. What the British added was above all the power of a unified and authoritarian state, which had acted because it saw the danger of drought and famine to its rule. Limited though it might be, irrigation in India was one of the greatest achievements of the British empire.[9]

For a decade and a half after gaining independence, Pakistan undertook the construction of only one major irrigation work, a canal that flows south of Lahore and served to blunt the Indian attack on the city on 6 September 1965. Successive governments that held office in the period before the arrival of the first military regime were either too preoccupied with other expensive projects such as the settlement of eight million refugees who had arrived from India in 1947, or did not have enough funds to commit to irrigation. It was only under Ayub Khan that the budgetary constraints were eased by the arrival of large amounts of American aid.

From about 1960 to 1976, water availability for canal withdrawals increased by an impressive 58 per cent, from 67 to 106 MAF. The increase occurred because of the construction of a barrage at Chashma and dams at Mangla and Tarbela. These works were completed in 1976. Since then—a period of thirty years—no major water storage project was undertaken while the gross storage capacity at the Chashma, Mangla and Tarbela reservoirs was depleted by 4.9 MAF by 2004. This happened because of the deposit of silt in the beds of the reservoirs, a process that will continue. In one study WAPDA estimated that by 2013, the three reservoirs will lose a storage capacity of 6.4 MAF.

This decline in the availability of water will occur while the country's population will continue to increase. In the early 2000s, Pakistan was heading towards a serious shortage of water. In 1951, per capita surface water availability for irrigation was estimated at 5,650 cubic meters; this declined sharply to only 1,350 cubic meters per head in 2002. The minimum amount that should be available is 1,000 cubic meters. Pakistan was clearly heading towards becoming what experts describe as a 'water short country.' By 2012, Pakistan will have reached the stage of 'acute water shortage.' One immediate consequence of this will be on the availability of food for an increasingly large population. However, there was a solution to the problem.

But tapping the water that flows to the sea in the Indus River was not the only option available for increasing agricultural productive. The other was a programme aimed at improving the efficiency of the system of irrigation. A large labour-intensive public works programme could be launched aimed at cleaning the tens of thousands of miles of irrigation channels that brought water to the land under cultivation. Labour intensive works could also be undertaken to line the canals with bricks and mortar in the sections where leakages occurred. Surplus rural labour could also be used to build farm-to-market roads.

Such a programme could be entrusted to the local bodies established by the local government development programme adopted by the regime of General Pervez Musharraf. It could be financed jointly by the state and the farming communities that would benefit enormously from this type of investment. That way the burden on the national exchequer would be reduced.

With so much land irrigated by water that flows through an expensive system of canals, Pakistan should move away from the production of food grains that had become a strategic necessity during the British period towards the development of high value added agriculture. A 'niche based' approach would help to make the transition.

3. Tapping Agricultures' Potential: Development of Niche Markets

Unfortunately Pakistan, one of the world's most populous countries, has not taken advantage of the window of demographic opportunity that has opened up in recent years. While this subject was discussed in Chapter 4, I would like to revisit it in the context of discussing the development of the agriculture sector.

Pakistan's private sector should now begin to direct its attention towards the opportunities that are coming its way as a result of the massive restructuring of the global economy brought about, in part, by the fundamental demographic change that is afoot in most parts of the developed world. In that context I should mention that sometimes casual observations can help to point a way towards economic progress. Some years ago when I worked as the World Bank's Vice President of Operations in Latin America, I had the opportunity to get to know the region well. As a part of my job I paid visits to many countries from Mexico and Central America in the north and Argentina and Chile in the south. On one of these visits—to El Salvador in Central America—I met a group of entrepreneurs who had developed an extraordinarily dynamic industry based on meeting America's growing demand for seafood. This group of El Salvadorians had decided that there was considerable value to be added if prawns—a favourite seafood in America—were not exported in raw form. Profit margins would be considerably higher if prawns already cooked on skewers were dispatched directly to supermarkets and restaurants. This turned out to be an amazingly successful business plan. It was also labour intensive and provided well paid jobs to thousands of people. And it created a unique set of opportunities for the country's transport sector.

How could Pakistan get into this kind of business? One answer to this question is based on another personal observation. In the summer of 2004, my wife and I drove close to a thousand miles in northern England and Scotland. We were struck by the fact that even in small towns the only thing that was palpably foreign and ethnic were *balti ghosht* restaurants. Given the cost of labour in Britain and given the presence of a reasonably affluent expatriate community from Pakistan settled in that country and already engaged in various businesses, a new line of activity could be developed. It was not inconceivable to imagine that the fare served in these mostly 'take-out' ethnic restaurants could be prepared and flown from Pakistan. Admittedly, Pakistan was a long way from the United Kingdom. But distance has not stopped flower growers in Ecuador from supplying florists in Miami and points beyond.

Even with air freight included in the business plan, it would still be attractive for entrepreneurs in Pakistan and Britain to construct a supply chain starting with kitchens in Pakistan and ending either with the shelves in grocery stores in the towns and cities in Britain, or on the tables in Britain's ethnic restaurants. This is an example of one of the many niches Pakistani exporters could develop. There are significant changes in lifestyles in the post-industrial societies that are opening new but not easily recognized niches in the economies of the western world. These could be exploited by countries such as Pakistan.

That is why more and more opportunities are available for the countries that have the labour force prepared to do the kind of work shunned by the workers in the West. It is for this reason that I believe there is profit in building a supply chain originating in Pakistan's kitchens with their preparations carted by planes to consumers in the West. These supply chains could incorporate specially equipped trucks and airplanes to ferry the produce from Pakistan to various points of distribution in Britain and other countries. These distribution points could serve grocery stores and restaurants scattered around the country. This is exactly what the prawn exporters were doing in El Salvador to serve the lucrative American market.

This was just one example of the way one part of the Pakistani production system could successfully exploit adding value to an important part of the agricultural economy (livestock, fruits and vegetables) by using the talent available (chefs, meal planners, food-packers) to transform raw material into finished products (cooked meals) and transport them by the cargo planes of domestic airlines (not just PIA but also privately-owned carriers) for distribution to a chain of restaurants and take-out stores that have become such an important part of the post-modern British lifestyle.

There are several other examples where such a strategy based on niche development could bear fruit. Let me mention one other possibility. The abundant availability of raw material (cotton fabrics) and talent (fashion designers) in Pakistan could create a niche in America and Western Europe.

We can notice the impact oriental fashions are having on western consumption. Take a look at the display windows of such large stores as Harrods, Selfridges, Marks and Spencer, Macys and you would recognize instantly that South Asian designers are having a major impact on what the young in the West are now wearing. Pakistan now has a fledgling fashion industry in cities such as Karachi, Lahore and Islamabad. This could go international with some help from the government.

What is the government's role in getting such a 'niche-based' strategy to work? Building the kind of complex supply chains I have described above requires skilled people. The government could help by setting up specialized institutions to train people in food product marketing, clothing design and air transport of delicate cargo. It could provide tax incentives to invite venture capitalists to invest in these new industries. It could improve financial regulations to help the banking industry and capital markets to promote the development of a host of new enterprises serving new markets. It could encourage the airline industry to develop the capacity to deliver perishable products quickly and reliably from production centres in Pakistan to centres of consumption in America and Europe. What is required is a vision supported by a strategy to turn Pakistan's large and young population into skilled entrepreneurs catering to the rapidly changing global market place, using the extraordinary potential of its bountiful agricultural sector.

4. Issues Concerning Land

There is no issue that should receive greater analytical and public policy attention than that of land and there is no issue that has been more ignored in recent years by policymakers as well as policy-thinkers in Pakistan. The last time serious attention was given to the set of issues that come together under the subject of land ownership was under President Ayub Khan. A high-powered commission was then set up to guide the government in formulating its policy towards land ownership in the countryside. That urban land policy was also worth the government's attention did not then occur to the policymakers since it had not attained the importance it was to acquire in the early 2000s.

The issue of land has many facets: who owns it and how is ownership distributed; who cultivates it and how are the returns divided between those who till the land and those who own it; how productive is the land and what are the reasons if productivity is lower than the potential; is there a market in land and how does it operate; in what way does the distribution of land affect politics and economics; to what extent does the pattern of land ownership influence the incidence of poverty and income inequality etc. Each of these subjects—and many others related to land—can keep analysts occupied for years and each one of them should be the basis for serious government policy. And yet, since the days of Ayub Khan—and to some extent since Zulfikar Ali Bhutto showed some interest in this area—land has been ignored as a subject of policy discourse and public policymaking. One reason for this is the continuing power of the landed elite.

There was a seeming paradox about the way one powerful elite used its influence to develop Pakistan's economic and political systems. The landed aristocracy was the main obstacle in Pakistan's movement towards a broadly representative system of government. Even when elections were held on a regular basis, which was the case in the period from 1985 to 2002, the group's grip over the countryside was too tight to allow the people's voice to be heard in the corridors of power. The legislators elected by the people, no matter to which party they belonged, worked for their narrow interests rather than for the welfare of their constituents. This behaviour led to widespread corruption on the part of the people's elected governments and made it possible for the military to intervene periodically. The obvious conclusion to be drawn from this is that the space the military created for itself in the country's political and economic systems would not have become available had the landlords not exercised such a paralyzing hold over politics.

And yet, this hold over the political process notwithstanding, the powerful rural elite did not influence resource allocation by the public sector in favour of the sector of agriculture. Consequently agriculture stagnated while public funds and public policy favoured other sectors of the economy. This was the paradox in Pakistan's economic and political development. The power large landlords wielded in Pakistan hurt the country economically and politically. To understand why it happened we need to better understand the politics and economics of land use in Pakistan. While agriculture is the subject of this chapter, I will broaden the scope of the discussion of land to include urban areas.

This analysis must begin with a description of the pattern of landholding in the country, not only in the countryside but also in the towns and cities. Landownership in many countries—and Pakistan was not an exception—was highly unequal, substantially more so than the distribution of income or consumption. One way of measuring inequality was to use the Gini coefficient that ranged between 0 and 1. Zero implied perfect distribution of whatever was being measured, income or assets. An estimate of 1 meant that all the income went to or all the assets were owned by one individual. In the World Bank's *World Development Report 2005*, Gini coefficients for land distribution were provided for fifty-eight countries including Pakistan.[10] Among these countries Norway, with a coefficient of only 0.18, had the most equitable distribution of land among the countries for which this information was available. The worst distribution was for Venezuela with a coefficient of 0.88. Pakistan, with an estimated Gini of 0.57, was among the countries with relatively more uneven distribution.

While the Gini is high for land distribution, the coefficient was lower for income in Pakistan's case as well as in the case of almost all countries. This means that the distribution of land, the most important income-producing asset in an important sector of the economy, was considerably more skewed than the distribution of income. There was a good reason for this seeming discrepancy. Land did not always produce incomes commensurate with its market value. It was owned for reasons other than economics: there was attachment to land, it was owned since it provided insurance against bad times, and there were also speculative motives involved. A good example of the non-economic value placed on land was the way people reacted to the government's suggestion that the town of Balakot, destroyed by the earthquake of October 2005, needed to be moved to a place that did not sit on the geological fault lines that threatened more tremors, some probably as severe as the one that destroyed the town. According to one newspaper account, 'in Balakot, despite the potential dangers of its location, residents are vigorously protesting the [government's decision]. Many said they had survived one earthquake and would take their chances on another, while others vowed to hang on to the land of their forefathers, which remains precious to them even in its current degraded condition.[11]'

In most countries—in particular in countries in South Asia—a significant proportion of land is owned by the government, and the state tends to use it to reward its supporters. The Mughal emperors did it; the Sikh rulers of the Punjab did it; both civilian and military governments in Pakistan have done it. The dispensations of land by the British and the Sikhs created the system of *jagirs* that was abolished by the government of Ayub Khan in 1959 when it instituted its programme of land reforms. However, the government's continued ownership of large amounts of land, in particular in the rapidly expanding cities, was affecting the structure of the economy as well as the way it was developing.

Complicating the issue in Pakistan was the ownership of vast tracts of prime land by the military in the cantonment areas right in the heart of several major cities in the country. The British administration had appropriated these lands to build bases for its army in various parts of their Indian domain. Since the areas that now make up Pakistan were strategically more important for the British than several other parts of India, the proportion of the cantonment land in total state land was much larger in Pakistan. Significant acreage from this land was developed by the military under the aegis of the Defence Housing Authority that had little to do with providing housing to military personnel and more to do with providing senior ranks with additional compensation for their service. This introduced a serious distortion in the compensation system for one group of officials that needed to be addressed as a part of land policy.

There were strong equity and efficiency reasons for reducing inequalities in land distribution, both rural and urban. Why was it a good public policy to reduce the size of farms and reduce also inequality in the distribution of land? Why was it necessary to provide security of ownership to those who till the land but not own it?

I have already mentioned why it was important for political development to reduce the economic power of the landed aristocracy. There were also good economic reasons for this public policy. For most crops, under normal availability of mechanical services, production was unaffected by the size of the farms. It was, as economists would say, neutral to size. However, when management requirements were substantial—this was the case for labour intensive crops, erratic weather conditions, frequent pest incidence—family farms, as opposed to larger wage-labour farms, could be more efficient because of advantages in supervising labour. Since the conditions cited above prevailed in Pakistan it would be good public policy to aim to reduce landholding inequality and reduce the size of farms.

There was a considerable amount of evidence available from many parts of the globe that productivity was higher for the land owned by small and medium size operators. The gap in productivity of small and large farms within a country could be enormous: it was estimated at 5.6 times higher in the case of Brazil and, while not as high, to be 2.75 times greater in Pakistan. The estimates were made by two researchers, R. Albert Berry and William Cline, who worked for the International Labour Office's programme on employment. The research was done in 1979 but the results remained valid.[12] It was bad economics not to give land to those who used it more productively. The reason why that did not happen was that land provided more than income; it gave social status and political power.

Productivity was also known to increase when a programme of land reforms moved farmers from being share croppers to owners. Another set of researchers found that productivity was 30 per cent lower in sharecropped land compared to the same sized land cultivated by owners.[13] On the impact of security of property some other analysts found that a land reform that gave farmers the right to sell, transfer, or inherit their land use rights, also increased agricultural investment, particularly the planting of multi-year crops.

But simply taking land away from the rich and giving it to the poor won't necessarily produce the results cited above. The state must do much more. It must also improve the economic circumstances in which the poor farmers work. In a comparison of land transactions in Indian and Bangladeshi villages during 1960–80, Mead Cain, a researcher, found that poor farmers who had access to safety net programmes used the land market to augment their holdings and undertook productivity-enhancing investments that included irrigation, use of better seeds and better production technologies.[14] A programme of land reform that did not provide for some kind of insurance to the farmers will not yield the kinds of dividends mentioned above.

The conclusion to be drawn from the evidence cited above—and a great deal more evidence was available to support it—was that for Pakistan to realize the full potential of its well-endowed agricultural sector and to pave the way for the development of a representative political system, land reform should be high on the policymaker's agenda of structural reforms. What kinds of attempts were made in the past and why did they not produce significant economic and political returns? What should the government do to realize the full potential of the agricultural sector and also ensure that the disproportionate power wielded by the large landlords—disproportionate to the contribution they made to the economy—did not inhabit political development? These were important questions for the formulation of public policy with respect to the ownership and use of rural and urban land.

I have placed land policy at the heart of the structural reform agenda Islamabad must pursue in order to bring about economic, political and social changes that will be durable and last way into the future. Various aspects of land policy—how much of it was owned; how it was owned and who were the various categories of people associated with it; the relationship between owners and cultivators; the functioning of the land markets in both rural and urban areas; the recording of various kinds of land rights, not just ownership but also various tenancy and rental arrangements—are the central elements of land policy.

The traditional way of viewing land policy was in terms of the ownership of rural land, in particular land under cultivation. However, this was a limited view which did not touch upon the contribution land made to development—not only economic development and growth but also with respect to social and political progress. A policy that aimed to change the nature of the relationship among different groups of people connected with land must encompass not only privately-held land in the rural areas but also governed-owned land and urban land.

The first of these is public land—land that the government owned and sometimes also operated. This must be an important component of land policy. In a country such as Pakistan where various invaders arrived, settled and governed for long periods of time, and where population density was low, governments tended to claim for themselves all the land not *demonstrably* owned by individuals or communities. It was in this way that the Mughals, the Sikhs and, finally, the British established their claim on large tracts of land. Each of these administrations used land grants to their supporters and sympathizers to expand their constituencies.

The discretion for granting land to individuals was entirely that of the administration—the royal courts in the case of the Mughals and the Sikhs, and the provincial authorities in the case of the British raj.

The precedence set by the British was followed by the series of administrations that held office in Pakistan.[15] While some government-owned land was used for settling the refugees who arrived from India in 1947, and some of it was given away to interested farmers following the implementation of such 'land colonization' schemes as the one implemented by the Thal Development Authority in the 1950s and 1960s, most allocations were done in ad hoc ways. In this the military played an important role. It granted large tracts of land—sometimes as much as 250 acres per recipient—to the retiring or retired officers in order to reward them for their services to the state.

There is a need to change that policy in favour of a more regulated and transparent system of allocation. When land becomes available for disposal, it should be auctioned and not allotted. Proceeds from auctions could be used to finance various government programmes including providing ex-servicemen with incomes to augment their pensions. Land grants on an ad hoc basis created perverse incentives and introduce serious distortions into the system of compensation for government employees, including military personnel.

Urban land is the second type of land that should be included in a wide-ranging and all-encompassing land policy. Very few developing countries modernized their regulatory polices with respect to urban land use. In several large cities, height regulations were strictly enforced which resulted in less than optimum use of land in the more congested parts. Lahore was a good example of a city in which land use was governed by antiquated laws. Most of Pakistan's large cities were 'flat' with few high-rise buildings. All major cities stretched over a large area with very few buildings more than three or four stories high. This form of city development imposed all kinds of costs on the economy: it created demands for extensive rather than intensive infrastructure. Roads had to be built, water pipes and sewerage systems had to be laid, electric power lines had to be erected to cover a large area. Mass transit had to be provided to bring in people who lived in places distant from their place of work. These types of investments were seldom made, with the result that urban services were poorly provided. That created costs for the economy and resentment among people.

The use of land in towns and cities also impacted on the availability of land in the countryside. Urban land-use policies permitted the continuous encroachment of cities on the surrounding countryside. Incomes from agriculture cannot compete with incomes available from the urban use of land, for housing, commerce and industry. Allowing cities to expand into the countryside reduces the amount of land available for agriculture. This was not a happy situation for a country such as Pakistan which had a large and increasing population and scarcity of good land. That continuous and mostly unregulated expansion of cities hurt agriculture can be seen from the way Lahore has expanded beyond its borders. This has been happening in the south-western parts of the city as new housing colonies have been built.

The best way of dealing with urban land policy is to fully involve the people who will be affected by it. Not only should land use be carefully defined, including matters such as the separation of residential and commercial land, heights of buildings, preservation of historical areas and buildings and the location of industries, but the policy must address environmental issues. Allowing a city to continue to expand creates long distance traffic which in turn results in air pollution.

Over the last several decades, developing countries have gained a lot of experience dealing with inequalities in the distribution of rural land. Initially the favoured approach was the establishment of ceilings on land ownership, expropriation of land above the prescribed ceiling, very little compensation to those who lost land, and distribution of the acquired land to landless peasants. This approach worked only if the government departments and institutions undertaking such programmes were in the hands of those who could not be influenced by the landed aristocracy. This condition was not met in Pakistan when attempts were made to deal with the problem of inequality in land ownership and to solve it by acquiring land and redistributing it.

This approach was followed in Pakistan on three occasions—in 1959 by the government of President Ayub Khan, and in 1974 and 1977 by the administration of Prime Minister Zulfikar Ali Bhutto. As in so many other things that produce inequalities in the distribution of wealth and income, dealing with a highly skewed distribution of landownership required more than state-mandated land distribution. In the three efforts made by Pakistan, the state decided to expropriate land beyond a certain ceiling, paying minimal compensation to the large owners whose land was to be acquired. Given the political clout possessed by the to-be-affected owners, it was inevitable that the programme of expropriation would come with a number of built-in loopholes. These allowed the owners to keep much larger holdings than permitted by the laws that were enacted as a part of the reform effort. The programmes were also corrupted during implementation, which was also inevitable. When the legal systems were weak and large landlords had influence over the bureaucracies assigned the task of implementing the reform programmes, the programmes could be easily subverted.

In retrospect, it appears that General Ayub Khan was much more serious about redistributing land in order to reduce inequalities in its distribution. His effort was more genuine than the two attempts made by Zulfikar Ali Bhutto. When Ayub Khan launched his programme, he was still not beholden to the landed aristocracy. That happened later when Nawab Amir Mohammad Khan Kalabagh was able to expand his political influence at the expense of the more moderate elements in the constituency that supported the military president. Kalabagh brought the landed aristocracy back to the centre stage of Pakistani economics and politics. Large landlords had been sidelined for a while because of their opposition, if not total hostility, to the idea of Pakistan.[16] Once back in power, they were able to stall all efforts to undertake land reforms, whereas across the border in India, the Congress

Party, which was more under the influence of urban economic interests, was able to move forward with a fairly draconian land redistribution policy. That move no doubt helped India to develop a democratic system of governance.

Expropriation is expensive if it comes with compensation determined at market prices for the land acquired. It is affordable, if compensation covers only a fraction of the market value of land. But such a policy is politically difficult to implement. This was the way Ayub Khan's government tried to redistribute land beyond a prescribed ceiling on landholding. Long term bonds were issued that had little value. Expropriation has only worked in revolutionary circumstances as in China, or when an invader was able to force change in the pattern of ownership as was done by the Japanese in Korea and Taiwan.

As already indicated, improving the legal structure and administrative arrangements would help to adopt programmes that aim to reduce the economic and political presence of large landholders in the countryside. Also the full productivity benefits of land reform cannot be realized without complementary inputs and training. This is one of the many conclusions reached by the World Bank in the *World Development Report 2006*. The Bank pointed out that putting land in the hands of inexperienced farmers without the needed support, often led to high rates of desertion. Wrote the Bank:

> More generally, a broader rural development strategy is required to complement land reform, because rural households get their livelihoods from several different sources. This has implications for the design of land reform (for example, determining viable farm size) and highlights the importance of investments that can facilitate off-farm employment such as education.[17]

If the type of land reforms attempted in Pakistan in the past did not achieve the required results, if the experiences of a number of other countries suggested that a wide ranging rural development programme must accompany any effort to redistribute land, then what public policy options are available to Pakistan? Brazil and

South Africa have tried with some success to use what is described as 'market based' land reforms. Large farmers were encouraged but not forced to reduce the size of their holdings. However, small owners or landless peasants were encouraged to augment their holdings or buy land for themselves by the provision of capital on easy terms for making land purchases. This approach helped to develop active land markets. Once they become operational, large landlords may be inclined to dispose off land they considered surplus for their needs. This was inevitably a slow process and took a long time to reduce inequalities in land distribution.

Perhaps a better approach is to use markets to redistribute land along with the imposition of ceilings on family holdings. Once the ceiling is prescribed the state should provide a period for making adjustment, using the market to dispose of the land beyond the established limit. The period of adjustment could last for some five to ten years. If smallholders wish to buy the land that large owners are obliged to sell, the state could provide them with the needed financial resources on concessionary terms.

Redistribution of land is not the only way to improve wealth and income equality in the countryside. Providing security of tenure to those who rent land or are sharecroppers, giving them access to capital for making improvements in the land they cultivate and allowing them a larger share in the output are some of the ways of helping this segment of the population.

5. Conclusion

The main argument of this chapter is that Pakistan has not adopted public policies to realize the extraordinary potential of its extremely well-endowed agricultural sector. The government's attention was diverted from agriculture to industry in 1949 when India launched a trade war with Pakistan. The sector never received public policy priority after that event as it had during the times of the British when the colonial administration used massive investments in irrigation to turn the provinces of Punjab and Sindh into the granaries of food-deficit India. The sector received some attention during the days of the reformist government headed by President Ayub Khan. It was during his time that Pakistan saw the first 'green revolution.' The sector continued to be neglected by the governments that took office after Ayub Khan.

Pakistan could achieve a high rate of economic growth and sustain it over time if it gave agriculture the priority it deserves. That could still be done if the government focuses its attention on at least three areas: develops irrigation, creates the environment for developing niche opportunities and adopts a policy aimed at redistributing land more equitably among the farmers. In irrigation there is the need to invest in new reservoirs on the Indus to compensate for the losses that have occurred because of the silting of the dams that were built in the 1960s. There is also the need to restore the productivity of the sector by improving the state of the irrigation network that was built by the British but was allowed to deteriorate. With greater availability of water for irrigation, the country should work to change the pattern of cropping and move away from the production of such land-extensive crops as wheat and sugar cane and more towards the production of high value-added crops including fruits, vegetables, flowers and dairy products. There are interesting niches available in the global market that Pakistan could exploit. Such a strategy would not only lift the rate of growth of the GDP, but will also help reduce the incidence of rural poverty. However, in order to make the transition towards a new agricultural sector, with a different structure, policymakers should also, once again, address the problem of considerable inequities in the ownership of land. A land policy needs to be developed that includes not only rural but also urban land.

There is no doubt that with the adoption of the right set of public policies and the establishment of institutions in both public and private sectors that support the modernization of agriculture in Pakistan, this sector could play an important role in helping the economy to attain high rates of growth. Globalization is changing the structures of economies all across the world. As incomes increase, both traditional agriculture and manufacturing are losing their importance. Pakistan needs to carefully review the global situation and the changes occurring in it, and then move forward with the development and modernization of its agriculture.

NOTES

1. The statement is attributed to Sardar Vallabhbhai Patel, at that time Home Minister in the government of Prime Minister Jawaharlal Nehru. Patel had bitterly opposed the creation of Pakistan and would have liked to see the annulment of the partition of British India.
2. Shahid Javed Burki, *Pakistan: First Fifty Years*, Boulder, Colo.: Westview Press, 1990.
3. This section is based on my article that appeared under the title 'A niche-based strategy' in *Dawn* on 9 March 2004.
4. This part is based on my articles published in *Dawn* under the title 'Kalabagh and the water crisis' on 17 January 2006, and 'Water: The coming crisis,' published on 24 January 2006.
5. David Fieldhouse, 'The metropolitan economics of empire,' in Judith M. Brown and Wm. Roger Louis, *The Oxford History of the British Empire; Volume IV: The Twentieth Century*, Oxford: Oxford University Press, 1999, p. 88.
6. Niall Ferguson, *Empire: How Britain made the Modern World*, London: Allen Lane, 2003, p. 53.
7. Amartya Sen, *Poverty of Famines: An Essay of Entitlement and Deprivation*, New York: Oxford University Press, 1983.
8. D.K. Fieldhouse, op. cit.
9. Ibid.
10. The World Bank, *World Development Report, 2005: Equity and Development*, Washington DC, 2005, Table A2, pp. 280–281.
11. Salman Masood, 'Balakot Journal: Quake-stricken town to move, saddening survivors', *The New York Times*, 20 April 2006, p. A4.
12. These estimates are from R. Albert Berry and William Cline, Agrarian Structure and Productivity in Developing Countries: A Study Prepared for the International Labor Office within the Framework for the World Development Programme, Johns Hopkins University Press, 1979.
13. Radwan Shaban, 'Testing between Competing Models of Sharecropping,' *Journal of Political Economy*, 95(5), pp. 893–920.
14. Mead Cain, 'Risk and Insurance: Perspective on Fertility and Agrarian Change in India and Bangladesh.' *Population and Development Review*, 7(3), pp. 435–474.
15. One well-researched account of the way the British colonized the land they brought under cultivation is to be found in Imran Ali, *The Punjab: Under Imperialism, 1885-1947*, Princeton, NJ: Princeton University Press, 1988.

16. In an earlier work I described the return of the landed aristocracy to the centrestage of politics as the process of 'indigenization'. See Shahid Javed Burki, *Pakistan under Bhutto, 1971-77*, London: Macmillan, 1980.
17. The World Bank, *World Development Report*, op. cit., p. 164.

6

The Diasporas' Economic Role

The development of the Pakistani diasporas in various parts of the world was the product of some remarkable demographic shifts that occurred in the country over a period of almost six decades. The areas that became Pakistan had always sent people to other countries to earn a decent living—at any rate, a living better than what was possible from the arid lands from which they came. The migrants were expected not only to support themselves but also send money to improve the living conditions of those they had left behind. A steady flow of migrants in one direction and remittance in the other had become a feature of the economic life of the parts of South Asia the British carved out of their large Indian domain to make Pakistan. That was on 14 August 1947.

Migrants from the areas that were now Pakistan had moved in many different directions: to East Asia, to the Far East, to the Caribbean, to the West Coast of Canada. But it was Britain that attracted the largest number. As its own young men were called to arms to fight the Germans and Italians in Europe and North Africa and the Japanese in East Asia, those from what was now Pakistan went to the midlands in England to man the textile factories.

Exactly how and why these shifts of people happened warrants further study. This is for the simple reason that the formation of the diasporas and their interaction with the home country are events of enormous significance not just for the history of the communities of Pakistanis living abroad, but also for the social, political and economic development of Pakistan.

Like the Jews, the Chinese and some Indians, some—but not all, Punjabis and Pathans are more likely to migrate than the Sindhis and Balochis—Pakistanis are also naturally diasporic people. They are prepared to move long distances in order to escape economic hardship or religious persecution and also to look for new opportunities. Of these early long-distance migrants it was only the Jews who displayed a strong sense of separate identity and nationhood. These impulses were strong enough for them to create a homeland for themselves against heavy odds. The Indian and Chinese communities for a long time took little interest in their respective countries of origin. The Chinese, living in various China towns in the western world, were almost totally out of touch with the homeland. This was also the case with the Indian communities in the Caribbean and various parts of Africa.

The Asian foreign communities were founded hundreds of years ago. Their isolation from the homeland may have been the result of poor communications in those periods.

The more recent migrants were different. No matter where they came from, they tended to remain in close touch with the places and people they had left behind. This became possible by the low cost of communication; it took a few pennies to make a telephone call to the homeland whereas a few decades ago the cost was a multiple of the daily wage. The same was true about the cost of travel. A return air ticket from the United States to Pakistan cost less than one-tenth of the annual minimum wage of a gainfully employed person. It was not surprising that, when the new migrants developed the financial wherewithal, they looked at their homeland as an important destination for their savings. This was what the large Pakistani diasporas in three continents—in the Middle East, in Britain and in the United States—began to do in the early part of the twenty-first century.

This would not be an unusual role for a diaspora; this type of contribution was made—and is being made—by the communities that originated in many countries. These included Israel, Ireland, Poland, China, the Philippines, India and Mexico. Pakistan joined this league of nations. In fact the total amount of remittances flowing into the developing world from the groups of immigrants living and working in various parts of the developed world in 2006 was estimated at more than $100 billion.[1] This was twice the amount of total foreign aid provided by rich nations to poor countries and about a quarter of the annual flow of foreign direct investment into the developing world. The fact that governments in the developing world invested so much time and effort in maintaining good relations with the providers of development assistance but spent practically no time at all studying their diasporas or working with them, was a good indication of the ignorance about the important role these communities were playing—or could play—in the development of their homelands.

The precise interest of the diaspora communities in their homeland is the product of several factors. These include the economic and social background of the immigrants, the nature and scope of the ties the overseas communities maintain with the country of their origin, the types of financial instruments that are available to the remitters, and the way the communities living and working abroad view their home country's economic prospects. It is also influenced by the social, cultural, economic and political environment in which the migrants live. Given these factors no stream of remittance was the same. A country hoping to economically benefit from the wealth of its citizens living abroad would do well to understand their economic interests.

The chapter builds upon several articles I contributed to *Dawn* since 2000 when I began to write for the newspaper on a regular basis. Using population as an economic asset rather than allowing it to become a burden was a recurrent theme in many of these articles. Migration was one safety valve available to growing people. However, given the difficulty in securing immigration visas to the United States since 9/11, developing the outsourcing industry in the country has become a more attractive option. This chapter will describe how the Pakistani diasporas were formed in three parts of the globe, how these communities began to interact with the homeland, the attempts made by some Pakistani administrations to tap into the wealth and income of the various diasporas, the role the government could play in benefiting from the presence of large communities in the world's developed parts, and the encroachment of radical Islam into these communities and how that might influence their contacts with the homeland. In Section 1, I will describe briefly the formation of the Pakistani communities in Britain, the Middle East and North America and the changes in the pattern of remittances sent by them to their home country. In Section 2, I will analyze in greater detail the development of the Pakistani community in the United States. This is by far the largest and wealthiest Pakistani diaspora in the world. In Section 3, I will suggest the direction public policy could go in taking advantage of the presence of large communities of Pakistanis in the United States. In Section 4, I will briefly review how the West's war against radical Islam began to influence some segments of the Pakistani communities in Britain and the United States. The chapter will end with a brief concluding section.

1. Formation of Diasporas and Engagement with the Homeland

Pakistanis began to form diasporas even before they became Pakistanis; large scale migration began immediately after the Second World War and has continued to this day. Why was Pakistan an active contributor to the cross border movement of people? One answer comes from the novelist Nadeem Aslam, himself a member of the large Pakistani diaspora in Britain. Aslam left his native Gujranwala along with his parents when he was only 14 years old. His father, an avowed communist, feared repression at the hands of the Ayub Khan government. His second novel, *Maps for Lost Lovers,* highly acclaimed in the English reading world, deals with a community of Pakistanis that lives in utter isolation in a desolate industrial town in England. He writes:

> Pakistan is a poor country, a harsh and disastrously unjust land, its history a book of sad stories, and life is a trial if not punishment for most of those born there: Millions of its sons and daughters have managed to find footholds all around the globe in their search for livelihood and semblance of dignity. Roaming the planet for solace, they've settled in small towns that make them even smaller still, and in cities that have tall buildings and even taller loneliness.[2]

Pakistanis first gained a foothold in Britain where they went to work for the textile mills and the transport sector. The Second World War and the loss of tens of thousands of young men left Britain seriously short of labour. The government and the mill owners turned to the populous colonies of Britain that had surplus workers to fill the gap. India was one such colony. The British recruiters went to the areas they knew well because of the soldiers they had enlisted for their army. Northern parts of the Punjab and western Kashmir were the two areas that had supplied the British Indian Army with recruits; after the war was over, they provided workers for the mills and the transport sector. A steady stream of migrants went to Britain even after Pakistan came into existence. This first wave of migrants was succeeded by another as those who had gone earlier began to form families. Spouses were imported from the villages and towns from which the first set of migrants came; sometimes even other family members joined.

This wave of migration continued until the mid seventies when two developments occurred to reduce it to insignificance. The British government tightened its immigration policy and a new destination of migration emerged nearer Pakistan, in the Middle East. Briefly another group of migrants moved from Pakistan to Britain. These were mostly doctors recruited to staff the National Health Service the British government was putting in place once it was finished with the post-war economic reconstruction and revival programme. This migration episode was short lived; it also ended because of the emergence of another, more attractive destination, the United States. In the extensive coverage given to the Pakistani community following the bombing of 7 July 2005 in which of the four suicide bombers who were involved, three were of Pakistani origin, it was estimated that the number of people who claimed to be descended from parents and grandparents from Pakistan was more than a million. There were in all 1.6 million Muslims said to be living in various parts of Britain. The Pakistanis constituted the second largest diaspora in Britain after the Indians who numbered about 2.5 million.

In the seventies the Organization of the Petroleum Exporting Countries (OPEC) in the Middle East increased the price of oil severalfold. The resultant windfall incomes fed an economic boom marked by the construction of new and elaborate infrastructure. Roads and highways, ports, airports, schools, universities and hospitals, offices and shopping centres were built in Saudi Arabia, Kuwait and the UAE. This construction activity would not have happened had these countries been unable to find workers. These were available in Pakistan. Pakistan was the preferred country of supply; it was Muslim and, therefore, adjustment would not be a problem in the campsites that were opened all over the region. Also a number of large companies that won contracts in the Middle East knew the Pakistani labour market. They had worked in Pakistan in the sixties to build the massive projects under the Indus Basin Replacement Works. Once again, workers were recruited from north Punjab, Azad Kashmir, and also the North West Frontier Province.

The migration to the Middle East was different from the one to the United Kingdom. It was more programmed. The workers went under a contract for a specified period of time, after which they had to return. They were required to live in workers' camps near the construction sites, were not expected to get assimilated with the native population, and were not allowed to bring family members. As I will discuss in Section 6 below, their only interaction with the native population was through the *imams* who preached at the mosques set up in the camps.

The people of Pakistani origin formed the third diaspora in North America, in Canada and the United States. As discussed in Section 2, the communities that constituted this large diaspora was made up mostly of professionals—doctors, engineers, economists, accountants etc.—who were unable to find jobs that matched their skills in the slow growing economy of Pakistan in the 'seventies'.

How did these diasporas react with the homeland? Initially the impact was through the supply of capital. Since the mid-seventies when this type of external flow became important for the Pakistani economy it was referred to as 'workers' remittances.' That was a correct description since the bulk of the money being sent then was coming from the millions of Pakistanis working in the Middle East. A very large number of these people were unskilled or semi-skilled workers labouring on thousands of construction sites all over the oil-producing and exporting countries of the Middle East. These workers went on short-term assignments that lasted for no more than three to five years. They lived in labour camps near the construction sites, saved most of what they earned, and remitted back to Pakistan most of what they saved. They returned home once the contract period was over.

There was an impression at that time that much of this flow of money was simply frittered away by those who received it. There was no doubt some waste; that always happens with windfall incomes. That notwithstanding, the remittances sent by the Pakistanis in the Middle East went straight to the friends and families of the workers and a good proportion of them were used for meeting the basic needs of the dependents who had stayed back. That the incidence of poverty declined in Pakistan by a significant amount during in the 1980s was largely the result of the flow of this money to the poor. But that was then. In the period after 2001—after the attacks on the United States by Islamic militants— the origin of remittances and the use to which they were put were entirely different from those earlier flows.

The first phase of the construction boom in the Middle East was mostly over by the end of the 1980s; it was brought to an abrupt end by the first Gulf War of 1991 when the United States intervened to expel Iraq from Kuwait. By then most of the workers who were employed on the construction sites were back in Pakistan. The next phase of the boom that saw enormous construction activities in Dubai, Bahrain and Qatar did not involve much labour from Pakistan. The people of Pakistani origin still resident in the Middle East mostly represented a different economic and social class; their pattern of savings and investments was different from those who worked in this part of the world a few decades earlier. They had, in other words, a different kind of relationship with the homeland. The Pakistanis living and working in the Middle East in the nineties and beyond did not send back as much money as was the case with the first wave of migrants.

One way of illustrating this fundamental change in diaspora economics is to look at the streams of remittances into the country over the last several decades. For a quarter century from 1975 to 2000, Saudi Arabia was the largest source of remittances into Pakistan. In the ten-year period between 1990–1991 and 1999–2000, Pakistanis living in Saudi Arabia sent a total of $4.796 billion to their homeland. This averaged $480 million a year. However, the amounts sent declined steadily from $682 million in 1990–1991 to only $310 million in 1999–2000. By the end of the decade of the 'nineties' the amount of remittances received by Pakistan from Saudi Arabia was less than one-half of the amount at the beginning of the decade. Not only did the amounts sent by the Pakistanis in Saudi Arabia decline, their proportion in the total also fell significantly. In 1990–1991, the Saudi Arabian remittances accounted for 37.4 per cent of the total; ten years later, the proportion had declined to only 28.5 per cent.[3]

During the same period the Pakistanis living in the United States began to increase the amount of money remitted back to the homeland. This flow cannot be called 'workers' remittances' in the strict sense of that term. The funds that constituted this stream were not emanating from the working class but from the class of professionals who had, over time, built large diasporas in North America. What motivated this group of people was not the provision of financial assistance to the people they had left behind. They were much more interested in making economic investments in their country of origin.

The stringent regulations introduced on money transfers after the terrorist attacks on the United States on 11 September 2001 had an impact on this flow of funds. In one year—between 2000–2001 and 2001–2002—remittances from the United States increased almost six-fold, from $135 million to $779 million. In the following year, they increased by another 60 per cent and reached a record of $1.24 billion.[4] They have stayed around that level after that. What explained the sudden jump in this type of financial flow?

The initial impetus no doubt came from the steps taken by the US Treasury following the terrorist attack. Instead of using the informal *hundi/hawala* channels for transmitting funds, the remitters were forced by new regulations to use official banking channels. Some black money that was available with the members of the diasporas also came under scrutiny and was probably pulled out of the United States and sent back to Pakistan. Some of the remitted money probably constituted capital flight—deposits held in the American banking system by the Pakistani businesses awaiting a turnaround in their country's economy. Some members of the Pakistani diasporas in the United States, troubled by the policies pursued by Washington in the Muslim world, may have sought new investment opportunities in their own country. All these factors contributed to the sharp increase in the flow of private funds from the United States to Pakistan.

But there was more to this story than this explanation suggests. There was enough anecdotal evidence available from around the United States to suggest that a profound change had occurred in the way the diasporas viewed Pakistan and the way they might become important players in Pakistan's economic progress.

How were they using their savings from both accumulated wealth and current income? How much of these savings were going to Pakistan and what was the likelihood of their increase? Would the diasporas be prepared to tap into their income and wealth to make investments in Pakistan? Was there a role for the Pakistani government in encouraging the diasporas' savings to flow to Pakistan? I will attempt answers to these questions later in this chapter.

Financial flows from the Pakistani communities in the United States could play a significant role in the economic and social development of the home country. This had begun to happen given the quantum jump in the level of remittances in the period after 11 September 2001. In 2003–2004, the total amount of remittances received by Pakistan was more than 4 per cent of the country's gross domestic product, equal to about one-quarter of the total amount of net investment. This flow contributed more than one percentage point to the increase in national income estimated at 6.4 per cent for 2003–4 and 8.6 per cent in 2004–5. In other words, the Pakistani diasporas had begun to contribute significantly to their homeland's economic development.

Neither the academic community nor government agencies took much notice of the economic background and medium and long-term economic interests of the Pakistanis resident in the United States. It is my belief that this community was poised to play a significant economic and social role in the future of their homeland. Since the contribution they could make will be more pronounced than that of the possible contributions of the two other Pakistani diasporas—the communities in Britain and the Middle East—it is worth the effort to develop a better understanding of these communities. What follows is an effort to disaggregate the large community of Pakistanis in North America into its various parts. This description is not based on deep research but drawn from informed guess work and personal knowledge about the broad economic characteristics of these diverse groups of people. It should provide a framework for future research into this important subject.

2. Pakistanis in the United States

When people in Pakistan talk about the growing American influence on their country, they are of course thinking of the way Washington may be affecting policymaking in Islamabad. That the administration headed by President George W. Bush has forged a close relationship with the administration of President Pervez Musharraf is a fact of life for Pakistan. But there is one other way in which America has begun to impact on developments in Pakistan. What I have in mind is the influence originating from an increasingly powerful group in America. The reference here is to the Pakistani diasporas in the United States made up of hundreds of thousands of Pakistanis resident in different parts of that country.

The growing economic and political weight carried by this community in the early 2000s should help to steady the relationship between Washington and Islamabad. Other diasporas have performed this role. This is particularly true of the powerful Jewish community in the United States that has kept Washington's relations with Israel on an even keel. Increasingly the non-resident Indians (NRIs) have begun to play the same role.

In the minds of many Pakistanis, the economic recovery that began in 2003 was the result of the large flows of foreign capital. This was true to some extent. Less well known and less well appreciated was the fact that the largest part of this flow was not from official sources such as the government of the United States or the World Bank or the Asian Development Bank. It came in the form of remittances sent by the Pakistanis living and working abroad.

How large was the Pakistani community in North America—in Canada and the United States—in the early 2000s and what was the level of their incomes, savings and investments? How much wealth had the community accumulated and to what use was it being put? There was little solid information available to provide good answers to these questions. I have suggested in some of my writings that the number of Pakistanis living in the United States and Canada is close to a million, about equal to those resident in Britain. That estimate was based on some of the information available from the US census but the problem with the official numbers was that they used the place of birth to identify the country of origin of the people living in the country. A state-by-state survey done by the Pakistan Embassy in Washington suggested a much smaller number. The Indians who claim the size of their North American community to be about 2.5 million believe that there are only 150,000 people of Pakistani origin in the United States. There was a reason why the Indians would put forward a smaller estimate for the size of the Pakistani diasporas; the larger the size the greater the political influence of the community. A similar debate had gone on for some time between the Jewish and Muslim populations of the United States. Organizations representing the former claimed that at most there are two to three million Muslims in the United States; the latter put their number at between six and eight million.

Even if we use a number of 0.75 million for the size of the Pakistani community in the United States, their economic presence with reference to the homeland would still be considerable. There are several ways of estimating the economic weight of this community. Since little information is available about this, I will use mostly guess work or information about other diasporas. If the average income per head of the members of the diasporas is $50,000—more than the average for the United States but a bit less than the average for the Indian community—the aggregate income per head of the community in the early 2000s was of the order of $37.5 billion. This was a little less than one-third of the revised estimate for Pakistan's gross domestic product. If this community saved one quarter of its annual income, the aggregate savings would amount to over $9.4 billion. This was equivalent to about one-half of net national savings of Pakistan estimated by the World Bank at 18 per cent of the gross domestic product.

How have the diasporas deployed their savings over time? As is the case with all immigrants, housing is generally the first destination of savings. I estimate the accumulated wealth of this community at about $100 billion. This asset was built over a period of three decades when Pakistanis began to arrive in the United States and Canada in large numbers. Of this, probably one-half, or $50 billion, was in housing. That translated into about 200,000 housing units that this community owned in the United States. About a quarter, or $25 billion, was invested in businesses, mostly small. The remaining $25 billion was in various kinds of financial assets.

The amount of total income of the Pakistani diasporas in the United States will continue to increase even if there was no addition to their numbers. This will happen since the total wealth of the community will keep on increasing, which in turn will produce additional income. We can, therefore, safely assume that the economic weight of the diasporas will continue to expand, probably at a rate larger than the rate of increase in Pakistan's GDP? How has this economic wealth begun to affect Pakistan and what was likely to happen in the future?

There is a rich mix of social and economic backgrounds among the North American Pakistani diasporas. The community in the Greater Washington area is dominated by the professional classes, a significant number of whom are employed in the public sector including the Federal Government, the World Bank, and the International Monetary Fund. There are also people from this community—in particular from the second or third generations— who have found jobs in the numerous think-tanks that operate in the area. A growing number of working class immigrants from Pakistan are resident in the northern part of the state of Virginia, next door to Washington.

Further up the East Coast are the Pakistani communities of New Jersey and New York which have a larger proportion of working classes than is the case with the other diasporas. As is common with other groups of immigrants, the members of this group had congregated in the businesses in which some of those that came earlier scored successes. Prominent in this group are taxi drivers, owners of newspaper kiosks, owners and workers in small retail businesses, and owners and waiters in ethnic restaurants.

Moving further north are the communities in Chicago and Detroit. Not unlike the Washington group, this diaspora also has a significant number of professionals—physicians and surgeons, engineers, lawyers, economists and accountants. Almost all of them work in private businesses, either self-owned or as employees in large firms. The Toronto Pakistani community in Canada—the largest Pakistani diaspora in that country—is basically an extension of the Chicago group.

The community in the San Francisco and Los Angeles areas is dominated by the people in the high-tech industry. As a result of the IT and dot.com booms of the nineties some of these people have experienced vertiginous upward economic mobility. The size of accumulated wealth and annual incomes of this community is considerably greater than the average for the communities in other parts of the continent.

Finally, the Pakistani community in the Houston–Dallas area is dominated by the people who had set up successful businesses; some of them in the oil sector while some others had taken advantage of the economic boom that had lasted for decades in the area. Since this part of the United States has a very strong presence of immigrants many of whom operate their own businesses, the Pakistanis have found an easier acceptance as business owners and operators.

These communities have different economic interests in Pakistan. The working class communities on the East Coast (Washington–Virginia and New Jersey–New York) are not unlike the Pakistani workers in the Middle East. While they earn considerably more but save less than the Pakistani workers in the Gulf States, they send a significant amount of remittances to their relatives and friends back in the homeland. A steady flow of about $150 million from the United States to Pakistan in the period before '9/11' was made up of this type of remittance. It was unlikely that the total amount of money originating with this group would grow in any significant way unless their number increased. The size of this component of the diaspora is unlikely to increase given the constraints imposed on the entry of people with low levels of skills into the United States following the terrorist attacks of 11 September 2001. These constraints are particularly severe for the Muslim world. The more well-to-do members of the various communities of Pakistanis identified above have come recently into the picture as active remitters, attracted by the booming real estate markets in various parts of Pakistan. How are they responding to the opportunities they see in the homeland?

All new human settlements, including the establishment of diasporas, go through a distinct life cycle. They are founded by the young and adventurous—people prepared to take risks and expend a great deal of energy to improve their economic prospects. The large Pakistani diasporas in North America are about three decades old when thousands of well trained professionals left their home country to look for opportunities abroad. They went either to Britain or came to the United States. Once they found jobs, they settled down and brought in their partners, mostly from Pakistan. When they started families, they bought homes near the place of work. Some of them took advantage of the provision in the US immigration law of that time to sponsor close members of their families to migrate as well. The word about the economic success of this first wave of migrants spread in the homeland and more people, mostly with similar social and economic backgrounds, also took the plunge. They generally went to the places where their friends or relatives had taken residence. This is the reason why diasporas even in a country as large as the United States exist in the form of highly concentrated clusters. Although public policy in the United States has not encouraged 'multi-culturalism' as was done in Britain, new non-white diaspora communities are not as well-integrated with the mainstream as happened with the migrants that arrived to the country in the early twentieth century. This fact has begun to worry social scientists such as Samuel P. Huntington who was of the view that the inability of the new entrants to integrate into the mainstream would change the culture of the United States from a white protestant country to one with several different cultures that don't happily coexist.[5]

Some thirty to forty years after the arrival of the first migrants, a large number of the founders of the diasporas have reached the age of retirement. Where would they like to spend the rest of their lives? Will they remain in the United States or re-locate themselves to Pakistan? Is America the right place to live out life or would Pakistan, with domestic help easily available and support of the larger family also at hand, be a better place to be in? These questions are being asked in the Pakistani diasporas as they mature. They have also become significant for two other reasons: changes in the American approach towards allowing new migrants from places such as Pakistan, and the on-going process of globalization which continues to knit the world together ever more closely.

With the cost of communications coming down every day, relocation no longer means a permanent change in the place of residence. It has now become possible for people with means to divide their time between the homeland and whichever place they have spent the productive years of their lives. It is in this context that decisions about investment in real estate are being increasingly made by the older members of the Pakistani communities in the United States. Other factors also weigh, in particular the impression that the country may have begun to turn the economic corner.

3. Tapping the Diasporas for Capital Flows to the Homeland

How can the authorities in Islamabad tap the large wealth and incomes of the expatriate Pakistanis living and working abroad? How can the resources available to the rich Pakistani community in North America, in particular, become available for economic use in Pakistan? Is there a role for the government at all in turning to the diasporas for promoting development at home?

The government's intervention in the past was not very helpful in bringing resources to Pakistan. In the mid-1970s, Prime Minister Zulfikar Ali Bhutto, having become aware of the enormous amount of aggregate income of the Pakistani workers in the Middle East, attempted to first channel the remittances through government owned banks and then tax them to generate resources for the public sector. He was told by his advisors that economic theory was on his side since some of the skills the workers were putting to use in the Middle East to earn large incomes were acquired in government institutions. This was then payback time. Even if the government could find an economic reason for making such a move, it had not counted on the deep-seated cultural antipathy of the citizens of Pakistan towards taxes. The workers simply stopped using government channels for sending remittances. They moved towards the *hawala* system, making it virtually impossible for the authorities to track incomes they could tax. Remittances moving through official channels declined significantly. A sobered government withdrew the tax.

The second attempt for tapping the non-resident Pakistanis was made by Prime Minister Nawaz Sharif. I may have contributed to this effort since in several conversations I had with the prime minister as I was concluding my own tenure as finance minister in 1996-97, I made him aware of the growing wealth of the Pakistani diasporas in North America. In early 1997, he dispatched Sartaj Aziz, his finance minister, to address a gathering of Pakistani physicians in the United States, to ask them to make contributions to a special Prime Minister's fund. The fund was being established to pay back a part of the rapidly increasing tax burden the country was carrying. This appeal to patriotism was rebuffed and an embarrassed Sartaj Aziz returned home empty-handed.

There are several lessons to be learned from these attempts. A government that presides over a weak system of tax administration cannot hope to tax incomes earned abroad by its citizens working in foreign lands. Even the United States, which probably has one of the most efficient systems of tax collection in the world, does not target the incomes of its citizens if they are living abroad. It only taxes foreign incomes when they are earned by its residents. Second, governments should not use a sense of patriotism to generate revenues for itself. There is, however, a bit of a history to support the view that on occasions such an approach can be justified. In the first decade or two after Pakistan's birth, the government was able to appeal to its citizens to contribute to various funds established for specific purposes such as refugee relief or help to the victims of floods. The generous contributions made by Pakistanis living abroad to the various relief efforts launched by the government and non-government organizations following the devastating earthquake of 8 October 2005 is a more recent example of how the diasporas can come to the help of the homeland in periods of crises. The earthquake took 80,000 lives and left more than three million people homeless. The diasporas, response was not limited to contributing money to the relief efforts; a number of doctors from Britain, Canada and the United States went to the affected areas to provide medical assistance.[6]

Nawaz Sharif's government was perhaps guided by these precedents. It did not succeed for the reason that reducing the burden of debt—especially when it was acquired by the government's own profligacy—was not going to give rise to charitable impulses. Reducing debt could not be seen as providing relief to the victims of natural or man-made disasters. A debt relief fund was not the same thing as funds for refugee rehabilitation or flood relief. Besides, in the 1990s, much of the enthusiasm that had prompted the first generation of Pakistanis to contribute to various relief funds had largely dissipated.

These experiences do not suggest that the governments have no role to play. They can make an important contribution by creating what economists now call an 'enabling environment' for investment. A government can contribute to the creation of opportunities which would be seen as attractive by potential investors. It can provide information through various mechanisms to the expatriate communities on the opportunities available in the homeland that could earn handsome dividends for the non-resident investor.

Governments can also target their citizens living and working abroad to raise funds through various kinds of bonds. This was done very successfully by India in the 1990s through the flotation of 'patriot bonds.' Although a sense of patriotism was invoked, billions of dollars flowed into these instruments not only because of the love of the homeland. Non-resident Indians bought the bonds for basically two reasons. They found the terms appealing and they had developed enormous confidence in their homeland's economic future.

For purposes of public policy it also makes great sense to treat remittances not as one homogeneous flow but as a stream made up of several different components. In planning to tap resources from expatriate communities, it is important to recognize that the members of these groups send back money for a variety of reasons. At least four of these are important for purposes of policy. The first, and by far the most important reason is to help family and friends who are still living in the homeland. This is the principal motivation for remitting money for low-income migrants or for the migrants who have relatives and friends in the home country in need of financial assistance. My guess is that some two-thirds to three-fourths of the current flow of remittances of some $4.5 billion received by Pakistan in the years 2004–2006 were provided in response to this need. This type of flow has considerable economic benefits. It is not wasted by the recipients, as was generally the belief in Pakistan in the 1970s and 1980s when billions of dollars flowed into the country's poorer areas. While this is a good subject for policy research, it would be safe to assume that a significant amount of this flow goes into poverty redressal and into human development. It is used for health care, education, shelter, clothing, and improving water supply. All these are basic needs that the poor are not able to adequately satisfy from their own meagre resources. I have argued in some of my earlier writings that remittances from abroad had a great deal to do with the sharp reduction in the incidence of poverty in the 1980s.[7]

There are at least two roles governments can play in facilitating this type of flow and in making its use more efficient. They can help to bring down the cost of transmission by requiring the banking system to reduce what is called the float—the time that elapses between the placement of the amount at a particular bank for remittance and the time when it is released to the beneficiary. This is a popular way for the banks to increase their incomes from handling remittances. The government's regulatory system can also prescribe the fee banks are allowed to charge these customers.

Governments can also help the recipients to handle the windfall incomes that remittances sometimes represent. They can introduce savings instruments the poor can use and which are easily accessible to them. Some countries use post offices to sell such instruments; in some other countries retail outlets have been allowed to charge a small commission for selling small denomination government bills to potential investors; in some places governments have used 'mobile banks' that travel from village to village or between small towns to sell such instruments. Regulatory systems should also encourage commercial banks and thrift institutions to reach the small savers.

The second type of remittance by non-residents working abroad was charity, a significant proportion of which was given to the poor by the members of the expatriate communities on home visits. Sending money home for *sadqas* was one example of this type of remittance. Some of this money also went into the funding of non-government organizations that had developed programmes of assistance the diasporas like. Giving for charity depended on the average incomes of the communities resident abroad; the higher the incomes more likely that this type of flow would go through organized channels.

Fund raising functions—dinners and various kinds of galas—became a part of the social life of the well-to-do expatriate communities in the United States in the early 2000s.[8] Most of these were sponsored by non-government organizations that had registered themselves with the authorities, and were allowed to receive contributions that are tax-exempt. In this way a dollar worth of contribution effectively pulled about 20 to 25 cents worth of US government money into charity. Some of the better organized non-government organizations that began life in Pakistan also set up affiliates in the United States to take advantage of this provision in the tax code. The Citizens Foundation, the Edhi Foundation and the Shaukat Khanum Memorial Cancer Hospital are three examples of Pakistan-based charities that periodically bring their fund-raising activities to the United States.

The third type of remittance is of relatively recent origin and is directed at providing resource-starved social sectors with additional funds. The NRI community are very active in this area. A group of wealthy expatriates from India who had made fortunes in the sectors of finance and high-tech founded a foundation that raised hundreds of millions of dollars to fund the establishment of a world-class business school in Hyderabad. The school was affiliated with the prestigious Wharton School of Pennsylvania University and the Kellogg School of Chicago University. Within a few years, the Hyderabad School succeeded in putting itself on the map for advanced training in business and financial administration. It was visited by George W. Bush, the US president, during his trip to South Asia in March 2006.

The Pakistani diasporas in the United States have yet to move in this direction. If anything, Pakistan needs institutions such as the Hyderabad School more than India. What has kept the Pakistani communities in the United States from venturing into this area is the same set of reasons that has inhibited human development at home in the first place. There is some recognition that without skill development, Pakistan would not be able to modernize its economy and become fully integrated into the global economic system. This has led the private sector to invest in building institutions such as the Lahore University of Management Sciences and the Beaconhouse University, also at Lahore. Institutions such as these could become the focus of charitable giving by the Pakistani communities in the United States.

Pakistani diasporas in America took some interest in assisting organizations that aimed to bring literacy to the more backward areas in the country. The third type of flow was composed of financial contributions for promoting social development in the homeland. As the word has gone around, spread by institutions such as the United Nations Development Fund in their annual *Human Development Report,* non-resident Pakistanis are becoming painfully aware of the fact that their country is fast losing the race to get better integrated into the global economy.[9] This could only happen if the quality of human resources could be dramatically improved. This would require a massive effort which was beyond the competence of the public sector and considerably greater than the government's financial capacity. This awareness has resulted in the establishment of a number of non-government organizations that enjoy a special tax status in the United States. When contributing to these organizations the donors can write off their giving against their incomes. In a way, therefore, these contributions are leveraged with money from the United States Treasury. This type of giving also has begun to attract reputable and well-established Pakistan-based organizations that are able to take advantage of tax relief available to potential donors to raise funds from the expatriate community.

The Association of Pakistani Physicians in North America—better known by its acronym, AAPNA—has played a pioneering role in this area. Some of the active members of this well established organization founded well-run non-government organizations that raise money from expatriates to establish and manage schools in several remote areas of the homeland. The innovative skills now being deployed by the management of the National Human Development Commission in Pakistan were learned by its founder[10] while doing charity work under the aegis of AAPNA.

The fourth flow as a constituent of the stream of remittances is of relatively recent origin. This pertains to investments in various forms of assets that hold promise for the financially savvy members of the community. For the moment much of this has gone into real estate and some has found its way into the stock market. This move towards sending money for investment in physical and financial assets is typical of maturing diasporas. It also signals an increase in confidence in the economic prospects of the home country.

There was first the word of mouth that conveyed to the diasporas that conditions at home were improving; that Pakistan may not, after all, be an unsafe place to go back to; that the returns on investment in land and houses were considerably higher than those available in the United States. Those who had gone for holidays to Pakistan returned with stories about the boom in the real estate market in several large cities, in particular Islamabad, Lahore, and Karachi. But it wasn't only the word of mouth that was spreading the good news about the home country. Respected newspapers also began to write about the economic boom in the country. In March 2005 *The New York Times* published a story about the economic boom in Pakistan in an important place in the newspaper—page three which carries the main foreign story of the day.[11] In the account written by Somni Sengupta, a writer based in New Delhi, the newspaper presented a fairly rosy picture of the Pakistani economy. It started with a story about a Pakistani entrepreneur 'British-born, New York-trained and married to a woman from

New Jersey, who had long dreamed of running his own restaurant. London was too expensive, New York was too risky. Karachi seemed just right'. This was news not only for the Americans who associated Karachi with sectarian violence, Islamic radicalism, and the kidnapping and gruesome murder of Daniel Pearl, the correspondent for *The Wall Street Journal*; it was also a pleasant break for Pakistanis, accustomed as they were, to reading negative stories about their homeland. 'I'm getting a lot of corporate heads, a lot of nouveau riche people who come from abroad who are not necessarily wealthy but are educated about cuisine,' said Mr Sheikh, the son of Pakistani immigrants to Britain who started the Karachi restaurant. 'People want high end products,' and Sheikh was prepared to provide them. The stage was now set for the return and flow of diaspora capital as well as diaspora's management and entrepreneurial talent into Pakistan's economy.

If the experience of other diasporas was anything to learn from, investments into Pakistan by the more well-to-do members of the communities in the United States will proceed through four phases. The first will be investment in real estate, motivated mostly by the desire to establish an alternative place of residence by the older members of the group. This began to happen in 2002, not because of 9/11 but because of the sharp downturn in the US financial markets. The diaporas, interest in investing in Pakistan was probably behind the boom in real estate and housing prices in several major cities of the country in the period 2002–2006. There were tens of thousands of expatriates looking to invest in the Pakistani housing market at that time. This fuelled the market and prices increased manifold in a number of major cities, in particular Islamabad, Lahore and Karachi. The return of the non-resident Pakistanis to their home country, even for part-time living, will bring in other developments. The move to construct new golf courses in places such as Lahore, Rawalpindi and Karachi may be in anticipation of this new demand. Other developments will also come, such as new retail outlets that can cater to the needs of this class of consumers, health care, restaurants and entertainment.

The second phase of this remittance was normally directed at the capital markets. Once again the enormous increase in the prices of the stocks quoted in the Karachi capital market in the first ten weeks of 2005 may have been caused in part by the arrival of portfolio investment by the members of the diasporas. This group was active as investors in the world's capital markets and they looked at the Karachi market as an opportunity for making handsome returns. Even though the market went through a severe decline in the spring of 2005, the diasporas did not lose heart and contributed to its revival in early 2006 when the KSE (Karachi Stock Exchange) index set new records.

The third flow from the diaspora usually took the form of investment in small businesses such as restaurants, retail outlets, fashion houses, medical practices and educational services. As already noted with reference to the article in *The New York Times* this type of investment was attracting members of the Pakistani communities resident outside the country. There was a considerable amount of anecdotal evidence to suggest that second and third generation Pakistanis living in Britain and the United States were looking at the homeland of their ancestors as a place where lucrative investments could be made.

The fourth flow involved large-scale investment in either green-field operations or the acquisition of established enterprises. Much of this activity happened in association with foreign firms. This was one way that foreign direct investment will began to flow into the country. This was the pattern followed by the expatriate communities of China and India. For Pakistan this last flow will be the most important one and will help to bring the Pakistani economy into the global mainstream. Some of that has begun to happen. Bestway, a large chain of grocery stores owned by Sir Anwar Pervez, a British businessman of Pakistani origin, had built a cement plant in what was once his homeland. He has also teamed up with Middle Eastern investors to buy the United Bank Limited, one of the large banks privatized by the government of President Musharraf in the early 2000s.

. Notwithstanding the unsuccessful attempts made by the administrations of Prime Ministers Zulfikar Ali Bhutto and Mian Nawaz Sharif to use the public sector for tapping the diasporas for raising resources, the government has a role to play. Good public policy in this area could benefit the people at home, revive the domestic economy, provide opportunities to the diasporas to get connected again with their homeland and, finally, open new investment opportunities in Pakistan for the well-to-do non-resident Pakistanis. What is that role?

Good policymakers while designing policies normally start by creating a 'matrix of choices' within which they can operate. In an earlier section of this chapter, I identified five geographical clusters in which the majority of the Pakistani community in the United States had located itself. Two of these were on the East Coast of the country, clustered around Washington and New York respectively. The third was in the northern mid-west around Chicago. The fourth was in the West Coast strip that ran down from San Francisco to San Diego and included the Silicon Valley and Los Angeles. The fifth was the cluster around Houston and Dallas in the state of Texas. In another section I identified four types of financial flows that normally originate from the diaspora communities. They include funds provided for family care, charitable giving, investment in real estate and the stock market and, finally, taking equity positions in old or new firms. If the five clusters in which most of the Pakistanis live in America were arrayed along a horizontal axis and the four types of flows they send back home were arranged along the vertical axis, and horizontal and vertical lines were drawn through them, the result would be a matrix made up of twenty 'decision boxes'. By way of examples let me identify three such boxes to indicate how the government could use the wealth and income of the diasporas for promoting development in Pakistan.

One such box was created by the intersection of economic interests of the community of Pakistanis resident, say in Chicago, and the opportunities available for investment in such existing assets as real estate and the stock market. For illustrative purposes let us look at the rapidly developing real estate business in Pakistan and how this could draw capital from the expatriate community. There were dozens of large property developers in the early 2000s who were looking for investors in housing schemes, office complexes, entertainment facilities including golf courses, and shopping malls. The newspapers published by the various Pakistani communities in the US carried prominent advertisements by these sponsors. They must know that there are many people of Pakistani origin living in the United States who would like to put their money in these kinds of ventures.

What is the government's role in this area? There are a number of things the public sector could do to ensure that the companies dealing with land and housing development had the capacity and the experience to operate in this area. They should be licensed to operate in these kinds of ventures and seek outside funds only if they can protect the title they are offering for sale against challenges and litigation. Pakistan did not have a good system of land records; registrations of transfers of property were still done by the *patwaris* using an antiquated system. Ordinary citizens could not go to central offices to verify who had the legitimate claim to a particular property as an owner, or as an occupant, or as a renter. Also title insurance was not available. This is normally provided by specialized institutions that do the checking of titles themselves and then, in return for a premium, take the responsibility for defending the claim of the title holder. Such institutions do not exist in Pakistan. They need to be established.

Having comfort about the quality of the title that was purchased, a buyer normally would want to leverage his or her investment by obtaining a loan to purchase an existing property or build a new one. Provision of this kind of finance is normally done by commercial banks or specialized institutions that deal only in mortgages. Lending for housing arrived in Pakistan following the privatization of large banks. The spread between the rate the banks paid to their depositors and the rate at which the borrowers were prepared to obtain money from the banks was large enough for most financial institutions to regard this kind of business as attractive. Accordingly an active market in housing finance developed in the country.

However, those who borrow for making investments in real estate like to obtain funding for relatively long periods of time. The banks cannot afford to keep long-term paper on their books, since the bulk of their own money comes from short-term deposits and transactions. The banks fear nothing more than what they call a 'maturity mismatch'—when they have short-term liabilities and long-term assets. The financial system has found a way of dealing with this conundrum. This is done by the development of specialized institutions that purchase mortgages the banks hold and bring them on their own books. This happens in what is generally referred to as the secondary market. The original holders of mortgages package them and sell them in large lots to the secondary market at a discount. In this way they achieve two ends: they make money quickly and they are not left holding assets which would be hard to liquidate if there is a crunch. Pakistan unfortunately does not have a secondary market of any consequence and this could cause a great deal of trouble, especially if the real estate comes under stress as it did in 2006 in most large cities of the country.

If the real estate market collapses as did the Karachi market in the spring of 2005, those who have taken out loans from the banks would not be able to service them. This would put the lending banks into a real quandary. It was this kind of situation that resulted in the banking crisis in Japan in the 1980s and 1990s from which the country took a decade and a half to recover. The government, to encourage the flow of funds into the housing and real estate market, must, therefore, facilitate the establishment of the institutions that provide comfort to the potential investor and spread around the risk.

Let me draw another 'decision box' to illustrate with some more examples what the government could do to facilitate investments by non-resident Pakistanis. If lines are dropped that start with the West Coast diaspora and cut the horizontal lines that include investment opportunities in new ventures, the result would be a box that connected with investment opportunities in the homeland. Some of the IT entrepreneurs from America's west coast are ready to invest in Pakistan provided the telecommunication network ensures them the type of connectivity they desire; provided there were an adequate number of people with appropriate skills available; provided the customers being served felt they could visit the places to which they have outsourced their operation. Some improvements were made in these areas particularly after the grant of two additional licenses to mobile operators and the privatization of the Pakistan Telecommunications Corporation but a great deal more need to be done. Those who have already made investments in Pakistan in businesses such as call centres, IT services, preparation of proprietary products, complain that skilled project managers are in short supply. There was even a suggestion that people with this background should be imported on temporary visas from India, where this industry has matured to the point that people are available who are prepared to work outside the country.

A third decision- and policy-making box involved the business community in the Houston–Dallas area, and their willingness to invest in new ventures in the more established areas of the economy. To facilitate this type of investment, Pakistan needs to create another set of financial institutions—those that specialize in the provision of private equity. These institutions generally take positions in established firms that are not yet listed on the stock market. These are mostly family-owned firms that have created businesses using their own savings and capital.

A private equity fund values the target company, takes a share in it, improves the quality of management, encourages the development of new products or new product lines, and finds new markets for the company's output. Private equity ventures do not linger for too long in the firms in which they take interest. Once they have turned around the firm, they move on and return the capital invested into them with profit. Exit is done either through listing in the capital market or by offering the reformed company for merging with or acquisition by larger enterprises.

Pakistan, with thousands of family-owned companies operating in all sectors of the economy, is ripe for this kind of capital infusion and corporate hand-holding. And the expatriate community with money to invest would be interested in putting their capital to work in the hands of experienced private equity entrepreneurs. The health service sector is one area crying out for this kind of association between local entrepreneurs who have invested in hospitals and clinics and the expatriate community, many of whose members have deep knowledge of the sector and have the resources to invest.

There is, therefore, a great deal of work to be done by the government before the large amount of funds available with the Pakistani communities living and working abroad can be put to use for benefiting the home economy. One way to make a start in this area is to establish a commission involving the government, the domestic business people and members of the expatriate community. The commission could be charged to develop concrete proposals and then sent on a road show to the areas in which the Pakistani community has a large presence.

4. Diasporas and Encroachment by Radical Islam

Pakistani diasporas have played a significant role in bringing radical Islam to the homeland. For several decades it was the community of Pakistanis in the Middle East that was instrumental in bringing a different type of Islam to the country of their origin. Later, the diasporas in Britain and the United States began to exert their influence. How these separate threads were woven into the fabric of the Pakistani society is an under-studied subject. What I have to offer here are simply thoughts that call for more research from a diverse group of social scientists—anthropologists, economists, political scientists, and sociologists.

As discussed in Section 1, the community of Pakistanis in the Middle East was initially dominated by mostly unskilled and semi-skilled workers who came from the North West Frontier Province and the northern areas of the Punjab. Poorly educated, they came under the influence of the *Wahabist imams* who preached and taught in the mosques visited by the migrant workers. This was the case in particular in Saudi Arabia where *Wahabism* was the official religion. Given that the migrant workers were an easy group to influence and the sermons calling for returning Islam to its original teachings resonated with it, they became an attractive target for conversion to fundamentalist Islam. Since these were temporary workers, they went back after a few years and entered the communities they had left behind. They returned with the zeal of new converts. The rise of radical Islam in north Punjab and the NWFP could be attributed in part to the influence of the returning migrants.

Radical Islam arrived in the Pakistani diasporas in Europe and North America from a different route. It came from two different directions. It came into the community of Pakistanis in Britain through the economic and social routes; the consequence of the inability—or the unwillingness—of the community to get integrated with the host population. In that respect the Pakistanis living in Britain were not unlike the North African Muslims who had taken up residence in France and whose frustrations exploded in the summer of 2005 in the riots that convulsed the European nation. But there was one fundamental difference in the way Europe, in particular France, sought to integrate the Muslim migrants into the culture of the country. The French demanded full integration to the extent that in 2005, in the glare of international publicity, the authorities banned the use of headscarves by Muslim women. This action agitated the community of French Muslims but the country's senior leaders, including President Jacques Chirac, refused to relent.

The British followed a different approach—that of multi-culturalism. This led to the creation of separate communities with little contact among them.

Perhaps the best description of the enclaves of isolation created by the community of migrants from Pakistan in Britain is in the already cited fictional account of Nadeem Aslam's book, *Maps for Lost Lovers*. I began this chapter with a long quote from his novel.

Aslam builds his story around the families originally from central Punjab who lived in a town called *Dasht-e-Tanhaii*.[12] Not able and not willing to get integrated with the British communities that surrounded them, this group of migrants refused to give up their culture or allow their religion to be encroached upon. Increasingly isolated, they suffered economic deprivation and social rejection. For such a group, Osama bin Laden's teachings resonated. He once described his followers and fighters as 'the nation of martyrdom: the nation that desires death more than those in the West who desire life.' As the young men mostly of Pakistani descent who carried out the bombings in the London underground transport system showed by their desperate actions, they yearned for martyrdom. Of the four bombers who carried out the attacks on 7 July 2005, three had travelled to Pakistan and at least one— perhaps even two—of them was known to have spent some time in a *madrassa* in the northern part of his parent's homeland.

It was through a different route that radical Islam gained a foothold among the Pakistanis resident in the United States. As America launched its war against international terrorism following the attacks of 11 September 2001, it focused much of its attention on the various Muslim communities that had established themselves in the country. Among these, the community of Pakistanis was large and exposed. The Pakistani diaspora in Britain had taken time to radicalize; the transformation in the United States was much more rapid, a reaction to the policies adopted by the administration of President George W. Bush. However, one particular Washington policy—the way America treated the people incarcerated in the prisons at Afghanistan's Bagram Base, Iraq's Abu Ghraib, and the Pentagon's Guantanamo Bay—created a common bond among the radical groups in these two otherwise distinct diasporas. To understand what has occurred and why these developments will have a lasting impact, I will deal with some specific events.

On 25 April 2006 a federal jury convicted Hamid Hayat, a 23-year old American of Pakistani origin, on terrorism charges. He was arrested in June 2005 and 'charged with providing material support to terrorism and lying about it after investigators said he attended a camp run by terrorists in Pakistan sometime between October 2003 and November 2004.'[13] On the same day, a judge released Umer Hayat, 48, Hamid's father, who had been charged with lying to investigators to conceal his son's activities. The jury failed to reach a verdict after eight days of deliberation. The older man was an ice-cream truck driver. The Hayats belonged to the farming town of Lodi in north California that had attracted the attention of the authorities after 9/11, mostly because of the presence of a significant number of mosque-attending people of Pakistani origin.

> But the Hayats, both United States citizens of Pakistani descent, were the only [Lodi] people charged, and the government never revealed what, if any, was the specific plot. Instead it portrayed the arrests as a preventive measure so that Hamid Hayat, who prosecutors said was committed to *jihad*, or holy war, could not carry out any orders.[14]

The Hayat case was a good illustration of three developments that were contributing to the radicalization of some parts of the Pakistani–American community. By turning to insiders for bringing suspects to the attention of the authorities, the communities were losing some of their cohesiveness, which then made them turn to outside influences to find some meaning. The case against the Hayats was built on the evidence provided by one Naseem Khan 'who recorded hundreds of hours of conversations with Hamid Hayat but proved troublesome at trial. Mr Khan revealed on the stand that he had been hired [by the government] after claiming Osama bin Laden's top deputy had been in Lodi, an assertion the government itself refuted.'[15]

Guantanamo proved to be another reason for the growing discomfort for the Muslim communities in America with the way they and their co-religionists were being treated by the American authorities. A moving account of the life and inhabitants of this prison in Cuba was written for *The Washington Post* by Mahvish Khan, a young American lawyer-journalist of Pakistani origin. 'My interest in the US military base in Cuba was sparked by an international law class I took last year at the University of Miami', she wrote. 'I wanted to become involved in what is going on there... Maybe part of my interest had to do with heritage. My Pushtun parents are doctors who met in a medical school in Peshawar... The very existence of the military detention camp at Guantanamo Bay seemed an affront to what the United States stands for. How could our government deny the prisoners there the right to a fair hearing? I didn't know whether they were innocent or guilty—but I figured they should be entitled to the same protections as any alleged rapist or murderer.'

During several visits to the prison, Khan met people consumed by frustration and a sense of helplessness. Among them was Ali Shah Mousavi, 'a physician from the Afghan city of Gardez where he was arrested by US troops two and a half years ago. He tells us that he had returned to Afghanistan in August 2003, after twelve years of exile in Iran, to help rebuild his *wathan*, his homeland. He believes someone turned him in to US forces just to collect up to $25,000 being offered to anyone who gave up a Talib or Al Qaeda member.' She also met Haji Nusrat, 80 years old, the oldest prisoner at Guantanamo Bay. 'A stroke left him partly paralyzed. He cannot stand up without assistance and hobbles to the bathroom behind a walker... During our meeting, Nusrat's emotions range from anger to despair.'[16]

Some segments of the Pakistani diaspora became increasingly disenchanted with America in part because of the policies pursued by the administration of President George W. Bush in its war against terrorism. How this group of people will ultimately relate to their adopted homeland would depend upon how this war evolves. There were some hopeful developments from their perspective as the American judiciary began to assert itself in favour of protecting the rights of the people who had come under suspicion. The judgment reached by the jury that tried Zacarias Moussaoui, a 37-year French citizen of Moroccan descent and the only person convicted in the United States for involvement in the 11 September attacks, gave the Muslim community some hope. He had entered the US in February 2001 and enrolled in flight schools in Oklahoma and Minnesota before being arrested for over-staying his visa. Moussaoui tried to persuade the jury to execute him, claiming that he had been ordered by Al Qaeda to fly a plane into the White House on 11 September 2001. This would have been the fifth plane to attack a prominent target in America. But the jury refused to oblige and sentenced him on 3 May 2006 to life imprisonment without parole. The sentence awarded to the French–Moroccan was well received by the US Muslim community and by the liberal media that had begun to worry about the erosion of human rights in the US as a part of the war against terrorism. But the problem created by the initiatives such as the prison at Guantanamo remained.

'The most important thing about the Moussaoui trial, however, was that it happened,' wrote *The New York Times* in an editorial.

'The proceedings—including the jury deliberations—were long and difficult, but they were also fair and in accordance with the rules of American justice. That is not the story of hundreds of other people, many far less complicit than Mr Moussaoui, who are languishing in the prison at Guantanamo because the United States rounded them haphazardly during the Afghan war and plunked them down in Cuba without any clear plan on what to do with them over the long run. So far only 10 of the 490 people still stashed away have ever been charged with anything. The rest were hauled up before military proceedings that were a joke....[17]

Given the fact that modern communications allow the diasporas to maintain close contacts with the homeland, this disenchantment with the West, especially the United States, was bound to influence Pakistan's social, political and economic development. For a number of decades the diasporas made a positive contribution to the development of the homeland. This will, of course continue, as the economic ties of those in the diasporas develop. Nonetheless, after 9/11 and the nature of the American response, this influence also took a negative tone: it undoubtedly contributed to the country's drift towards Islamic radicalism and obscurantism.

5. Conclusion

The Pakistani citizens living and working outside the country have played an important role in the economic and social life of their homeland for the entire time the country has been independent. Over time, they also became politically active, particularly after some of the more important leaders who were opposed to the government in power took refuge in the countries that had a large Pakistani presence—Benazir Bhutto settled in a long exile in Dubai; Mian Nawaz Sharif, having first gone to Saudi Arabia in 2000, shifted to London in 2006 and Altaf Hussain made his home in Britain. These leaders continue to lead their respective parties from exile. In spite of the political activity that was generated by the presence of these leaders among the diasporas, it was the economic and social impact on Pakistan that was the most profound influence.

The economic role changed over time. The diasporas initially contributed to the development of the economy and also to poverty alleviation by sending large amounts of capital as remittances to families and friends back in Pakistan. On occasion the amounts remitted by the members of the diasporas amounted to as much as 10 per cent of the gross domestic product. Later, however, particularly after 11 September 2001, the diasporas began to send money for different reasons. As there was some increase in unease with the environment that surrounded them, some affluent members of the Pakistani communities in Britain and the United States started making investments in the home country. The economic revival that began in 2003 also created a favourable environment for the flow of capital from the diasporas to Pakistan. While that was a positive development, the increase in confrontation between the West and Islam not only in America but also in Europe—a development predicted by the political scientist Samuel P. Huntington, in a highly influential book,[18]—began to generate a reaction among the Muslim communities in these countries that could prove to be of great significance for Pakistan.

NOTES

1. These numbers are hard to estimate since a significant amount of money does not move through formal banking channels but uses the informal *hawala* and *hundi* mechanisms. In these the remitter hands over the money to a person who has agents for distributing it in the currency used in the remitter's homeland. The agent charges a fee usually less than that taken by banks and the money flows faster. Fearing that *hawalas* and *hundi* mechanisms were used by terrorist organizations to raise money from the members of the diasporas who were sympathetic to their cause led to the adoption of regulatory mechanisms by the West—in particular the United States—to discourage these type of flows.

2. Nadeem Aslam, *Maps for Lost Lovers*, London: Faber and Faber, 2004, p. 9.

3. Government of Pakistan, *Pakistan Economic Survey, 2004–05*, Ministry of Finance, Islamabad, Statistical Annex.

4. Ibid.

5. Samuel P. Huntington, *Who Are We? The Challenge to America's National Identity*, New York: Simon and Schuster, 2005.

6. I covered the subject of the October 2005 earthquake in a series of articles for *Dawn*. See 'Protecting the vulnerable'; 'Quake: Thinking long term', 13 December 2005; 'Rebuilding Azad Kashmir', 20 December 2005.

7. See Shahid Javed Burki, *Pakistan under Bhutto, 1971–77*, London: Macmillan, 1980 and Shahid Javed Burki, *Pakistan: A Nation in the Making*, Boulder, Colo.: Westview Press, 1986.

8. To mention a few examples of these types of events and how they are crowding the social calendar of the Pakistanis in the United States, three fund-raising functions were held by different organizations in the suburbs of Washington: by Karachi University Alumni Association to raise funds for scholarships to low income deserving students who were admitted to the institution on 9 September 2006; by the Human Development Foundation on 15 September 2006, to support the work of the National Commission on Human Development; and a day later by a new charity that was set up to help street children in the country.

9. According to the UNDP *Human Development Report 2005*, Pakistan ranked 137th in the Human Development Index among 177 countries on which the agency reported results. See UNDP, *Human Development Report, 2005: International Cooperation at a Crossroads: Aid Trade and Security in an Unequal World*, New York: Oxford University Press, 2005, Table 1, pp. 222–224.

10. Dr Nasim Ashraf who worked as a physician in the Washington area before relocating himself in Islamabad, Pakistan.

11. Somni Sengupta, 'Pakistan is booming after 9/11 at least for the well-off', *The New York Times*, 23 March 2005, p. A3.

12. Nadeem Aslam, *Maps for Lost Lovers*, New York: Alfred A. Knopf, 2005.

13. Randal C. Archibold and Jeff Kearns, 'In California terror case, a mistrial for a father, but a son is guilty', *The New York Times*, 26 April 2006, p. A17.
14. Ibid., p. A17.
15. Ibid., p. A17.
16. Mahvish Khan, 'My Guantanamo Diary: face-to-face with the war on terrorism', *The Washington Post, Outlook*, 30 April 2006, pp. B1 and B5.
17. *The New York Times*, 'Due process', 4 May 2006, p. A30.
18. Samuel P. Huntington, *The Clash of Civilizations and the Remaking of World Order*, New York: Simon and Schuster, 1996.

7

An Economic Solution for the
Kashmir Problem

Why include a chapter on Kashmir in a book concerned with public policy in the field of economics? The question has a simple answer. The Kashmir dispute with India has had a profound impact on the Pakistani economy and also on its society. In terms of the economic consequences of the country's preoccupation with Kashmir ever since it gained independence some sixty years ago, it is not only the large expenditure on defence that matters. As I will argue below, the opportunity cost of the dispute has been significant in many other ways. This is particularly the case now as the process of globalization works its way towards South Asia. The Kashmir problem continues to create uncertainty about Pakistan's future and adversely affects its ability to attract foreign capital and foreign businesses into the country. My main argument in this chapter is that Pakistan may have to change its stance with respect to the dispute in order to buy a better future for itself. Also, the growing tension between the West and the Muslim world has a significant impact on the environment in which Pakistan must now deal with the problem of Kashmir.

There is no doubt that the terrorist attacks of 11 September 2001 on the United States produced a new world political order.[1] And there is also no doubt that this fateful event changed the way nation-states work with one another and with the United States. The administration of President George W. Bush in a policy statement issued in September 2002, a year after the terrorist attacks, signalled its intention to launch pre-emptive strikes if the United States determined that its security was threatened. The policy statement also declared that 'America must stand firmly for the non-negotiable demands of human dignity.' With these pronouncements the world's remaining super-power was indicating that it had the right to intervene outside its own borders without the sanction of any international authority if it decided that such an action was required for its own security. This message was not lost on other powerful nations across the globe.

Protagonists in a number of world-wide conflicts attempted to recast their roles in light of the changes after 9/11. Powerful states, wishing to impose order in the areas where their authority was being challenged, became considerably more assertive, especially if those who posed the challenge were militarily weaker and especially if those who challenged central authority could be labelled as terrorists. This happened in the case of the Russian attempt to put down the insurrection in Chechnya. The Kremlin was able to describe the Chechen separatists as terrorists, especially since there was an active involvement of the *jihadi* groups in the struggle by the Chechens against Russian domination. It also happened in the case of the Israeli–Palestinian conflict. The Palestinian suicide bombers were often labelled Islamic terrorists. That may also have happened in Kashmir where India had fought an insurgency against its rule since 1989. The Indians were also able to pin the label of terrorism on some of the people who had taken up arms against their rule of Kashmir, especially those who had infiltrated across the border from Pakistan. But India had to contend with Pakistan, albeit economically and militarily weaker than itself but strong enough to resist a major escalation of conflict in Kashmir. That notwithstanding, 9/11 changed the environment in which India and Pakistan were pursuing their very different objectives in the state of Jammu and Kashmir.[2] It is in the light of this change in environment that I will suggest in this chapter that an opportunity may have finally arisen which could lead India and Pakistan towards finding a solution—if not a solution then at least a working arrangement—for the long festering problem of Kashmir.

Both countries should recognize that by continuing to push their old strategy in pursuit of their interests in Kashmir they may be seen to be stoking the fires of Islamic extremism the Washington was keen to extinguish, and both should appreciate that the perpetuation of the conflict in Kashmir was exacting a heavy economic toll, which may seriously affect their future economic prospects. There was no doubt that Pakistan had paid a heavier price than India for its continuing involvement in the Kashmir dispute. But India had also suffered. Recognition of the cost of the Kashmir dispute led both Islamabad and Delhi to rethink their strategies towards the disputed area. In the fall of 2003—two years after the terrorist attacks on the United States and about eighteen months after India and Pakistan almost went to war once again over the disputed territory of Kashmir—both Islamabad and New Delhi seemed ready to look for new ways for resolving this long-enduring territorial dispute.

The Kashmir issue had not only soured relations between India and Pakistan, the two largest economies of South Asia, it also had a profound influence on all of South Asia, slowing down the sub-continent's economic growth and inhibiting regional integration. That could change if the leaderships of India and Pakistan were to turn their attention to launching a process that would begin to improve the economic well-being of the South Asian citizenry including the people of the two Kashmirs, one controlled by India and the other under the authority of Islamabad.

A solution to the problem may be found in creating new ground realities involving cooperation between India and Pakistan. This would have to be done not in one giant leap—an approach preferred by Pakistan—but in several small steps, as favoured by India. These steps could begin with the attempts to better the lives of the people of Kashmir on both sides of the 'line of control' (LOC). The LOC was effectively the border between India and Pakistan since the agreement between Prime Ministers Indira Gandhi of India and Zulfikar Ali Bhutto of Pakistan, signed at Simla in 1972, but it has not been recognized as such by Delhi and Islamabad. There was little prospect that the final solution for the problem would be to convert the LOC into an international border, a position India favours but Pakistan vehemently opposes. Instead it may be possible to turn this into a 'soft border' for a number of years—even for decades—while the various parties to the dispute agree to greater cooperation among themselves in the areas of economics and trade. If the various sides involved in this dispute decide to proceed on the route proposed here, they may have to journey a long time. It is also not certain as to the type of destination they will reach. Nonetheless, there is a very good reason to embark on this journey.

This chapter[3] has eight sections. The section following the introduction provides a brief history of the Kashmir dispute, focusing on the decision by the British to apply a different criterion for allocating princely states to the successor countries of India than they did to the provinces they directly governed. Had they used the same criterion—of allowing accession on the basis of which of the two communities, the Hindus and Muslims, constituted the majority—the dispute over Kashmir would not have risen and the story of South Asia would have been very different. Section 2 provides a couple of premises for the main argument in this chapter: that the Kashmir dispute can be resolved by adopting a different approach from the one pursued for almost sixty years by the parties to the conflict. Section 3 suggests some reasons why the early 2000s present an opportunity for thinking out of the box to resolve a dispute that has soured relations between India and Pakistan from the time they became independent. Section 4 provides a brief overview of the main events that have occurred since India and Pakistan launched the programme of 'confidence building' begun in January 2004. Section 5 provides an estimate of the cost to Pakistan of the Kashmir dispute in both economic and social terms. The calculations offered are based on how the country's economy would have performed had Kashmir not become a dispute. Section 6 suggests why India and Pakistan should take what I call the 'development route' for resolving this dispute. Section 7 provides the details of the type of programme that could be launched to rebuild the insurgency-torn economy of the state. The chapter ends with a brief concluding section.

1. The Background

There are several reasons why the West, in particular the United States, should be concerned about the situation in Kashmir. The Kashmir problem has been around for as long as India and Pakistan, the protagonists in the dispute over the ownership of this territory, have been independent. The dispute owes its origin to the untidy way in which the British government chose to partition their Indian domain between the successor states of India and Pakistan. They used the census of 1941 to assign the Muslim areas to Pakistan and left the rest for India. However, they decided to leave the future of the several hundred princely states in the hands of their rulers, but there was an expectation that those with Muslim majorities would accede to Pakistan while the remaining would be assimilated in India. One of the important unanswered questions about the way the departing British chose to partition the Indian subcontinent is why did they not apply the same formula to assigning the princely states to the two successor countries as they did for the provinces directly administered by them. If they had done that, Kashmir without Jammu would have become part of Pakistan while Jammu, Hyderabad and Junagadh would have automatically gone to India.

The formula adopted worked for all but three states—Hyderabad, Junagadh and Kashmir. The princes who ruled the first two states were Muslims but the majority of their populations were Hindu. In Kashmir the situation was just the opposite. India used its military to resolve the Hyderabad and Junagadh problems. Once it was clear that the ruling princes of Hyderabad and Junagadh would not readily accede to India, Delhi resorted to the use of force to bring them into the Indian union. It could adopt that approach since these states were surrounded by India. The case of Kashmir was different, since that state bordered not only India but also Pakistan and China.

When the Hindu maharaja of Jammu and Kashmir hesitated in making his decision about accession, both India and Pakistan tried to force his hand. In Pakistan's case force was literally applied. A rag-tag army of Pushtun warriors was dispatched across the border to conquer Kashmir. This it did on 26 October 1947, a few weeks after India and Pakistan became independent, which provoked Kashmir's Hindu ruler to sign the accession instrument in favour of India. That brought both the Indian and Pakistani armies openly into the conflict. After a brief but sharp war, the United Nations arranged a ceasefire in early 1949 and the Security Council passed the first of many resolutions on Kashmir. The resolution promised that the future of the state would be determined ultimately in a plebiscite which would ascertain the wishes of the people of the state whether they wanted to be part of Pakistan or remain with India. The option of being independent was not offered to the state's citizens. The plebiscite was never held but continued to be the basis on which Pakistan asserted its claim to the state.[4]

Mohandas Karamchand Gandhi—Mahatma Gandhi—seeing that the dispute over Kashmir could turn into a long and unsolvable struggle and result in a tragedy for the entire population of South Asia, tried to persuade the leadership of new India—in particular Jawaharlal Nehru, the country's first prime minister—to apply to the state of Jammu and Kashmir the logic on the basis of which British India was partitioned. 'I have been severely reprimanded for what I have said concerning Kashmir,' Stanley Wolpert, one of his many western's biographers, reports Gandhi telling his associates in Delhi in early 1948.

> The advice I give is the kind of advice the humblest man can give… Kashmir is a Hindu State, the majority of its people being Muslims… It seems obvious to me, as it should seem obvious to others… that if Sheikh Abdullah [Kashmir's prime minister] cannot carry with him the minority [Hindu] as well as the majority [Muslim], Kashmir cannot be saved by military might alone.' But Mahatma Gandhi's peaceful solution for the Kashmir conflict, formulating an honourable way for India to extricate itself from the costly and deadly war, was completely ignored by Nehru.[5]

In his biography of Jawaharlal Nehru, Wolpert quotes a conversation between the Indian prime minister and India's high commissioner (ambassador) to Pakistan as follows:

Nehru's High Commissioner to Pakistan Sri Prakash sensibly suggested that perhaps the wisest thing to do about Kashmir, since it was mostly Muslim, would be to let Pakistan have it. "I was amazed," Nehru thundered, "that you hinted at Kashmir being handed over to Pakistan... The fact is that Kashmir is of the most vital significance to India... Kashmir is going to be a drain on our resources, but it is going to be a greater drain on Pakistan".[6]

By the time the United Nations intervened and arranged a ceasefire, the two opposing views about Kashmir's future had jelled. Pakistan regarded the action by the Hindu ruler of the state unjustified since Kashmir was a Muslim majority area and should have acceded to Pakistan. For India, even though its leaders had accepted the idea of partition on the basis of religion, the prospect of dividing yet another area on a religious basis militated against the concept on which Indian nationhood was founded. The Indians regarded their country as a multiethnic secular national state. Josef Korbel, chairman of the United Nations Commission on India and Pakistan (UNCIP) until 1949, argued in his book *Danger in Kashmir* that

> the real cause of all the bitterness and bloodshed, all the venomed speech, recalcitrance and the suspicion that have characterized the Kashmir dispute is the uncompromising and perhaps uncompromisable struggle of two ways of life, two concepts of political organizations, two scales of values, two spiritual attitudes that find themselves locked in deadly conflict, a conflict. in which Kashmir has become both symbol and background.[7]

Even this short description of the genesis of the Kashmir problem would provoke a debate in India and Pakistan. Was the accession instrument signed by the Maharaja a legal document that could be sanctioned under the provisions of the India Independence Act of 1947? That act passed by the British parliament, along with the India Act of 1935, were the basis on which India was partitioned and remained the documents under which the two successor states were governed for as long as they did not write their own constitutions. Did the Security Council really intend to leave the final status of the state open until a plebiscite was conducted under the auspices of the United Nations? What were precisely the conditions that had to be fulfilled by the two sides before the United Nations could authorize a vote in the territory? Was the invasion of the state from the Pakistani side really carried out by an army of Pushtun tribesmen or were these people Pakistan's soldiers fighting under a camouflage? Did the Pakistani army need to depart from the areas it occupied before India could agree to a plebiscite? Had India by holding several elections in the state—even if some of them were conducted under a great deal of official pressure—effectively determined the wishes of the people? None of these questions—and all of them are important and need answers for a resolution of the dispute—had an unambiguous answer.

The real point of this chapter is not to provide answers to these questions by opening this debate. The purpose is not even to suggest that had the British carried out India's partition in a cleaner way by not giving the princes the right to choose between India and Pakistan, there would not have been a Kashmir problem. After all, the British could have applied the same logic for assigning the states to the two successor countries that they used to allocate the areas they ruled directly. In that case India would not have needed to use force to incorporate Hyderabad and Junagadh into its territory, and Kashmir would have automatically become part of Pakistan. Or, as was the case with the provinces of Bengal and Punjab, the State of Jammu and Kashmir could have also been partitioned along religious lines. This approach was suggested publicly by Pakistan's President Pervez Musharraf in the fall of 2004. But he was rebuffed by the Indian leadership. These remain weighty questions and issues, and they will continue to engage historians for a long time to come. The purpose of this chapter is not to write one more history of the Kashmir dispute but to propose a new approach towards resolving the issue.

2. The Premise

The main thrust of this chapter is to argue that by leaving the Kashmir problem unattended, the world was taking a great risk. The risk was as great as was taken in the case of the Middle East by letting the conflict between the Israelis and the Palestinians continue to fester. Similarly, when, in 1989, the Americans decided to leave the future of Afghanistan in the hands of the warlords who had successfully fought against the Soviet Union's occupation of their country, they helped create the environment which eventually led to the emergence of the Taliban regime in Kabul and the terrorist attacks of 11 September 2001 on the United States.

The Kashmir problem, left unresolved, could create another breeding ground from which Islamic radicals could begin to find recruits for their various causes. That this could happen would perhaps be disputed by those who argue that the Muslim population of Kashmir would not be radicalized, since the type of Islam it practiced was different from the faith of the people who supported Al Qaeda and other militant groups. There has been an extraordinary amount of religious harmony in Kashmir for centuries; the area's population practiced what they called *Kashmiryat*, a code of tolerance. But as the novelist Salman Rushdie laments in *Shalimar the Clown*, his novel that centres on Kashmir, a great deal of water has flown down Kashmir's many rivers for *Kashmiryat* to regain the hold it once had on the state's society.[8] It would not be prudent, therefore, to draw comfort from the argument that Islam in Kashmir would never breed extremism. The same was once said about the Palestinians, the most secular people in the Arab world. In an election in December 2005, the Palestinians elected Hamas, an avowedly religious party that was declared to be a terrorist organization by the United States, Europe and Israel. In fact the same could be said about the type of Islam that was once the religion of the vast majority of the people of Pakistan. Islam practiced in Pakistan was not the austere and fundamentalist religion that became the main base of support for Al Qaeda. In the early 2000s—for reasons beyond the scope of this book and chapter—Pakistan's population was also being radicalized; in several parts of the country, a gentle and accommodating Islam was yielding space to an austere, radical and extremist religion that was at the centre of what the political scientist Samuel P. Huntington called the 'clash of civilizations'.[9]

Kashmir in the early 2000s had all the ingredients needed to cook the radical-extremist broth. It had suffered from an insurgency that had gone on for more than a decade and a half and had claimed between 30,000 and 80,000 lives, depending on who was keeping the count. Most of the lives lost were in the brutal warfare that did not distinguish combatants from non-combatants. As a result of this prolonged conflict, the state's economy had suffered greatly. For a decade and a half Kashmir was been one of the slowest-growing regional economies in South Asia. It was among the poorer states of India. The part of the state held by Pakistan had done somewhat better since it had not been the scene of an insurgency and since a large number of people from the area had migrated to other parts of Pakistan or had gone abroad. But even this area suffered when it was hit by an earthquake on 8 October 2005 that took 84,000 lives and left more than three million people without shelter. Economic stagnation brought poverty and unemployment to the area.

Among those who have suffered the most in the Indian part of Kashmir are the young who account for more than one-half of the state's total population of some eleven million people. As the conflict drags on, the young see few prospects for themselves in the future. Their frustration offered opportunities to a number of radical Islamic leaders who were looking to build support for themselves. They will not hesitate to exploit this opportunity. If the conflict continues, politics in the state would very likely radicalize. It cannot be in India's interest to have a highly alienated Muslim population sitting in close proximity to its own large population of Muslims, estimated at some at 138 million.[10]

It cannot be in Pakistan's interest either to keep a dispute on simmer so that the *jihadi* groups could continue to find new recruits for their cause. And, it is certainly not in the interest of the rest of the world to allow another area peopled by a large

Muslim population to become the breeding and recruiting grounds for various Islamic causes. The world could not afford another group of people prepared to lay down their lives for furthering what they believed to be an 'Islamic cause.' It was in the interest of the civilized world to move towards finding a solution for the Kashmir population or, at least, finding a way to bring peace to this troubled region.

Was there a way out of this conundrum? Of the many ways of approaching the Kashmir problem, there were three that hold some promise. First, to let the dialogue inaugurated between India and Pakistan beginning in January 2004 to run its course in the hope that both sides would eventually begin to see that it was in their long-term interest to settle this dispute and concentrate public resources, not on building their respective militaries, making them stronger and deploying large number of armed personnel in troubled spots such as Kashmir, but in spending public funds on economic development and improving the welfare of their citizens. Second, they should persuade the world's major powers, in particular the United States, to get actively involved in pushing the two sides to the dispute—or three sides, if the Kashmiris were recognized as having interests that are separate from those of India and Pakistan—to move towards a resolution to the dispute. Third, they should initiate a set of activities in the state aimed at improving the economic condition of the people of the region.

The first option has many costs. For as long as the two countries continue to talk to one another and if these talks are stretched over a long period of time as India seems inclined to do, there will be no significant economic developments on the ground. Continuing economic stagnation will breed resentment especially among the young, and, most likely, push them towards Islamic extremism. And, as discussed below, a series of developments since January 2004, while encouraging, may not result in laying the ground for a final solution.

The second is really not an option since India has declared unequivocally on many occasions that it would not welcome or encourage outside involvement in finding a solution to the Kashmir problem. This point of view was put forward vigorously by Jaswant Singh, former foreign minister of India and regarded as a good friend of the United States in a statement in October 2004. Singh was contesting the story put out by Colin Powell, then US Secretary of State, in which he suggested that his country had acted to defuse tensions between India and Pakistan in 2001–2002. For decades New Delhi refused to accept the label of a 'dispute' to describe the nature of the Kashmir problem. It could not be called a dispute, maintained New Delhi, since the Maharaja of Kashmir decided the accession to India according to the procedures laid down in the 1947 partition agreement. This is why the third option needs to be seriously explored.

How to focus on creating better economic opportunities for the people of the state so that they begin to prepare the ground for the resolution of the problem? This may be done by agreeing on a programme that would involve all parties to the dispute to bring about economic change from which there could not be any turning back. This could be done in two ways. The first is to tinker at the margin; to do a number of small things in the state—particularly in the Indian part—so that visible economic benefits begin to convince the people that it is in their long-term interest to place their faith in non-radical solutions.[11] Chinese sages say that all long journeys begin with small steps. However, the steps on which the people of Kashmir should be made to embark must not be so tiny that their patience runs out. This is then the moment for adopting some brave new initiatives; for taking a few leaps into the future that would induce India, Pakistan, and the people of Kashmir to move forward not by just a small distance but by long strides. What are these brave initiatives? The main purpose of this chapter is to answer this question in some detail.

3. An Auspicious Moment for Finding the Final Solution

For a number of reasons the early 2000s presented the right moment for adopting a well-articulated plan to solve the Kashmir problem. Pragmatists rather than ideologues were in power in both New Delhi and Islamabad. This group included President Pervez Musharraf who had been greatly chastened by the events since 11 September 2001 and had begun to view the Kashmir problem from an entirely different angle. The two assassination attempts on him in December 2003 were orchestrated and carried out by the people who had once worked closely with the Pakistani armed forces and the Inter-Services Intelligence (ISI), the powerful intelligence agency associated with the military. As discussed below, President Musharraf was working hard to reorient his government's position towards Kashmir in order not to allow the exponents of radical Islam to create more space for themselves in Pakistan. There were other people in leadership positions in Pakistan who were similarly inclined as President Musharraf.

According to *The Economist*, Shaukat Aziz's appointment as Pakistan prime minister in September 2004:

> brings a curious, and in many ways pleasing symmetry to governance in the subcontinent's two nuclear-armed giants. Both will now have prime ministers who are technocrats: Mr Aziz hails from Citibank; India's Manmohan Singh was a much-respected academic economist. Both were drafted into politics late in life before getting the top job. And the fact that two such even-tempered and practical people are in charge should bring a more profound recognition of the huge benefits, in the form of trade and investment, that could accrue to both countries if their relations were conditioned more by economics and less by the destructive politics of Kashmir.[12]

Islamabad's approach to the problem of Kashmir appeared to have significantly changed after 11 September 2001. There was realization that the past way of dealing with the issue had cost the country a great deal. The support Islamabad provided the radical groups operating in Kashmir against India had contributed to the rise of Islamic extremism in the country. The cost to Pakistan of the lingering dispute was not only the rapid growth of Islamic radicalism in the country. As discussed in a later section, the economic costs that could be attributed to the dispute were also considerable. Shaukat Aziz, a technocrat, and then the prime minister, would have liked to see real economic progress on his watch. Having succeeded in stabilizing the economy with the help of the International Monetary Fund and the two multilateral development banks, the World Bank and the Asian Development Bank, he looked for ways to set the economy on a course that could yield rates of economic growth comparable to those achieved by India since the mid-1980s. That would require large doses of foreign direct investment to augment low domestic savings in Pakistan. These won't become available if tension persists between India and Pakistan and if Islamic extremists continue to disturb the peace in the country. It would help Pakistan's standing in international financial markets if there were a palpable improvement in relations between South Asia's two largest countries. Moving towards a resolution of the Kashmir dispute would be an important contribution to achieving this objective.

There was also a change of heart in India. Although the first few steps towards rapprochement with Pakistan were taken by Atal Bihari Vajpayee, India's former prime minister, it was doubtful that he would have been able to persuade his party to yield any ground whatsoever to Pakistan. The Bharatiya Janata Party (BJP) Vajpayee then led, had deep roots in Hindu fundamentalism. That the BJP would have been constrained against acting in a manner that would have resolved the Kashmir dispute over time was demonstrated time and again. President Pervez Musharraf maintained that he was willing to begin to initiate a political process that would have resulted in the easing of tensions between the two countries provided India was prepared to recognize that the issue of Kashmir had to be addressed. It was with that intention that he went to Agra in July 2001 for a summit meeting with Prime Minister Vajpayee. According to the Pakistani president, the radical wing of the BJP effectively vetoed Vajpayee's attempt to find a way that would bring the two sides closer to a final solution.[13] The BJP radicals struck again in 2005 when they reacted negatively to the statements by Lal Krishna Advani, who succeeded Vajpayee as the party's leader after its defeat in the general elections of 2004. Advani visited

Pakistan in early 2005 and, while laying a wreath at the tomb of Mohammad Ali Jinnah, Pakistan's founder, said some warm words about the Muslim leader. The extremely negative reaction to Advani's comments forced him to resign as BJP's president. Although he was persuaded to stay on, this reaction to the pronouncements of a leader who had always been regarded as a hardliner with respect to India's relations with Pakistan demonstrated once again the narrowness of the space within which the BJP could operate. Most likely the BJP would have balked at making meaningful concessions to Pakistan.

There were better prospects of peace between India and Pakistan after the return of the Congress Party to power in May 2004. This was for several reasons, not just the removal of the constraints imposed by the Hindu radicals on the BJP government in developing a working relationship with Pakistan. The Congress Party fought for and received the mandate to address the problem of persistent poverty and growing income inequality in the country. To achieve these goals it knew that it must increase public sector expenditure on social services which could be done by reducing non-development expenditure. Reducing defence expenditure would be helpful. While India wanted to play a larger role in South Asia as a regional power and this would mean modernizing its army, Kashmir was a drain since the continuation of the insurgency meant the maintenance of a large force on active duty. It was in the interests of the Congress government not to have its attention diverted towards Kashmir and not to have to commit a large amount of public money to maintaining more than half a million soldiers in the state. In the early 2000s, India was faced with a large fiscal deficit, which had cast a deep shadow on its economic prospects. Reducing the expenditure on Kashmir, incurred to maintain such a large military presence in a battle ready state, was an expensive and draining proposition. Any relief on this score would have considerable economic benefits.

There are other reasons why India seemed inclined to find a workable solution for the problem of Kashmir. It was seeking a role for itself as a global power. It tried hard to get a permanent seat in the reformed Security Council, and joined hands with Brazil, Germany, and Japan at the time of the United Nation's summit in September 2005 to realize that ambition. It wanted to be perceived not only as a regional power but as a country that had the economic strength and the military might to be counted, if not quite equal, then at least in the same league as the United States, the European Union, China, Japan, and Russia. Being embroiled in a dispute such as Kashmir reduced its stature on the global scene.

After a decade and a half of using its immense military power to suppress the insurgency in Kashmir, India seemed to have come to the conclusion that it should search for other solutions to the problem. The use of force would not serve its purpose. In a newspaper article, the historian Niall Ferguson suggested that insurgencies can be suppressed with the use of overwhelming force. His conclusion was based on a comparison of the way the Americans sought to stabilize Iraq after invading the country in 2003 with the way the British handled resistance in that country in the 1920s, 'Thus back then [in the 1920s], ratios of Iraqis to foreign forces was, at most, 23 to 1. To arrive at that ratio today, about one million American troops would be needed.' Applying the same arithmetic to the Indian attempt to pacify Kashmir meant that with half a million soldiers present in Kashmir India should be able to meet its objective. However, it was unable to do what Britain did then. 'The British were able to be ruthless: they used air raids and punitive expeditions to inflict harsh collective punishment on villages that supported the insurgents.'[14] World opinion and India's global ambitions do not allow the exercise of that option. Besides the Congress Party also had the strong support of the country's Muslim population that would like to see the issue of Kashmir resolved peacefully and not by the use of great force against fellow Muslims. India's nearly 140 million Muslims don't wish to have an unstable and radicalized Muslim Kashmiri population located right next to them. Strategic calculus seemed to point New Delhi toward a non-military option.

4. Some Developments, 2004–2006

The first step in the move toward resolving the Kashmir dispute was made by the then Prime Minister Atal Bihari Vajpayee in a speech delivered in Srinagar on 18 April 2003. Speaking in Urdu, he offered a 'hand of friendship' to Pakistan and its leader, President Pervez Musharraf. 'We are again extending the hand of friendship, but hands should be extended from both sides' the Indian leader told a crowd of several thousand people bused in by the state government to the Sher-e-Kashmir Cricket Stadium in Srinagar. The speech drew an immediate positive response from Pakistan's then prime minister, Zafarullah Khan Jamali, and Sheikh Rashid Ahmed, minister of information. 'Pakistan will go two steps forward if India will take one step,' said the information minister, who often spoke for President Pervez Musharraf.

Vajpayee was in a way returning to the situation in July 2001 when he entertained Musharraf to a summit meeting in Agra, a city with a number of rich reminders of the Muslim presence in India, including the Taj Mahal. His initiative, however, was seemingly vetoed by the hardliners in his administration, in particular Deputy Prime Minister Lal Krishna Advani. 'We would have made a breakthrough then had Vajpayee better prepared the ground in his party,' President Musharraf told me in a conversation in 2004.[15] The Pakistani president repeated this claim in *In the Line of Fire*, his memoir published in September 2006.[16]

In between the collapse of the Agra summit and Vajpayee's statement in Srinagar, India and Pakistan came very close to another war over the disputed territory. The Indians amassed hundreds of thousands of troops on their side of the border after the 13 December 2001 attack on the parliament compound in New Delhi. The attack was blamed on Pakistan's ISI and the *mujahideen* it was allegedly training to fight against India in Kashmir. Pakistan answered the Indian mobilization with one of its own, and amassed hundreds of thousands of troops on its side of the border. For sometime it appeared that India and Pakistan would go to yet another war over Kashmir. It took intense diplomatic activity on the part of the West—in particular the United States—to diffuse the tension and persuade New Delhi and Islamabad to pull their troops back from the border. The West was fearful that a war between the two long-time hostile nations could result in the use of nuclear weapons, an impression Pakistan's Pervez Musharraf did little to dispel since militarily Pakistan was in a much weaker position than India. The Pakistani president believed that he needed to threaten India to avert a conventional war his military could not sustain, let alone win.

From the fear of nuclear confrontation in the early months of 2002 to the offer of a hand of friendship a year later, the speed at which tensions eased between the two long-term South Asian rivals was—at least initially—almost breath-taking. There was a realization on both sides of the border that there was much greater wisdom in working out the differences between the two countries through dialogue rather than military confrontation. Both sides had also begun to appreciate the high economic rewards peace would inevitably bring.

The next step towards peace was taken at Islamabad in early January, when Prime Minister Vajpayee along with other heads of state and governments of the SAARC nations went to Pakistan's capital to attend the twice-postponed twelfth Summit of the organization. The Islamabad summit broke two new grounds. The SAARC nations agreed to launch the SAFTA on 1 January 2006.[17] And, on the sidelines of the summit, Prime Minister Atal Bihari Vajpayee and President Pervez Musharraf signed a joint statement in which

> both leaders welcomed the recent steps towards normalization of relations between the two countries and expressed the hope that the positive trends set by the CBMs (Confident Building Measures) would be consolidated. Prime Minister Vajpayee said that in order to take forward and sustain the dialogue, violence, hostility and terrorism must be prevented. President Musharraf reassured Prime Minister Vajpayee that he will not permit any territory under Pakistan's control to be used to support terrorism in any manner. President Musharraf emphasized that a sustained and productive dialogue addressing all issues would lead to positive results. To carry the process of normalization forward,

the [two leaders] agreed to commence the process of the composite dialogue in February 2004. [They] are confident that the resumption of the composite dialogue will lead to a peaceful settlement of all bilateral issues, including Jammu and Kashmir, to the satisfaction of both sides. The two leaders agreed that the constructive dialogue would promote progress towards the common objectives of peace, security and economic development for our people and for future generations.[18]

There were a number of interesting nuances in the joint statement issued from Islamabad. As President Musharraf was to do over and over again, he overruled the bureaucracy in his foreign office to agree to the statement. The traditionalists in Islamabad were especially troubled by the fact that the Pakistani president had virtually conceded that the insurgency in Kashmir was being sustained by the *mujahideen* trained by Pakistan and infiltrated into the Indian side of Kashmir from its side of the border.[19] The two sides also agreed to launch a 'composite' dialogue, an Indian term to signal that it was prepared to discuss Kashmir within the scope of an agenda that included eight items of interest to both sides. In return for this concession by India, Pakistan shed its claim that the Kashmir problem was central to finding a lasting peace between the two countries. The dialogue itself was to begin with discussions among middle level bureaucrats from both sides to deal with issues such as the restoration of diplomatic relations between the two countries, the resumption of flights by the national airlines over each other's territory, the resumption of train and bus services, and the release of prisoners (mostly fishermen who had mistakenly entered the other country's territorial waters). However, the bureaucracy got stuck in the well-worn grooves when there was an opportunity to break new ground.

This happened with the suggestion that a bus service should be inaugurated between Srinagar, the capital of the part of the state controlled by India, and Muzaffarabad, the capital of the Pakistani part of Kashmir. Such a bus service would bring an enormous amount of immediate relief to tens of thousands of Kashmiri families split by the division of the state in the late 1940s. But it took time to make progress since India demanded that the persons crossing the LOC must carry Indian passports. This was not acceptable to the Pakistani side since, Islamabad argued, the use of passports would give the signal that Pakistan had accepted the LOC as an international border. 'A dispute, left to be resolved by bureaucrats, won't make much progress. I had to intervene personally to get our bureaucracy to work towards the resumption of the bus service,' President Musharraf said to me in a conversation in the spring of 2005.[20]

With the dialogue stuck in the bureaucratic corridors, it was not surprising that the situation on the ground began to deteriorate as the summer of 2004 drew to a close. According to one analysis in a western newspaper,

> eight months after India and Pakistan initiated formal negotiations to end more than half of a century of hostility, much of it bearing on their competing claims to Kashmir, there has been little discernible reduction in human rights abuses by Indian security forces that have been waging a counterinsurgency campaign in the region since 1989, according to human rights monitors, Kashmiri political leaders and government data.[21]

On the Pakistani side, President Musharraf began to display some impatience with respect to the progress made in the composite dialogue being conducted by his officials and ministers and their counterparts in New Delhi. No progress was made in the talks held in early September 2004 between Natwar Singh, a veteran diplomat who had joined the Congress-led government as the country's new foreign minister, and Khurshid Mahmud Kasuri, his Pakistani counterpart. The talks were held in New Delhi.

In the midst of this impasse, President Pervez Musharraf decided to lay down a new roadmap. On 25 October 2004 at a Ramadan fast-breaking dinner at the residence of his minister of information he seemed to move two steps forward. First, he said that just as a settlement on the basis of the LOC was unacceptable to Pakistan, he recognized that a plebiscite to determine the future of the state would never be acceptable to India. This was a brave move on his part since no Pakistani leader before him had publicly declared that Pakistan would be prepared to give up on this long-standing demand. Second, the Pakistani president started to indicate that his government was considering other options. He noted that Kashmir had seven regions, two in the area under Pakistan's control and five in the Indian part of Kashmir. He suggested that some or all of these regions should be demilitarized and their status changed. The result of these moves could be independence, 'condominium' between India and Pakistan, or a UN mandate. 'India responded with chilly formality, saying it was not prepared to discuss Kashmir through the media. But at least it did not rule out talking on these lines. It probably calculates that General Musharraf needs to start building a constituency in Pakistan for a radical change in the country's negotiating position. He needs one: his opponents have already accused him of plotting a "sell-out" in Kashmir,' commented *The Economist*.[22]

The initial Indian reaction may have been chilly but it seemed to move in the direction suggested by the Pakistani leader. In a wide-ranging speech on 11 November, a few days before his first visit to Kashmir, Prime Minister Manmohan Singh indicated that his government had decided to reduce the number of troops present in the state. 'Mr Singh's statement, which surprised many senior officials in New Delhi, is the most significant step in months by either side to create a more positive climate for the nine month old peace process between India and Pakistan,' wrote the *Financial Times*.[23] There were indications that troop reductions would be substantial. While announcing the reduction, Singh, as a gesture to the hardliners in his country, warned that India could reverse its position 'if the levels of [terrorist] infiltration and terrorist violence increases.' Nonetheless, he told the *Financial Times* in an interview, he was 'willing, I think, to look at all options—to think about a new chapter and a new beginning between our two countries. I believe that when dealing with seemingly intractable problems one has to be confident of one's own sincerity in trying to find a solution.'[24]

On 17 November, Prime Minister Manmohan Singh addressed a public meeting in Srinagar, the capital of the Indian Kashmir. He struck a clear contrast to the tone of Atal Bihari Vajpayee, his predecessor, who had 'extended the hand of friendship' to Pakistan in a rally in the Kashmiri capital in April 2003. 'An economist with a technocratic background, Mr Singh made no attempt at the rhetorical flourishes for which Mr Vajpayee was famed. Nor did Mr Singh address any direct message to Islamabad' wrote Edward Luce of the *Financial Times*.[25] His speech was aimed at the people of Kashmir. 'I have come to you to say that we can make a new beginning, with dignity and self-respect. Together we can build a new Kashmir that can become once again a symbol of peace prosperity and cultural pluralism,' he told his audience which was restive at times. Singh's speech was interrupted when sections of the crowd chanted 'remove unemployment' and 'we want jobs'. Following his address, he indicated that he would be prepared to pull back more troops from the state if terrorist violence continued to decrease. India had finished work on a 780 km electronic fence along the Line of Control and felt confident that it could stop infiltration of Islamic militants into the state from the Pakistani side of the border. But it still needed Pakistan's cooperation.

The Indian prime minister, taking cognizance of the fact that Kashmir had been ravaged by the decade and a half long insurgency and that its economy was a shambles, held out a financial olive branch to the area's citizens. He proposed a new economic plan focused on a 'new vision of development' promising more than $5 billion in economic assistance to the state. The plan included an end to the four-year freeze on government recruitment, the largest employer in the state. The plan also included new investment in infrastructure, particularly electricity generation. Manmohan Singh, in other words, laid down the first plank of the structure proposed in this chapter. This structure would be erected on economic foundations and would aim to restore health to the state's economy. The plan's details are discussed in a later section.

A couple of weeks after Singh's visit to Srinagar, Shaukat Aziz, the Pakistani prime minister, went to Delhi for his first detailed meeting with his Indian counterpart. The meeting produced no break-through and the two sides to the dispute seemed to be returning to their earlier positions. That this was indeed the case was made more evident when the Foreign Secretaries of the two countries, the top bureaucrats in Delhi and Islamabad, met in the Pakistani capital in the closing days of 2004 to review the progress they had made since the resumption of bilateral talks. The joint statement issued following the talks indicated no significant progress; there was only the desire to continue with the dialogue.

In my discussion with Prime Minister Manmohan Singh in early December 2004, the Indian leader seemed frustrated at the lack of progress.

> I told General Pervez Musharraf that history has placed us in positions from which we can really help our people. We are 'accidental leaders;' neither of us expected to be in the seats we currently occupy. We owe it to the citizens of our two countries to spend our resources on economic development, on social improvements, and on poverty alleviation. I hope we won't waste this opportunity. I know he has many constraints; but so do I. No Indian prime minister can surrender any part of the country's territory. I certainly will not do that. There cannot be any territorial adjustments as a part of a solution to the problem of Kashmir. I hope you will communicate this message to General Musharraf when you meet with him next.[26]

These minor setbacks notwithstanding, tangible progress continued to be made. The most significant step since the statement by Vajpayee in April 2003, and the joint statement issued by President Musharraf and Prime Minister Atal Bihari Vajpayee in January came on 7 April 2005. A bus service was started on that day linking Srinagar and Muzaffarabad. This happened with much fanfare on the Indian side and less enthusiasm from the side of Pakistan. Islamic militants warned the passengers who wished to travel from Indian Kashmir that they were risking their lives if they continued with their plans. These warnings had some effect; only nineteen of the thirty passengers who had booked seats from India actually took the bus and travelled from Srinagar to Muzaffarabad.

Ten days after the resumption of the bus service, President Musharraf travelled to Delhi and held a summit meeting with Prime Minister Manmohan Singh. The Pakistani leader virtually forced the meeting on the Indians, inviting himself to watch the last cricket match of the series played by the national teams from the two countries. Progress was made at this meeting, with both sides reiterating that they wished to continue taking steps towards normalization. The two leaders 'determined that the peace process was now irreversible' and in that spirit they 'addressed the issue of Jammu and Kashmir and agreed to continue these discussions in a sincere and purposeful and forward-looking manner for a final settlement... They also agreed to pursue further measures to enhance interaction and cooperation across the LOC... [They] pledged that they would not allow terrorism to impede the peace process.' A notable advance made in this discussion was the focus on trade as a way of creating a conducive environment for bringing about peace in the region. 'Both leaders agreed that enhanced economic and commercial cooperation would contribute to the well-being of the peoples of the two countries and bring a higher level of peace and prosperity [to] the region.'[27]

The Delhi statement was couched in broad, non-specific terms. Other than declaring that the process of peace was now irreversible, the two sides had nothing tangible to offer, at least not in public. General Pervez Musharraf, somewhat less encumbered by domestic politics, continued to propose broad outlines of a possible solution. In an interview with *The Economist*, he suggested that the 'core dispute over Kashmir could be resolved within a year, and should be settled while he and Manmohan Singh... are still in office. A settlement, he suggests should be guaranteed by the international community.' He was perhaps referring to the possibility of opening both parts of Kashmir to India and Pakistan through trade and movement of people, when he talked about the 'growing irrelevance of borders in the modern world.'[28]

Manmohan Singh, the Indian Prime Minister, was also in search of ideas that could break new ground. In a meeting with the press to discuss the performance of his government during his first year in office he said:

> I have said to President Pervez Musharraf that India will never accept another division of our country on religious lines. I told him that I have no mandate to negotiate or redraw boundaries of our country. Within these limitations, we have to search for a solution… We are dealing with problems which have defied solutions for 57 years. I do not want to minimize the difficulties that lie ahead. It would be much too presumptuous on my part to give a timetable.[29]

The two countries continued to take small but meaningful steps towards improving relations. On 1 June, a delegation of nine separatist leaders from the Indian part of Kashmir crossed the 'peace bridge' constructed to allow buses to ply between the two parts of the state and began a week-long visit to Pakistan. The visit was allowed by India after an invitation was issued by President Musharraf. The delegation represented the liberal wing of the All-Parties Hurriyat Conference (APHC), an alliance of Kashmiri groups that had supported the insurrection but had split into two factions, one supporting the peace-dialogue between India and Pakistan while the other not believing that such a dialogue would lead to a resolution of the dispute. In their first meeting with the press after arriving in Muzaffarabad, the delegation emphasized that they would not countenance 'a sell-out of the blood of 80,000 people killed in fifteen years of uprising in Occupied Kashmir.'[30]

On the same day that the Kashmiri delegation arrived in Azad Kashmir, Lal Krishna Advani, then president of Bharatiya Janata Party (BJP), began a visit to Pakistan at the head of a large delegation and declared that 'the emergence of India and Pakistan as two separate, sovereign and independent states is an unalterable reality of history.' The purpose of the statement was to put to rest the often expressed fears in Pakistan that Advani's party, having opposed the creation of Pakistan, wished to dismember it. He reminded his audience that the peace process underway was initiated by the government headed by the BJP. As already indicated, this and other statements made by Advani during this visit caused an uproar within the ranks of his party.

The Indian stance towards Pakistan seemed to harden during the state visit by Prime Minister Manmohan Singh to Washington in July 2005. In several interviews he gave in the American capital, the Indian leader expressed unhappiness that Pakistan had not stopped all infiltration into the Indian part of Kashmir and had not dismantled the centres that trained the infiltrators. His suggestion that Pakistan's nuclear assets were not in secure hands drew a sharp response from President Musharraf. India and Pakistan seemed to have returned once again to verbal duelling. The only new sign of progress was the decision by the Indian prime minister to meet with the Kashmiri leaders who had visited Pakistan earlier in the year. The meeting was held in New Delhi in September 2005 in which Prime Minister Manmohan Singh once again expressed the hope that the number of Indian troops present in the state would be reduced.

On 15 September 2005 President Pervez Musharraf met once again with Prime Minister Manmohan Singh, their third formal meeting, this time in New York on the sidelines of the United Nations summit of world leaders. The two leaders met for more than four hours; they kept the press waiting until after midnight but did not issue any joint declaration. The only positive development was that the Indian prime minister accepted the invitation to visit Islamabad before the end of the year. It appeared that the two countries were once again stuck in a cul-de-sac. Even the visit by Singh did not materialize. Pakistan continued to invite the Indian leader to visit the country but the Indians were not prepared to oblige.

Terrorism once again took a heavy toll in India–Pakistan relations when a number of commuter trains were bombed in Mumbai in July 2006. Almost 200 people were killed. There was suspicion of the involvement of Lashkar-e-Taiba, a Pakistan-based group that was active in Kashmir and had carried out operations in India. The assault of December 2001 on the Indian national assembly compound was also traced to this group. The Mumbai bombings led to the postponement of the dialogue between the two countries.

In September, while President Pervez Musharraf was visiting the United States and Prime Minister Manmohan Singh was in Latin America, the chief of the Mumbai police announced that he had 'solved' the bombing case. He had found evidence of the direct involvement of Pakistan's ISI. This revelation, although not confirmed by New Delhi, further strained the relations between the two countries. This was unfortunate since the two leaders had met a few days earlier in Havana, Cuba on the sidelines of the summit of the leaders of the Non-Aligned Movement and agreed to work together to tackle the menace of terrorism. However, some comfort could be drawn from the fact that Islamabad and New Delhi agreed to go ahead and hold discussions between the secretaries of external affairs in November 2006.

The most promising development of the discussions that had been held since early 2004 was the entry of Kashmiri leaders as participants in the on-going dialogue about the future of their state. This opening offered an opportunity to explore other avenues for making progress. Economic cooperation and trade involving the three sides to the dispute—India, Pakistan and the people of Kashmir—was one such avenue that needed to be explored. But for the three sides to pursue this avenue they will have to think and act boldly.

5. Kashmir Dispute's Economic Cost[31]

Economic costs associated with the long-enduring Kashmir conflict and the resultant slowdown in the rate of economic growth can be estimated by using counterfactual analysis. This can be done by estimating the cost of the conflict and likely benefits that would have resulted had relations between the two countries been more amicable. We can distinguish between four different costs of the conflict and then estimate the benefits that would have accrued to the economy and to society had India and Pakistan been on better terms with each other. The four areas of likely benefit include reduced military expenditures; increase in intra-regional trade, in particular trade between India and Pakistan; a larger flow of foreign direct investment; and an investor friendly domestic environment.

There is no doubt that in the absence of the Kashmir dispute, military expenditure as a proportion of the GDP would have been lower in the case of Pakistan than of India. Small countries in the neighbourhood of large states tend to spend less on defence if the relations between them are cordial. In 2002, Argentina, for instance, spent only 1.1 per cent of its GDP on defence compared to 1.6 per cent for Brazil. For Canada the proportion was only 1.1 per cent compared to 3.4 per cent for the United States. Even Bangladesh that had uneasy relations with India, the country's much larger neighbour, spent only 1.1 per cent on defence.[32] If Pakistan had spent 2.5 per cent on defence—a proportion roughly equivalent to that of India—it could have saved as much as 3 per cent of the GDP a year. Compounded over this period, the amount saved would be equivalent to four times the country's gross domestic product.

What would have been the consequence if this entire amount had been invested in the economy? Assuming that the rate of return would have been the same as realized from investments in the past, additional capital flows into the economy would have significantly added to the rate of growth of the economy. Put in another way, military expenditure maintained at a level of 2.5 per cent a year with the savings utilized at an incremental capital ratio of four— which means that investment equal to 4 per cent of the GDP would raise the rate of the GDP growth by 1 per cent—would have increased the long-term GDP growth rate by as much as 0.75 per cent a year. This addition to the rate of the GDP growth compounded over a period of fifty-five years would have meant an increase of more than 50 per cent in the size of the GDP.

While a smaller amount committed to military expenditure would have directly contributed to increasing the GDP growth, conflict with India also hurt Pakistan by reducing trade as a proportion of its economy. India's initial antipathy towards Pakistan was not the result of the Kashmir dispute. The first generation of Indian leaders—in particular Jawaharlal Nehru, the country's prime minister and Sardar Vallabhbhai Patel, the powerful home minister in the first Indian cabinet—were angry at Mohammad Ali Jinnah, Pakistan's founding father, and his political associates. Jinnah and his colleagues stood in the way of the realization of the Hindu leadership's dream of a united India. The Indian leaders were also convinced that they could get Pakistan to return to the Indian fold by increasing the economic cost of separation.[33] It was this reason and not because of Kashmir that India launched its first trade war against Pakistan in 1949. However, Kashmir later worsened relations between the two countries and progressively loosened the strong economic links that had existed between the two parts of British India before they became independent states.

Had the two countries continued to trade at the levels of the exchanges that occurred before independence, the rate of increase in international trade in the case of Pakistan would have been of the order of 8 to 10 per cent a year, rather than the average 6 per cent achieved over the last quarter century. This too would have contributed to increasing the rate of the GDP growth. The World Bank maintains that growth in trade leads to increase in the GDP by a perceptible amount. It is not an exaggeration to suggest that by maintaining trade with India at the levels of the late 1940s, Pakistan would have added another one-third to half a percentage point to its GDP increase. This would have meant an additional one-third increase in the current level of the GDP.

The other important outcome of good relations with India would have been a greater flow of foreign direct investment (FDI) into the country. The contribution large FDI flows make to the development and modernization of the economies of East Asia is well recognized. South Asia had not benefited from the increased availability of these flows in a large part because of the security problems associated with the Kashmir conflict. There were other reasons as well-among them the less open economic policies followed by the countries in South Asia for nearly four decades.

However, even when these policies were abandoned in favour of greater openness—and they were in the early 1990s—foreign capital had still not become an important component of investment for the South Asian region. This was particularly the case for Pakistan.

Better relations with India and greater amounts of intra-regional trade would have brought in additional foreign direct investment into the country, adding significantly to the relatively low level of domestic savings and domestic investments. In 2002, Pakistan received $823 million FDI compared to $3 billion for India. Both countries did poorly in that area compared to those in East Asia. For instance, Malaysia received $3.2 billion, Thailand $2.4 billion, South Korea $2.0 billion, and the Philippines $1.1 billion. Foreign investors stayed away partly because of the less open economies of the region but also because of the virtual absence of intra-regional trade and a deep concern about security. If these concerns were not there, both India and Pakistan would have attracted amounts of capital to the order of perhaps $10 billion for the former and $2 billion a year for the latter. Two billion dollars of foreign flows would be equivalent to 3 per cent of Pakistan's GDP.

Pakistan has had a long history of poor domestic savings rates which translated into low rates of investment unless foreign capital was available. In the 1990s while domestic savings increased from 11 to 13 per cent—from 1990 to 2002—gross capital formation declined by four percentage points, from 19 to 15 per cent of GDP. The 8 per cent savings-investment gap was covered by foreign flows in 1990; the decline in foreign flows brought investment closer to domestic savings by 2002. Had foreign private capital been available in 2002 to the extent suggested above—in the neighbourhood of $2 billion a year—this would have brought investment back to the levels of the late 1980s. Foreign flows amounting to about 3 per cent of the GDP would have added about 0.75 per cent to the rate of economic growth.

A serious investment gap emerged between Pakistan and India in the 1990s at the height of the insurgency in Kashmir. According to a study carried out by Ijaz Nabi and his associates at the World

Bank, private investment in India and Pakistan was about the same in 1982–1991. However in 1992–2001, private investment in Pakistan was six percentage points lower than in India. A part of this gap—say about 75 per cent—could be attributed to the deterioration of the investment climate in Pakistan caused by the rise of Islamic militancy in the country, which in turn was associated with the Kashmir problem. These factors lowered investment rates in Pakistan by 4.5 percentage points compared to that in India. This implied loss in growth of at least one percentage point of the GDP. Stable relations with India would have brought economic and perhaps also political stability to Pakistan. This would have produced a better investment climate in the country and contributed to higher levels of domestic savings and investment. This would have also contributed to increasing the rate of GDP growth.

By aggregating the four positive consequences for the Pakistani economy if the country had not gotten embroiled in the Kashmir dispute, it would appear that the country's long-term growth rate could have been some 2 to 2.5 percentage points higher than that actually achieved. A higher rate of growth of this magnitude, sustained over a period of half a century, would have increased the gross product by a factor of between 3.5 and 4.5. Pakistan's gross domestic product could have been three and a half times larger than that in 2004–5—$450 billion rather than $ 110 billion—and its income per capita would have been $2900 rather than $710 had the country been at peace with India.

This estimate, of course, is a very rough order of magnitude. It is based on a series of heroic assumptions about the efficient use of resources diverted from military to development expenditure; about a significant increase in trade with India and a higher level of trade contributing to economic growth; about Pakistan becoming an attractive area for foreign direct investment; and about domestic savings and investment increasing with the presence of tranquility in the region. Even if half of the benefits estimated above had been actually realized, they were sizeable and they would have changed the economic, political and social complexion of Pakistan. In sum a good case can be made that Pakistan in particular has paid a very heavy economic, social and political cost for continuing to keep the Kashmir case on the front burner. This is a good time to take a very hard look at the cost-benefit calculus of the position the country has adopted in the past over the dispute in Kashmir.

The situation began to change largely because of the promise of peace between India and Pakistan. New investments have begun to flow into the country in particular from the Arab world; Pakistan's own private sector has become active; the rate of economic growth has picked up perceptibly; the incidence of poverty has begun to decline; Pakistan seems ready to join other fast-growing Asian economies. All or some of these developments would be at risk if Kashmir was allowed to intervene once again in the form of a dispute that attracted extremist elements in both countries. They will try to derail the process on which India and Pakistan got engaged, starting in January 2004. It is in the interest of both Delhi and Islamabad to resist those attempts.

6. Taking the Development Route[34]

Two rounds of bombings in London's underground railway system in July 2005 once again invited speculation on the motives that inspired young men to give their lives in order to create chaos. There were added worries of such trends when the British police in August 2006 thwarted an alleged plot to bomb American jumbo airliners *en route* to the United States from London. This plot involved a couple of dozen men of Pakistani origin. According to one view the Muslim communities in Britain, already alienated by the failure of the society in which they lived to offer them full accommodation, had turned to violence to draw attention to their anger. This was probably what President Musharraf meant when, on the 21 July 2005 address to the nation, he invited the British to look at their own failure before casting stones at Pakistan.

While Pakistan's culpability in the crimes committed in London was confined to its tolerance for some of the *madrassas* that taught hatred against all those who did not accept their narrow point of view, the country's long and ongoing involvement in the Kashmir dispute had already had a number of unanticipated consequences. It was reasonable—but very short-sighted—on the part of strategists in Islamabad to rely on the zealotry promoted by some of the madrassas in order to balance India's military advantage. As a result of that strategy Pakistan may have stalled India in Kashmir but it had also bought a serious problem for itself. In the early 2000s Pakistan was in the eye of the Islamic extremism storm partly the result of the Kashmir strategy. The time had come to switch to some other approach to achieve progress on Kashmir rather than continue to hope that *jihad* would eventually rescue the people of the state from their miserable plight.

Economics could succeed where politics had failed in ultimately resolving the problem of Kashmir. A two-pronged approach—simultaneous focus on economic development and on inter-regional trade—could introduce a new dynamic in the two parts of the state. It could induce the people of Kashmir to get absorbed in working towards their economic betterment and forego the temptation to resort to violence in order to settle their score with India. At the same time, by getting involved in the economic development of Kashmir, both India and Pakistan would begin to recognize that there were much richer rewards from the pursuit of this strategy than the mindless encouragement of militancy (on the part of Pakistan) or the suppression of insurgency by the use of excessive and brutal force (on the part of India).

How would economics really work? In a study prepared for the United States Institute for Peace and published in the fall of 2006, I proposed a multi-sectoral development programme, the details of which are developed in Section 7 below, to accelerate the rate of economic growth in the Indian-occupied areas of Kashmir. A similar programme could be launched in Azad Kashmir, concentrating on the same sectors as those proposed for the areas under India's control. According to my very rough calculations the two programmes together would cost some $25 billion—$20 billion for the Indian side and the remaining $5 billion for Azad

Kashmir—and could be implemented over a period of ten years, say from 2006 to 2016.

The estimates used by me were rough orders of magnitude. I had two reasons for providing them. One reason was to underscore the point that a programme developed to improve the economic prospects of the two parts of Kashmir would involve the commitment of large amounts of financial resources in order to produce the desired results—to convince the alienated people of the part of Kashmir under the control of India that the world was prepared to come to their assistance. This would not be done by supplying them with arms and military training but by giving them the resources for their economic uplift.

Given the amount of money that will be needed to be spent in order to produce a palpable difference in the lives of the people, for them to give up doing what they have done for the last decade and a half—to give up arms and a resort to violence, and turn to serious economic work—the international community will have to foot a significant part of the bill. This, as I will note below, was done once before to solve a dispute between India and Pakistan that at that point seemed intractable. In 1960, India and Pakistan signed the Indus Water Treaty to divide between them the waters of the Indus River system. The programme incorporated in the treaty included the construction of two large dams in Pakistan and a number of link canals to transport water among the tributaries of the Indus. The works cost more than \$2 billion in average 1960 prices, equivalent perhaps to \$10 billion in the prices of the early 2000s. The bulk of this expenditure was met by a consortium of donors led by the World Bank.[35]

There is, therefore, a very good precedence to turn to the international community to use economics to resolve a difficult issue. This was done almost half a century ago when there was considerable acrimony between the two countries soon after they gained independence. At one time it appeared that they might resort to an all-out war in order to decide their opposing claims on the waters that flowed down from the Himalayas through Kashmir and into the plains of the Punjab. The Punjab was now divided into two parts, each had a stake on the waters of the system.

The Indus Water Treaty of 1960 was the product of farsightedness on the part of the leaderships of the two countries, in particular President Mohammad Ayub Khan of Pakistan who recognized that the only way to settle the dispute was to aim for four objectives: develop a system-wide development plan, have the plan incorporated into an international treaty, establish a mechanism for the resolution of disputes that would inevitably arise between the two countries, and convince the international community to meet a large part of the expenditure that would be required to implement the plan. The Indus Basin Replacement Works that were formulated within the context of the treaty were ambitious in scope and provided what each country needed. Something similar will be needed for the formulation and implementation of the Kashmir Development Plan.

Secondly, I suggest that there are areas in the economy of Kashmir that could develop reasonably quickly and provide a significant increase in well-remunerated jobs and therefore could produce a noticeable increase in incomes, particularly for the state's youth. But there is one other objective a successful programme of Kashmir's development must satisfy: to link the state's economy with those of India and Pakistan in a way that neither country will have a reason to resort to force in the area. By focusing on the development of the energy sector and supplying surplus electric power to both Pakistan and India, the plan proposed by me would tie Kashmir's resources not only with its own development but with the growth and development of India and Pakistan as well.

A consensus has developed among economists around the globe that the world is now seriously faced with an energy problem. Given the rapid growth of China and India—and, to some extent, also Pakistan—the demand on the world's increasingly limited supplies of fossil fuels is bound to increase. Foreseeing that this would happen, world oil and gas markets have registered a pronounced increase in both spot and long-term prices. Both were at historical high levels in the summer of 2006. The development of the state's energy resources could be a central element in the programme of economic development for the two parts of Kashmir.

A great deal of further work needs to be done to develop the programme in detail. It would require a considerable amount of expertise and deep knowledge of various sectors. It could be formulated by multilateral development agencies such as the World Bank and the Asian Development Bank where such knowledge and expertise resides. The two agencies could also help to mobilize the required resources and oversee the programme's implementation. The experts may come up with a different set of sectors to concentrate on than those proposed by me. They may also propose a different timeline for the programme, stretching out over a longer period of time or condensing it into a shorter period. And their cost estimates were bound to be different than those made by me.

Since January 2004, the senior leaders of India and Pakistan have spent a great deal of their time and the energies of their diplomats on building confidence on both sides of the border so that the two countries could live in peace and harmony. There was an assumption that this would eventually lead to some accommodation on Kashmir. This was, however, a passive approach that may not produce the results both sides wanted. A more visionary strategy was required, of the type that was adopted in 1960 to solve the problem associated with the division of waters in the Indus River system.

What would be the economic impact of the $25 billion development plan proposed in this chapter? What are the likely consequences in the Indian part of Kashmir and in Azad Kashmir on the economic rates of growth, on the levels of employment, on the incidence of poverty, and on bringing about their greater integration with the global economy? A simple model suggests some answers to these questions. This level of investment, spread over a ten year period on both sides of the present divide, should yield $50 million of additional income a year. This would correspond to an increase of 9.5 per cent a year in the Gross State (or Provincial) Domestic Product (GSDP) of both parts of Kashmir. The combined gross product of the two sides was of the order of $5.6 billion, $4.4 billion for the part held by India and $1.2 billion for the parts that are with Pakistan. The income per head of the two parts was about the same, $400 a year.

The total population of Kashmir in 2005 was fourteen million, with eleven million on the Indian side of the border and three million on the Pakistani side. This was likely to increase to 17.5 million by 2016. A 9.5 per cent growth in the GSDP would mean that the size of the combined economies would grow in constant terms to $14 billion, increasing per capita income to $800, bringing it close to the anticipated incomes in both India and Pakistan. This is not an impossible target to achieve considering that the state economy had grown at a rate well below the Indian average. The same was true for Azad Kashmir, the Pakistani part of the state.

An important feature—in fact that should be a condition for international help for the programme—would be the agreement by the two countries that they will be willing to incorporate the state of Kashmir and the territory of Azad Kashmir into a sub-regional trading arrangement. Such an arrangement could be a corollary to the SAFTA, which became partially operational on 1 January 2006 and fully on 1 July of the same year.

7. A Development Plan for Kashmir

It is obvious that Pakistan cannot afford to pay either the economic price for prolonging the dispute or continue to tolerate extremism to distort its society and corrupt its political system. Given all this, what are the options available to Islamabad *at this time*? I would like to emphasize the 'at this time' aspect of this question. In 2005–6, the Pakistani economy was at the point of fulsome recovery; the country had also begun to attract the interest of foreign investors as vividly demonstrated by the privatization of Habib Bank and Pakistan Telecommunications that were acquired by foreign investors. India seemed ready to do a deal with Pakistan on Kashmir in order to free itself from a dispute which had also been costly for it. By remaining unresolved the Kashmir issue would come in India's way as it began to assert itself as a global power. In Pakistan, President Pervez Musharraf openly acknowledged that Islamic extremism was his greatest problem. The western world exposed to the expression of violence by the extremists—not only in the United States but also in Madrid and London—could not possibly tolerate them in their midst. This then was the right time to seriously ask the question about the right Pakistani approach towards Kashmir.

Should Pakistan abandon its long-standing demand that the problem of Kashmir could only be resolved by the state's citizens expressing their will openly as was agreed at the United Nations in 1949? Or should Pakistan, awed by the multiple cost of keeping the issue alive, abandon the people of Kashmir to their fate and to political expediency? Neither of these approaches is practical; the second one in particular can not be sold to the people of Pakistan even when they are fully educated about the cost of the dispute and how they will be hurt by letting it fester. The only feasible option appears to be to follow the way the ever-practical people of East Asia have dealt with territorial disputes. The Chinese tolerated the virtual independence of Taiwan for almost as long as Pakistan has lived with the issue of Kashmir. They were prepared to continue with the status quo for as long as Taiwanese 'virtual independence' remained exactly that: virtual.

The South Koreans are not particularly interested in reuniting with their brethren in the north, hoping that whenever that happens it would not be destructive for their own economy and political system. What these examples have to teach is the value of patience.

There are times when it is much more prudent not to force solutions for which the environment is not ready. Such is the case with the Kashmir problem in the early 2000s. If Pakistan can not force a solution that would fully satisfy its moral commitment, and political and strategic interests, how should it approach the problem of Kashmir at this time? One way out is to allow the gradual integration of the Kashmiri economy into its own system. The ongoing effort to build a free trade area in South Asia over a period of a decade offers a unique opportunity for laying the ground for the resolution of the Kashmir problem. Under this approach, a beginning would be made within the SAFTA framework already agreed upon among the SAARC countries. An economic development programme for the state of Kashmir could be formulated that would rely heavily for its success on greater trade among India and Pakistan and the state of Kashmir.

Since such a plan would cost tens of billions of dollars to implement, it would require the active support of the international community. However, a development plan focused on the state's physical and human endowment would only work if it gained political acceptance from the parties involved in the dispute. For that to happen it must not change the political status of the state for some time to come, otherwise it will not be acceptable to India. At the same time, it must not suggest that the Line of Control would become the international boundary. That would not be acceptable to Pakistan. Even with these two constraints in place there is enough space left within which an ambitious plan could be formulated. The plan would have to be ambitious to achieve its three objectives: increase economic welfare for the citizens of Kashmir, initiate a process that could ultimately lead to the resolution of the dispute, and draw foreign support for its implementation.

For the plan to be ambitious in scope as well as in its objectives it has to fully involve the state's people, the governments and people of India and Pakistan, and the international community. The main focus of the plan should be to develop exchanges— movement of people, goods and services among the three geographical entities, Kashmir, India and Pakistan. The aim should be to develop an integrated market in the region, which could later develop into a common market. Such a market could later encompass other parts of South Asia. A plan of economic and trade integration involving Kashmir and the contiguous parts of India and Pakistan could become a stepping-stone towards the establishment of the free trade area in South Asia envisioned in the

Islamabad Declaration issued by the leaders at the twelfth SAARC summit on 6 January 2004.

The plan could be built around five central elements: developing the state's water resources with a view to generating electric power; rebuilding and expanding the tourism industry; developing forestry and high-value-added agriculture; improving physical infrastructure; and developing the human resources to engage the young in the more productive sectors of what would essentially become a new economic system.

The first element would involve reinterpreting rather than renegotiating the Indus Water Treaty of 1960 that distributed the waters of the Indus River system between India and Pakistan. The main aim of the treaty was to make a sufficient amount of water available in the eastern rivers so that the irrigation system that relied on these rivers and served many parts of Pakistan would not go dry. The treaty was remarkably successful in that it prevented a major confrontation between India and Pakistan on the issue of the use of water from the large Indus system. Kashmir's accession to India had made the country sit on top of the system of irrigation the British had built in order to turn the part of Punjab that was now a province of Pakistan into a granary for colonial India. India had plans to use its upper riparian status to irrigate the deserts of Rajasthan with water drawn from the Indus tributaries. Soon after gaining independence it began work on the Bhakra dam project to bring new land under cultivation in Rajasthan. This would have resulted in a serious reduction in the amount of water flowing into Pakistan. With the treaty in place India was in the position to achieve that objective without reducing the availability of water flowing through Pakistan's rivers and canals.

From Kashmir's perspective, the treaty froze the development of water and hydro-power resources for its own people. The question is whether the treaty could be reinterpreted not to reduce the flow of water to Pakistan but to jointly develop hydroelectricity to benefit both Pakistan and Kashmir. This could be done on the basis of a careful study of the power potential of the Indus system for the purpose of developing it so that it brings benefits to the power-short regions of Kashmir, Pakistan and northern parts of India. An important component of this plan would be to build an integrated power grid to serve the three areas. This plan could aim to create the capacity for generating between 5,000 and 7,500 megawatts of additional power for use in the three areas. The total cost to be incurred over a ten-year period, say from 2005 to 2015, would be of the order of $10 billion.

Both India and Pakistan were working separately to develop the hydroelectricity potential of the rivers flowing through their parts of Kashmir. The Indian efforts resulted in creating considerable apprehension in Pakistan that the authorities in New Delhi were attempting to subvert the Indus treaty. Islamabad had serious concerns about the Wullar Lake, Baglihar Dam and Kishenganga Dam projects. It saw all these as attempts to draw more water from the tributaries of the Indus River than India was allowed under the 1960 treaty. Unable to have its concerns resolved by India on the issue of the Baglihar Dam, Pakistan invoked a provision in the 1960 treaty that allowed for external arbitration in case a dispute concerning water distribution in the system cannot be resolved by the two governments working on their own.

There is, therefore, an urgent need to summon experts from both sides to develop a plan that would tap the power potential of the rivers in Kashmir without disturbing the water distribution agreement of the Indus Water Treaty. This would be best done within the scope of a sub-regional treaty, overseen by an international agency such as the World Bank. International involvement would be helpful not only because of the large amount of money that would be required, but would also be useful since it would keep all the parties involved on track. A sub-regional arrangement would be needed since the amount of power that could be ultimately generated would be far in excess of the future demand of the state of Kashmir. There will be the need—and an opportunity—to sell the surplus power through a regional grid to India and Pakistan, which could be built inexpensively by connecting the elaborate systems that already exist on both sides of the border.

Kashmir's second major potential—tourism—used to be the source of a significant amount of capital flow into the state as well as the source of employment for the area's workforce. It also provided the state with links to the outside world. Kashmir became a major destination for Indian tourism in the 1980s; by 1981 the number of visitors from India had reached 600,000. The state also attracted some foreigners but not in the number that could have visited the area given its many attractions. The proportion of foreign tourists remained about one-tenth of the total. The year before the beginning of the insurgency in the mid-1980s, tourists visiting the state almost reached the level of three-quarters of a million. This was to be the peak year for tourism in the state. Thereafter the number of visitors declined rapidly contributing to the economic problem faced by the area. A major consequence of the insurgency that has lasted for a decade and a half resulted in the destruction of the infrastructure that supported tourism, in addition to turning visitors away from the state on account of lack of security.

The plan proposed here aims to turn Kashmir along with Pakistan's northern areas into destinations for international tourism and not just an attractive place to visit for tourists from India and Pakistan. This way Kashmir and its adjoining areas would get reconnected with the world and this would help to wean away the young from the destructive forces unleashed by Islamic extremism.

Tourism is the fastest growing part of the service sector in the global economy; there are new consumers entering the sector as populations age and personal incomes increase. There are reports that some 100 million Chinese may be prepared to join the tourist trade as consumers. Pakistan's northern areas and Kashmir would offer attractive places for the Chinese to visit since much of that country's ancient history has roots in these areas. The same applies to the tourists from Japan and other East Asian countries. To achieve this would require considerable amounts of investment in developing the infrastructure and training people to manage the industry. The infrastructure required include roads that could take heavy traffic, airports, hotels and restaurants. New museums would need to be built and the sites that would have appeal for the East Asian tourists—Kashmir was once an important centre of Buddhism—will need to be developed. An investment of some $5 billion would be required over a period of ten years—most of it from the private sector—to get tourists in large numbers to come to the area. Benefits would flow to Kashmir, and the northern parts of India and Pakistan.

Kashmir's third major economic assets were its forestry and orchards. Once again the products offered by these sectors had considerable external demand not only in the West but also in China. Kashmir had the raw material and skills needed to develop a high-value-added furniture industry, again one of the more rapidly growing items of international trade in manufactures. With security returning to the area it would be possible to engage major transnational corporations that specialize in manufacturing and distributing products in this sector to develop this part of the economy. Much of the investment required could come from these corporations; they would also be able to provide management expertise and improve project design. Resource commitment by the public sector would not be large although the state will need to establish training institutions needed to develop the skills that would be required. India could help in this respect, using its well-organised institutional infrastructure to provide technical assistance.

The state's reputation as an 'orchard of the East' is based on a combination of good soil, appropriate altitude and a supporting climate that makes the land attractive for cultivating a wide variety of fruits that have markets in the West and in the Middle East. To achieve full potential in this area the government, with help from transnational corporations, will need to develop an integrated development programme with detailed costs and cost sharing. The total amount of expenditure envisaged for this sector is of the order of $4 billion over a period of ten years.

Before India and Pakistan gained independence, Kashmir's physical infrastructure—mostly roads—catered to tourism. The state was not part of the area the British had either regarded as strategically sensitive (as was the case with Punjab, the North West Frontier Province and, to a lesser extent, Balochistan) or economically important (as was the case with the Punjab and Sindh provinces). Strategic and economic consideration had resulted in massive investments by the British to develop roads, railways, and irrigation systems in the Punjab and Sindh. There were no such compulsions present in the princely state of Jammu and Kashmir. The small amounts of investments that were made aimed to facilitate the movement of tourists into the area, most of them British. The tourist infrastructure existed around Srinagar, the state capital, and the main link to it was from Rawalpindi, a British garrison town in the north-western part of the Punjab province.

The road from Rawalpindi climbed steeply towards Murree, hugging the foothills of the Himalayas. After reaching a height of seven thousand feet it wound down towards Muzaffarabad, a small city in the western part of Kashmir, situated on the confluence of two mighty rivers, the Neelum and the Jhelum. From Muzaffarabad the road crossed the Jhelum and went on first to Baramula and then to Srinagar. There were also road links, albeit less travelled ones, between Jammu and Sialkot in Pakistan. The only railway link was between Sialkot and Jammu. On the Indian side, the railway system terminated at Pathankot short of the boundary with Jammu and Kashmir. In other words, Kashmir's natural communication links were with Pakistan.

Under the development plan proposed here, these links will be restored and improved. A programme for infrastructural development in the state will have two components: the development of communications within the state will serve not only the major centres of economic activity centred on high value agriculture, forestry and tourism, but will also require better connections for the state with the world outside. Most of this will have to be through Pakistan, exploiting the road and railway networks that already exist in that country. Pakistan's well-developed Karakoram Highway that links Islamabad with Kashgar in western China provides an easy access to Kashmir via the roads to

Rawalpindi and along the Neelum River to Abbottabad. The railway link between Sialkot and Jammu that is in a stage of advanced disrepair could be put back to use, linking the state with the railways systems of India and Pakistan through the city of Lahore.

Pakistan's recent investment in a modern airport in Lahore could bring in feeder services from Srinagar, Jammu and other cities in the state to points in India and the world outside. Lahore already has a well-developed facility for handling air cargo for export for some of the items that would be of interest to a revived Kashmiri economy. Woollen shawls, animal skins and wooden artifacts are delicate products that need to be air-freighted. This could be done through Lahore.

The programme of infrastructure development suggested here is less ambitious than that for the development of energy resources. It is estimated to cost $3 billion spread over a ten-year period from 2005 to 2015.

An important component of the Kashmir development plan would be to improve the quality of human resources in the state by providing education and skills to the young that would help them to participate in the modern economy. The quality of human resources has suffered a significant decline since the beginning of insurgency in the state. One way of assessing the impact is to use the human development index (HDI) developed by the UNDP for use in the organization's Human Development reports. India has used the methodology developed by the UNDP to estimate HDIs for its states. According to the Indian Planning Commission, the ranking of the state of Jammu and Kashmir declined from nineteen among thirty-two political jurisdictions in 1981 to twenty-one in 1991. The Commission's *Human Development Report, 2001* did not estimate the value for Kashmir. In 1981, the HDI index for the state was calculated at 0.337 as against the Indian average of 0.302. Chandigarh, with a value of 0.550 had the highest ranking, while Bihar at 0.237 was the lowest ranked. In 1991, Kashmir's HDI was estimated at 0.402 with Chandigarh, still in the first place at 0.674 and Bihar still in the last place at 0.308. The overall value for India was 0.381. The state did particularly poorly in terms of literacy. In 2001, the literacy rate was only 54.5 per cent for the entire population while it was 60.1 per cent for males and 41.8 per cent for females. On this score, the state ranked 33rd among thirty-five jurisdictions in all of India. The Indian average for that year was 65.4 per cent—75.9 per cent for the male population and 54.2 per cent for females.

Before the start of the insurgency, the state's economy had a very small modern component. Much of the non-agricultural employment was in the tourist industry. The development of the modern sector was affected because the uncertainty created by the insurgency discouraged new investment. Tourism suffered a major setback because of the poor security situation. The revival of the state's economy, if undertaken according to the plan proposed here, would create entrepreneurial and employment opportunities in several sectors. To prepare the population to participate in these sectors would require large amounts of additional investment in education. It would also need the establishment of specialized institutions linked with those already working in India and Pakistan as well as in more advanced countries. The total cost of this effort is estimated at $2 billion over the ten year period between 2005 and 2015.

How would such a plan be financed and implemented? The massive effort needed to invest in Kashmir to rebuild the state's economy and develop economic and trade links with Pakistan would need a great deal of money, beyond the capacity of Pakistan. But a precedent exists for finding foreign finance for this kind of initiative. In the 1960s India and Pakistan working together were able to attract capital from multilateral development agencies and bilateral donors to finance the replacement works to divide the waters of the Indus River. Foreign help became available since the objective was to find a peaceful solution to a problem that could have resulted in a war between India and Pakistan. A plan that promised peace in Kashmir will also be of interest to donors.

8. Conclusion

There is an impression in Islamabad that India may have lost interest in finding a solution to the problem of Kashmir since it was emboldened by the development of a new relationship with the United States. An agreement was concluded with America during President George W. Bush's visit to Delhi in March 2006 to allow Delhi access to nuclear technology denied to those who had not joined the Nuclear Non-Proliferation Treaty. Could it be that having virtually gained the near superpower status and virtual entry into the Nuclear Club of five states as its sixth member, Delhi feels less compelled to accommodate Pakistan?

Nobody should have expected that the warming of relations between India and Pakistan would proceed on an upwardly sloping curve; that each act of benevolence by the one side will be reciprocated by the other. Years of ill-feelings and suspicion could not be washed away for good, and within a short period of time Pakistan could not become Canada to India's United States. It will take time before the two countries begin to live in peace and harmony, and start to concentrate their attention on bettering the lives of their people rather than spending untold resources on a military face-off.

The process of change could not have been a smooth one especially when the environment in which it was taking place was constantly changing, most of the time to Pakistan's disadvantage. India continues to gain respect as a responsible player in the international system. It has a buoyant economy, a working political system, and a growing pool of talented people who are being put at the service of the global economy. Pakistan, on the other hand, has to deal once again with the perception that it is at the frontline of the *jihadi* campaign being fought by stateless and mostly faceless people against the West and in particular against the United States. When a face was acquired by this set of people to Pakistan's great consternation it turned out to be a Pakistani one—of the four men who killed fifty-two people in London on 7 July three were of Pakistani origin. All three had visited Pakistan and at least one of them had spent some time at a Pakistani *madrassa*. These events seriously affected the environment in which Pakistan was operating in the early 2000s.

It is clear that the window of opportunity available to Pakistan to rebuild its relations with India on a different foundation and to get a different strategy to work for itself on Kashmir is getting narrower. As the 'perception gap' between the way the world perceives India and Pakistan widens, it will weaken Islamabad's bargaining position. The compulsion for India to accommodate Pakistan will be reduced if this trend continues. That had already happened. It is important that this time Islamabad moves with intelligence and alacrity. How should it proceed especially with respect to Kashmir?

A new policy concerning Kashmir could be built on four 'recognitions' of mistakes made in the past. The first is the recognition that the dispute over Kashmir was the result of the messy way the British partitioned their Indian domain. Had the principle on which the British Indian Empire was divided been applied to the 'princely states,' Kashmir, being a predominantly Muslim area, would have automatically become part of Pakistan. By granting choice to the princes the British, perhaps quite deliberately, sowed the seeds of what became an all-consuming passion for both India and Pakistan. However, it is futile to base public policy on a perceived wrong done way past in history.

Second, having been frustrated by Delhi's unwillingness to abide by the resolutions of the United Nations that called for a plebiscite in the state to settle its future, Pakistan tried to use force to move Kashmir to its side. That did not work and as India became stronger economically and militarily, Pakistan turned to *jihad* as a way of forcing the Indian hand. In using this tactic it was encouraged by the way the *jihadis* had humbled a superpower in Afghanistan in the bitterly fought war in the 1980s. There was considerable temptation for Islamabad to encourage the same tactics in Kashmir especially after draconian measures were adopted by the Indians in the state to suppress the growing opposition to their presence. The Indian tactics alienated most of the population and fairly large segments of the population were prepared to take up arms against the Indians to assert their rights. This presented Pakistan with an opportunity by encouraging the insurgency. But this approach could not be continued as the world became increasingly concerned with Islamic extremism.

Third, while encouraging *jihad* in Kashmir was tempting for Pakistan, there was a tremendous cost attached to the pursuit of this strategy. There were two elements to the cost. One was the growing diversion of scarce resources into military expenditure, especially when gross mismanagement by a series of politicians in the 1990s weakened the economy. The other was the prestige acquired by the extremists in Pakistan as their sacrifices in Kashmir against heavy odds were greatly appreciated by large segments of the Pakistani population. Once again, the country had to recognize that public policy that encouraged Islamic extremism posed enormous dangers.

Fourth, after the terrorist attacks of 11 September 2001 alerted the international community to the extreme dangers involved in allowing weak states to use dedicated religo-nationalists to press their demands, Islamabad came under pressure to curb the groups it had supported. The involvement of young men of Pakistani origin in the bombings in London on 7 July 2005 has brought additional focus to bear on the operation of these groups. Pakistan has to recognize that it has to move quickly to create an environment that does not encourage Islamic extremism to throw deep roots into the country's soil.

For these reasons—and there were several more—it is now the time for Islamabad to focus on an entirely different approach. This will have Pakistan work with India to develop, help finance, and implement a programme of economic development that has three distinct objectives. One, to increase employment opportunities for Kashmiri youth and thus address the problem of poverty. Two, to closely tie the economies of both parts of Kashmir with those of India and Pakistan. Three, to involve the international community in developing, financing and watching over the implementation of such a plan. An integral component of this approach is to agree with India for the need to launch a sub-regional trade arrangement that provides free and easy access, including transit rights, to the goods and commodities produced by Kashmir as well as to the people of the state. This could be done within the agreed framework for SAFTA which the seven countries of SAARC agreed to launch on 1 January 2006. That decision was taken in Islamabad at SAARC's twelfth summit. In 2007, Afghanistan was admitted as the eighth member of the group.

An India–Pakistan–Kashmir regional trade pact could go beyond that envisaged within the context of the SAFTA. It could focus not just on allowing tariff-free access among the participants for the goods they produce. It could also include the sectors excluded for the time being from SAFTA. Of particular relevance for such an arrangement would be the sector of services and the movement of people. Including Kashmir as a separate autonomous entity within a sub-regional trade arrangement would allow free access to potential tourists from Pakistan to Kashmir and India, and Indians and Kashmiris to Pakistan. The Chinese should also be able to use the already established land links between their country and Pakistan to gain access to the attractions Kashmir had to offer.

The free movement of people between Kashmir and Pakistan would reverse the constraints on travel that resulted from the long-enduring conflict involving the state. Such a movement could integrate the sizeable handicraft industry that existed on both sides of the Kashmir divide. Before the partition of British India and the conflict over Kashmir, the Kashmiri handicraft industry, including wool-weaving and wood-working, had strong links with similar activities in the border cities of Rawalpindi and Sialkot. Those links could be re-established.

Would such an arrangement be practical; would India and Pakistan be prepared to work on it as a way of finding a lasting solution for the long enduring problem? India seemes inclined to move towards such an option. In a wide ranging discussion with the press following the visit to Delhi by Shaukat Aziz, the Pakistani prime minister, in late November 2004, Natwar Singh, then India's foreign minister, said that 'the two countries could settle the Kashmir dispute only if they strengthened ties, increased trade and brought people on the two sides closer to prepare them to accept a compromise.' A similar hope was expressed by the Indian prime minister and the Pakistani president after their April 2005 summit in Delhi.

A sub-regional trade arrangement involving India, Pakistan and Kashmir could only be concluded if Delhi was prepared to grant the state economic and political powers that go beyond those given to the other states in the Union. This would imply much greater autonomy than given to Jammu and Kashmir in Article 370 of the Indian Constitution. India seems willing to do that. 'We have made it clear... as far as regional autonomy is concerned, the sky is the limit,' Natwar Singh said in the statement from which I have already quoted. Pakistan seems to be moving in the same direction. In an interview with the magazine *The Economist*, in May 2005 'General Musharraf talked of offering the people of Kashmir "something between autonomy and independence, like self-governance." This could be "over-watched" by all three parties.'

Some cooling off in the relations in 2005–6 notwithstanding, the two countries seem committed to using economics and trade to create a new realty. One such reality could be created by setting into place a tripartite trade relations involving India, Pakistan and Kashmir. This could be done within the framework of the SAFTA.

NOTES

1. A vast amount of published material has become available on various aspects of 9/11. From the perspective of the United States, the most authoritative account remains the report prepared by a special commission to investigate the circumstances that led to the terrorist attacks, to explore their consequences, and to suggest what the United States should do in order not to be surprised again. See *The 9/11 Commission Report: Final Report of the National Commission on Terrorist Attacks Upon the United States*. New York: W.W. Norton, 2004. A number of books have also been published detailing how 9/11 affected American policy towards the Muslim world. See in particular Phil Rees, *Dining with Terrorists: Meeting with the World's Most Wanted Militants*, London: Macmillan, 2005; Lawrence Wright, *The Looming*

Tower: Al-Qaeda and the Road to 9/11, New York: Alfred Knopf, 2006; and Ron Suskind, *The One Percent Doctrine: Deep Inside America's Pursuit of its Enemies,* New York: Simon and Schuster, 2006.

2. There are several ways of referring to Kashmir. The official name for the state in India is Jammu and Kashmir. However, the Indians refer to the area occupied by Pakistan since the UN mandated cease-fire as Pakistan Occupied Kashmir or simply POK. In Pakistan the area under its control is called Azad (free) Kashmir, or AK, while the area under India's control is referred to as the Indian Occupied Kashmir.

3. This chapter builds upon the material published in a series of articles contributed by me to *Dawn* in 2005. These include, 'Kashmir trap: a way out,' 7 June 2005; 'Cost and gain of Kashmir,' 28 June 2005; 'Kashmir: A new strategy,' 5 July 2005; 'Taking the development route,' 12 July 2005; 'Kashmir: Taking the development route,' 2 August 2005; 'Kashmir disputed economic cost,' 'What to do about Kashmir?'; "Kashmir: The economic option;' 'Kashmir: A sub-regional trading arrangement;' 'Kashmir: The economic option II.'

4. There is a fairly rich literature on the Kashmir problem, most of it written by historians from India and Pakistan, each looking at the genesis of the problem from their country's perspective. Among those who have analyzed the problem from a more neutral angle are Josef Korbel, *Danger in Kashmir,* Princeton, NJ: Princeton University Press, 1954 and Victoria Schofield, *Kashmir in the Crossfire,* London: I.B. Tauris, 1996. Korbel served as the chief of the United Nations mission in Kashmir in the late 1950s.

5. Stanley Wolpert, *Gandhi's Passion: The Life and Legacy of Mahatma Gandhi.* New York: Oxford University Press, 2001, pp. 250.

6. Stanley Wolpert, *Nehru: A Tryst with Destiny,* New York: Oxford University Press, 1987, pp. 423–24.

7. Josef Korbel, *Danger in Kashmir,* Princeton, NJ: Princeton University Press, 1966.

8. Salman Rushdie, *Shalimar the Clown,* New York: Random House, 2006.

9. Samuel P. Huntington, *The Clash of Civilizations: Remaking of World Order,* New York: Simon and Schuster, 1996.

10. The Indian Census Commission reported on 7 September 2004 that the Muslim population was increasing at a rate much faster than that of the majority. In the 1991–2001 decade the number of Muslims increased by 32.5 per cent compared to an increase of 32.9 in the previous decade. The rate of increase in the Hindu population was declining; in 1991–2001, the number of Hindus increased by 21.7 per cent.

11. This approach was adopted by Tezzy Schaeffer and Wajhat Habibullah in the two papers presented at a workshop organized by the US Institute of Peace in 2004. Habibullah's paper, 'The Political Economy of the Kashmir Conflict: Opportunities for Economic Peace building and for U.S. Policy,' was subsequently published by the United States Institute of Peace, Washington, DC, in June 2004 as Special Report 121.

12. *The Economist*, 'India and Pakistan: The technocrats take over', 28 August 2004, p. 10.
13. In a conversation with the author in February 2004.
14. Niall Ferguson, 'Cowboys and Indians,' *The New York Times*, 24 May 2005, p. A25.
15. Conversation with President Musharraf on 19 February 2004, at Islamabad.
16. Pervez Musharraf, *In the Line of Fire: A Memoir*, New York: Simon and Schuster, 2006.
17. See Chapter 3 for a discussion on SAFTA.
18. As reported in *The Hindu* (India), and *Dawn* (Pakistan), 7 January 2004.
19. Interview with a senior official of the Ministry of Foreign Affairs, Pakistan in March 2005.
20. Interview with President Musharraf in Islamabad, 3 March 2005.
21. John Lancaster, 'In Kashmir, abuses bruise hopes for peace', *The Washington Post*, 6 September 2002, p. A18.
22. *The Economist*, 'India and Pakistan: Commando diplomacy,' 30 October 2004, p. 66.
23. Edward Luce, 'India to cut troop numbers in divided state', *Financial Times*, 12 November 2004, p. 7.
24. Edward Luce, 'India's premier goes to Kashmir to talk peace, *Financial Times*, 18 November 2004, p. 12.
25. Ibid., p. 12.
26. Conversation with the author in New Delhi on 15 December 2004. I communicated Prime Minister Singh's message to President Musharraf on 3 March 2005.
27. Text published in most major newspapers of India and Pakistan, including *The Hindu*, 20 April 2004, and *Dawn*, 20 April 2004.
28. *The Economist*, 'Pakistan's leader: Getting comfy with the general,' and 'India and Pakistan: In from the cold,' 28 May 2005, pp. 43–44.
29. Rama Lakhshmi, 'Indian leader says Pakistan must do more to rein in extremists,' *The Washington Post*, 31 May 2005, p. A13.
30. The delegation was led by Mirwaiz Omar Farooq, Chairman All-Parties Hurriyat Conference; Yasin Malik, Chief of the pro-independence Jammu and Kashmir Liberation Front; and Abdul Ghani Bhat who had said earlier that he would never visit Pakistan, accusing it of having caused a rift in the APHC. The radical wing of the alliance, led by Syed Ali Geelani, was not represented in the delegation. Geelani had opposed the resumption of the bus service across the Line of Control. The figure of 80,000 used by the delegation as an estimate for the number of people killed in the insurgency was much higher than other counts.
31. This section draws upon the material first published in my article in *Dawn* under the title of 'Cost and gain of Kashmir', 28 June 2005.

32. The data on military expenditures is from The World Bank, *World Development Indicators, 2005*, Table 5.8, pp. 298–300.
33. I have discussed this aspect of Pakistan's relations with India in Chapter 2.
34. This section draws upon the material first presented in my article in *Dawn* under the title of 'Taking the development route' published on 2 August 2005, p. 7.
35. For a comprehensive analysis of the Indus Waters Treaty see Aloys A. Michel, *The Indus River: A Study of the Effect of Partition*, New Haven, Conn.: Yale University Press, 1967.

8

A Concluding Word: Some Public Policy Imperatives

In the foregoing chapters I have attempted to provide an overview of the Pakistani economy and how it has functioned and developed over time. Four themes run through this work. I will bring them all together in this chapter in order to suggest how Pakistan could steady its economic performance and move towards a more prosperous future.

First, over the last sixty years—ever since the country's birth on 14 August 1947—the Pakistani economy and its politics have been on two separate roller-coasters. The economy has had many ups and downs and the political system has alternated between civilian and military rules. This constant up and down movement hurt the political system as well as the economy. Neither developed to the point where stability could be ensured.

Second, in spite of some impressive gains made by the economy over the last four years, its foundations remain weak. Without support from the outside that comes in mostly as official and private capital flows, the economy is likely to revert back to what is essentially its long-term structural rate of growth. This I estimate at about 4.5 per cent increase in the GDP and about 2.3 per cent growth in per capita income. Third, in spite of the weaknesses in the various supporting structures of the economy there are some 'positives' on which a robust economy could be built over the next couple of decades. Fourth, to move the economy on to a new growth trajectory—to climb to a growth rate of 5 to 6 per cent in per capita income and 7 to 8 per cent in the GDP—there will need to be comprehensive changes in public policy. A strategy needs to be developed with the full support of the public that builds on some of the positives and also makes use of some of the 'potentials.' At this time, notwithstanding the pronouncements of the government—not just by the president himself but also by various senior officials of the administration—there is no well-defined strategy in place to achieve the economy's potential.

Fifth, and finally, it is not correct to deal separately with the domains of economics, politics and society as if these do not intersect and interact. This is what the government headed by General Musharraf has tended to do with the result that the political and social implications of economic development are not fully understood. Nowhere is this more evident than in the growth in income and wealth inequalities as well as the unequal access to economic opportunities. These inequalities affect not only individuals but also different regions in the country. Left unaddressed, inequalities can have serious consequences for political and social development.

In this chapter, I will first recapitulate the first three themes in order to lay the ground for what I believe should be the appropriate focus of public policy. The approach the government needs to adopt should cover not just its own actions but also how it works with the private sector. In a world increasingly defined by what is called 'globalization,' Islamabad's policymakers should also take full cognizance of the environment in which the country finds itself. Finally, since economics is often influenced by politics and by the way society works, public policy must also address the reform of the political structure and the development of the society. I will conclude this chapter by developing the last two themes.

I will begin with a quick overview of the way the economy remains dependent on help from the outside. This help was available in the past whenever the United States wished to recruit a partner for some of its endeavours in the area to which Pakistan belongs. It is for this reason that the economy did well during prolonged periods of military rule. This was not necessarily the case because the military rulers were better economic managers. The economy performed well since the military was able to attract large amounts of foreign capital to the country. Foreign money came in as the military was willing to work with the United States in areas of great strategic concern to Washington.

During the period of General (later Field Marshal) Ayub Khan (1958–69), Pakistan became a close ally of the United States in the the latter's attempt to stop the spread of communism in Asia. It joined a series of alliances arranged by America—the Central Treaty Organization (CENTO) that included a number of countries from the Middle East, and the South East Asia Treaty Organization (SEATO) that encompassed the nations to Pakistan's east. In fact, Pakistan was the link that connected these two alliances. In return for Pakistan's willingness to be thus associated, it was handsomely rewarded by Washington and large doses of military and economic assistance flowed into the country during the first seven years of Ayub Khan's military rule. It was only after Islamabad's ill-advised move into Kashmir in the summer of 1965 that Pakistan woke up to the rude shock that the support available from Washington was contingent on not straying from the course laid out by the Americans. The *mujahideen's* move into Kashmir led to the seventeen-day war with India from 6 to 23 September and the flow of American aid stopped. It was resumed later but not in the generous amounts provided before 1965. According to one estimate, foreign savings (foreign capital flows) in 1964–65 were equivalent to 10.5 per cent of the GNP, almost equal to national savings calculated at 10.6 per cent of the gross national product.[2]

President Ayub Khan had discovered that the relationship he had forged with the United States was not based on mutual interest but on the interest of Washington alone. This is not what he expected. In his address to the joint sitting of the US Congress in 1961 while on a visit to Washington, he had emphasized the need to build alliances on the basis of common interests. As he recalled half a dozen years later in his autobiography, 'I reminded the Congress of their responsibilities and world obligations. There was applause when I said, 'the only people who will stand by you are the people of Pakistan,' but before the applause died down, I added, 'provided—provided you are prepared to stand by them. So, I would like you to remember that, whatever may be the dictates of your commitments, you will not take any steps that might aggravate our problems or in any fashion jeopardize our security. And as long as you remember that, I have no doubt in my mind that our friendship will grow in strength.'[3] This did not happen. President Ayub Khan titled his biography *Friends not Masters* to underscore that point. But in any relationship of unequals, friendship alone cannot be the basis of relationship. This point was emphasized by Zulfikar Ali Bhutto, once Ayub Khan's foreign minister, who split with his leader on this issue. Bhutto's riposte to Ayub Khan's biography came with the title, *The Myth of Independence*.[4]

Nevertheless, the flow of American money after the war with India was over and a peace treaty had been signed at Tashkent augmented by the funds provided by the World Bank helped accelerate the rate of growth of the GDP from a paltry 3.1 per cent a year in the 1950s to 6.7 per cent in the 1960s. The impact on the increase in income per head of the population was significant. Before the advent of military rule, the GDP per capita barely increased—it grew by 0.6 per cent a year. While no count was then kept of the number of people living in poverty, there can be no doubt that they increased in the first decade after independence but declined under Ayub Khan. During the latter period, per capita income increased by an impressive 3.8 per cent a year.

The brief civilian interlude in 1971–77 that interrupted the rule by the military, slowed economic expansion to 4.4 per cent a year and the increase in income per head to a mere 1.3 per cent a year. Zulfikar Ali Bhutto was in power during this time and delivered a severe shock to the economy by taking it through a profound structural change. But that was not the entire reason for the slowdown. Without large external flows, Pakistan had returned to its structural rate of growth. The country just did not save enough and invest enough to do any better. There were other structural flaws that constrained economic growth. These included poorly developed human resource, poorly developed physical infrastructure, and an institutional base that could not propel the economy at rates much faster than the rate of population increase.

The return to power by the military in July 1977 once again created the circumstance that brought back external capital. This did not happen immediately since General Ziaul Haq's coup against the government of Prime Minister Zulfikar Ali Bhutto disturbed the West, in particular the United States. Ayub Khan's venture into politics two decades earlier was received with considerable enthusiasm since a number of influential development thinkers— economists as well as political scientists—had concluded that the developing world needed a steady hand at the helm only the military could provide. This thinking encouraged dozens of military leaders to intervene in Africa, Asia and the Middle East. But once in office the military had performed less well than anticipated. By the time the men in uniform returned to the corridors of power in Islamabad in 1977, the Western view of military rule had swung to the opposite direction. The military was no longer viewed as a promoter of development; it was seen, instead, as an obstacle to social, economic and political advance in the developing world.

General Ziaul Haq did not, therefore, initially endear himself to the West; his decision to execute Zulfikar Ali Bhutto further reduced his welcome. However, the situation changed dramatically with the Soviet Union's invasion of Afghanistan in 1979. Pakistan once again became a front-line state in America's war against communism. The Pakistani president played his cards well. His rejection of President Jimmy Carter's offer of assistance to Pakistan as 'peanuts', prepared the ground for a much larger flow of funds when, in January 1981, the reins of power changed hands in Washington. The Republican Party President, Ronald Reagan, was prepared to engage his country more fully with Pakistan if the latter provided full assistance to the CIA-led proxy war in Afghanistan. This Islamabad was happy to do, and aid began to flow once again. President Ziaul Haq was now welcome in Western capitals; he was feted in America and Europe as a champion of the free world. Buoyed by external flows, in particular the assistance from the United States, the GNP growth rate bounced back to 6.4 per cent a year during 1977–88 and income per head increased to 3.3 per cent a year.

The Zia period ended shortly before the withdrawal of the Soviet Union from Afghanistan. The Soviet pullout also resulted in the total loss of US and Western interest in Pakistan. Official capital flows declined. Foreigners were no longer able to camouflage Pakistan's structural weaknesses, and the country returned to its structural growth rate of just over 4 per cent a year. In 1988–99, the GNP increased at the rate of 4.1 per cent and the income per head of the population grew by only 1.2 per cent. Prime Minister Nawaz Sharif's decision to test a series of nuclear devices in May 1998 brought Pakistan under Western sanctions and further isolated the country. It was in these inauspicious circumstances that General Pervez Musharraf brought the military back to politics. Once again, its intervention was treated with hostility in all Western capitals, in particular the United States. When President Bill Clinton visited Islamabad for a few hours after a stay of several days in India in March 2000, he showed disdain for Pakistan's new military leader by refusing to shake his hand in public. His recollection of his meeting with President Musharraf was condescending.

> In my meetings with Musharraf, I saw why he had emerged from the complex, often violent culture of Pakistani politics. He was clearly intelligent, strong, and sophisticated. If he chose to pursue a peaceful, progressive path, I thought he had a fair chance to succeed but I told him I thought terrorism would eventually destroy Pakistan from within if he didn't move against it.[5]

The terrorist attacks on the United States on 11 September 2001 returned the United States to Pakistan. It has become a cliché to say that 9/11 changed the world; for Pakistan the change was certainly sudden and dramatic. By now the warning that the US would bomb Pakistan back to the Stone Age has been heard the world over after its revelation by President Pervez Musharraf while he was launching his memoir, *In the Line of Fire,* in the United States. There is no doubt that the American threat worked.[6] Pakistan abandoned the Taliban regime in Afghanistan, facilitated America's conquest of the country that had harboured Osama bin

Laden, and took an active part in Washington's war against terrorism and Al Qaeda. It was handsomely rewarded. Washington helped to reduce Pakistan's large debt burden and provided both military and economic assistance. Foreign savings as a proportion of the GDP became positive after having remained negative for three years at the start of the Musharraf period. It had become negative on account of the large amount of debt service Pakistan was paying because of the build-up of external debt. In 2005–6, foreign savings were estimated at 3.7 per cent of the GDP and one-fifth of the GDI.

As a consequence, the economy perked up; not immediately as had happened during previous takeovers by the military but after a time lag which was the consequence of the programme of economic stabilization imposed upon the country by the IMF. The IMF did to Pakistan what it had done to a number of other countries; it stabilized the economy by squeezing growth out of it.[7] Growth returned only after the IMF's programme was concluded. Starting with the year 2002–3, the rate of GDP increase crossed the structural rate and continued to accelerate till it reached 8.6 per cent growth in 2004–5. In the seven-year-period during which President Musharraf has been in charge, the GDP increased by 42.4 per cent which translates into an annual growth rate of 5.2 per cent a year, or 3.2 per cent per head of the population.

This quick overview of the close connection between the availability of external capital flows and economic growth raises some obvious questions: was the recovery of the economy in the latter part of the Musharraf period built on endogenous factors or was it still the consequences of copious amounts of foreign assistance and other types of external flows received since 9/11? What will happen if America once again loses interest in Pakistan or if it chooses to walk out of Afghanistan once more, or if it increases its reliance on India as a more reliable strategic partner in South Asia? What will be the consequences of the change of political command in Washington if the Democratic Party—never a friend of Pakistan—gains power not just in Congress as it did following the mid-term elections of November 2006 but also wins back the White House in 2008? In other words, what will happen when in 2009 President George W. Bush who, more than most chief executives in America's recent history, honours friendship, returns to his ranch in Crawford and hands over the presidency to a successor who may be less charitable towards Pakistan? Will Pakistan be able to sustain the shock of cessation of or a drastic reduction in the flow of official capital?

There is some substance to the argument put forward by President Pervez Musharraf that his management of the economy has brought about important structural changes. The general concludes his memoir with a question: 'What more must be done to sustain Pakistan on a path of progress and prosperity?' He provides the answer in the form of a seven-point programme of reform which has three elements related to the promotion of economic development. 'We have to sustain our huge economic growth through better irrigation and agriculture, increase foreign direct investment for industrial growth, and enhanced exports. We must convert Pakistan into a regional hub of trade and energy. All this has to be done while our fiscal deficit is kept in check.' These statements, however, provide mostly a vision; they don't constitute a strategy. That said, he recognizes that growth, even if it could be sustained, needs to benefit not just the elite but the masses. 'We have to transfer our economic gains to the people through alleviation of poverty, creation of jobs and control of inflation. We have to improve the quality of life by providing *everyone* [my italics] with access to electricity, clean drinking water, and natural gas.' These are worthy goals but reaching everyone with these basic services will need a great deal of money which the government does not have and is unlikely to mobilize. But he continues in the same vein, turning to other basic needs. 'We have to concentrate all our energies on developing human resources through improved education and health facilities at every level.'[8] Once again these are worthy aims but the question remains as to how all this will get done.

This brings me to the second theme I have explored in the various chapters of the book: that the foundations of the Pakistani economy would remain weak, hidden by the generosity of the country's friends during moments of *their* stress. Once that support is withdrawn, the rate of GDP growth will return to what I have called its structural rate. The sustainable rate now is probably half a percentage point more than before the start of the Musharraf period. It is probably of the order of 4.5 per cent a year rather than 4 per cent. This slight increase is the result of what I would like to describe as the 'positives' in the economy.[9] Some of these are the result of the reforms started in the 1990s but continued—in fact accelerated—during the Musharraf period. That notwithstanding, the economy is not in a position to achieve anything close to the rate of growth the Musharraf government believes is sustainable way into the future.

Before recounting the various positives present in the economy, it would be useful to discuss the many structural weaknesses that result in a low rate of growth when foreign savings are not available. In this context it is useful to recall that development economists, learning from experience, now include a longer array of determinants of growth than those that were initially identified. In the 1950s and 1960s when economists began to appreciate that they had to search for ways to promote growth in the newly emerging economies of Africa and Asia, they focused on two factors, labour and capital. Labour was abundantly available but capital was in short supply. To produce growth, the countries coming out from under the weight of colonialism had to be provided with money additional to what they could generate at home through domestic savings. There had to be copious amounts of external capital flows and they had to be made available on the terms the developing countries could afford. This finding paved the way for the use of concessional official flows as an instrument for producing growth.[10]

However, the flow of aid did not always yield growth. Economists and practitioners of development began to look for other contributing factors. They recognized several of these. Prominent among them were the quality of human capital, institutional development, and the quality of social capital. Human capital had to be developed by investing not just in primary education but also in higher education and by training people to work in the modern sectors of the economy. Social capital, a term used to describe how individuals relate with one another, was seen as a contributor to growth and development. Institutions were of critical importance. Among those that were required were a legal system that ensured quick settlement of disputes, a policy framework that could maintain law and order, a system for recording land and property rights that unambiguously assigned ownership, a regulatory system that provided protection to consumers from what could become predatory behaviour of private enterprises, health safety laws that also protected consumers, and checks against political and bureaucratic corruption. In fact, the list of the determinants of growth and development to which economists now subscribe is even longer than the one I have enumerated above. Without focus on them in the context of a broad economic strategy, this wish list is not likely to be realized.

In reading the way President Musharraf has looked at the economy's future I am reminded of a long discussion I had with President Hugo Chavez of Venezuela soon after he was elected to the position he now occupies. President James Wolfensohn of the World Bank had many rich friends in Venezuela; they were worried about their future under Chavez. They wanted the World Bank to exert pressure on the man who was soon to become president not to adopt radical economic policies. I was then Vice President in charge of the World Bank's operations in Latin America. I flew to Caracas where I first met with the president who Chavez was set to succeed. The president told me that what he feared the most was the radicalization of both economics and politics once Chavez took charge. I then met with the president-elect and spent several hours with him at the Army Club. He said that Venezuela's traditional political elite had brought a great deal of misery to the poor; it had only enriched itself. He was gong to change that by bringing universal education, health care and other social services to the poor, and he was intending to do that quickly. 'How will you do that,' I asked the president-elect. 'Do you have a strategy that would include the establishment of institutions to provide services to the poor, and do you have some idea of where all the resources you will need for achieving such an ambitious programme will come from?' He said it was his job to have a vision; he left all the details to his economic advisors. Some of them were present in the room and they nodded their heads to indicate their assent to the approach the president-elect wished to follow once he had assumed office.

Once in office, Hugo Chavez pursued his vision. He not only committed his country's own abundant resources, he also obtained help from some of the countries that were friendly towards him. Hundreds of Cuban doctors are now working in the Venezuelan health system. Chavez often speaks about the revolution he has brought to his country. But he and his country have paid a heavy price. According to the World Bank's *World Development Indicators 2005*, Venezuela has done very well in improving some of the indices that measure social development. The share in total income of the poorest tenth of the population in 1990–2003 was estimated at 3 per cent compared to a miserable 2.3 per cent for Brazil; the proportion of underweight children declined from 5 per cent in 1989–94 to 4 per cent while not much change occurred in several Latin American countries; the primary school completion rate increased from 81 to 90 per cent; the ratio of female enrolment in primary and secondary schools increased from 90 per cent in 1990/91 to 105 per cent in 2002/03; the child mortality rate declined from 27 per 1000 in 1990 to 21 in 2002; the maternal mortality rates fell to 96 for 100,000 live births in 2000; and births attended by skilled health staff were estimated at 85 per cent of the total in 2000–3.[11]

These numbers spell a fairly significant improvement in social development in a country where the poor who also happened to be ethnically different from the rich had been neglected by the state for long—perhaps for ever. President Hugo Chavez changed all that but the change came with great cost. In 2002–3, the year when the president was confronted by the opposition mostly from the privileged segments of the population, gross domestic product declined by 9.4 per cent and by another 11.4 per cent in the year that followed. These were the years when the president directed huge amounts of subsidies and public sector expenditure towards the poor. In two years, the size of Venezuela's GDP was reduced by almost one-quarter.[12]

But Venezuela compared to Pakistan is a country rich in resources with a resource (oil) whose international price continues to increase as the demand for it continues to grow. Pakistan also has resources—I call them 'positives'—but they need to be developed and nurtured before they can be put to use for developing the country's human capital. Therefore, President Musharraf's vision and promise to give everyone access to some of the more basic human needs would be realized—if it gets realized at all—over a much longer period of time and with the help of a carefully crafted strategy of reform and development that is still to be put together by the regime. To reach that objective he will have to overcome the structural weaknesses in the economy and build a future that makes good use of the positives in the economy. The point of providing the Venezuelan example is to emphasize that a country that does not have a rich base of resources such as Pakistan has to make a great deal of sober effort to increase the rate of increase in GDP and to have the increase flow to the poorer segments of society and the poorer regions of the country. If this effort was made, the rewards would be impressive, since Pakistan has some 'positives' on which it can build a relatively strong economy.

My list of positives includes a vibrant banking sector that has begun to play an active role in revitalizing the economy and in activating a number of sectors that remained dormant for lack of finance. The banking sector is now under the control of the private sector and is managed by professionals. It has diversified its asset base by lending large amounts to tens of thousands of new customers. Also among the positives is the sector of agriculture that has begun to produce high value-added crops for domestic consumption as well as export. It makes little sense for Pakistan to commit so much land and use so much water to grow crops that don't yield as much income as would vegetables, fruits and flowers. With the rapid development of the food and agricultural processing industry (activities supported by the banking sector), the share of the value added crops has begun to increase in total agricultural output.

A large and young population is another positive feature of Pakistan's economic landscape. I differ from those economists that treat a growing population as a burden rather than as an asset. But they can only be an asset if the youth are educated and trained to help modernize the economy. The World Bank devoted its 2007 *World Development Report* to the subject of 'development and next generation.' According to the report:

> The situation of young people today presents the world with an unprecedented opportunity to accelerate growth and reduce poverty. First, thanks to the development achievements of past decades, more young people are completing primary school and surviving childhood diseases. However, to succeed in today's competitive global economy, they must be equipped with advanced skills beyond literacy to stay healthy; they must confront new disease burdens, such as sexually transmitted diseases and obesity. Second, lower fertility rates in many countries means that today's youth will enter the workforce with fewer nonworking dependents, and thus fewer to support.[13]

The young can also earn foreign exchange by servicing the parts of the global economy that are now facing severe shortages of skilled workers.

The fourth positive is the large Pakistani diaspora scattered over three continents and earning incomes that aggregated are equivalent to a significant proportion of the homeland's gross domestic product. Not only that, the members of the diaspora save more than the entire amount saved by the country of their origin and they now seem to be ready to commit some of this to the development of the homeland. As the World Bank notes in a recently concluded study, remittances by migrants should reach $268 billion in 2006, over twice as much as in 2000. Workers from developing countries account for most of this flow: they are expected to send $199 billion in 2006, compared with $85 billion six years ago. Remittances have been the largest source of external capital flow into Pakistan. The Bank estimates the flow into the country to be the seventh largest among developing countries, below that of Mexico, India, China, the Philippines, Morocco and Lebanon. At an expected $5 billion it is equal to that of Bangladesh. It is the sixth highest in terms of the proportion of the country's GDP, estimated at 4.2 per cent.[14] The money that is flowing back from the diaspora is no longer mostly in the form of remittances; it is also coming as investment in various kinds of assets in Pakistan. However, the important development in the case of Pakistan is that this flow is increasingly from the United States rather than Saudi Arabia. America is now the largest source. Experience from many countries—China, India and Mexico among them—suggests that the involvement of the diaspora in making investments in the homeland can lead other investors. Foreigners have been shy to come to Pakistan, concerned about the situation with respect to security. Some of these perceptions are highly exaggerated and can be countered if the members of the diasporas begin to lead the way. Foreigners with capital to invest in the developing world will follow once the diasporas establish a beachhead.

Could these 'positives' enhance Pakistan's economic future? The answer is 'yes' provided Islamabad begins to factor them into a well-thought-out and articulated growth strategy. Unfortunately there are few indications that this is being done. In this context I should emphasize that public policy needs to cover a wide front in order to lift the rate of growth beyond what I have indicated above is the 'structural level'—the rate that is plausible given the structure of the economy and the society.

In thinking about economic growth and in thinking about sustaining it at a high level and in order to achieve these outcomes without depending on outside assistance, Islamabad's policymakers will have to recognize that there have to be simultaneous movements on a number of fronts, not just on the economic front. Political and social development must proceed at a faster rate than appears to be currently planned by those who hold power in the country.

In a recent book, *Adam's Fallacy: A Guide to Economic Theology*, economist Duncan Foley correctly maintains that it is misguided to argue that 'the pursuit of self-interest is guided by objective laws to a socially beneficent outcome in the economic realm unlike all the rest of social life.' This assertion is 'morally problematic and has to be weighed against other ends.'[15] Progress won't occur unless political and social development occurs along with economic growth.

Once before in its history, Pakistan seemed to have arrived at the stage of Rostowian take-off. About that time economist W.W. Rostow had published his authoritative account of how traditional societies modernize. That was in 1965 when Pakistan's first military administration seemed to have created most of what Rostow had identified as the preconditions for take-off. Rostow wrote:

> The idea spreads not merely that economic progress is a necessary condition but some other purpose, judged it to be good, be it national dignity, private profit, the general welfare, or better life for children ...New types of enterprising economic men come forward—in the private economy, in government, or both—willing to mobilize savings and to take risks in pursuing profit or modernization.[16]

Pakistan nicely fitted this description.

Forty years later, in 2005, Pakistan once again reached that point; pre-conditions for achieving take-off seemed to have reappeared. To quote from Rostow again, this happens when

> banks and other institutions for mobilizing capital appear. Investment increases... The scope of commerce, external and internal widens. And, here and there, modern manufacturing enterprise appears, using the new methods. But all this activity proceeds at a limited pace within an economy and a society still mainly characterized by traditional low-productivity methods, by the old structure and values, and by the regionally based political institutions that developed in conjunction with them. In many cases, for example, the traditional society persisted side-by-side with modern economic activities, conducted for limited economic purposes...[17]

In the year after 2005, the rate of economic growth slackened and the pre-conditions for take-off were overcome by political and social developments. To go back to Rostow for the third time,

> although the period of transition—between the traditional society and the take-off—saw major changes in both the economy itself and in the balance of social values, a decisive feature was often political. Politically the building of an effective centralized national government—on the basis of coalitions touched with new nationalism in opposition to the traditional landed interests...was a decisive aspect of the preconditions period, and it was, almost universally, a necessary condition for take-off.[18]

At the time of this writing (the winter of 2006–2007), Pakistan is once again being overwhelmed by forces that can only be described as anti-modern.

Will Pakistan once again lose the opportunity for making its economy work or will it be beaten once again by forces its leaders have done little to bring into a national political and social framework that promises cohesion rather than antagonism and eventual dispersion? I will leave the readers with this final question.

NOTES

1. In his memoir published in September 2006, President Pervez Musharraf claims that his stewardship of the economy has ensured a steady rate of growth in the future. See Pervez Musharraf, *In the Line of Fire: A Memoir*, New York: Simon and Schuster, 2006.
2. Parvez Hasan, *Pakistan's Economy at the Crossroads: Past Policies and Present Imperatives*, Karachi: Oxford University Press, 1998, Table 1.5, p. 29.
3. Mohammad Ayub Khan, *Friends not Masters: A Political Autobiography*, Karachi: Oxford University Press, 1967, p. 137.
4. Zulfikar Ali Bhutto, *The Myth of Independence*, Karachi: Oxford University Press, 1969.
5. Bill Clinton, *My Life*, New York: Alfred A. Knopf, 2004, p. 903.
6. The American version of the way Pakistan was pulled back into the Washington orbit is provided at some length by Bob Woodward in the first

of the three books he wrote on the presidency of George W. Bush and how it fought the threat posed by Islamic extremists. See Bob Woodward, *Bush at War*, New York: Simon & Schuster, 2002, pp. 58–59.

7. For a critique of the IMF's approach in the developing world, see in particular Joseph Stiglitz, *Globalization and its Discontents*, New York: W.W. Norton, 2002, and William Easterly, *The White Man's Burden: Why the West's Effort to Aid the Rest Have Done so Much Ill and So Little Good*, New York: The Penguin Press, 2006.

8. Pervez Musharraf, *In the Line of Fire*, op. cit., p. 337.

9. I wrote a series of articles for *Dawn* in late 2006 on what I termed the 'positives' in the Pakistani economy. See Shahid Javed Burki, 'More stress on positives' (*Dawn*, 26 September 2006, p. 7); 'Building on the positives' (*Dawn*, 3 October 2006, p. 7); 'Population as a resource' (*Dawn*, 10 October 2006, p. 7); 'Contribution of expatriates', *Dawn*, 17 October 2006, p. 7); and 'A resurgent private sector', (*Dawn*, 31 October 2006, p. 7).

10. For a quick overview of the thinking of the economists who became the pioneers of development economics as a discipline see, Gerald M. Meier 'The Formative Period' in Gerald M. Meier and Dudley Seers (eds.), *Pioneers in Development*, New York: Oxford University Press, pp. 3–24.

11. The World Bank, *World Development Indicators 2005*, Table 1.2, pp. 26–28.

12. The World Bank, *World Development Indicators 2005*, Table 1.1, p. 24.

13. The World Bank, *World Development Report, 2007: Development and the Next Generation*, Washington, DC, 2006, p. 2.

14. As reported in *The Economist*, 'Migrants' remittances', 25 November 2006, p. 106.

15. Duncan K. Foley, *Adam's Fallacy: A Guide to Economic Theology*, New York: Belknap Press, 2006. pp. 28–32

16. W.W. Rostow, *The Stages of Economic Growth: A Non-Communist Manifesto*, Cambridge: Cambridge University Press, 1960, p. 6.

17. Ibid., p. 7.

18. Ibid., p. 7.

Index